# Contents

*The population figures quoted in this guide are based on the 1990 US census.*

*Addresses, telephone numbers, opening hours and prices published in this guide are accurate at the time of publication. We apologize for any inconvenience resulting from outdated information. Send us your comments:*
**Michelin Travel Publications, One Parkway South, Greenville, SC 29615.**

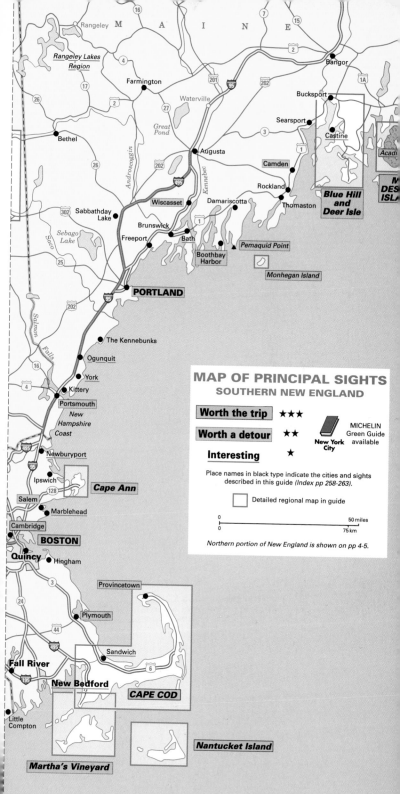

# MAP OF PRINCIPAL SIGHTS
## SOUTHERN NEW ENGLAND

| | |
|---|---|
| **Worth the trip** | ★★★ |
| **Worth a detour** | ★★ |
| **Interesting** | ★ |

**New York City** — MICHELIN Green Guide available

Place names in black type indicate the cities and sights described in this guide (Index pp 258-263).

☐ Detailed regional map in guide

```
0                    50 miles
0                    75 km
```

*Northern portion of New England is shown on pp 4-5.*

MAINE

Rangeley
Rangeley Lakes Region
Farmington
Waterville
Great Pond
Bethel
Bangor
Bucksport
Searsport
Castine
Augusta
Camden
Rockland
Blue Hill and Deer Isle
Acadi
M DES ISLA
Androscoggin
Kennebec
Sabbathday Lake
Wiscasset
Damariscotta
Thomaston
Sebago Lake
Saco
Brunswick
Freeport
Bath
Boothbay Harbor
Pemaquid Point
Monhegan Island

PORTLAND

Salmon Falls
The Kennebunks
Ogunquit
York
Kittery
Portsmouth
New Hampshire Coast
Newburyport
Ipswich
Cape Ann
Salem
Marblehead
Cambridge
BOSTON
Quincy
Hingham
Provincetown
Plymouth
Sandwich
Fall River
New Bedford
CAPE COD
Little Compton
Martha's Vineyard
Nantucket Island

ATLANTIC OCEAN

3

## MAP OF PRINCIPAL SIGHTS
### NORTHERN NEW ENGLAND

**Worth the trip**  ★★★

**Worth a detour**  ★★

**Interesting**  ★

MICHELIN Green Guide available

Place names in black type indicate the cities and sights described in this guide *(Index pp 258-263)*.

Detailed regional map in guide

0 ____ 50 miles
0 ____ 75 km

*Southern portion of New England is shown on pp 2-3.*

MAINE

*Flagstaff Lake*

*Rangeley Lakes*

*Kennebec*

*Penobscot*

95

Bucksport

15

Ellsworth

172

Searsport

3

**Bar Harbor★**
*(2 nights)*

**★★Camden**

**★★★ MOUNT DESERT ISLAND**

**★★Blue Hill and Deer Isle**

*Androscoggin*

*Sebago Lake*

★Wiscasset

1

**★Bath**

27

130

**★Pemaquid Point★★**

*Saco*

209

**★★Boothbay Harbor**

**Portland★★**

95

9

Kennebunkport

**Ogunquit★**

York★

**Portsmouth★★**

1

*New Hampshire Coast*

Newburyport★

**Cape Ann★★**

**Salem★★**

**BOSTON★★★**
*(2 nights)*

93

3

**★★Provincetown**

**Plymouth★★**

**★★★Cape Cod National Seashore**

495

★Brewster

6

Sandwich

6A

Chatham★

195

28

**★New Bedford**

**Cape Cod★★★**

Falmouth★

*Nantucket Island*

*Martha's Vineyard*

ATLANTIC OCEAN

## REGIONAL DRIVING TOURS

**New York to Montreal:**
376 miles – 3 days

**Southern New England:**
704 miles – 7 days

**The Coast North of Boston:**
522 miles – 7 days

**Vermont and New Hampshire:**
984 miles – 8 days

◯  ○  Towns described in this guide
*(Index pp 258-263)*

Suggested overnight stop

**Newport ★★**  City map in this guide

**Cape Cod★★★**  Regional map in this guide

0 — 40mi
0 — 60km

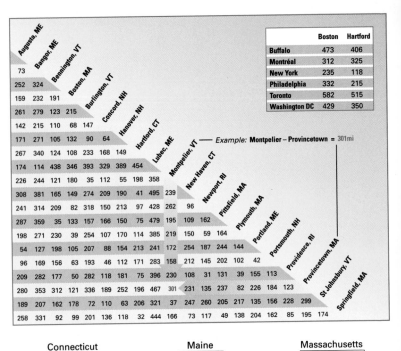

|              | Boston | Hartford |
|--------------|--------|----------|
| **Buffalo**      | 473    | 406      |
| **Montréal**     | 312    | 325      |
| **New York**     | 235    | 118      |
| **Philadelphia** | 332    | 215      |
| **Toronto**      | 582    | 515      |
| **Washington DC**| 429    | 350      |

Augusta, ME
73 Bangor, ME
252 324 Bennington, VT
159 232 191 Boston, MA
261 279 123 215 Burlington, VT
142 215 110 68 147 Concord, NH
171 271 105 132 90 64 Hanover, NH
267 340 124 108 233 168 149 Hartford, CT
174 114 438 346 329 389 454 Lubec, ME
226 244 121 180 35 112 55 198 358 Montpelier, VT
308 381 165 149 274 209 190 41 495 239 New Haven, CT
241 314 209 82 318 150 213 97 428 262 96 Newport, RI
287 359 35 133 157 166 150 75 479 195 109 162 Pittsfield, MA
198 271 230 39 254 107 170 114 385 219 150 59 164 Plymouth, MA
54 127 198 105 207 88 154 213 241 172 254 187 244 144 Portland, ME
96 169 156 63 193 46 112 171 283 158 212 145 202 102 42 Portsmouth, NH
209 282 177 50 282 118 181 75 396 230 108 31 131 39 155 113 Providence, RI
280 353 312 121 336 189 252 196 467 301 231 135 237 82 226 184 123 Provincetown, MA
189 207 162 178 72 110 63 206 321 37 247 260 205 217 135 156 228 299 St. Johnsbury, VT
258 331 92 99 201 136 118 32 444 166 73 117 49 138 204 162 85 195 174 Springfield, MA

—— *Example:* **Montpelier – Provincetown = 301mi**

**FALL FOLIAGE TOURS**

1 Outside Boston
2 Northern Vermont and New Hampshire
3 Central Connecticut
4 The Berkshires and Southern Vermont
5 Central Maine
6 Coastal Maine
*(see maps pp 10-13)*

## List of Maps and Plans

# FALL FOLIAGE TOURS

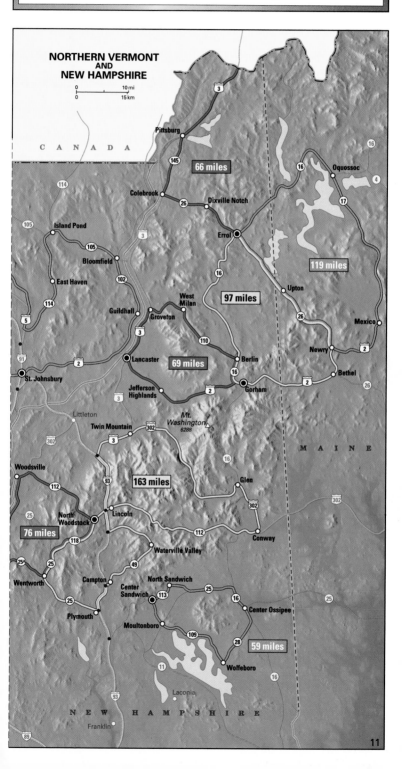

**Legend:**
- Suggested routes
- **211 miles** Tour distance
- ○ Town/village along tour
- ◉ Starting point of tour
- 95 Interstate Highway
- 3 US Route
- 118 Other route

**NORTHERN VERMONT AND NEW HAMPSHIRE**

Scale: 0–10 mi / 0–15 km

CANADA

- Pittsburg
- 145 — **66 miles**
- Colebrook — 26 — Dixville Notch
- 114
- 105 — Island Pond
- 105 — Bloomfield
- 102
- East Haven
- 114
- 5
- 91
- Guildhall
- Groveton — West Milan
- 110
- **69 miles** — Lancaster
- 2 — St. Johnsbury
- Jefferson Highlands
- 3
- 16 — Oquossoc — 4
- 17
- Errol
- 16
- **97 miles**
- **119 miles** — Upton
- 26 — Mexico
- Newry — 2
- Berlin — Bethel — 26
- 16 — Gorham — 2
- Littleton
- Twin Mountain — 302 — Mt. Washington 6288
- 302
- 3
- 16
- MAINE
- Woodsville
- 112
- 93 — **163 miles**
- Glen
- 25
- North Woodstock — Lincoln — 112 — Conway — 302
- 302
- **76 miles** — 118
- Waterville Valley
- 25
- 49
- Campton — North Sandwich
- Wentworth — 25 — Center Sandwich — 113 — 25
- 25 — Plymouth
- Moultonboro — 109 — 16 — Center Ossipee — 25
- 28 — **59 miles**
- 11 — Wolfeboro — 16
- Laconia
- 93
- NEW HAMPSHIRE
- 89 — Franklin

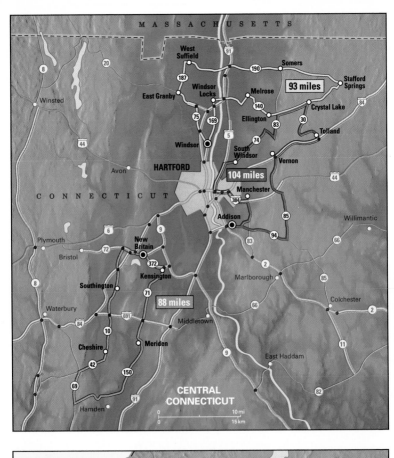

### CENTRAL CONNECTICUT

MASSACHUSETTS

West Suffield
Somers
Stafford Springs
187
190
East Granby
Windsor Locks
Melrose
**93 miles**
Crystal Lake
75
169
140
Ellington
83
30
Tolland
Windsor
5
74
Vernon
HARTFORD
South Windsor
**104 miles**
Manchester
Willimantic
384
Avon
85
CONNECTICUT
Addison
94
Plymouth
6
9
New Britain
83
66
Bristol
372
Kensington
Marlborough
85
Colchester
Southington
71
**88 miles**
Waterbury
691
Middletown
66
10
East Haddam
Cheshire
Meriden
9
42
150
82
69
91
Hamden

Winsted
8
20
44

0 — 10 mi
0 — 15 km

### CENTRAL MAINE

0 — 10 mi
0 — 15 km

201
Jackman
6
15
The Birches
CANADA
Greenville
Coburn Gore
West Forks
6
27
201
15
Abbot Village
Dover-Foxcroft
MAINE
Sangerville
16
23
7
Stratton
16
Bigelow
27
Bingham
7
Rangeley
4
Kingfield
Solon
**212 miles**
11
4
Madrid
16
Newport
17
27
North Anson
Skowhegan
2
Pittsfield
142
**144 miles**
Norridgewock
95
Weld
156
Farmington
2
Waterville
Mexico
Dryden
139
2
108
201

12

# Introduction To New England

---

*"New England is the authorized version of America: her land and people chapter and verse for more than three hundred years."*

Poet David McCord
Address in 1960 at
Old Sturbridge Village

# NEW ENGLAND'S NATURAL ENVIRONMENT

Framed by the White Mountains to the north and the Green Mountains to the west, New England's gently rolling hills and valleys taper off to an irregular rockbound coastline edged with sandy beaches to the south. Vast woodlands coupled with an extensive river and stream system complete the picture.

The region's major mountain ranges are remnants of higher peaks that were formed 300 million to 500 million years ago. Much younger in geologic age, the numerous ponds, lakes, U-shaped valleys and winding ridges owe their existence to the Laurentide ice sheet and associated glaciers that covered this portion of the North American continent until about 10,000 years ago.

**Formation of New England** – During the Paleozoic era (240–570 million years ago), the earth's crust, composed largely of gneiss, was submerged beneath inland seas. Layers of sediment accumulated on the sea floor until the Eurasian and North American tectonic plates collided, causing the earth's crust to heave upward. Consequently, the sea floor buckled along the Canadian Shield and rose above the water as a mass of parallel folds. The intense heat and pressure accompanying the uplift and folding of these peaks (ancestors of the Green Mountains and the Taconic Range) transformed the sedimentary sandstone and limestone into metamorphic rocks, consisting primarily of schist and marble.

During the same era, domes of Precambrian, largely granitic, rock pushed upward into the folded sections of rock, forming New Hampshire's Presidential Range. These ancient mountains probably reached the elevations of the present-day Alps or Himalayas. Since then, erosion has worn the mountains down to a dissected plain. Repeated uplifts and cycles of erosion, coupled with the scouring of subsequent glaciers, created the principal features of New England's landscape.

**A Glaciated Landscape** – The last of four stages of continental glaciation that occurred during the first part of the Quaternary Epoch ended some 10,000 years ago. About 1.5 million years ago at the dawn of the Pleistocene Period, the climate became increasingly colder and snow accumulated, spawning the beginning of the most recent Ice Age. The weight of the top layers of snow, compacted by repeated melting and refreezing, eventually compressed the lower tiers into crystalline ice.

When the ice reached a thickness of 150ft to 200ft, the lower layer, no longer able to support the intense pressure, began to spread. Moving southeastward from the Labrador peninsula in Canada to Long Island, New York, the enormous Laurentide ice sheet stretched across the northeastern part of the Appalachians, and came to a halt along a line roughly parallel to New England's present southern coastline.

Glaciers scoured the walls and floors of narrow valleys, widening them into U-shaped valleys called notches. Abrasive materials carried along the bottom of the ice chiseled and striated the granite and other bedrock. Boulders, now scattered across New England, were plucked from exposed mountain sides. Glacial detritus formed natural dams, often blocking valleys and creating ponds and waterfalls as the ice dissipated. Large isolated blocks of ice left in the wake of receding glaciers eventually melted, giving rise to the kettle lakes (named for their rounded shape) that dot the region.

Near the coast, glaciers mounded sticky clay deposits to form low-lying oval hills (known as drumlins) such as Bunker Hill and World's End *(p 149)*. When the ice finally melted, it left behind enormous moraines consisting of a mixture of unsorted rock fragments ranging from huge boulders to tiny clay particles. The formation of CAPE COD, MARTHA'S VINEYARD, NANTUCKET, BLOCK ISLAND and Long Island has been attributed to these prominent ridges of debris, which remained above sea level when the ocean invaded the low-lying land.

## Major Geographic Features

**Appalachian Mountains** – The Appalachians, extending about 1,600mi from Canada's St Lawrence Valley to Alabama, form the spine of New England. Several parallel ranges with a primarily north-south orientation make up the northeastern Appalachian system.

**The White Mountains** – These once heavily glaciated mountains, characterized by rocky, cone-shaped summits and U-shaped valleys, claim the highest peak in the northeastern US: Mt Washington (6,288ft).

**The Green Mountains** – The most prominent peaks in Vermont form a north-south ridge through the center of the state. Composed of ancient metamorphic rocks, including Vermont's rich marble deposits, this mountain chain extends into Massachusetts, where it is known as the Berkshires.

**The Taconic Range** – Extending along the common border of New York and Massachusetts, and into southern Vermont, this range, comprised primarily of schists, includes Mt Equinox in Vermont and Mt Greylock in Massachusetts.

**The Monadnocks** – Several isolated mountains, called monadnocks, the remnants of ancient crystalline rock more resistant to erosion than the surrounding rock strata, dominate the countryside. Mt Monadnock in New Hampshire exemplifies this type of relief; its name has been adopted by geographers to describe similar formations found elsewhere. Other monadnocks include Mts Katahdin and Blue in Maine, Mts Cardigan and Kearsage in New Hampshire, and Mts Wachusetts and Greylock in Massachusetts.

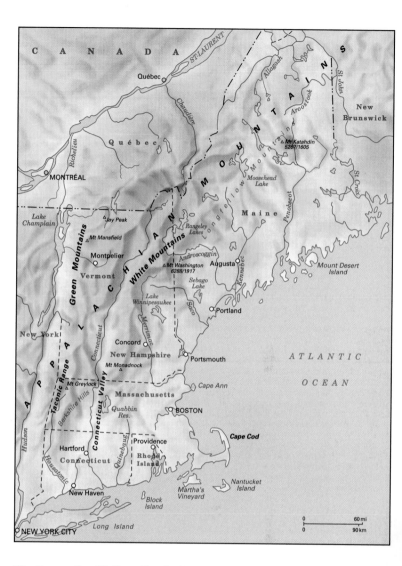

**The Connecticut Valley** – New England is bisected by this 400mi-long, north-south incision carved by the Connecticut River. The valley follows a fault that is punctuated by several craggy basalt ridges (Mts Sugarloaf and Holyoke) rising above the valley floor in Massachusetts and north of NEW HAVEN, Connecticut. The valley's abundance of fossils (p 161) reflects its rich geologic past.

**The Coast** – In the north the coast is jagged and indented, with countless peninsulas and bays following a northwest-southeast orientation, a vivid reminder of the direction of the Laurentide ice sheet. Melting glacial waters together with a rising sea level inundated this land, hiding most of the glacial landforms and creating a coastline of elongated bays and hundreds of offshore islands. South of PORTLAND, Maine, the broad, flat coastal plain gives way to sandy beaches. The estuaries and lagoons of quiet water protected by barrier beaches have given rise to vast salt marshes that provide food and resting grounds for birds and waterfowl in the Atlantic Flyway. Farther south enormous accumulations of sand cover the glacial moraines of Cape Cod and the islands, creating the landscape that typifies the Cape.

**Climate** – Mark Twain once observed that "there is a sumptuous variety about the New England weather, that compels admiration—and regret.... In the spring I have counted 136 different kinds of weather inside of 24 hours." This varied climate results from the fact that the region lies in a zone where cool, dry air from Canada meets warm, humid air from the southeast. Annual precipitation averages 42in, and the seasons are sharply defined.

**Winter** is cold, particularly in the north where temperatures range from -10°F to 10°F (-23°C to -12°C), and the annual snowfall in the mountains ranges from 90 to 100in. A period of variable temperatures, **spring** in New England is brief. In the north, the two- to three-week interval between winter and summer, when the snow melts and the ground thaws, is known as "mud season." Flooding can make driving on country roads hazardous during this time.

A pattern of hazy or foggy days alternating with showers followed by clear weather characterizes the humid **summer**. Daytime temperatures peak at 90°F (32°C); evenings are cool along the coast, in the mountains and near the lakes. **Autumn**, with its sunny days and cool nights, is the season when "leaf lookers" travel to New England to view the spectacular fall foliage. A cool spell in late September is often followed by **Indian summer**, a milder period when the leaves take on their most brilliant color.

Northeasters, coastal storms accompanied by high tides, heavy rain (or snow in winter) and gale-force winds, can occur at any time of year, especially off the coast of Maine. Mean temperatures for northern and southern New England vary and are affected by differences in altitude.

## Vegetation

With more than 70 percent of the region's surface covered by woodlands, New England's landscape is appealing in the summer for its thick cover of green, and even more so in the fall for its blazing leaf colors. The forests consist of a combination of deciduous trees and evergreens. The most common deciduous trees are the beech, birch, hickory, oak, and sugar or rock maple. Among the conifers, the white pine is found throughout southern New England, while hemlock, balsam fir and spruce forests abound in the north. The latter are exploited by the large paper-making companies.

**Fall Foliage** – Dramatic and unforgettable, the blazing New England foliage transforms the countryside into a palette of vivid golds (birches, poplars, gingkos), oranges (maples, hickories, mountain ash) and scarlets (red maples, red oak, sassafras and dogwoods), framed by the dark points of spruce and fir trees. What makes the scene especially impressive are the flaming crimsons and scarlets of the maple trees that cover New England. The Indian summer climate, with its crisp, clear sunny days followed by increasingly longer and colder nights, catalyzes the chemical reaction that halts the production of chlorophyll in the leaves, and causes the previously concealed pigments—yellowish carotene, brown tannin, and red anthocynin—to appear.

Leaves begin to change color in the northern states in mid-September and continue to change until mid-October, and until late October in the south. However, the first two weeks in October remain the most glorious period, when bright color blankets the New England landscape. In all six states, information centers provide foliage reports by telephone *(p 253). Driving itineraries for selected foliage tours begin on p 10.*

Willard Clay/Dembinsky Photo Assoc.

New England's fall foliage

**The Sugar Maples** – Capable of adapting to a cold climate and rocky soil, the sugar or rock maple is found throughout Vermont and New Hampshire. In early spring when the sap begins to rise in the maple trees, farmers insert a tube, from which a bucket is suspended, into the trunk. The sap that collects in the bucket is transferred to an evaporator in a nearby wooden shed called a sugarhouse, where it is boiled down into syrup. It takes 30 gallons of sap to produce one gallon of syrup. Modern technology has simplified this process; now, plastic tubes lead directly from the tree to the sugarhouse. *Visitors are welcome at many of New England's sugarhouses p 253.*

**Marshes and Bogs** – Because of its glacial origin, the soil in New England is often swampy. Vast marshlands, distinguished by tall grasses and reedy plants, line the region's coast. Bogs, wetlands characterized by the high acid content of the soil, support plants such as sedges, heaths, orchids, Labrador Tea, sphagnum moss and, in low-lying sandy areas, cranberries. Dead matter accumulating in the bog is prevented from decaying because of the acidic environment, and over a period of time this material is transformed into peat. Gradually the surface of the bog may be covered with a thick, soggy mat of sphagnum moss. Peat deposits will support trees and shrubs, and eventually vegetation will fill in the bog, converting it into dry, forested land.

**Wildflowers** – By late spring the mantle of snow has almost disappeared and the flowers in the woods, along the roadside, in the fields and mountains burst into bloom. The magnificent **rhododendron** and **laurel** bushes lend pink accents to the dark green woods. During the summer the roadsides are alternately tinted with the orange of the flowering **Turk's-cap lily**, the yellow of the tall-stemmed **goldenrod**, the pale blue of the multitude of tiny **asters** and the purplish hue of broad, swaying patches of **lupine**. Hundreds of species of more familiar wildflowers, including buttercups, daisies, sunflowers, Queen Anne's Lace and lily of the valley, adorn the fields and grassy meadows. In moist, marshy areas, look for the delicate **lady's-slipper**, a small pink or white member of the orchid family, and the greenish **Jack-in-the-pulpit**, so named because of the curved flap that gives the flower its appearance of a preacher in a pulpit.

| Rhododendron | Laurel | Turk's-cap lily | Jack-in-the-pulpit |

| Goldenrod | Aster | Wild lupine | Lady's-slipper |

*By permission of Houghton Mifflin Co,* A Field Guide to Wildflowers, *Peterson & McKenny*

# Wildlife

There are virtually no forms of wildlife unique to New England, yet several species of animals are typical of the region's fauna.

**The Forests** – The **white-tailed deer**, the favorite game of hunters, is found in many parts of New England. This species of deer, characterized by its white, bushy tail, inhabits the northern spruce and fir forests together with **black bears** and **moose** *(illustration p 78)*. The region's largest mammal, the moose boasts an enormous set of antlers and may be encountered in the middle of forest roads.
In ponds and streams, colonies of **beavers** *(illustration p 259)* toil, felling trees with their teeth to build dams. Their structures often create deep ponds or cause flooding in low-lying areas. Swampy zones are thus created where trees cannot survive; dead tree trunks identify these ponds.
Among the other forest inhabitants are the masked **raccoon**, the **porcupine** with its protective bristly quills, the black-and-white-striped **skunk**, and the **red squirrel**. The **chipmunk**, a member of the squirrel family, is a small mammal that frequents settled areas as well as woodlands.

**The Coast** – **Sea gulls** and **terns** are ever-present along the coast, always searching for food on boats, on the beaches, in inlets and marshes and on the piers that line the waterfront. The **great cormorants** are larger in size and live principally on the rocky sea cliffs that they share with several species of **seals**.
Coastal marshes serve as the feeding and resting grounds for hundreds of species of birds. Located along the **Atlantic Flyway**, broad stretches of salt marshes, such as those west of Barnstable Harbor on Cape Cod, are frequented by large numbers of birdwatchers during the spring and fall migrations. Flocks of **Canada geese**, their graceful V-formation a familiar sight in the New England sky during migratory seasons, rest in these tranquil areas. **Puffins** *(p 254)* may also be seen.

# TIME LINE

## Exploration

| | |
|---|---|
| **1000** | Norse sailors reach the shores of present-day Newfoundland. |
| **1492** | Christopher Columbus lands on the island of San Salvador. |
| **1497** | **John Cabot** explores the coast of North America. English claims to land in the New World are based on his voyages. |
| **1509** | Henry VIII becomes king of England. |
| **1524** | **Giovanni da Verrazano** explores the coast of North America for France. |
| **1534** | Henry VIII establishes the Church of England. |
| **1558** | Elizabeth I accedes to the English throne. |
| **1602** | English explorer **Bartholomew Gosnold**, sailing south along the New England coast, names Cape Cod, the Elizabeth Islands and Martha's Vineyard. |
| **1604** | The Frenchmen **Samuel de Champlain** and **Pierre de Gua**, **Sieur de Monts**, founders of Acadia (New France), establish a colony on St Croix Island (p 74) and explore the Maine coast. |
| **1605** | Capt **George Weymouth** returns to England from Maine with five American Indians. |
| **1607** | Virginia Colony, the first permanent English settlement in North America, is established at Jamestown. **Sir John Popham** and **Sir Ferdinando Gorges** finance an expedition to start a colony on the coast of Maine (p 64). |
| **1608** | Samuel de Champlain founds Quebec City. |
| **1613** | The Jesuits establish a mission on Mt Desert Island, Maine. |
| **1614** | **Capt John Smith**, sailing for a group of London merchants, returns to England with a cargo of fish and furs. The term "New England" is used for the first time in his account of the voyage, *A Description of New England*. Dutch navigator Adrian Block names Block Island. |

## Colonization

| | |
|---|---|
| **1620** | The Pilgrims arrive on the **Mayflower** and establish Plymouth Colony, the first permanent English settlement in New England. |
| **1625** | Charles I becomes king of England. |
| **1626** | Roger Conant leads a group to Cape Ann and organizes the Puritan colony of Salem. |
| **1630** | **Boston** is founded by Puritans led by **John Winthrop**. |
| **1635** | **Thomas Hooker** leads a group of settlers from Massachusetts Bay Colony to the Connecticut Valley and founds Hartford Colony. |
| **1636** | **Harvard College** established. **Roger Williams** flees the intolerance of Massachusetts Bay Colony and establishes Providence, Rhode Island. |
| **1638** | **Anne Hutchinson** and William Coddington found Portsmouth, Rhode Island. |
| **1638-1639** | The Connecticut Valley towns of Hartford, Windsor and Wethersfield join to form Connecticut Colony. |
| **1653** | Oliver Cromwell is appointed Lord Protector of England. |
| **1660** | The Restoration: accession of Charles II. |
| **1662** | A royal charter unites the New Haven and Connecticut Colonies. |
| **1689** | Accession of William III and his wife, Mary. |
| **1702** | Anne becomes queen of Britain. |
| **1713** | By the Treaty of Utrecht, France cedes Acadia, Newfoundland and the Hudson Bay territory to Britain. |
| **1714** | George I accedes to the British throne. |
| **1763** | The Treaty of Paris ends the French and Indian War (1756-1763): France cedes Canada and territories east of the Mississippi to Britain. |

## Independence

| | |
|---|---|
| **1765** | Passage of the **Stamp Act**, a direct tax levied by Britain on the American colonies without the consent of the colonial legislature. |
| **1766** | Stamp Act is repealed. |
| **1767** | Parliament passes the **Townshend Acts**, which levy duties on colonial imports of tea, paper and glass. |
| **1770** | The majority of the Townshend Acts are repealed, but the tax on tea remains. Friction between the colonists and the British leads to the Boston Massacre (p 97). |
| **1773** | In response to the British refusal to repeal the tax on tea, colonists stage the Boston Tea Party (p 97) at Boston Harbor. |
| **1774** | Parliament passes the five **Intolerable Acts**, four of which were directed against the citizens of Massachusetts in retaliation for the Boston Tea Party the previous year. Colonists who oppose Britain's policies hold the **First Continental Congress**. |
| **1775** | Outbreak of the **American Revolution**:<br>April 18 – Ride of Paul Revere (p 97).<br>April 19 – Battles of Lexington and Concord (pp 143 and 150).<br>May 10 – Siege of Fort Ticonderoga (p 225) by Ethan Allen and the Green Mountain Boys, along with Benedict Arnold and his men.<br>June 17 – Battle of Bunker Hill (p 97).<br>July 3 – Washington is named Commander-in-Chief by the Continental Congress. |
| **1776** | March 17 – British troops evacuate Boston.<br>July 4 – **Declaration of Independence** is adopted. |
| **1777** | Battle of Bennington (p 223).<br>Vermont declares its independence and adopts its own state constitution. |
| **1780** | French forces led by General Rochambeau arrive in Newport, Rhode Island to aid the American revolutionaries. |
| **1781** | Colonists defeat British troops led by General Cornwallis at Yorktown, Virginia. |
| **1783** | End of the American Revolution; Britain recognizes the independence of the 13 colonies. |

| | |
|---|---|
| **1788** | Ratification of the US Constitution. |
| | Connecticut, Massachusetts and New Hampshire are admitted to the Union as the fifth, sixth and ninth states, respectively. |
| **1789** | **George Washington** is chosen as the first President of the US. |
| | The French Revolution begins. |
| **1790** | Rhode Island becomes the 13th US state. |
| **1791** | Vermont, the last New England colony to join the Union, is admitted as the 14th state in the US. |

## 19C and 20C

| | |
|---|---|
| **1812** | US declares war on Britain. |
| **1814** | The Treaty of Ghent ends the War of 1812 on Christmas Eve. |
| **1815** | The defeat of French Emperor Napoleon Bonaparte at the Battle of Waterloo on June 19 leads to his abdication and exile. |
| **1820** | Maine enters the Union as the 23rd state. |
| **1837** | Queen Victoria begins her 64-year reign. |
| **1845** | Famine strikes Ireland. |
| **1851-1852** | Harriet Beecher Stowe's novel *Uncle Tom's Cabin* appears in serial form in the abolitionist paper *The National Era*. |
| **1861-1865** | **Civil War.** |
| **1865** | John Wilkes Booth assassinates President Lincoln at Ford's Theatre in Washington DC on the night of April 14. |
| **1905** | The Treaty of Portsmouth, ending the Russo-Japanese War, is signed at the Portsmouth Naval Base in Kittery, Maine. |
| **1914-1918** | **World War I.** |
| **1917** | US declares war on Germany. |
| **1921** | Italian immigrants Nicola Sacco and Bartolomeo Vanzetti are tried for murder in Dedham, Massachusetts. |
| **1929** | Stock market crash signals the start of the Great Depression. |
| **1932** | Franklin Delano Roosevelt is elected 32nd President of the US. |
| **1939-1945** | **World War II.** |
| **1941** | US declares war on Japan following the December 7 attack on Pearl Harbor. |
| **1944** | Bretton Woods Conference is held in New Hampshire *(p 197)*. |
| **1954** | World's first nuclear-powered submarine is constructed at Groton, Connecticut. |
| **1961** | At age 43, John F. Kennedy from Massachusetts becomes the youngest man ever to be elected US president. |
| **1963** | President Kennedy is assassinated in Dallas, Texas on November 22. |
| **1966** | Massachusetts State Attorney General Edward W. Brooke is the first black elected to the US Senate since Reconstruction. |
| **1976** | The Liberian tanker *Argo Merchant* runs aground near Nantucket Island and spills 7.5 million gallons of crude oil into the North Atlantic. |
| **1980** | Boston celebrates its 350th anniversary. |
| **1983** | *Australia II* wins the America's Cup by defeating the American yacht *Liberty* in the best of seven races off the coast of Newport, Rhode Island. |
| **1985** | Vermont voters elect the nation's first foreign-born woman governor, Madeleine M. Kunin. |
| **1988** | Democratic candidate Michael Dukakis, former governor of Massachusetts, loses the US presidential election to George Bush. Dukakis receives 46 percent of the nation's popular vote. |
| **1990** | Twelve works of art, valued at $100 million, are stolen from the Isabella Stewart Gardner Museum *(p 121)* in Boston. |
| **1991** | Bridgeport, Connecticut becomes the largest US city to file a petition of bankruptcy. The city's petition is denied. |
| **1992** | Mashantucket Pequot Indians open Foxwoods, a resort casino in Ledyard, CT. |
| **1993** | The Norman Rockwell Museum at Stockbridge opens in western MA. |
| **1994** | Harvard University, the most generously endowed of private universities ($6 billion) launches largest fund-raising drive in the history of higher education. |
| **1995** | Boston's Museum of Fine Arts *(p 118)* announces layoffs and restructuring to reduce $4.5 million deficit. |

Craig Alness (f/STOP PICTURES)

Revolutionary reenactment, Portsmouth

# ECONOMY

The economic evolution of New England paralleled that of the area's mother country. A period of intense agricultural activity was followed by maritime prosperity and then industrialization, which formed the backbone of the economy through the 19C and into the 20C. After World War II the region fell into an economic slump, due to the movement of many of its factories to the South. As a result New England turned to new, diversified, high-value industries, such as electronics, as its principal sources of revenue.

## Industry

In the 19C profits accumulated from trade, shipping and whaling, and the influx of immigrants from Europe and Canada, which provided the large labor force needed for industrialization, fostered New England's growth into one of the world's leading manufacturing centers.

**The Mill Towns** – The region's many waterways compensated for the lack of raw materials and fuel by providing the power necessary to operate factory machinery. Mill towns, supporting factories that specialized in a single product, sprung up on the banks of rivers and streams. Textiles and leather goods were made in Massachusetts and New Hampshire, precision products such as clocks and firearms were manufactured in Connecticut, and machine tools were produced in Vermont. The large manufacturing centers in the Merrimack Valley, LOWELL, Lawrence and MANCHESTER, developed into world leaders in textile production. Strings of brick factories, dwellings and stores still dominate these cities.
During the 20C most of these industries moved south to the Sun Belt, but the region remained a leader in the manufacture of woolen cloth. The production of machine tools and fabricated metals has now replaced textiles, and the shoe industry is important in New Hampshire and Maine.

**The New Industries** – The rebirth of New England after World War II was linked to the development of its research-oriented industries, which could draw on the region's excellent educational institutions and highly trained personnel. These new industries, located essentially in the Boston area (on Route 128), in southern New Hampshire and in HARTFORD, contributed to advances made in space and computer technology and electronics. Their existence gave rise to the production of high-value goods, such as information systems, precision instruments and electronic components, and provided an increasing number of jobs. BOSTON, known for its medical research firms, is also home to producers of medical instruments and artificial organs.

## Insurance

Insurance has been an important business in New England since the 19C, when investors offered to underwrite the risks involved in international shipping. Every boat that sailed out of port represented a gamble; it could return with valuable cargo, or it could sink, eliminating forever all hopes of profit. With the decline of sea trade, the insurance industry expanded to include losses due to fire, and the center of the industry shifted inland. Hartford, Connecticut, a national insurance center, is the seat of some 40 companies. The modern office towers built in Boston to serve as headquarters of the John Hancock and Prudential insurance companies are the tallest structures in New England, symbolizing the importance of this industry to the economy.

## Education

Traditionally renowned as a national center of culture and learning, New England is home to three prestigious ivy-league universities (Harvard, Yale and Dartmouth) and two choice preparatory schools (Phillips Exeter Academy in Exeter, New Hampshire and Phillips Academy in Andover, Massachusetts). The concentration of schools, academies, and some 258 institutions of higher learning in the six-state area makes education a significant contributor to the economy. Small businesses in cities (WORCESTER, NEW HAVEN, PROVIDENCE), towns (MIDDLEBURY, HANOVER, BRUNSWICK, Amherst), and regions (PIONEER VALLEY, Greater Boston) depend on the revenue generated by the schools within their borders. In Massachusetts, where education is a major source of income, the state's 80 private colleges alone generated $10 billion of revenue in 1991.

## Tourism

Tourism ranks with manufacturing as one of New England's major industries. Mountain and seaside resorts in New England have been welcoming visitors for over a century, and with the growing popularity of winter sports since the 1940s, the region has developed into a year-round vacation area. Fine handicrafts, fashioned by artisans working in New Hampshire, Vermont and along the coast, abound throughout New England. Their sale depends to a great extent on tourists.

## Agriculture

Despite the poor soil and rocky, hilly terrain, subsistence farming was an important activity until the mid-19C. In the spring settlers cleared land to ready it for planting. The mounds of rock they removed from the soil were used to build the low stone walls that appear to ramble aimlessly through the woods. Farming reached a peak in New

England between 1830 and 1880 with 60 percent of the region under cultivation. After 1880 the opening of the fertile plains south of the Great Lakes drew farmers westward. They abandoned their farms, and the forests gradually reclaimed the land. Today only six percent of the surface of New England continues to be devoted to agriculture, while 70 percent of the region's land (90 percent in Maine and 80 percent in New Hampshire) remains covered with woodlands. Despite this fact, certain areas have been successful in cultivating single-crop specialties.

**Dairy and Poultry Farming** – The major portion of income from agriculture is provided by dairy and poultry farming. The region's dairy farms supply milk products to the sprawling urban areas of southern New England. Dairy farms, well-suited to the terrain, predominate in Vermont, where large red barns with their shiny aluminum silos dominate the landscape.

Poultry farming is practiced throughout the region. Connecticut and Rhode Island focus on raising chickens. In fact Rhode Island is famous for raising a breed of chicken called the Rhode Island Red. Vermont's turkey farms—their buildings well lit, temperature-controlled and equipped with modern machinery—are busiest during the holiday seasons, particularly around Thanksgiving.

**Specialty Crops** – Shade-grown **tobacco** is raised in the fertile Connecticut River Valley. Firm and broad-leafed, this tobacco, grown beneath a layer of netting and hung in large sheds to dry, is used as the outer wrapping of cigars. Fruit is cultivated in many areas: apple, peach and pear orchards extend along the banks of LAKE CHAMPLAIN and abound on the sunny slopes of New Hampshire, in the Connecticut and Nashua Valleys and in Rhode Island. Maine leads all other states in production of **blueberries** (80 million pounds in 1992), and the sandy bogs on Cape Cod *(p 138)* and in nearby areas yield the nation's largest crop of **cranberries**, the small, red berries traditionally served as part of the Thanksgiving Day feast.
Maine's other specialty crop is **potatoes**, grown in the fertile soil of Aroostook County. The state's potato industry ranks third in size after Idaho's and Washington's.
In the fall visitors to rural New England can purchase locally raised **pumpkins, gourds** and **Indian corn** at roadside stands *(p 253)*.

**Forests** – Despite the enormous area that they cover, New England's deciduous and coniferous forests are not significant as sources of income because of large-scale deforestation of the region throughout the 19C, and current federal and state protection of vast tracts of land. Only the commercial timberlands owned by the large paper companies in northern Maine and New Hampshire constitute important sources of revenue. A major portion of the timber harvested is processed into wood pulp for the mills in Maine (Millinocket, BUCKSPORT, Woodland, Rumford) and New Hampshire (Berlin), with Maine's factories ranking among the world's leading paper producers. Other plants and mills transform timber into a variety of wood products, including lumber, veneer, furniture and boxes. The production of **maple syrup** is a traditional springtime activity in Vermont, New Hampshire and Maine.

## Fishing

As early as the 15C, European fishermen were drawn to the rich fishing grounds off the coast of New England. These shallow, sandy banks (such as George's Bank), extending 1,500mi east to west off Cape Cod, teemed with fish. The fishing industry was so vital to New England that fishermen were exempt from military service, and the Massachusetts Bay Colony adopted the cod as its symbol.
Commercial fishing has been especially important to the ports of Gloucester, NEW BED-FORD and Boston. Modern techniques of filleting, freezing and packaging fish, and larger, more efficient vessels have made New England a leader in the packaged and frozen seafood industry. However, the region's fishing industry has seen dramatic curtailment over the past three decades, stemming from overfishing (particularly of cod, flounder, tuna and haddock), pollution and insufficient conservation. More recently, stringent federal regulations have been proposed to reduce stock depletion.
Lobstering ranks as an activity approaching an art in Maine, where it is practiced by thousands of DownEast lobstermen, who can often be observed in a variety of craft, checking their traps in the offshore waters. Maine lobster is a delicacy that is available in markets across the nation.

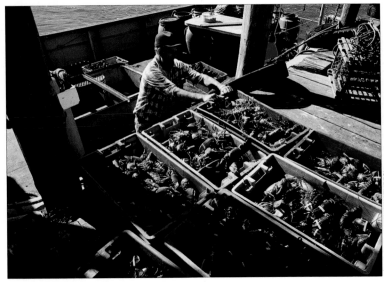

John Lazenby (f/STOP PICTURES)

Unloading lobster

# NEW ENGLAND AND THE SEA

New England has been closely related to the sea ever since the colonists turned from the rocky soil to the offshore waters for their food. At first the colonists erected weirs, similar to those used to this day by the Indians in Maine to snare fish near the shore. Not until the mid-17C did Yankee vessels sail in large numbers to the Grand Banks, the fishing grounds off the southern coast of Newfoundland, which teemed with cod, haddock and pollack. The Sacred Cod, hanging in the Massachusetts State House (*p 105*), symbolizes the important role played by the cod fisheries in the history of Massachusetts. New England's fisheries became the backbone of the region's trade with Europe, and boatyards sprang up along the coast from Connecticut to Maine to construct fishing and cargo vessels.

Fisheries, trade and shipbuilding prospered, reaching their zenith in the mid 19C. The south (Connecticut, Rhode Island and southeastern Massachusetts) was home to the Yankee whaling fleet; ports along the northern coast of Massachusetts and New Hampshire led the trade with the Orient (the China Trade *p 167*) and the shipbuilding industry. With its protected inlets and thick forests, the Maine coast focused on wooden shipbuilding. Between 1830 and 1860, nearly one-third of the boats launched in the US were built in Maine.

Small coastal villages grew into sophisticated urban centers, as merchants, shipmasters and sea captains accumulated great wealth and built the handsome Federal and Greek Revival homes that still stand in SALEM, NANTUCKET, PORTSMOUTH, NEWBURYPORT, NEW BEDFORD, PROVIDENCE and other seaport cities.

Several large museums preserve New England's seafaring past. Mystic Seaport and the whaling museums in New Bedford, Nantucket and Sharon recall the Yankee whaling tradition. In Salem the Peabody Essex Museum presents the story of New England's trade with the Orient, and the Maine Maritime Museum and the Penobscot Marine Museum portray the history of shipbuilding in Maine.

## Whaling

During the 19C whale oil was used to light homes and streets across America and Europe. New Bedford and Nantucket, leading whaling centers, were busy day and night with vessels arriving, departing or preparing for a whaling voyage. Herman Melville's novel *Moby-Dick* (1851) vividly re-creates New England's whaling days.

**A Prized Catch** – Since history has been recorded, man has been fascinated by this warm-blooded, air-breathing mammal that roams the world's oceans. The order Cetacea, to which all whales belong, includes the largest animal that has ever lived: the blue whale. A mature blue whale can attain a length of 100ft, and weigh up to 150 tons. Whales can be divided into two groups: toothed and toothless (baleen).

**Toothed** whales are predators that feed on fish. Averaging 63 tons, the **sperm whale** was the species on which New England's whaling industry depended. This animal was hunted in large numbers because it was a source of rare products. Spermaceti, a solid waxy substance, was used to make fragrant

Scrimshaw - Whale's tooth

Courtesy Mystic Seaport Museum

candles. Obtained in liquid form from a cavity in the whale's head, sperm oil provided fuel for oil-burning lamps. One male sperm whale yielded more than 1,800 gallons of oil. Ambergris, a substance found in the intestines of the whale, was used commercially in the manufacture of perfumes.

**Baleen** whales, such as the **right whale**—considered the "right whale to hunt" since it floated when it was dead—live on plankton sifted out of the sea by the long, comb-like sheets of baleen, a horny material hanging from the roof of the animal's mouth. The plastic of the 19C, flexible baleen furnished the raw material for corset and umbrella stays, buggy whips and a variety of other products.

**A Meteoric Industry** – Indians were hunting whales long before the first settlements were established. The colonists learned how to hunt inshore whales by observing the Indians. They built tall watchtowers and set up large black cauldrons, called tryworks, in which the whale fat was melted down, on the beaches. In the 18C the discovery of sperm whales in deep ocean waters led to the construction of larger vessels that were outfitted for long ocean voyages. By 1730 Yankee whalemen had moved the tryworks from the beaches to the decks of whaling vessels so they could process whales at sea. In the late 18C Nantucket boasted a fleet of 150 whaling vessels; in its heyday, New Bedford was home port to nearly 400. NEW LONDON, PROVINCETOWN, Fairhaven, MYSTIC, Stonington and Edgartown also launched their own fleets. Shipyards turned out sturdier ocean-going vessels, factories manufactured spermaceti candles, tons of baleen were dried in the fields and thousands of barrels of whale oil were stored along the wharves. Whale ships built, owned and commandeered in New England sailed the oceans from Greenland to the North Pacific, from the Azores to Brazil, and from Polynesia to Japan. Many languages could be heard as seamen from international ports-of-call walked the streets of New England's waterfront districts.

The decline of the whaling industry in New England was precipitated by the discovery of petroleum in Pennsylvania in 1859 and the loss of nearly half of New England's whaling fleet during the Civil War years. In 1861 the Union Navy purchased 39 whale ships to form the "Stone Fleet," a group of vessels that were loaded with blocks of granite and sunk in the harbors of Savannah, Georgia and Charleston, South Carolina to prevent blockade runners from entering those channels. The Confederate ship *Shenandoah* destroyed an additional 21 whaling vessels in the North Pacific Ocean in 1865. After the war New England sent out fewer and fewer whalers, until in 1971, whale hunting was finally outlawed in the US.

## Maritime Commerce

New England's maritime commerce with Africa, Europe and the West Indies brought prosperity to many of its coastal ports in the early 18C, but not until after the Revolution, when Americans were free to trade with the Orient, did Boston, Providence, Portsmouth, Salem and other cities develop into rich centers of the China Trade.

**China Trade** – Boats sailing to the Far East rounded Cape Horn, then generally made detours to ports along the way to obtain returns—goods that could be traded in China for silks, porcelains and tea. Furs were acquired along the northwest Pacific coast, sandalwood from the Sandwich Islands, and the delicacy *bêche-de-mer* (sea grub) from the Polynesian Islands. Later, when opium replaced furs as returns, boats called at ports in India and Turkey to barter for the illicit drug before continuing to China.

Other exotic products obtained along the route were pepper purchased in Sumatra, sugar and coffee from Java, cotton from Bombay and Madras, ivory from Zanzibar, spices from Indonesia and gum arabic from Oman.

Until 1842 **Canton** was the only Chinese port open to foreign trade. Vessels anchored about 10mi outside the city at **Whampoa Reach**. Several weeks or even months could be spent visiting shops and factories, and bartering with Chinese merchants before the foreign vessel, filled with a cargo of luxury items, set sail for home.

The museums and historical houses of New England exhibit countless examples of Chinese decorative arts and furnishings brought back to America from the Orient during the years of the China Trade.

**Ice: A Unique New England Industry** – The ice trade developed in the 19C when ice was harvested north of Boston and in Maine, and shipped to the southern states, the West Indies and as far away as Calcutta to be used for refrigeration. Ice was harvested in the winter, when the rivers, lakes and ponds were frozen over. Snow was cleared with the aid of oxen or horses. The ice field, marked off into squares, was cut into blocks weighing up to 200lbs each. Packed in sawdust and stored in nearby ice houses until the first thaw, the ice was then transported by boat to its destination. Boats with specially constructed airtight hulls were used to prevent the ice from melting. The ice business prospered until the introduction of mechanical refrigeration in the late 19C.

## Shipbuilding

The wooden sailing vessel has been the basis of New England's shipbuilding tradition since 1607, when the pinnace *Virginia* was built by the short-lived Popham Colony on the banks of the Kennebec River in Maine.

**Early Days** – As the colonists established their first settlements, shipyards began to dot the coast. At first they built small, one-masted ketches and fishing sloops, followed in the early 18C by two- and three-masted schooners capable of crossing the Atlantic. The schooner enjoyed a long and glamorous career in the waters off the New England coast. When English dominance of American trade led to widespread smuggling by the colonists, it was the schooner, with its simple rigging, ease-of-handling, and ability to evade British revenue ships, that carried many an illicit cargo safely into port. During the American Revolution, armed, privately owned schooners (privateers) were authorized by the Continental Congress to capture enemy vessels. The schooner remained in service as a cargo carrier until the end of World War I.

**Age of the Clipper Ship** – With the opening of Chinese ports in the 1840s, Americans clamored for Chinese goods. Knowing that American customers would pay high prices for the freshest teas from the Orient, shrewd shippers demanded faster vessels to transport this perishable commodity in the shortest possible time. The clipper—derived from the word *clipper,* describing any person or thing that traveled quickly— was designed to meet their needs. Between the mid-1840s and mid-1850s, these three-masted vessels, with their lean hulls, narrow bows and acres of canvas sails, became famous for the great speeds they could attain. During the California Gold Rush, clippers—with names such as *Lightning, Flying Cloud* and *Eagle Wing*—carried miners and supplies from the Atlantic coast, around Cape Horn, to San Francisco, as well as sailing the long ocean routes to the Orient.

The major boatyards working to turn out these ships were located in New York, Boston and BATH, Maine, and the master designer was **Donald McKay** of East Boston. Of the approximately 100 vessels that made the voyage around Cape Horn in less than four months, 19 of them, including the *Flying Cloud*, were built by McKay. The first ship to round the Cape to San Francisco in under 90 days, the *Flying Cloud* set a record of 89 days on her maiden voyage in 1851, and repeated it three years later. Her record was never surpassed by a ship under sail.

**Last Sailing Ships** – From the 1850s to the early 1900s, the ports of Maine specialized in the production of commercial wooden sailing vessels: the **down-easter** and the **great schooner**. The down-easter, a three-masted square-rigger, had the long clean lines of a clipper, and could attain comparable speeds. Unlike the clipper, the down-easter had a large, deep hull that offered greater carrying space and made it a more profitable means of transporting cargo.

The down-easters and two- and three-masted schooners were used in shipping until the 1880s, when boat builders discovered that four-masted schooners, though larger, cost little more to operate. The construction of the great schooners—four-, five- and six-masted vessels—followed. These ships hauled large bulk cargoes (coal, lumber, granite, grain) from the East Coast, around Cape Horn and up to the West Coast. Striving to compete with the steamboat, Maine shipyards turned to the production of a small fleet of steel four-, five- and six-masters. The days of sail were numbered, however: the efficient, regularly scheduled steamer triumphed.

# POPULATION

New England's population of 13 million inhabitants is unevenly distributed; the majority live in the southern half of the region, where the largest cities (BOSTON, WORCESTER, PROVIDENCE, SPRINGFIELD, HARTFORD and NEW HAVEN) are found. The large waves of immigrants who arrived in the 19C brought with them a diversity of cultures that is still reflected in the ethnic character of the population today.

**The Many Faces of New England** – The **Indians** of the Algonquin nation were the first to inhabit the region. They were woodland Indians, who farmed, hunted, fished and camped along the coast. Their numbers had already been greatly reduced by disease and tribal warfare when the Europeans settled here in the 17C. The largest group, the **Narragansett** tribe of Rhode Island, was virtually wiped out by the English colonists at the Battle of the Great Swamp *(p 202)* during King Philip's War. Present-day descendants of the **Passamaquoddy** and **Penobscot** tribes live on reservations at Pleasant Point and Old Town in Maine. The circular traps, or weirs, that they constructed offshore to trap fish are visible as you drive along the north coast of Maine. Members of the **Wampanoag** tribe make their home on Cape Cod and Martha's Vineyard.

Descendants of the 17C and 18C Puritan settlers dominated New England's population until the mid-19C. Hard work, frugality and "Yankee ingenuity"—the talent for making the best of any situation—characterized these early New Englanders, some of whom amassed great fortunes in trade and shipping, and later in industry and finance.

The population remained basically homogeneous until the 1840s, when the potato famine in Ireland caused thousands of **Irish** to emigrate to New England, where they found work in the mills. The **Italians** followed in the 1870s, and at the end of the 19C, **French Canadians**, attracted by jobs in the region's factories, began to settle here. Communities of **Portuguese** fishermen from the Azores developed in coastal ports such as Gloucester, PROVINCETOWN and QUINCY, while successive waves of immigrants brought **Swedes**, **Russians** and other **Eastern Europeans** to the cities and factory towns. As Boston's **African-American** community vacated the North End for Beacon Hill, the Irish, followed by the Jews and eventually the Italians, made the North End their home. Each ethnic group formed its own cohesive neighborhood, where the unity of language, culture and religion drew them together. Irish, Italians and Jews tended to settle in or near the large cities, while the Portuguese continue to reside in the coastal areas, maintaining traditions, such as the celebration of the blessing of the fleet *(Calendar of Events pp 244-245)*. French names are common in New Hampshire, Maine and Vermont, where French Canadians form a significant part of the population. People of Swedish, Russian and Eastern European extraction chose to live in Maine and the rural areas. The majority of the region's black and **Hispanic** populations reside in southern New England.

*Other Michelin Green Guides available in English are:*

| | | |
|---|---|---|
| *California* | *Belgium* | *Regions of France:* |
| *Canada* | *Switzerland* | *Atlantic Coast* |
| *New England* | *Greece* | *Brittany* |
| *Mexico* | *Italy* | *Burgundy* |
| *Quebec* | *Portugal* | *Châteaux of the Loire* |
| *Great Britain* | *Spain* | *Dordogne* |
| *England:* | | *French Riviera* |
| *   The West Country* | *City Guides:* | *Île-de-France* |
| *Scotland* | *New York* | *Normandy Cotentin* |
| *Ireland* | *Washington, DC* | *Normandy Seine Valley* |
| *Netherlands* | *London* | *Provence* |
| *France* | *Paris* | |
| *Germany* | *Rome* | |
| *Austria* | | |

# ARCHITECTURE

New England's identity is justifiably architectural: it is indeed the classic calendar image of white-spired churches, trim red barns and weather-beaten farmhouses, well-preserved by a cold climate and fierce pride in local history. Best known for its colonial architecture, the region nevertheless retains a rich heritage of building traditions from all periods, ranging from practical Indian dwellings to the magnificent seaside estates of the Gilded Age and the visually striking high rises of post-Modernism. In the 20C New England's prestigious universities attracted such leading modernists as Walter Gropius, Le Corbusier, Eero Saarinen, Philip Johnson and I.M. Pei who, in turn, re-shaped the architectural tenor of such cities as BOSTON, CAMBRIDGE and NEW HAVEN and placed New England in the forefront of contemporary design.

**Native American** – The traditional Algonquin dwelling was not the familiar tipi of the Great Plains but the **wigwam**, a domed or conical hut made of bent saplings covered with reed mats or bark. Quick and easy to build, these snug shelters were adopted as temporary housing by the first Massachusetts colonists until they could construct timber-framed homes. Wigwams built in the traditional manner may be seen at Pioneer Village (p 170) and at the Institute for American Indian Studies (p 51).

**Early Colonial** – The prevailing early colonial dwelling was the 2-story **post-and-beam house**, a post-medieval form characterized by a steeply pitched roof originally designed to support thatch. Several examples dating from c.1660 to 1720 still exist

in Connecticut (Buttolph-Williams House p 62) and in such early Massachusetts Bay towns as IPSWICH (Parson Capen House p 150) and at Plimoth Plantation (p 164). Settlers of these areas came almost exclusively from East Anglia, a region in southeast England where wood construction was common. Finding unlimited timber supply in the new country, they logically continued a building technique that was already familiar. The typical house plan comprised two large multipurpose rooms with exposed beams and a massive center chimney hugged by a narrow

Early Colonial

stairway leading to chambers above. Clad in shingles or clapboard siding, the exterior featured small casement windows with diamond-shaped glass panes imported from England. Often intersecting gables provided more space to the second story (Iron Works House p 128), which might have a slight overhang, or jetty, trimmed with decorative pendants (Stanley-Whitman House p 43). When the steep roof extends almost to the ground over a rear kitchen lean-to, the house is known as a **saltbox** (Fairbanks House p 128). Built low to be braced against shoreline winds, the smaller, 1 1/2-story **Cape Cod cottage**, another common early colonial house type, features a pitched or bowed roof.

In erecting a house the heavy hand-hewn framing pieces, usually of pine or oak, were numbered (Roman numerals can still be spotted on attic rafters), fitted on the ground and then lifted into place in an all-hands effort called a "raising."

By court decree all 17C New England villages were laid out according to a similar plan with the houses set around a park-like central **green**, or common, to provide protection against Indians and assure close proximity to the **meetinghouse**, the largest building in a settlement. A deliberate departure from the traditional Anglican church, the Puritan meetinghouse was an original architectural form—a square wooden structure with a hipped roof and crowning belfry (Old Ship Church p 149). It served both as church and town hall, reflecting the close ties between politics and religion in the 17C.

**Georgian** – This term generally refers to an English architectural style developed by such noted architects as Christopher Wren and James Gibbs and popularized in America from about 1720 until the Revolution (during the reigns of Kings George II

Georgian

and III) largely through pattern books and British-trained builders. The Georgian style was inspired by the new fashion for Italian Renaissance architecture—especially that of Andrea Palladio. Based primarily on the design principles of ancient Rome, this style incorporated, unlike medieval building, the Classical orders, especially Doric, Ionic and Corinthian.

Dignified and formal, the high-style Georgian house proved ideally suited to the tastes of a growing mercantile class. Mansions in wood, stone or brick soon appeared in every major port city (Portsmouth p 190). Crowned by a pitched, hipped or gambrel roof, the house featured a symmetrical facade accentuated with even rows of double-hung windows. Often a central projecting pavilion front with a Palladian window and a pedimented portico graced the entryway. Heavy quoins (stone or wood blocks) typically marked the corners, and the elaborate front door was topped by a round-arched fanlight and a sculptural pediment.

A central-hall plan with end chimneys accommodated larger rooms (now with specific uses such as dining and music), robust wood carving and plaster decoration, and colorful paint treatments. In rural farm towns the Georgian house frequently retained the old center-chimney plan but boasted ornate exterior features, such as the heavy swan's neck door pediments used in the Connecticut River Valley *(illustration p 146)*.

Several Georgian public buildings were designed by **Peter Harrison** (1716-1775), perhaps America's most important colonial builder/architect. Harrison's Redwood Library in Newport *(p 212)* is based on a Roman temple. His Touro Synagogue *(p 211)*, also in Newport, and King's Chapel in Boston *(p 109)* are notable for their interior paneling. During this period many New England churches gained their familiar front towers and steeples, often adapted from the published designs of Wren (Trinity Church *p 211*) or Gibbs (First Baptist Church in America *p 216*).

## Federal

**Federal** – Popular from about 1780 to 1820, this British Neoclassical style, sometimes called Adam style, was first adopted in America by an affluent merchant class, primarily Federalists who retained close trade ties to England even after the Revolution. Bostonian **Charles Bulfinch** (1763-1844) was New England's best-known Federal-period architect, responsible for Beacon Hill's Massachusetts State House *(p 105)* and Harrison Gray Otis House *(p 107)*. Another proponent of the Federal style, **Samuel McIntire** (1757-1811) designed several public buildings and houses in Salem. His Gardener-Pingree House *(p 169)* is typical of the 19C seaport town's many elegant 3-story Federal houses built of narrow, butter-smooth bricks with low, hipped roofs crowned by handsome cornice-line balustrades.

Like its Georgian counterpart, the high-style Federal mansion, often with bowed or rounded walls (Gore Place *p 128*) was symmetrical and its central door was topped by a Palladian window (Harrison Gray Otis House *p 107*). But the overall appearance was far lighter and more conservative, sometimes sober, with proportions elongated, exterior decoration reduced and fanlights flattened from half-rounds into ellipses.

Federal

The style is most notable for its refined interior decor, influenced by the work of British architect **Robert Adam**. Oval and round rooms were introduced, along with graceful freestanding staircases and exquisitely decorated fireplace mantels and surrounds, carved with delicate garlands, urns, wheat sheaves and other classical motifs inspired by recent discoveries at Pompeii and Herculaneum. Extremely popular, Federal-style design eventually spread to even the most modest of farm- and village houses and churches throughout New England (look for the telltale elliptical front door fanlight).

## Greek Revival

**Greek Revival** – Coinciding with several popular English books on Greek archaeology, the Greek Revival style came to America via England and was popular here from about 1820 to 1845. While the Georgian and Federal styles were based on Roman prototypes, the new architectural mode adhered to ancient Greek orders and design principles, notable for squarer proportions, a more monumental scale and less surface ornament. Imitative of Greek temples, buildings in the style were almost always white and usually featured the so-called "temple front." This 2-story portico with Doric, Ionic or Corinthian columns supported an unbroken triangular pediment at the roof line.

Among the educated elite the Greek Revival style represented a symbolic link between the republic of ancient Greece and the new American nation. It was adopted for many impressive public buildings, including marble or granite courthouses, banks, libraries (Providence Athenaeum *p 218*), churches (Church of the Presidents *p 166*) and temples of trade (Providence Arcade *p 218*), as well as for domestic architecture. Elegant Greek Revival-styled mansions appeared in affluent towns and seaports (Whale Oil Row *p 59*).

Greek Revival

Among the major designers of the period were **Alexander Parris** (Quincy Market *p 111*) and **Robert Mills** (Customs House *p 160*). **Asher Benjamin**, who wrote some of the most influential builder's handbooks in America, designed many New England churches (Old West Church *p 107*) and fine homes (Nos. 54-55 Beacon St *p 105*). Through handbooks such as his, the style was also adopted for simple clapboard farm- and village houses throughout the region. On more modest farmhouses the triangular roof gable was turned to face front and the corner boards suggested the columns.

**19C Vernacular** – A distinctive feature of rural New England is the **covered bridge** (West Cornwall *p 50;* WINDSOR *p 240*). In 1820 noted New Haven architect Ithiel Town (Center and Trinity Churches *p 57*) patented the **lattice truss**, the interwoven framework visible on the inside of the bridge. The roof, of pine or spruce, was designed to protect the structural elements from harsh weather. The **connected farm**, a complex of attached houses, barns and animal sheds prevalent in northern New England in the mid-19C, developed as old outbuildings were moved from farm property and added to the main residence. The attached buildings commonly housed cottage industries such as canning and weaving, which were important supplements to farm income.

Along the coast 19C **lighthouses** mark harbor entrances and dangerous shoals. These structures originally included a tower and beacon, first lit with oil lamps and parabolic reflectors, as well as housing for the keeper, who was often the nearest US customs agent. The keeper's role has now been lost to automation. Occupying dramatic sites, some decommissioned 19C lighthouses have been converted to private homes, but numerous lights can be visited by the public (Sheffield Island *p 60;* Owl's Head *p 88*).

Still visible in many industrial towns are 19C **textile mills**, originally powered by water turbine (steam power became common in the 1850s). Manned largely by cheap immigrant labor, mills were designed as self-contained complexes and typically included railroads, parks, canals, churches and employee housing. Punctuated by rhythmic rows of windows and an occasional clock tower or smoke stack, these granite- or brick-walled buildings, usually five or more stories, can stretch for miles along a riverfront. Some complexes now contain museums (Lowell National Historic Park *p 151*); others have been converted to house small business and retail outlets (Amoskeag Manufacturing Complex *p 185*).

**Victorian Eclecticism** – During the Victorian era (1837-1901), classical design was abandoned in favor of a broad range of styles, many inspired by the dark, romantic architecture of medieval Europe. Pointed-arch windows, steeply pointed gables and gingerbread cornice boards are hallmarks of the picturesque **Gothic Revival** style (Kingscote *p 209*) also seen in board-and-batten **Carpenter's Gothic** villas and cottages (Roseland Cottage *p 62*). Other Victorian-era styles include **Italianate** (square towers, flat or low-pitched roof and broad porch; Victoria Mansion *p 86*); **Second Empire** (mansard roof, ornate cornice and round dormers; Old City Hall *p 109*) and **Queen Anne** (turrets, spindlework, asymmetrical porches, bay windows and gingerbread trim; Oak Bluffs *p 153*). In the early 1870s Boston architect **Henry Hobson Richardson** developed **Romanesque Revival** (also known as Richardsonian Romanesque), a distinctly American style rooted in the medieval architecture of France and Spain. His masterpiece, Trinity Church (*p 114*), exemplifies the characteristic squat columns, round arches and heavy rough-cut stone. Favored for seaside resorts were the **Shingle** style

Italianate

(dark wood shingles, towers and piazzas, steeply pitched roofline and asymmetrical facade; Hammersmith Farm *p 209*, Newport Casino *p 213*) and **Stick** style (gabled roof, rustic woodwork with diagonal bands, contrasting paint colors, decoratively shaped shingles; Newport Art Museum, *p 212* and Mark Twain House *p 47*).

**Turn-of-the-Century** – Late in the 19C architects trained in the academic principles of the prestigious Ecole des Beaux-Arts in Paris rejected the eccentric Victorian styles in favor of "correct" interpretations of historic European architecture, notably French Baroque, English Neoclassicism and Italian Renaissance (Renaissance Revival). Typical of the highly decorative **Beaux-Arts** style are great estates such as The Breakers (*p 207*) and Marble House (*p 208*) by the fashionable society designer **Richard Morris Hunt** and grandiose public buildings (Boston Public Library, *p 115*). Both were modeled on Italian Renaissance palaces. Beaux-Arts buildings are typically of stone (marble or granite) and feature ornate statuary, heavy facade ornamentation and rows of paired columns alternating with arched windows.

Developing at the same time was the **Colonial Revival** style, which drew on America's own colonial architecture, reinterpreted on a larger scale. A Palladian window, classical columns, swan's neck pediments and a large entry portico are typical features.

Promoted by such pretigious architectural firms as **McKim, Mead and White** (Rhode Island State House *p 218*), the style was used primarily for neo-Georgian town houses and country estates from about 1900 to 1920 (North and South Streets, Litchfield, *p 50*).

**Contemporary Architecture** – New England attracted many of the European architects who brought the **International style** to America in the 1930s, including **Walter Gropius** (1883-1969), founder of the German design school known as the **Bauhaus**. Representative of **early modernism**, which rejected ornament and historical references and embraced machine-age technology and materials, is the 1938 Gropius House *(p 145)*, a streamlined cubic design incorporating the then new materials of glass block, acoustical plaster and chrome. Among other innovative modernist works is **Eero Saarinen**'s 1955 M.I.T. Chapel *(p 134)*. Its brick cylindrical shape presents a distinct contrast to the chaste white wooden church of the New England green. The heir of early modernism was the so-called **glass box** design, ubiquitous in the 1960s in the construction of multistoried urban apartments and public buildings. An unusual example is the 1963 Beinecke Library at Yale University *(p 55)* by **Gordon Bunshaft** of **Skidmore, Owings and Merrill** designed with self-supporting walls of translucent marble. Many glass boxes appeared in New Haven, Boston and other New England cities during periods of widespread urban redevelopment that resulted in the demolition of older buildings. In concert with the growing preservation movement of the last two decades, innovative design programs have, however, helped save endangered structures and rehabilitate the blighted market and waterfront districts in such cities as Boston, Salem, Newburyport, NORWALK and BURLINGTON.

International style

Since the early 1970s innovators Robert Venturi, Robert Stern and Philip Johnson and others have developed **post-Modernism**, a movement promoting a deliberate return to ornament. Familiar historical motifs such as the classical pediment are often playfully exaggerated, used as the dominant crowning element of a building, for example. The Palladian window is simplified, even caricaturized, or the classical column is reduced to a plain shaft, topped by a ball rather than a traditional capital. Unexpected exterior color combinations are another feature. In recent years New England campuses and city skylines, notably Boston (222 Berkeley St and 500 Boylston St *p 117*), Providence and Hartford, have become national showcases for buildings in the style, which emphasizes scale, compatible materials and the relationship of a building to its neighbors.

# SCULPTURE

Sculpture consisted predominantly of folk art—shop and trade signs, weathervanes, figureheads—until the 19C, when American sculptors, studying in Italy and at the Ecole des Beaux-Arts in Paris, were exposed to the grandeur of classical sculpture. **Daniel Chester French** (1850-1931) *(p 174)* and **Augustus Saint-Gaudens** (1848-1907) *(p 192)* trained abroad and exerted a strong influence on American sculpture from the period following the Civil War until the early 20C. Each obtained numerous public commissions for war memorials and statues during his lifetime. French became known early in his career for his statue of the *Minute Man* (Concord, *p 144*), while the monumental seated *Lincoln* (Lincoln Memorial in Washington DC) is recognized as his most impressive achievement. Saint-Gaudens executed delicate, bas-relief portrait plaques and monumental sculptures, such as the Shaw Memorial in Boston *(p 105)*, for which he is best remembered.

Although both spent much of their careers in Italy, Boston native **Horatio Greenough** (1805-1852) and Vermont-born **Hiram Powers** (1805-1873) aided significantly in establishing Neoclassicism in American sculpture. Powers' *The Greek Slave* (1843) *(p 56)* was the most popular sculpture of its time both in the US and in Europe.

**John Rogers** (1829-1904) of Salem studied in Rome, though briefly. Influenced by the American scene, Rogers modeled small sculptured clay groups depicting events of historical and topical interest *(The Slave Auction)* and everyday living *(Checkers at the Farm)*. His 80 "Rogers groups" as they were known were reproduced by the thousands and gained immediate popularity.

# FURNITURE

American furnishings were influenced from colonial days through the 19C by European, and in particular, English designs. Carpenters in rural villages copied the pieces the colonists had brought with them across the ocean, or reproduced from memory the furniture they had known in England. Early American cabinetmakers turned to imported style manuals as guides to making contemporary furniture.

**Pilgrim** – Furniture made between 1620 and 1690—tables, chairs, bible boxes and chests—is heavy and rectilinear, reflecting the medieval influences of the English Tudor and Jacobean styles. Oak is the principal wood used. The Connecticut-made Hadley, Guilford and Sunflower chests ornamented with carved and painted floral designs or geometric motifs are characteristic of this period.

William and Mary

**William and Mary** – This style was in vogue from 1689 to 1702 during the reign of William of Orange and his wife, Mary. The Flemish influence and contact with the Orient introduced such techniques as *japanning* (floral or scenic designs on lacquered wood surfaces), and turning (wooden pieces shaped on a lathe). Japanned highboys, chests with bold turnings, and chairs with caned or leather backs were popular during these years.

**Queen Anne** – Curved lines, such as the gracefully shaped cabriole leg, are a stylistic feature of the years between 1720 and 1750. Maple, walnut and cherry are the woods typically used; decoration is minimal. A Queen Anne chair is distinguished by its cabriole legs and vase-shaped back splat.

Queen Anne

The **Windsor chair**, unrelated to the Queen Anne style, was imported from England in the early 18C and remains popular in America. The Windsor is defined by its spindles inserted between a plank seat and curved upper railing. The comb back, bow back and writing table are variations of the original low-back Windsor.

**Chippendale** – London cabinetmaker Thomas Chippendale borrowed elements of French rococo and Chinese art in creating the wide range of furniture forms illustrated in his design manuals. Pieces from the period 1750 to 1785 are generally fashioned of mahogany, with curved legs (ending in the ball-and-claw foot) and chair backs pierced with lacy fretwork. Adornment consists of rich carving, elaborate brasses and finials. The **Goddard** and **Townsend** families of Newport were among the most celebrated cabinetmakers working in this style. Their blockfront case pieces, carved with the shell motif *(illustration p 217)*, are adaptations of Chippendale's designs.

Windsor

**Federal** – Inspired by British architect **Robert Adam**, and English cabinetmakers **George Hepplewhite** and **Thomas Sheraton**, the style that won favor from 1785 and 1815 is defined by light, straight lines and refined decoration: veneers, inlay and marquetry in contrasting woods. The square, tapered leg, fluted, reeded or ending in a spade foot, is common. Chair backs in the Hepplewhite style resemble a variety of shapes, including an oval, shield, heart or wheel; Sheraton chair backs are rectilinear. Cabinetmakers working in the Federal style included John and Thomas Seymour and John and Simeon Skillin of Boston. The eagle, adapted from the Great Seal of the US, is a popular motif. Looking glasses with gilt frames surmounted by a flat cornice or a delicate urn and floral sprays, and shelf and mantel clocks produced by New England clockmakers *(p 48)*, relieve the restrained classical interiors. The girandole mirror, ornamented with an eagle, is a favorite accessory.

Chippendale

**Empire** – Imported from Europe, this heavy, massive style, popular from 1815 to 1840, was inspired by Greek and Egyptian antiquity. Bronze, gilt, winged and caryatid supports, lion's-paw feet, rolled backs on chairs, and sofas with upswept ends distinguish this style.

**Victorian** – Furniture of the period between 1840 and the late 19C, inspired by a variety of styles including Gothic, Elizabethan, Renaissance and French rococo, is heavy and ornate. Upholstered chairs and sofas are overstuffed and velvet coverings are typical. Balloonback and fiddleback chairs, and tables with marble tops were popular.

Hepplewhite

**Shaker Furniture** – Produced primarily from 1800 until the middle of the 19C, Shaker chairs, tables and cupboards *(p 148)*, simple and functional, are admired for their clean, pure lines and superb craftsmanship. Shaker chairs are recognized by their ladder backs, and seats made of rush, cane, splint or woven webbing.

# PAINTING

From the beginning of the colonial period to the late 17C, painting was appreciated primarily for its practical uses for trade signs and portraiture. The artist often sketched only the face of his subject from life, then completed the remainder of the picture in a stylized manner. Highlighting this genre of portrait, which is appealing for its simplicity and charm, is the painting of *Mrs. Elizabeth Freake and Baby Mary* that now hangs in the Worcester Art Museum in Massachusetts.

**18C Development** – The arrival of Scottish painter **John Smibert** (1688-1751) in America in 1729 initiated the era of professional painting. At his Boston studio Smibert instructed his students in the art of portraiture as it was practiced in Europe. His works, such as *Bishop Berkeley and his Entourage* (Yale University Art Gallery, New Haven) served as models for the Americans who studied with him, including Newport artist **Robert Feke** (1705-1750) and **John Singleton Copley** (1738-1815), America's first important portraitist. Copley painted the well-known persons of his day (*Paul Revere*, Museum of Fine Arts, Boston), render-

ing his subjects amazingly lifelike by his keen attention to detail and surface texture.

**Gilbert Stuart** (1755-1828) was the most important American painter of the period. Although he is best remembered for his portraits of George Washington, Stuart in fact painted only three portraits of the president from life, using these as models for his later works.

In the late 18C many Americans traveled to London in order to study with their countryman **Benjamin West** (1738-1820) who was born in Springfield, Massachusetts and became a leader of the Neoclassical movement. **Samuel F. B. Morse** (1791-1872), a fine portraitist before he devoted himself to the invention of the telegraph, studied with West, as did **Ralph Earl** (1751-1801), who spent seven years in London, yet retained the simplicity of his native American folk

*Mrs. Elizabeth Freake and Baby Mary*
(c.1671) Artist unknown

style. It was also under West's guidance that **John Trumbull** (1756-1843), son of the governor of Connecticut, executed a series of historical paintings (*The Battle of Bunker Hill; Signing of the Declaration of Independence,* Yale University Art Gallery), which ultimately made Trumbull famous. He was later commissioned by Congress to decorate the rotunda of the Capitol in Washington DC.

**19C** – Until the 1800s demand was primarily for portraits, with folk artists such as **William Matthew Prior** (1806-1873) and **Erastus Salisbury Field** (1805-1900) active at mid-century. Following the American Revolution, the opening of the West led to an increased awareness of the vast scale and beauty of the nation, and the American scene became a popular theme for artists. Painters of the **Hudson River school** in the 1820s followed the lead of **Thomas Cole** and **Albert Bierstadt** by setting up their easels outdoors and painting directly from nature. Their favorite New England subjects were the WHITE MOUNTAINS and the CONNECTICUT VALLEY. Born in HARTFORD, **Frederick Edwin Church** (1826-1900), whose major works were of New England landscapes, studied with Cole. The sea was a source of inspiration for other artists. **Fitz Hugh Lane** (1804-1865), living in Gloucester, illustrated in soft, glowing tones the serene beauty of the sea and the offshore islands. New Bedford artist **William Bradford** (1823-1892), fascinated by maritime themes and the northern lights, depicted the rising and setting of the Arctic sun, and whalers sailing among icebergs (New Bedford Whaling Museum).

Beginning in the 1860s, Americans began to live and study abroad for longer periods of time. **James McNeill Whistler** (1834-1903), a native of Lowell, became known in London for his delicate riverscapes of the Thames. **William Morris Hunt** (1824-1879), influenced by the French schools, opened a studio in Boston where he introduced artists to the principles of naturalism as reflected in the landscape paintings of the Barbizon school. Some years later, Italian-born **John Singer Sargent** (1856-1925) traveled extensively in Europe and won acclaim as the portraitist of the international social set *(illustration p 121)*. The grace and elegance he imparted to his subjects made him the most sought-after artist of his day.

The career of the self-taught watercolorist and master of the naturalist movement, **Winslow Homer** (1836-1910), began during the Civil War, when Homer served as an illustrator for *Harper's Weekly*. He is known for the large canvases of the sea that he painted during many summers at Prout's Neck, Maine.

**20C** – In the present century several painters, each with their own distinctive style, have been identified with New England. **Grandma Moses** (1860-1961), who did not begin to paint until she was in her 70s, illustrated themes associated with rural New England *(Sleigh Ride; Sugaring-Off)*. The vivid coloration and charm of her works, a collection of which can be seen at the Bennington Museum in Vermont *(p 224)*, are reminiscent of America's folk artists.

**Norman Rockwell** (1894-1978), for many years an illustrator for the *Saturday Evening Post,* painted a chronicle of American life. Rockwell's vision of the persons and events he depicted was always tempered by his warmth, keen attention to detail, and sense of humor. His principal works can be viewed in STOCKBRIDGE. Born in 1917 **Andrew Wyeth** has spent several summers in Maine, where he painted his dramatic canvases exploring the relationship between man and nature. Wyeth's compositions, executed in a lucid, realistic style, are simple and uncluttered, as is his celebrated painting *Christina's World*. The Farnsworth Art Museum in Rockland *(p 87)* exhibits a large group of his works.

# FOLK ARTS

In rural New England, isolated from the mother country, necessities for daily living were handmade by the farmers themselves or by tradesmen who received a modest fee for their services. The tools, household utensils, cloth, weathervanes and furniture they produced revealed the tastes, flair and loving attention to detail of their creators. Today these items are admired for their unsophisticated charm, and for the picture of early rural American life they present.

**Quilts** – Quilted bed coverings, consisting of a top and bottom layer of cloth stitched together with sheets of cotton or wool batting in between, were essential during the long, cold New England winter. Often finished in a geometric or floral motif, the quilt became one of a rural household's few decorative accessories. Because of the scarcity of material, quilts were often fashioned from scraps of leftover cloth. These patchwork quilts were either **pieced** (scraps were cut into geometric shapes and sewn together) or **appliquéd** (small pieces of cloth were sewn onto a broad layer of cloth to form a specific design).

Quilting had a pleasant social aspect as well: the **quilting bee.** When the top layer of a quilt was completed—perhaps it was a **wedding quilt** for a young woman planning to be married, or a **freedom quilt** to be presented to a young man on his 21st birthday—the women gathered at one house to stitch the quilt together. The assembly was often the most difficult part of making the quilt, and after the quilting bee, the quilters would hold a party to celebrate its completion.

**Stencils** – This early decorative technique, which uses pre-cut patterns and paint to embellish furniture, implements, cloth, floors and walls, brightened the interiors of many homes. Wall stenciling added color to the otherwise plain white plaster or wooden plank surfaces, and in the 19C was a low-cost alternative to expensive imported wallpapers. The painter could choose from a large selection of motifs: geometric figures, flowers, baskets of fruit, and the symbolic eagle (liberty), pineapple (hospitality), willow (immortality) and heart and bells (joy). The popular "fancy" chair, produced by **Lambert Hitchcock** at his factory in RIVERTON, was decorated with hand-painted stenciling.

**Weathervanes** – When most New Englanders farmed or went to sea, weathervanes were important as indicators of changes in the weather. The simple profile of a weathervane, carved from wood or cut from metal, topped most buildings of any significant height. A weathervane made to crown a church spire might be in the shape of a cockerel or fish, the symbols of early Christianity. In rural areas the silhouette of a cow, horse or sheep rose above farm buildings, while along the coast, the whale, clipper ship and mermaid were popular. New England's famous grasshopper weathervane *(p 110)*, atop the cupola of Faneuil Hall, has been the symbol of the port of Boston since the 18C. The **whirligig,** a carved three-dimensional figure with paddle-like arms, was a whimsical variation of the weathervane. Large whirligigs indicated wind speed and direction, while smaller ones served as children's toys.

Courtesy Mystic Seaport Museum

Ship figureheads

**Figureheads, Trade Signs and Shop Figures** – During the age of sail, carvers sculpted figureheads, sternboards and other accessories for new vessels. A small figure representing the wife or daughter of the ship's owner ordinarily adorned a whaling vessel, while figures (generally female) with windblown hair were carved as graceful extensions of the prows of clipper ships *(see the collections in the maritime museums in Mystic, CT; New Bedford, Nantucket and Salem, MA; and SHELBURNE, VT).*

Ship carvers also produced trade signs and shop figures as a sideline. These brightly painted, hand-carved signs and figures, an early form of advertising, illustrated the specialty of a shop: a mariner holding a sextant was associated with a nautical instrument maker, and a sign bearing a large boot indicated a cobbler's shop. The streets of the Old Port Exchange in Portland *(p 85)* are lined with similar eye-catching signs. Among the large number of **cigar store figures** produced in the 19C, the most familiar was the image of the Indian, a reminder that tobacco was a native product. Ranging from 2ft to 7ft in height, the Indian usually wore a headdress of tobacco leaves that were often mistaken for feathers.

**Glass** – Until the mid-19C most glass manufactured in New England was in the form of window glass and glass containers. Handmade glassware was a luxury only a few could afford. However, Deming Jarves and his workmen at **Sandwich** *(p 170)* made available, for the first time, attractive glassware at affordable prices. The factory at Sandwich became famous for pressed glass with patterns that resembled lace. Despite large-scale production of pressed glass, the art of glassblowing continued to thrive. Of the numerous glass factories operating in New England during the 19C, those in Massachusetts—the New England Glass Co, Boston and Sandwich Glass Co, and Mount Washington Glass Works—were unrivaled for the beauty of their products. Items varied from tableware to decorative art glass *(described below)*, and may be seen at the Sandwich Glass Museum *(p 171)*, at Old Sturbridge Village *(p 174)* and in the Bennington Museum in Vermont *(p 224)*.

**Burmese Glass** – This opaque glass, in hues ranging from coral pink to yellow, was made between 1885 and 1895 by Mount Washington Glass Co. Pink coloring was made possible by gold in the glass mixture.

**Peachblow** – This technique is similar to that used to make Burmese glass, but featured shades from opaque white to rose. Soft matte, satiny finishes result from an acid bath. Peachblow, made by the New England Glass Co (1886-1888), was known as Wild Rose.

**Lava Glass** – This shiny black glass, the first American art glass, was invented and patented by Mount Washington Glass Co in New Bedford. The first pieces of lava glass were made from volcanic pumice.

**Amberina** – Ranging from pale amber to rich ruby in color, this transparent glass was dubbed Amberina by the New England Glass Co and Rose Amber by the Mount Washington Glass Co. The amber glass mix contained a small amount of gold which, upon reheating a portion of the glass, resulted in a ruby color.

**Pomona** – The designs and frosted appearance of this expensive, transparent glass were originally achieved by covering the piece with wax, scratching through the wax with an etching device, then applying acid, which ate through the glass to create the frosted effect. Designs were stained, then the piece was fired at a high temperature.

**Scrimshaw** – Perfected by New England sailors in the 19C, scrimshaw, the art of etching the surface of the teeth or jawbone of a whale *(illustration p 25)*, or the tusks of a walrus, is considered by some the only art form indigenous to America. The tooth or tusk was allowed to dry. Then the surface was polished with shark skin and the picture or design to be etched—depicting whale hunts, detailed ship replicas, port scenes—was incised onto the bone with a jackknife or sail needles. Ink, soot or tobacco juice was applied for color. The scrimshander's skill was reflected in the intricately detailed ornamentation of jagging wheels (used to crimp the edges of pie crusts), bird cages, inlaid boxes and other items. Exceptional scrimshaw collections can be found at the whaling museums in New Bedford *(p 159)*, Nantucket *(p 157)* and Sharon *(p 129)*.

**Decoys** – Wooden decoys sculpted and painted to resemble geese, ducks, shore birds and waterfowl have been used since colonial times to lure birds within range of the hunter. The practice originated with the Indians, who used heaps of mud, reeds and skins filled with grass to attract waterfowl. By the 19C decoy-making had developed into an art form. Craftsmen portrayed birds with increasing realism, taking into consideration the natural conditions where the decoys would be used. In Maine, where the sea is rough and the wind strong, decoys were large and heavy, and had a flat bottom and low head to ensure stability; in Massachusetts Bay, where the waters are calmer, the decoys were lighter. Purely decorative decoys, such as the shore birds and miniatures carved and painted by **A. Elmer Crowell** of Massachusetts, illustrate the more elegant forms of this art. Craftsmen along the coast from Cape Cod to Maine still engage in producing these lures. The Shelburne Museum owns a fine collection of over 1,000 decoys *(p 238)*, including examples of Crowell's work.

**Gravestones** – The Puritans, who found little time for the frivolities of art during their daily life, have left outstanding examples of the skill of their early stonecutters in the rows of gravestones that stand in New England's old burial grounds. The designs were initially symbolic and plain. In the 17C the hourglass, sun, scythe, winged skull, hearts and cherubim (symbols for life, death and resurrection) were typical motifs. Throughout the 18C realistic portraits and detailed scenes of the death of the deceased became popular. The romantic tendencies of the 19C were represented by extensive use of the weeping willow and the urn, classical symbols for death.

The old cemeteries in BOSTON, LEXINGTON, NEWBURYPORT and SALEM, NEW LONDON and NEWPORT contain splendid examples of gravestone art.

# LITERATURE

The literature produced in the colonies in the 17C and 18C consisted primarily of histories and religious writings: sermons, pamphlets, diaries and journals. The *History* of *Plimoth Plantation* by William Bradford, Governor of Plimoth Plantation between 1621 and 1657; and a *Journal* account of life in the Massachusetts Bay Colony written by its first governor, John Winthrop (1588-1649), remain the principal records of this period. The clergyman **Cotton Mather** (1669-1728) wrote hundreds of sermons, scientific tracts and treatises including his monumental *Ecclesiastical History of New England*. Inventor, statesman, philosopher and scientist **Benjamin Franklin** (1706-1790), of Boston, was highly regarded at home and abroad for his satire of British policies in America. His *Poor Richard's Almanac* was found in most New England homes.

**Coming of Age** – In the 19C a literature distinctly American in theme, idea, character and setting emerged in New England. The Transcendental movement, based on belief in the mystical union of all nature, gained popularity under the leadership of **Ralph Waldo Emerson** (1803-1882), who lectured throughout the US. His essay on *Nature* (1836), states the ideals and principles of Transcendentalism.

**Henry David Thoreau** (1817-1862), a disciple of Emerson, put the tenets of Transcendentalism into practice by living a solitary existence for two years at Walden Pond in CONCORD. *Walden* recounts his life in the woods. Transcendentalism inspired experiments in communal living such as Brook Farm near Boston and Fruitlands *(p 147)*. The voice of this movement was sounded in the literary magazine, *The Dial,* which Emerson and Margaret Fuller founded in 1840. Bronson Alcott, whose daughter **Louisa May Alcott** (1832-1888) became famous for her novel *Little Women*, contributed to *The Dial*.

Attracted by Transcendentalism **Nathaniel Hawthorne** (1806-1864) lived at Brook Farm for a brief time. As a writer, he helped establish the short story and the psychological novel as significant American literary forms. Hawthorne's Puritan ancestry is reflected in the gloomy atmosphere and moralistic themes of his short stories and novels such as *The House of the Seven Gables (p 168)* and *The Scarlet Letter,* a symbolic study of the effects of sin on mankind's soul. Influenced by Hawthorne's technique, **Herman Melville** (1819-1891) wrote his masterpiece *Moby-Dick* while living in the BERKSHIRES.

Many writers supported the abolitionist movement. **William Lloyd Garrison** (1805-1879) published the anti-slavery newspaper, *The Liberator,* for more than three decades until the adoption of the 13th Amendment. The best-selling novel *Uncle Tom's Cabin* by **Harriet Beecher Stowe** (1811-1896) exposed the cruelties of slavery.

With the expansion of the nation came a heightened awareness of regional differences, and the introduction of a literary genre depicting local color, scenery and speech. Hartford resident **Mark Twain** (1835-1910) *(p 47)* was a master of the new regional literature. His popular works, *Tom Sawyer* and *Huckleberry Finn,* portrayed life on the Mississippi River. The novel *The Country of the Pointed Firs* by **Sarah Orne Jewett** (1849-1909) presents a poetic account of the people and countryside of Maine.

History was a favorite subject of New Englanders. Although nearly blind, Salem native **William Hickling Prescott** (1796-1859) wrote several volumes about Spanish history; **George Bancroft** (1800-1891), a Massachusetts teacher, produced the *History of the United States*, the first major work of its kind. **Francis Parkman's** (1823-1893) ten-volume study of the conflict between England and France in the New World spans four decades. Bostonian **Henry Adams'** (1838-1918) nine-volume history describes the shaping of the nation's character. In 1828 **Noah Webster** (1758-1843), a native of New Haven, published the first *American Dictionary of the English Language*.

**20C** – In the 20C the American theater won international acclaim through the works of playwright **Eugene O'Neill** (1888-1953), whose close association with the Provincetown Players began in 1916 when his play *Bound East for Cardiff* was produced in PROVINCETOWN. New England was the setting for his *Desire Under the Elms, Mourning Becomes Electra* and the Pulitzer prize-winning, *Beyond the Horizon.* Other New England authors include native-born John P. Marquand, Kenneth Roberts, William Dean Howells, and writers who adopted New England as their second home Edith Wharton, Pearl Buck, Norman Mailer, Alexander Solzhenitsyn.

**Poetry** – **Henry Wadsworth Longfellow** (1807-1882), born in PORTLAND, taught modern languages at Harvard. One of the most widely read poets of his day, Longfellow chose American folk heroes, such as Hiawatha, Evangeline, Paul Revere and Miles Standish as the subjects of many of his poems. Longfellow's contemporary **John Greenleaf Whittier** (1807-1892) was a spokesman for the abolitionist cause and wrote poetry that portrayed life in rural, pre-industrialized New England.

**Emily Dickinson** (1830-1886), an Amherst resident who remained a recluse most of her life, wrote verses rich in lyricism and sensitivity. Best known for his poems about nature, **Robert Frost** (1874-1963) lived on a farm in New Hampshire from 1901 to 1909, and later spent his summers in Vermont. His verse, inspired by New England's people and landscapes, exhibits a refreshing simplicity, as illustrated in his poem *Stopping by the Woods on a Snowy Evening*. Originally from Massachusetts **Amy Lowell** (1874-1925) moved to England in 1913, where she met Ezra Pound and became a leader of the Imagist movement, which experimented with creating concrete images, free of the unrestrained imagery and sentimentality that characterized 19C verse.

In more recent times the poetry of **e.e. cummings** (1894-1962), a native of CAMBRIDGE, is distinguished by his unconventional use of typography and punctuation. Another New England-born poet whose work has made a significant impact on modern poetry is **Robert Lowell** (1917-1977), whose early verse reflects New England's historical and ethical traditions.

# CULINARY TRADITIONS

New England has a well-deserved reputation for simple, hearty fare, but the cuisine here can also be remarkably varied. In addition to shellfish, the region boasts delicious game meat, including venison and grouse; farmland produce; good local wines; and regional specialties ranging from maple syrup and Vermont cheddar cheese to saltwater taffy and **Boston cream pie** (actually a custard-filled cake glazed with chocolate). Country inns and taverns serve traditional Yankee fare, while eat-in-the-rough **clam shacks**, dockside lobster pounds and shoreline dinner halls offer the best in seafood dining experience.

**Native American Traditions** – Many local dishes trace their roots to the New England Indians, who were the first to make maple sugar, **cranberry sauce**, **Johnnycakes** (these fried cornmeal patties are popular in Rhode Island) and **Indian pudding**, a hot dessert of molasses, cornmeal, cinnamon and nutmeg. Slow-cooked **Boston baked beans** flavored with molasses and salt pork also derive from a native recipe, as does their traditional accompaniment, **brown bread**, made with equal parts of rye and wheat flour and cornmeal, and steamed in a tin can rather than baked.

**Fish and Shellfish** – Brook trout is a popular freshwater fish, while swordfish and tuna (grilled with lemon), **bluefish** and **striped bass** (baked or broiled) are saltwater favorites; straight from the fisherman's catch, these fish are so fresh that they need little seasoning. **Lobster**, found in the cold waters off Rhode Island, Massachusetts and Maine, was so common in the 1600s that it was considered one of the lowliest menu items. Now scarce, it is the king of shellfish, served baked or boiled with lemon and butter, in rich stews, bisques and pies, hot and buttered on a bun (lobster roll) or chilled with mayonnaise (lobster-salad roll).

Larry Lefever/Grant Heilman Photography

**Blue mussels** grow in clusters around shoreline rocks; try these tender mollusks steamed in wine and herbs or grilled with garlic. Equally popular are **clams**, harvested by rake from the sandy bottoms of warmwater bays and salt ponds. They are delicious steamed with butter, batter-fried, deep-fried in light, puffy **fritters** (a Rhode Island specialty) or baked and stuffed with bread crumbs and seasonings. Varieties include the thin-shelled, long-necked steamer; large hardshelled quahogs (KOE-hogs); and littlenecks and cherrystones, two types of young quahogs eaten raw on the half shell with lemon and a cocktail sauce spiced with horseradish. Fall and winter are the seasons for **bay scallops** (sauteed in butter and lemon) and **oysters** (raw on the half shell).

The famous New England **clambake** is another Indian custom. To make this all-in-one shoreline meal—served up from a beach-dug pit—potatoes, onions, unhusked corn, chicken, lobsters and clams are layered in seaweed over charcoal-heated stones for hours of slow steaming. (The classic clambake typically feeds up to 100 people, but restaurants offer a smaller version cooked in a steamer pot.)

**Chowders and Stews** – Thought to have originated with settlers from the Channel Islands, **chowders** are thick, slow-simmered soups made from milk and vegetables. Corn chowder is a regional specialty. Fish chowder usually features cod or haddock; steamers or quahogs, potatoes and onions (never tomatoes) are key ingredients of **clam chowder** (made, in Rhode Island, with clear clam-juice broth rather than milk). The **New England boiled dinner** is an autumn dish of corned beef (brisket cured in salt brine) and stewed late-season garden vegetables (turnips, beets, cabbage and carrots). The dish, traditionally made on Monday, simmered all day while the wash was done; leftovers went into **red flannel hash** (named for the beets) for meals the rest of the week.

**Fresh Produce** – Seasonal favorites include fiddlehead ferns (spring), and strawberries (early summer), savored in strawberry shortcake. Maine is famous for its blueberries; indeed, no trip to New England is complete without sampling blueberry pancakes, pie, muffins or a type of pudding called **blueberry slump**. Late summer produces vine-ripened tomatoes, corn on the cob and pumpkins (used for soups and pies). Add to these classic farmstand offerings preserves made from wild beach plums and Concord grapes. In autumn stop at a pick-your-own orchard for cider and some of the best apples grown in the US (Cortland, Granny Smith, Macoun and McIntosh).

**Maple Syrup** – Come early spring, maple trees are tapped for sap, cooked down into a sweet syrup used for baking and as a topping for pancakes, waffles and ice cream. Vermont and New Hampshire lead New England in maple syrup production. The best quality is Grade A light amber, followed by Grade A medium and dark ambers.

## FURTHER READING

### Non-Fiction

**Appalachian Mountain Club guidebooks** *(Appalachian Mountain Club)*
**Bed and Breakfasts in New England** by Bernice Chesler *(Globe Pequot Press, 1994)*
**Boston Globe Historic Walks in Old Boston** by John Harris *(Globe Pequot Press, 1993)*
**Country Inns and Back Roads of New England** *(Berkshire Traveller Press, 1994)*
**Fifty Hikes in New England series** (available for CT, ME, MA, NH, VT) *(Countryman Press, Inc, 1994)*
**Guide Book of the Long Trail** *(Green Mountain Club, 1995)*
**New England: Land of Scenic Splendor** *(National Geographic Society, 1989)*

### Fiction

**The Bostonians** by Henry James (1886)
**Captains Courageous** by Rudyard Kipling (1897)
**The Country of the Pointed Firs** by Sara Orne Jewett (1896)
**The House of the Seven Gables** by Nathaniel Hawthorne (1851)
**The Last Puritan** by George Santayana (1935)
**The Late George Apley** by John P. Marquand (1937)
**Moby-Dick** by Herman Melville (1851)
**The Outermost House** by Henry Beston (1928)
**The Scarlet Letter** by Nathaniel Hawthorne (1850)
**Two Years Before the Mast** by Richard Henry Dana (1840)

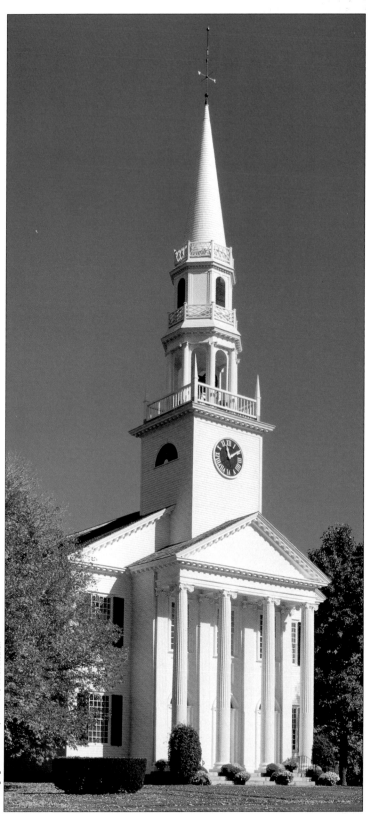

First Congregational Church, Litchfield / ©Dick Dietrich

# Connecticut

**Area:** 5,009sq mi
**Population:** 3,287,116
**Capital:** Hartford
**Nickname:** The Constitution State
**State Flower:** Mountain Laurel

This rectangle extending about 90 miles east to west and 55 miles north to south bears the name of the river that divides it almost in half: the *Connecticut*, an Indian word meaning "beside the long tidal river." Small colonial villages scattered throughout the state offer a pleasing contrast to the densely populated industrialized centers in the Hartford region and to the cities of Stamford, Bridgeport, Stratford and New Haven on the south shore. The affluent communities in southwestern Connecticut's Fairfield County (Greenwich, Ridgefield, New Canaan) are, in essence, "suburbs" of New York.

The state is predominantly rural; two-thirds of its woodlands are included in the state park and forest system. To the south, on the shores of Long Island Sound, sandy beaches separate the former whaling ports of New London, Mystic and Stonington. The idyllic Litchfield Hills, rising in the northern part of the state, are an extension of the Green Mountains and the Berkshire Hills.

## The Constitution State –

Connecticut's first settlers were staunch Puritans who found the atmosphere in Boston too liberal. They arrived from Massachusetts in 1633 by the Connecticut River, and within two years had founded the towns of Hartford, Windsor and Wethersfield.

In 1639 these towns joined to form Hartford Colony, later to become Connecticut Colony. The Fundamental Orders of Connecticut, statutes drawn up and adopted January 14, 1639 as the basis of government in Hartford Colony, is the first constitution drafted in the New World—thus the state's nickname, the Constitution State.

## Economy –

Benefiting from the wide range of products developed by the state's inventors, Connecticut has traditionally been a prosperous manufacturing center, and in 1989 ranked first in the nation in per capita income. Mechanical innovations introduced by Connecticut clockmakers *(p 48)* made clockmaking one of the state's earliest industries and put a clock in almost every home in America.

In the 19C the production of firearms became an important business. The Colt .45 revolver, developed by Hartford entrepreneur **Samuel Colt**, and the Winchester rifle, were made in Connecticut. During the same period, **Eli Whitney** manufactured his revolutionary new cotton gin in New Haven and introduced the use of standardized parts at his firearms factory nearby. Danbury became known for its hats, Torrington and Waterbury for brass items, and Meriden for its fine silverware.

Connecticut continues to obtain a great part of its income from industry. Electrical goods, tools, chemicals, plastics, jet engines, helicopters and nuclear submarines are its leading

Larry Lefever/Grant Heilman Photography

products. The Electric Boat Division of General Dynamics at Groton *(p 43)* builds submarines for the nation's fleet. A number of corporations (General Electric, Union Carbide, Xerox) and insurance companies maintain headquarters in the state.

Locally marketed poultry, fruit and dairy products are major sources of agricultural income. Broadleaf tobacco, used for cigar wrapping, is shade-grown in the Connecticut and Farmington Valleys. Picturesque tobacco sheds identify these flat regions.

# BRIDGEPORT

Map of Principal Sights p 2        Tourist Office ☎203-854-7825

This heavily industrialized and populated center on Long Island Sound was the home of **Phineas T. Barnum**, the colorful showman promoter, and former mayor of Bridgeport. Barnum's world-famous, three-ring circus toured America and Europe in the 19C and won acclaim as "The Greatest Show on Earth." A statue of Barnum surveys the harbor from Seaside Park at the end of Main Street.

Manufacturing, government, service industries and wholesale and retail activities support the local economy. Bridgeport's manufacturing plants produce machinery, transportation equipment and primary and fabricated metals.

Prominent among the city's educational institutions is the **University of Bridgeport**.

**Barnum Museum** – *820 Main St. Open year-round Tue–Sat 10am–4:30pm, Sun noon–4:30pm. Closed major holidays. $5. ☎203-331-9881*. This ornate building is as eccentric as its creator; the circus memorabilia it houses reflects Barnum's exuberant personality. Highlights include costumes and furnishings that belonged to Tom Thumb, the first major attraction of the circus, and the **Brinley Miniature Circus** of more than 3,000 hand-carved figures. A contemporary wing features temporary exhibits on 19C industrial history and art as well as American popular culture.

## EXCURSION

**Ferry to Port Jefferson, Long Island, NY** – *Departs from Bridgeport Harbor year-round daily 7:30am–9pm (9:30pm Fri & Sun). One-way 1hr 15min. $31 (car & driver). ✗ Bridgeport & Port Jefferson Steamboat Co. ☎203-367-3043.*

# ★ CONNECTICUT VALLEY

Map of Principal Sights p 2        Tourist Office ☎203-347-0028

Wide, shallow and bordered by unspoiled countryside, the Connecticut River flows into a multitude of coves and boat harbors as it ends its more than 400mi journey downstream to Long Island Sound. Villages such as Old Lyme and Old Saybrook have retained their early character thanks to a sandbar at the mouth of the river that has always prevented deep-draft vessels from entering these waters.

There are several ways to explore the valley: by land, following the itinerary below through small riverside towns, and by river, taking a cruise from East Haddam, Deep River or Essex. In the summer a ferry ride *(3hrs, p 42)* from Haddam to Long Island is available.

## FROM I-95 TO MOODUS    *26mi. Allow 4hrs. Map p 42.*

*From I-95, Exit 69 (Old Saybrook), take Rte 9 to Exit 3 in the direction of Essex.*

★ **Essex** – Pop 2,500. Established in 1645, Essex developed into an important shipbuilding center by the early 18C, and in 1775 produced Connecticut's first warship, the *Oliver Cromwell*. Today Essex attracts a sophisticated summer crowd who berth their yachts and cabin cruisers at local marinas. The town's main street consists of interesting shops, art galleries and the Old Griswold Inn, which has been operating since 1776. A former warehouse at Steamboat Dock houses the **Connecticut River Museum**, with maritime exhibits including a model of the *Oliver Cromwell (open year-round Tue– Sun 10am–5pm; $4; ☎203-767-8269).*

**Valley Railroad** – *Exit 3 off Rte 9. Departs from Essex Station mid-Jun–mid-Sept daily 10am–4:15pm (Sat 6:45pm, Sun 5:30pm). Late Apr–mid-Jun Wed 2–3:30pm & weekends 10am–4:15pm. Mid-Sept–Oct Wed–Sun 10am–4:15pm. Train service to Chester (round-trip 1hr) with connecting river cruises from Deep River to East Haddam (train & cruise: round-trip 2hr 30min). $8.50 (train only), $14 (train & cruise). ✗ Valley Railroad Co. ☎203-767-0103.* Rides on the railroad's early 20C steam train afford views of the valley landscape and the Connecticut River.

*From Essex take Rte 9 to Exit 6, then Rte 148 to the ferry that crosses the river.*

**Chester-Hadlyme Ferry** – *Departs from Chester Apr–mid-Dec daily 7am–6:45pm. Closed Thanksgiving Day. One-way 5min. $2.25 (car & driver). State Bureau of Aviation & Ports. ☎203-566-7635.* During the crossing there is a good view of Gillette Castle, perched high on a hilltop above the east bank.

*Take Rte 148, then turn left, following the signs for Gillette Castle.*

★ **Gillette Castle State Park** – *Open late May–mid-Oct daily 8am–5pm (castle 10am–5pm). Mid-Oct–mid-Dec weekends only 10am–4pm. $4. ☎203-526-2336.* The castles of the Rhine Valley inspired the design of this bizarre stone castle built in 1919 by actor **William Gillette**, who drew up the plans for the castle and decorated each of the 24 rooms himself. Furniture that slides on metal tracks and other devices were developed by Gillette, who had a fascination for gadgetry. The 190-acre estate offers splendid **vistas★** of the Connecticut River and the valley below. *Picnicking and hiking trails.*

*Take Rte 82 to East Haddam.*

**East Haddam** – Pop 6,676. This small town with beautiful old homes is proud of its little red **schoolhouse** where Nathan Hale once taught, and of being the site of the **Goodspeed Opera House**, a Victorian-style opera house dating from the era when New York-to-Connecticut steamers called at East Haddam. *Musicals are presented from Apr–Dec. Ticket information* ☎203-873-8668.

*River cruises (one-way 3hrs) operate between Marine Park in Haddam (2.5mi north of East Haddam, on the other side of the river) and Long Island Jun–Aug Tue–Sun 9am. Sept Sun 9am. $15.* ✗ ♿ *Camelot Cruises.* ☎203-345-4507.

> *Follow Rte 149, which offers good views of the river before turning northeast.*

**Moodus** – Facing the Moodus green is the **Amasa Day House** (1816), which contains well-preserved examples of the floor stenciling laid over a century ago *(open late May–Labor Day Wed–Sun 1–5pm; closed major holidays; $3;* ☎203-873-8144*).*

## COVENTRY — Pop 9,820

Map of Principal Sights p 2  Tourist Office ☎203-928-1228

This small town in rural northeastern Connecticut was the birthplace of the American patriot **Nathan Hale** (1755-1776). Hale, a school teacher by profession, was commissioned an officer in the Connecticut militia at the outbreak of the Revolutionary War. After participating in several military operations in New England, he volunteered for the perilous mission of gathering intelligence about the British troops on Long Island. Young Hale was discovered by the British and hanged as a spy on September 22, 1776. The last words he spoke on the scaffold, "I only regret that I have but one life to lose for my country," are among the most memorable in the annals of American history.

**Nathan Hale Homestead** – *2299 South St. Open mid-May–mid-Oct daily 1–5pm. $3.* ♿ ☎203-742-6917. Nathan Hale never lived in this ten-room dwelling, which was built in October 1776 by his father on the site of the home where Hale was born. The family homestead until 1832, the house contains Hale family memorabilia and period furnishings.

**Caprilands Herb Farm** – *534 Silver St. Open year-round daily 9am–5pm. Closed major holidays.* ☎203-742-7244. More than 300 different types of herbs are cultivated on the 20 acres of this farm, which has been the family estate of Adelma Grenier Simmons since 1929. Visitors are free to wander through the restored 18C barn, the specialty gardens and the greenhouse. The 18C farmhouse is the setting for a daily luncheon and lecture program *(Apr–Dec. $18; check-in 11:15am; reservations suggested* ☎203-742-7244*).*

## ★ FARMINGTON — Pop 20,608

Map of Principal Sights p 2  Tourist Office ☎203-520-4480

Beautiful 18C and 19C residences line the streets of this elegant HARTFORD suburb on the Farmington River. Several of these early structures on Main Street are part of a well-known school for girls, **Miss Porter's School.**

★ **Hill-Stead Museum** – *35 Mountain Rd. Visit by guided tour (1hr) only, May–Oct Tue–Sun 10am–4pm; rest of the year 11am–3pm. $6.* ♿ ☎203-677-9064. In 1900 Theodate Pope Riddle, one of America's early woman architects, worked with the firm of McKim, Mead and White to design this Colonial Revival country house for her father, wealthy industrialist Alfred Atmore Pope. The design of the sunken garden is based on a plan by Beatrix Jones Farrand. Hill-Stead's attractive furnishings and European and Oriental objets d'art lend a pleasant, lived-in atmosphere to this

CONNECTICUT

museum that is set on 150 acres. Pope's interest in the Impressionists led him to purchase a large number of the works of art displayed, especially the fine paintings by Monet *(Haystacks)*, Manet *(The Guitar Player)*, Degas *(The Tub; Jockeys)* and several canvases by Whistler and Mary Cassatt.

**Stanley-Whitman House** – *37 High St. Visit by guided tour (45min) only, May–Oct Wed–Sun noon–4pm; Mar, Apr, Nov, Dec Sun noon–4pm. Closed major holidays. $3.* & ☎203-677-9222. The influence of the European building styles on American Colonial architecture is seen in this house (c.1720) with its overhang, decorative pendants and central chimney. Inside there are furnishings and handcrafted items of the period.

# GROTON                                                              Pop 9,837

*Map of Principal Sights p 2*                        Tourist Office ☎203-444-2206

This small industrial city on the east bank of the Thames River, opposite NEW LONDON, is the home port of the US Atlantic submarine fleet. The US Naval Submarine Base *(not open to the public)* contains more than 270 buildings; subs are berthed and repaired at the Lower Base beside the river. Sailing vessels, merchant ships, tugboats and sightseeing boats also ply the waters of Groton's busy deep-water harbor. Boatyards on the Thames turn out many different types of ships, but it is Groton's largest employer, the Electric Boat Division of General Dynamics—builder of the world's first nuclear-powered submarine—that is best known. Each year, in June, the Thames River is the site of the colorful Yale-Harvard regatta.
Above the river, on the grounds of **Fort Griswold State Park**, rises the **Groton Monument**, a stone obelisk that commemorates the patriots who were killed when British troops captured Fort Griswold *(p 58)* in 1781.

**Nautilus Memorial** – *Berthed at a pier adjacent to the Submarine Base. From I-95 Exit 86 take Rte 12 north, then follow the signs. Open mid-Apr–mid-Oct Mon, Wed–Sun 9am–5pm, Tue 1–5pm; rest of the year Mon, Wed–Sun 9am–4pm. Closed Jan 1, Thanksgiving Day, Dec 25.* & ☎203-449-3174. With the launching in 1954 of the *Nautilus,* the world's first nuclear-powered vessel, submarine technology entered the atomic age. The *Nautilus* established new submerged records for speed, distance and underwater endurance and in 1958 became the first submarine to reach the North Pole.
Decommissioned in 1980, the 320ft ship is now the principal attraction at the USS Nautilus Memorial/Submarine Force Library and Museum complex. The torpedo room, control room and other sections of the vessel may be viewed.
Exhibits in the **museum** present the story of underwater navigation, the *Nautilus* and life aboard a sub. Operational periscopes allow visitors to practice sighting.

# GUILFORD                                                          Pop 19,848

*Map of Principal Sights p 2*                        Tourist Office ☎203-347-0028

In 1639 Minister Henry Whitfield arrived here with 25 families and bought the land that became Guilford from the Menunketuck Indians. Commerce and the fishing, milling and shipbuilding industries developed in this small town, which grew rapidly because of its location on the main road between New York and Boston. Guilford's 18C and 19C homes and lovely green reflect its early prosperity.

**Henry Whitfield State Museum** – *Old Whitfield St. Open Feb–mid-Dec Wed–Sun 10am–4:30pm; rest of the year by appointment only. Closed Jan 1, Thanksgiving Day, Dec 25. $3.* & ☎203-453-2457. In a land where wood was plentiful, Reverend Whitfield, inspired by the dwellings of northern England, built his home of stone. The first dwelling (1639) built in Guilford, it served as a garrison and meeting hall. Restored to its 17C appearance and decorated with 17-19C furnishings, the house is the oldest stone dwelling in New England.

**Hyland House** – *84 Boston St. Visit by guided tour (45min) only, Jun–Labor Day Tue–Sun 10am–4:30pm; mid-Sept–mid-Oct weekends only 10am–4:30pm. Closed Columbus Day & Monday holidays. $2.* ☎203-453-9477. This typical "saltbox" *(p 28)*, built in the late 17C, is furnished with American antiques of the period. The parlor is noteworthy for its fine wood paneling.

**Thomas Griswold House** – *171 Boston St. Visit by guided tour (30min) only, mid-Jun–mid-Sept Tue–Sun 10am–4pm. Mid-Sept–mid-Oct Sat 10am–4pm, Sun noon–4pm. $1.* ☎203-453-3176. Inhabited by five generations of the same family (1774-1958), this beautifully restored classic saltbox house features its original double-batten door (solid vertical planks held by horizontal boards) constructed in defense against Indian attacks. Two fireplaces are restored to their original dimensions. The period rooms contain furniture from the 18C to 19C. Note in particular two fine examples of the "Guilford" corner cabinet.

## ★★ HARTFORD

Map of Principal Sights p 2

Tourist Office ☎ 203-520-4480

This Yankee city, the capital of Connecticut, is easily recognized from a distance by tall office towers rising beside the Connecticut River. These modern buildings contain the headquarters of numerous insurance companies, as Hartford is a major national insurance center.

Manufacturing plays an important role in the city's economy. Pratt and Whitney Aircraft, the Colt Industries (the Colt revolver credited with "winning the West" was manufactured in Hartford during the 19C) and producers of typewriters, precision instruments and computers are located in the Greater Hartford region. The blue, star-speckled, onion-shaped dome of the **Colt factory** is a landmark visible from I-91. Extensive revitalization of Hartford's downtown area during recent decades includes the construction of new shopping and business complexes, notably, Constitution Plaza and the Civic Center. The landmark Cheney Building, renamed The Richardson in honor of the renowned architect *(p 30)* who designed it in 1877, now houses a shopping mall and apartments. The downtown skyline is graced with several striking examples of 1980s architecture such as One Corporate Center.

### HISTORICAL NOTES

**From Good Hope to the Connecticut Colony** – Hartford's location on a waterway navigable to the sea led the Dutch to establish a trading post, named Fort Good Hope, on this site in 1633. Because of the region's abundant supply of furs and timber, Puritans from the Massachusetts Bay Colony settled in the area two years later. Their village grew quickly, and in 1638 it joined with Wethersfield *(p 62)* and Windsor to form Hartford Colony. The **Fundamental Orders of Connecticut,** the governing document drawn up by members of Hartford Colony in 1639, is regarded as the New World's first constitution. In 1662 Hartford Colony became the Colony of Connecticut.

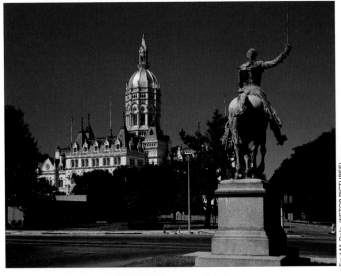

State Capitol from Bushnell Park

**The Charter Oak** – The independence of the Hartford Colony was guaranteed by the Royal Charter of 1662. In 1687, however, the royal governor, Edmond Andros, demanded the return of the charter. According to legend, during a meeting that took place one evening to discuss the matter, someone suddenly extinguished the candles and, in the darkness, fled with the charter. The charter was hidden in an oak tree where it remained until Sir Edmond returned to England a few years later. The tree, which became known as the Charter Oak, fell during a storm in the 19C. A variety of items made from the Oak are on view in the city's museums. The number of objects supposedly made from the tree is so large that it prompted Mark Twain to remark there is "a walking stick, dog collar, needle case, three-legged stool, bootjack, dinner table, tenpin alley, toothpick, and enough Charter Oak to build a plank road from Hartford to Salt Lake City." The original charter remains intact and is on display with the Fundamental Orders at the State Library *(p 47)*.

**An Insurance Center** – Hartford's insurance industry originated in the 18C when a group of men agreed to cover a shipowner's losses if his vessel did not return home safely. As shipping began to decline in the 19C, the industry shifted from marine to fire insurance.

On October 31, 1835, more than 600 buildings were destroyed by fire in New York City. The enormous number of claims filed forced many New York insurance firms into bankruptcy. The astute president of the Hartford Fire Insurance Co traveled to New York on a snowy winter night to assure his policyholders that their claims would be honored. The company promptly paid the claims, and its business boomed. Its consistently good record in the wake of subsequent disasters in Boston and Chicago gave rise to the city's sobriquet "Insurance Capital of the Nation." The approximately 40 insurance companies located in Greater Hartford today employ over 10 percent of the labor force throughout the metropolitan area.

## DOWNTOWN  *4hrs. Map p 46.*

**Hartford Civic Center** – *Trumbull St. Visitor information booth.* Completed in 1975, this concrete-and-glass structure is Connecticut's major convention center and the entertainment hub of Hartford. In addition to the 14,500-seat coliseum, the assembly hall and 10,000sq ft of exhibition space, the complex has an enclosed shopping mall, adjacent hotel and underground parking facilities. A pedestrian walkway links the center to CityPlace.

Diagonally across from the Civic Center, on Church Street, lies the **Hartford Stage Company**, a simple elongated building (1977) with a smooth, patterned exterior. *Performances are presented by the company in its 489-seat theater Sept–Jun. For information* ☎203-527-5151.

**CityPlace** – *185 Asylum St.* This is Connecticut's tallest building, a 39-story, office-retail tower (1984) with setbacks and a granite-and-glass exterior that blends well with its surroundings. Designed by Skidmore, Owings and Merrill, CityPlace contains an atrium where exhibits and concerts are offered year-round.

★ **Old State House** – *800 Main St. Open year-round daily 10am–5pm. Closed Jan 1, Dec 25. Visitor center has maps and brochures for Hartford and the state* ☎203-522-6766. This elegant Federal-style building (1792) with its graceful staircases, arches, balustrades and classical pediments was designed by Charles Bulfinch, the architect of the state houses of Maine and Massachusetts *(pp 65 and 105)*. The legislative chambers on the second floor contain original furnishings.

★ **Constitution Plaza** – The modern 12-acre plaza completed in the 1960s provided Hartford with new office buildings, shops, an open mall, and added a striking landmark to the city's skyline: the **Phoenix Mutual Life Insurance Building**. This elliptical, glass-sheathed tower is referred to as "the Boat" because of its shape. The plaza is the site of the Hartford Festival of Light, an annual lighting display held every evening from late November to January 1.

**Travelers Tower** – *1 Tower Square.* This building is the home of the Travelers Insurance Co, which began, as its name suggests, by insuring travelers. In 1864 the company's first policyholder insured his life for $5,000 "against accident while on a four-block walk home for lunch from his place of business." For this he paid a premium of 2 cents.

From the **observation deck** there is a **view★★** of the Hartford region *(visit by 30min guided tour only, May–early Oct Mon–Fri 10am–3pm; closed major holidays; advance 1-day reservation required; 100 steps to climb;* ☎203-277-3011).

★★ **Wadsworth Atheneum** – *600 Main St. Open year-round Tue–Sun 11am–5pm. Closed Jan 1, Jul 4, Thanksgiving Day, Dec 25. $5.* ✕ �&. ☎203-278-2670. Founded in 1842, this museum, whose initial collection consisted of landscapes by such artists as John Trumbull, Frederick Edwin Church and Thomas Cole, now houses a broad spectrum of ancient and modern art. In addition to paintings by the Hudson River school, highlights include European porcelains, 19C European paintings and the comprehensive Nutting collection of 17C furniture.

The present building is the result of several additions to the original Gothic Revival structure, completed in 1844, to house the library and art gallery established by Daniel Wadsworth. Donations and bequests funded subsequent additions to the original structure: the Colt Wing (1907), Morgan Memorial (1910), Avery Memorial (1934) and Goodwin Wing (1969). An interesting blend of traditional and modern architecture styles, the complex comprises the museum, a theater and art library.

**Main Floor** – Hilles Gallery contains selections from the permanent collection of 20C art. On display are paintings by Picasso, Mondrian and Dali as well as sculpture by Giacometti, Calder, Hepworth and David Smith, among others. In **Avery Court** an 8ft-tall figure of Venus, sculpted in the 16C by Pietro Francavilla, graces the indoor fountain. MATRIX gallery is reserved for temporary exhibits of contemporary art. **Morgan Great Hall★** and adjacent galleries feature Asian, Greek, Roman and Egyptian antiquities, European Medieval and Renaissance works and 17-19C European and American painting and sculpture. The Costume and Textiles exhibit is also here. Huntington Gallery features the museum's collection of 19C **European paintings**, one of its major strengths. Canvases by Monet *(Beach at Trouville)*, Renoir *(Monet Painting in his Garden at Argenteuil)*, Toulouse-Lautrec *(Jane Avril Leaving the Moulin Rouge)* and Degas are presented together with works by Manet, Ingres, Delacroix *(Turkish Women Bathing)*, Cézanne, Vlaminck, Vuillard and Bonnard. Also in this gallery is Goya's *Gossiping Women*.

**Second Floor** – The Amistad and Fleet Galleries of African-American Art present selections from the museum's collection of art and artifacts from the 18C to 20C. Several rooms in the Morgan Wing are devoted to 17C and 18C painting. Among the prominent Spanish, Italian, French and Dutch masters represented in the collection are Caravaggio *(Ecstasy of Saint Francis),* Rembrandt, Rubens, Zurbaran *(Saint Serapion),* Boucher, Chardin and Anthony Van Dyck.

The museum's comprehensive collection of **Meissen**, Sèvres, Worchester and other porcelain is exhibited in the Continental Porcelain Gallery in the Morgan Wing. Collections of English silver and ceramics are also located on this floor.

**Third Floor** – Traveling exhibits are staged in the Austin Gallery.

★ **American Collection** – Second and third floor galleries in the Avery Wing contain the museum's collection of American art spanning the early colonial period to the 20C. Included are portraits by John Singleton Copley *(Mrs. Seymour Fort),* Ralph Earl *(Chief Justice Oliver Ellsworth and His Wife),* Rembrandt Peale and Thomas Eakins, as well as historic subjects and genre paintings by Benjamin West, Trumbull *(Signing of the Declaration of Independence)* and Homer *(The Nooning).* These galleries also house a spectacular group of landscape paintings by members of the **Hudson River school** *(p 33),* including Cole *(Mount Etna From the Ruins of Taormina),* Bierstadt *(In the Mountains–Yosemite Valley),* Church, and more recent works by noted 20C artists such as Andrew Wyeth *(Chambered Nautilus).*

Displayed in the galleries on the second floor is the distinguished **Wallace Nutting Collection**★★ of early American Colonial furniture. Note the elaborately carved chests, ironwork, and domestic implements and utensils gathered by this retired Congregationalist minister (1861-1941), who greatly admired the furniture of the Pilgrim century, and acquired the items found in these galleries to serve as models for his furniture reproduction company. Author of over 20 books on antique furniture, he restored half a dozen houses including the Wentworth-Gardner House *(p 191),* the Saugus Iron Works House *(p 128)* and the Webb House *(p 62).* Rounding out the American section is the Hammerslough collection of silver with its great variety of forms, including porringers, saltcellars, skewers and strainers.

In Burr Mall outside the museum, between the Atheneum and the Municipal Building, is the giant, red stabile **Stegosaurus [1]** by Alexander Calder. On the triangular open space diagonally across from the Atheneum, note Carl Andre's controversial sculpture **Stone Field [2]**, a group of 36 boulders arranged in a geometrical pattern.

★ **Connecticut State Capitol** – *Illustration p 44. 210 Capitol Ave. Open Apr–Oct Mon–Fri 8am– 5pm, Sat 10am–3pm, rest of the year Mon–Fri 8am–5pm. Closed major holidays.* ※ & 🅿 ☎*203-240-0222.* This array of turrets, finials, gables, porches and towers, designed by Richard Upjohn, was the talk of the town when it was built in 1879. Rising above heavily sculpted walls, the capitol's golden dome overlooks **Bushnell Park**, designed originally by Frederick Law Olmsted.

The hand-painted columns, elaborate stenciling, courtyards, stained-glass windows, marble floors and balconies of the **interior★** all produce a startling effect. The capitol houses the legislative chambers and offices of state officials. Legislative offices are located in the 5-story **Legislative Office Building**, which is joined to the capitol by both a terraced walkway and an underground concourse.

**State Library** – *231 Capitol Ave. Open year-round Mon–Fri 9:30am–5pm. Closed major holidays.* ✗ ૯ ☎*203-566-4777.* This building, across from the capitol, houses the State Library *(east wing)*, the state's supreme court *(west wing)* and the State Museum *(center wing)*. Museum exhibits include Colt firearms, revolving displays of Connecticut history and the Fundamental Orders of Connecticut *(p 44)*.

**Bushnell Memorial Auditorium** – *Trinity and Capitol Aves.* Concerts, opera, ballet, films and plays are presented in this brick Colonial-style building erected in 1930 as a memorial to The Reverend Horace Bushnell (1802-1876).

## ADDITIONAL SIGHTS *2hrs*

★★ **Mark Twain House** – *351 Farmington Ave. Take I-84 west to Exit 46. Turn right on Sisson Ave, then right on Farmington. Visit by guided tour (1hr) only, Jun–mid-Oct Mon–Sat 9:30am–5pm, Sun noon–5pm; rest of the year closed Tue. Closed major holidays. $6.50.* ૯ ▫ ☎*203-493-6411.* Today a memorial to the well-known author, this delightful house was one of the comfortable Victorian dwellings that stood on **Nook Farm**, a "nook" of woodland beside the north branch of the Park River. In the 19C a community of writers lived in this pastoral setting, including Mark Twain and Harriet Beecher Stowe, whose homes have been restored and may be visited.

Mark Twain House, Hartford CT

Mark Twain *(p 36)*, the pen name of Samuel Clemens (1835-1910), commissioned this whimsical Stick-style Victorian house in 1874. A high-spirited and good-natured individualist, Twain smoked 20 cigars a day, slept backwards in his bed in order to face its carved headboard, and did most of his best writing in the Billiard Room. New inventions intrigued him—he owned the first private telephone in Hartford. His hospitality was legendary, and he counted among his closest friends General Sherman and Rudyard Kipling. He wrote seven of his most successful works, including *The Adventures of Tom Sawyer* (1876) and *The Adventures of Huckleberry Finn* (1884), during his residency in this house (1874-1891).

Outside, a profusion of open porches, balconies, towers, brackets and steeply pitched roofs give the structure a free, irregular shape. Inside, the splendid decoration done in 1881 has been restored: note in particular the silver stenciling, elaborately carved woodwork and exquisite wall coverings.

**Harriet Beecher Stowe House** – *73 Forest St. Visit by guided tour (1hr) only, Jun–mid-Oct & Dec Mon–Sat 9:30am–4pm, Sun noon–4pm; rest of the year closed Mon. Closed Dec 24 & major holidays. $6.50* ૯ ▫ ☎*203-525-9317.* Near the Twain house stands a simple Victorian cottage, which was the writer's home from 1873 until her death (1896). Mrs Stowe, whose novel *Uncle Tom's Cabin* led to an unprecedented attack on slavery, wrote several novels about New England.

Lacy gingerbread motifs adorn the plain facade. The light, airy interior contains furnishings that belonged to Mrs Stowe.

Next door is the handsome **Day House** *(also featured on the tour)*, which houses the Nook Farm research library and changing exhibits. Katharine S. Day was Mrs Stowe's grandniece and a prime force in preserving the farm's structures.

## EXCURSIONS

** **American Clock and Watch Museum** – *100 Maple St in Bristol, 18mi southwest of Hartford. Take I-84 to Exit 31. Follow Rte 229 to the right for 3mi. Turn left on Woodland St. Open Apr–Nov daily 10am–5pm. Closed Thanksgiving Day. $3.50. & ☎203-583-6070.* In the 19C America's clockmaking industry was centered in the Bristol area, where in 1860 alone, more than 200,000 clocks were produced. The neighboring towns of Terryville and Thomaston were named for Connecticut clockmakers **Eli Terry** and **Seth Thomas**. By using standardized wooden parts, Terry made it possible to turn out a moderately priced timepiece. His innovation, the small, compact **shelf clock**, was easily carried by Yankee peddlers who sold thousands of these lightweight timepieces in states east of the Mississippi.

Most of the clocks and watches in the museum's collection were produced in Connecticut. The Annex contains novelty clocks and timepieces easily identified by their shape: acorn, banjo and tall case clocks. *A video (20min) chronicles the history of clockmaking.*

* **Wethersfield** – *5mi south of Hartford by I-91. Description p 62.*

* **Dinosaur State Park** – *West St in Rocky Hill, 10mi south of Hartford. Take I-91 to Exit 23, turn left at the light. Open year-round daily 9am–4:30pm (exhibit center closed Mon). $2. & ☎203-529-8423.* The park offers a good opportunity to observe, intact and at its original site, an area covered with more than 500 dinosaur tracks *(see also p 161).* The size of the impressions and the 4ft-long pace suggest that the two-legged dinosaurs that made these tracks were probably 8ft tall and about 20ft long. A full-scale model of *Dilophosaurus,* the dinosaur considered the best match for these tracks, and a model of Coelophysis, some skeletal remains of which have been found in the Connecticut Valley, are part of the exhibit. A geodesic dome constructed in 1977 protects the excavated site and accompanying displays. In the casting area, visitors may make plaster casts of actual tracks *(open May–Oct daily 9am–3:30pm; visitors must provide their own materials; call for information).*

* **Farmington** – *10mi west of Hartford by I-84. Description p 42.*

* **Old New-Gate Prison and Copper Mine** – *In East Granby, 14mi northeast of Hartford. Take I-91 north to Rte 20 west. Turn right onto Newgate Rd. Open mid-May–Oct Wed–Sun 10am–4:30pm. $3. ☎203-653-3563. Rubber-soled shoes advised.* This former copper mine was worked until the mid-18C when financial setbacks induced the owners to sell the property to the colonial government. The government transformed the mine into the state's first prison in 1773. Here, robbers, counterfeiters, horse thieves, and later, Tories and British prisoners of war were held captive. Walking through the cold, damp mine tunnels buried deep within the earth, visitors can imagine the despair of those prisoners who, as a precaution against escape, were forced to sleep in these sunless subterranean passageways.

* **New Britain Museum of American Art** – *56 Lexington St in New Britain, 15mi southwest of Hartford. Take I-84 to Exit 35 onto Rte 72. Follow signs to New Britain and take Columbus Blvd Exit. Turn left at traffic light onto Lake St. At the stop sign, turn right and then immediate left onto Lexington St. Open year-round Tue–Sun 1–5pm. Closed major holidays. & ☎203-229-0257.* The holdings of this small museum illustrate trends in American art from the colonial period to the present. The 18C portraitists (Trumbull, Stuart, Smibert), the Hudson River school, the eight artists of the Ash Can school (including Sloan, Henri, Luks), and such renowned 19C and 20C masters as Homer, Whistler, Wyeth and Cassatt dominate the collection. Thomas Hart Benton's series of murals *Arts of Life in America* (1932), painted originally for the Whitney Museum of American Art in New York City, has been permanently installed here. *"Looking at Art," a museum publication ($5) available at the museum shop, is helpful for viewing the collection.*

**Talcott Mountain State Park** – *8mi northwest of Hartford. Leave Hartford on Rte 189, then follow Rte 185 to park entrance. Open Labor Day–Nov daily 10am–5pm. Mid-Apr–Labor Day Thu–Sun 10am–5pm. ☎203-677-0662. Facility information p 251.* A 1.3mi trail leads up to the Heublein Tower *(round-trip 1.5hrs),* which affords a sweeping **view**★ across the Farmington Valley to Hartford, and south to Long Island Sound.

**New England Air Museum** – *Bradley International Airport in Windsor Locks, 14mi northeast of Hartford. Take I-91 north to Rte 20 west, then Rte 75 north. Open year-round daily 10am–5pm. Closed Thanksgiving Day & Dec 25. $6.50. & ☎203-623-3305.* Located in two spacious buildings on the west side of Bradley Airport, the museum displays some 70 aircraft, which trace the history of aviation. Among the earliest exhibits is the 1909 Blériot XI, one of the first to be produced on a broad scale. Developments of later decades are highlighted by a large number of military aircraft. Helicopters are also on view; note the large Sikorsky Seabat used for rescue missions in Antarctica.

**Suffield** – *18mi north of Hartford by I-91 north, Rte 20 west, then Rte 75 north. Description p 61.*

The heart of the Housatonic Valley lies in the thickly wooded and hilly northwest corner of Connecticut, between the foothills of the Taconic Mountains and the Berkshire Hills. The valley is peaceful, with no raucous entertainment districts, glaring neon signs or noisy highways. Quiet country roads lead to small colonial villages, across covered bridges and through parks and forests. Trails (including the Appalachian Trail) crisscrossing the region's parks and forests are used by skiers in the winter and hikers during the milder seasons. Alongside these trails, streams and falls mark the path of the Housatonic as it flows downstream to Long Island Sound. The beauty of the valley and its proximity to New York have made the area a favorite of artists, writers and business people.

Jonathan Wallen

The area experienced a brief period of prosperity in the 18C when iron ore was discovered in the Litchfield Hills. Forges were built and operated until coal fields were discovered in Pennsylvania. Ruins of the old furnaces still remain in several villages, although they are usually hidden by the woods that have grown up around them.

## FROM BULLS BRIDGE TO WEST CORNWALL
*24mi. 3hrs. Map p 50.*

This itinerary follows Route 7, once a major route linking Montreal and New York.

*Begin at Bulls Bridge, 3mi north of Gaylordsville, on Rte 7. Turn left onto Bulls Bridge Rd, which passes over a covered bridge that spans the Housatonic River. After crossing a second bridge, turn right onto Schaghticoke Rd.*

**Schaghticoke Road** – *The first mile of this narrow road is largely unpaved.* The road follows the river as it winds through wooded terrain that is offset by patches of gnarled ledges and rock formations bordering the riverbed. After 1mi, the road arrives at the Schaghticoke Indian Reservation and passes an old Indian burial ground. The inscription on one of the stones reads simply: *Eunice-Mauwee – A Christian Indian Princess 1756-1860.*
The road passes the buildings of **Kent School**, a prestigious private secondary school (525 students).

*Turn left onto Rte 341.*

**Macedonia Brook State Park** – *Follow Rte 341 for 1mi, then turn right and follow the signs. Open year-round daily 8am–dusk.* △ *(reservations suggested)* ☎*203-927-3238. Facility information p 251.* The park, with its rocky gorge, streams, and brook, offers camping, fishing and hiking.

*Take Rte 341 to Kent.*

**Kent** – Pop. 2,918. Nestled among the hills bordering the Housatonic River, Kent is the home of artists and craftspeople whose works are often displayed in shops in the village center.

★ **Sloane-Stanley Museum** – *On Rte 7, 1mi north of junction of Rtes 7 & 341. Open mid-May–Oct Wed–Sun 10am–4pm. $3.* ⚊ ☎*203-927-3849.* Located near the ruins of the Old Kent Furnace (19C), this museum contains a fine collection of early American wooden and iron tools, acquired and artistically arranged by American artist Eric Sloane (1905-1985). A video (30min) on Sloane is available for viewing.

*Follow Rte 7 north.*

**Kent Falls State Park** – *Entrance on Rte 7. Open year-round daily 8am–dusk.* △ ⅊ *(reservations suggested). $5/car.* ☎203-927-3238. *Facility information p 251.*

Steps to the right of the falls lead to a point from which the cascades can be viewed from above. From this point, one can cross the bridge and descend to the parking lot by following a path (30min) through the woods.

Route 7 passes through **Cornwall Bridge**, where the local general store is a welcome sight to hikers on the Appalachian Trail.

**Housatonic Meadows State Park** – *Entrance on Rte 7. Open year-round daily 8am–dusk.* △ *(reservations suggested)* ⅊ ☎203-927- 3238. *Facility information p 251.* The **Pine Knob Loop Trail** *(round-trip 2hrs from the parking lot on the west side of Rte 7)* leads to the summit of Pine Knob (1,160ft) where there are views into the Housatonic Valley.

*Return to Rte 7 and continue north to West Cornwall.*

★ **West Cornwall** – This tiny village with several shops and restaurants is known for its picturesque **covered bridge**, built in 1864 and recently restored.

## ★★ LITCHFIELD

Pop 1,378

*Map of Principal Sights p 2*

Tourist Office ☎203-567-4506

A photographer's paradise in Indian summer when the trees are afire with color, Litchfield is a small, reserved New England village with broad streets and stately clapboard dwellings dating from the 18C. The nation's first law school and first institution of higher learning for women (Miss Pierce's School) were established in Litchfield during this early period. In the 19C the railroad and industrial development bypassed the center of town, a fact that accounts for Litchfield's having one of the loveliest and best-preserved ensembles of early American architecture in the nation.

**The Green** – North, South, East and West Streets meet at the green, dominated by Litchfield's **First Congregational Church** *(illustration p 39)*. Nearby, the **Litchfield Historical Society** organizes exhibits related to life in 17C and 18C Litchfield *(open mid-Apr– Nov Tue–Sat 11am–5pm, Sun 1–5pm; $2;* ⅊ ☎203-567-4501*)*. Many handsome dwellings will be found along **North** and **South Streets**; most are privately owned and are accessible to the public only during the Historic Homes Tour in mid-July.

**Tapping Reeve House and Law School** – *82 South St. Open mid-May–mid-Oct Tue–Sat 11am–5pm, Sun 1–5pm. $2.* ☎203-567-4501. The home of Tapping Reeve, founder of the nation's first law school (1775), stands near the one-room schoolhouse where he taught classes.

★ **White Memorial Foundation and Conservation Center** – *2mi west of Litchfield by Rte 202 west. Grounds open year-round daily.* ☎203-567-0857. Varied vegetation and landscapes abound on this 4,000-acre preserve, which is owned and operated by the White Memorial Foundation. A map of the center's hiking trails and historic buildings may be purchased at the museum *(open year-round Mon–Sat 9am–5pm, Sun noon–4pm)* or Foundation office *(on the grounds)*.

**CONNECTICUT**

## EXCURSIONS

★ **Bellamy-Ferriday House and Garden** – *On the green in Bethlehem, 6mi south of Litchfield via Rtes 63 and 61. Visit by guided tour (30min) only, May–Oct Wed, Sat, Sun 11am–4pm. $5.* ☎ *203-266-7596.* This 2-story clapboard Georgian-style house, graced with a Palladian portico, was built c.1745 and enlarged and embellished over the next 200 years. The interior includes vernacular furnishings from the area.

Dotted with white barns and orchards, the grounds feature a 1912 garden with lilacs, peonies, magnolias and roses in season.

**Institute for American Indian Studies** – *38 Curtis Rd in Washington, 11mi southwest of Litchfield. Rte 202 west 6mi, then Rte 47 south 3mi to Washington. Take Rte 199 south 2mi to Curtis Rd and follow signs to the institute. Open Apr–Dec Mon–Sat 10am–5pm, Sun noon–5pm, rest of the year Wed–Sat 10am–5pm, Sun noon–5pm. Closed major holidays. $4.* ☎ *203-868-0518.* This small museum in a peaceful woodland setting honors the culture and history of Connecticut Indians. Exhibits include clan emblems, handcrafted splint baskets and a longhouse.

A short nature trail leads to a re-created Algonquin encampment, complete with several **wigwams**.

## ★★ MYSTIC
Pop 2,618

Map of Principal Sights p 2          Tourist Office ☎ 203-444-2206

The village of Mystic, on the Mystic River, has been a shipbuilding center since the 17C. In the 1850s clipper ships reflecting the glory of America's maritime era were built in Mystic yards. At about the same time, whaling became a major industry on the coast and Mystic's fleet grew to include over 18 whaling ships. Many of the fine homes lining Gravel, Clift and High Streets were home to sea captains and sailors during this period. Local boatyards turned to the construction of pleasure craft in the early 20C, and during World War II, Navy ships were built there.

Today Mystic is known primarily as the site of Mystic Seaport, a museum-village that re-creates the atmosphere of America's maritime past.

### ★★ MYSTIC SEAPORT    *1 day*

Mystic Seaport is a living replica of a 19C waterfront community. This popular attraction has grown from a collection of nautical memorabilia displayed in a renovated mill to a complex of some 60 buildings covering 17 acres.The tall ships, the village center and the working shipyard add to the authenticity of the setting. Museum buildings house marvelous collections of marine art and artifacts.

**Visit** – *From I-95 Exit 90, follow Rte 27 south. Open Jan–Mar daily 10am–4pm. Apr–late Jun & Sept–late Oct daily 9am–5pm. Late Jun–Aug daily 9am–8pm. Late Oct–Dec daily 9am–4pm. Limited exhibits Thanksgiving Day. Closed Dec 25. $15. Schedule of daily events and map distributed at entrance.* ✗ ᗒ ☎ *203-572-5315.* Begin your visit at the Visitor Services building at the main entrance. A video *(shown continuously)* offers a good introduction to the seaport.

The 1908 steamboat **Sabino** makes trips *(30min)* on the river *(mid-May–mid-Oct daily 11am–4pm, late Jun–late Aug 6pm; $3 in addition to museum admission; 1hr 30min evening cruise available one hour after the last departure* ᗒ*).*

**The Village and Waterfront** – The heart of the village is the waterfront. Along the wharves and adjacent streets are shops and businesses commonly found in a 19C seaport:

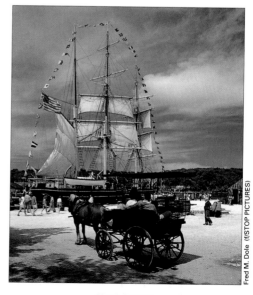

Fred M. Dole (f/STOP PICTURES)

Mystic Seaport

the bank, printer, tavern, ship's chandlery, the shops of the craftsmen who worked to outfit the vessels, and the ropewalk—the incredibly long cordage company building where the miles of rope necessary for rigging large vessels were made. Youngsters will particularly enjoy the **Children's Museum**, where they may participate in games and shipboard activities that were popular during the sailing era. Three impressive, fully rigged sailing vessels are moored at the waterfront:

★★ **The Charles W. Morgan** – The *Morgan*, sole survivor of America's 19C whaling fleet, has been declared a National Historic Site. During 80 years of service, the *Morgan* made 37 voyages, a number of which lasted three to four years. Visitors may board the ship to examine the officers' cabin and gigantic tryworks, the cauldrons used to melt whale fat.

**The Joseph Conrad** – This Danish-built training vessel (1882) has sailed under the Danish, British and American flags. Property of Mystic Seaport, the *Conrad* now serves its original function as a training ship.

**The L.A. Dunton** – This graceful schooner, built in 1921, typifies the fishing vessels that once sailed from New England to the Grand Banks off Newfoundland in the 1920s and 1930s.

**Henry B. du Pont Preservation Shipyard** – All kinds of boats from the seaport's vast collection are restored here. Visitors may observe craftsmen at work from a platform on the second level.

**Mystic River Scale Model** – The exhibit features a large model of Mystic in 1853.

**Stillman Building** – The 3-story building contains outstanding **collections★** of ship models and scrimshaw. A film *(10min)* dating from 1917 depicts the rigors of a whale hunt.

**Wendell Building** – This building houses the seaport's rich collection of wooden ship figureheads★ *(illustration p 34)*.

## ADDITIONAL SIGHT

★★ **Mystic Marinelife Aquarium** – *55 Coogan Blvd. Open year-round daily 9am–4:30pm (Jul–Labor Day 7pm). Closed Jan 1, last week in Jan, Thanksgiving Day, Dec 25. $9.50. & ☎203-572-5955.* Living specimens of marine animals and plants are grouped into more than 45 major exhibits demonstrating aquatic communities, habitat and adaptation.
**Seal Island**, a 2.5-acre outdoor complex, features seals and sea lions in settings constructed to resemble their natural habitats. The **Penguin Pavilion** houses a colony of African black-footed penguins. *Dolphins and whales exhibit natural behaviors in demonstrations presented daily in the indoor theater.*

## EXCURSION

★ **Stonington** – *Pop 1,287. 4mi east on Rte 1, then Rte 1A.* This is one of the prettiest coastal villages in Connecticut. The early character of this former shipbuilding center is preserved by the lovely old homes lining Stonington's tree-shaded streets. From the stone lighthouse, there is a view to Fishers Island, which is privately owned.

**Old Lighthouse Museum** – *7 Water St. Open Jul–Aug daily 11am–5pm. May–Jun & Sept–Oct Tue–Sun 11am–5pm. $3. ☎203-535-1440.* Seasonal exhibits in the old lighthouse are nostalgic reminders of Stonington's days as a shipbuilding center and sealing and whaling port. Artifacts date from the 17-19C and include portraits, whaling tools and scrimshaw. Visitors may climb to the lighthouse tower for a view encompassing three states: Rhode Island, New York, and Connecticut.

> *"You can always tell the Irish,*
> *You can always tell the Dutch,*
> *You can always tell a Yankee;*
> *But you cannot tell him much."*
>
> —Eric Knight, from *All Yankees Are Liars*

Map of Principal Sights p 2                    Tourist Office ☎203-777-8550

CONNECTICUT

Seen from I-95, New Haven appears to be a city of manufacturing facilities and tall office towers, such as the unusual cylindrical-towered **Knights of Columbus Building** framed by the red basalt ridges of East Rock and West Rock Parks. Only by leaving the interstate and driving toward the green can visitors discover the serene residential streets (Whitney Avenue, Hillhouse Avenue, Prospect Street) and the ivy-covered buildings of Yale University.

## HISTORICAL NOTES

The first planned city in America was founded in 1638 by a group of Puritans led by The Reverend John Davenport and Theophilus Eaton. New Haven was at first an independent colony. Efforts to develop the settlement's economy were unsuccessful, and in 1662 New Haven was made part of Connecticut Colony.

In the 18C New Haven's founders realized their dream when the colony flourished because of its deep-water harbor. The War of 1812 brought an end to this prosperous period in New Haven, as it did in other ports throughout New England.

The face of the town changed forever with the arrival of the railroad in the 19C. Industry and manufacturing developed, and immigrants came by the thousands to work in Connecticut's clock, firearms and carriage factories. One of the many innovative men in New Haven was **Eli Whitney**, who is recognized as the father of mass production. Whitney introduced the use of standardized parts as the basis of the assembly line in his arms factory outside the city.

By the mid-20C, burdened by the problems of unplanned industrial growth and increasing competition from the suburbs, the city rapidly deteriorated. Projects focusing on the revitalization of the downtown area, as well as the suburbs, were undertaken in the 1960s, resulting in the rehabilitation and construction of schools, homes and parks. Today New Haven—a blend of both traditional and modern architectural styles—is recognized as an interesting example of urban renewal.

**A Cultural Center** – The presence of Yale University, with its museums, libraries and programs of music, theater and dance, has made New Haven a prominent cultural center. The wide range of fine shops and restaurants adds to the city's cosmopolitan flavor. The New Haven stage, once a proving ground for Broadway productions, has become well known in its own right.

**Long Wharf Theater** – 222 Sargent Dr. ☎203-787-4282. Located in a former warehouse, this theater has been the recipient of a Tony Award.

**Shubert Performing Arts Center [1]** – Map p 55. 247 College St. ☎203-624-1825. The Shubert's varied program of performances includes Broadway-bound productions, Broadway road shows and concerts.

**Palace Performing Arts Center [2]** – Map p 55. 246 College St. ☎203-789-2120. Musicals and classical and popular concerts are presented at this 2,037-seat concert hall, formerly the Roger Sherman Theater.

**Yale Repertory Theater [3]** – Map p 55. 1120 Chapel St. ☎203-432-1234. The "Rep" focuses on plays written by young playwrights, and on modern interpretations of the classics.

**New Haven Symphony Orchestra** – 33 Whitney Ave. ☎203-776-1444. One of the finest in the nation, the city's resident symphony orchestra performs at Woolsey Hall [G] on the Yale campus.

Concerts are also staged at the **Yale School of Music [4]** (map p 55) ☎203-432-4157.

## ★★ YALE UNIVERSITY    1 day. Map p 55.

This Ivy League school is one of the oldest and most distinguished institutions of higher learning in the US. The university was founded in 1701 by a group of Puritan clergymen who wished to provide Connecticut with an educational institution where young men could be trained to serve the church and state. The school they established, known at first as the Collegiate School, was located in Saybrook. In 1716 the school was moved to the New Haven green, and two years later the Collegiate School was renamed Yale for its benefactor, the wealthy merchant **Elihu Yale**.

**Organization** – The university's 10,600 students, 4,000 faculty members, and staff represent a community of over 25,000 persons. Undergraduates are divided among 12 colleges, each of which has its own library, dining room, dormitories, social activities and athletic programs. Graduate programs are offered by Yale's schools of Art, Architecture, Divinity, Drama, Forestry and Environmental Studies, Arts and Sciences, Law, Medicine, Music, Nursing, and Management.

Yale gained university status in 1887, long after its Medical School (1810) and Law School (1824) were established. The nation's first Ph.D. degrees were awarded by Yale in 1861 and, before the turn of the century, women were admitted to the Ph.D. program. Women have been admitted to the undergraduate school since 1969.

**Architecture** – The architectural diversity that characterizes the Yale campus is dominated by the **Gothic** style with its medieval turrets, spires, massive towers, leaded stained glass and cathedral-like stone buildings. The **Georgian** influence is also significant, although the facades of most of these handsome structures are visible only from their courtyards.

Since the 1950s Yale has commissioned leading architects of the day to design the university's most recent, modern structures: **Louis Kahn** (the Yale Art Gallery and the Yale Center for British Art); **Paul Rudolph** (School of Art and Architecture); **Eero Saarinen** (Morse and Ezra Stiles Colleges, the Yale Co-Op and the Ingalls Hockey Rink); **Philip Johnson** (Kline Biology Tower); and **Gordon Bunshaft** (Beinecke Rare Book and Manuscript Library).

## Walking Tour

*Begin at the visitor center within Phelps Gate [A] on College St (open daily 10am–4pm; 1hr guided tours of the campus available Mon–Fri 10:30am & 2pm, weekends 1:30pm; ☎203-432-2300).*

*Enter the Old Campus.*

**Old Campus** – This is the site of Yale's earliest college buildings. **Connecticut Hall [B]** is the university's oldest structure. A statue of Nathan Hale, a Yale alumnus, stands in front of this simple Georgian hall where Hale lived as a student.

*Cross the Old Campus and exit onto High St.*

Across High Street is the landmark **Harkness Tower [C]** (1920), a 221ft Gothic Revival bell tower heavily ornamented with carved figures of famous Yale alumni, among them Noah Webster and Eli Whitney.

*Turn left on High St, pass under an arch, then turn right onto Chapel St.*

The **Yale University Art Gallery**, Louis Kahn's first major work, stands facing his last creation, the **Yale Center for British Art**. Both buildings present interesting conceptions of museum architecture from the point of view of building materials, light and the use of space. *For descriptions of the museums' collections see pp 56-57.*

*Continue to York St.*

The former Gothic Revival-style church on the left is the **Yale Repertory Theater [3]** *(p 53)*, home of the Yale Repertory Company, a professional acting troupe in residence at the university. Diagonally opposite stands Paul Rudolph's high rise **School of Art and Architecture**. Seemingly seven stories high, the building actually has 36 levels that are visible only from the interior.

Harkness Tower, Yale University

*Turn right onto York St and continue about halfway down the street.*

★ **Pierson and Davenport Colleges** – These elegant Georgian buildings hidden beyond the colleges' medieval-style, street-side facades may be seen from the courtyards. On the opposite side of the street stands **Wrexham Tower [D]**, designed after the church in Wales where Elihu Yale is buried.

*Cross Elm St and continue on York St. At no. 306 York St, walk through the narrow passageway on the left.*

★ **Morse and Ezra Stiles Colleges** – Saarinen's design for this ensemble of contemporary buildings was inspired by an Italian hill town. A continuous play of light and shadows is created throughout the day by the maze of stone passages with their vertical planes, geometric forms and sharp angular turns. Nearby is another of Saarinen's works, the **Yale Co-Op** (now known as the West Co-Op, since an adjacent building, the East Co-Op, has been constructed).

On Tower Parkway, across the street from Morse and Ezra Stiles Colleges, is the **Payne Whitney Gymnasium**, one of Yale's cathedral-like structures.

*Continue along Tower Pkwy, which becomes Grove St, to High St.*

Note the massive Egyptian Revival-style **gate**★ at the entrance to Grove Street Cemetery. Its architect, Henry Austin, was responsible for several of the 19C houses on Hillhouse Avenue *(p 57)*.

*Return via Grove St to York St. Turn left onto York St, then left onto Wall St.*

**Sterling Law Buildings** – Law students live in this group of buildings similar in design to the English Inns of Court where students during the 16-18C studied law. Portraits of police and robbers have been carved in stone above the windows.

*Cross High St.*

★ **Beinecke Rare Book and Manuscript Library** – *121 Wall St.* The exterior walls of this library (1961, Gordon Bunshaft) are composed of a granite framework fitted with translucent marble panels. Enter the library and observe the unusual effect produced by the sunlight streaming through the marble slabs. A **Gutenberg Bible** and changing exhibits are displayed on the mezzanine.
Isamu Noguchi's **sculptures [5]** of geometric shapes anchor the sunken courtyard, which fronts the library.

YALE UNIVERSITY

I-95 / Shore Line Trolley Museum

Facing the library are several buildings erected to celebrate Yale's bicentennial: **Woodbridge Hall [E]** offices, the **University Dining Hall [F]** and **Woolsey Hall [G]** auditorium. The rotunda, **Memorial Hall [H]**, contains a large group of commemorative plaques. On the plaza, near Woodbridge Hall, note Alexander Calder's red stabile *Gallows and Lollipops.*

*Return to the corner of Wall and High Sts and turn left onto High St. A number of small statues ornament the rooftops of buildings along this street.*

**Sterling Memorial Library** – *120 High St.* This is Yale's main library, yet at first glance its stained-glass windows, frescoes and archways suggest a cathedral. The **Cross Campus Library [J]**, located beneath Cross Campus *(to the left)*, was built underground to allow the green to remain intact. Gracing the Cross Campus entry plaza is a granite **fountain sculpture [6]** honoring Yale women by **Maya Lin**, a former Yale student and designer of Washington DC's Vietnam Veterans Memorial.

## Museums

**★★ Yale University Art Gallery** – *1111 Chapel St. Open Jan–Jul, Sept–Dec Tue–Sat 10am–5pm, Sun 2–5pm. Closed major holidays.* ☎203-432-0600. This gallery was founded in 1832 with a gift of about 100 works of art by the patriot artist **John Trumbull**. The museum contains two interconnected units: a 1928 building in the Italian Romanesque style, and the 1953 addition designed by Louis Kahn. The new gallery uses movable partitions to display the collections.

**Ground Floor** – The collection of ancient art features a Mithraic Shrine (Temple to the Sun God) with elaborate paintings and reliefs from **Dura-Europos**, an ancient Roman town in Syria. A selection of Greek, Etruscan and Egyptian vases and sculpture includes *Leda and the Swan* (370 BC), a Roman copy of a Greek original attributed to Timotheos. Equally noteworthy are the stone, clay, and jade artifacts in the growing **pre-Columbian** collection. The group figurines provide glimpses into the daily life of the period.

**First Floor** – Special exhibits and contemporary art are found on this floor. Noteworthy in the Sculpture Hall is Richard Serra's site-specific *Stacks* (1990), two steel monoliths placed 60ft apart. The Albers Corridor features a rotating selection of the gallery's 74 paintings and 110 prints by artist Joseph Albers, who chaired Yale's art department for ten years (1950-1960).

**Second Floor** – In addition to Impressionist paintings, the 19C collection includes works by Manet *(Young Woman Reclining in Spanish Costume)*, Courbet *(Le Grand Pont)*, Van Gogh *(Night Cafe)*, Millet, Corot, Degas and Matisse.
In the section devoted to early modern art, the visitor will find works by Marcel Duchamp *(Tu'm)*, Stella *(Brooklyn Bridge)*, Magritte *(Pandora's Box)* and Dali *(The Phantom Cart)* and canvases by Tanguy, Ernst, Klee and Kandinsky.
The Ordway Gallery contains changing exhibits of 20C art. Paintings by Picasso *(Coquillages sur un Piano; Femme Assise)*, Renoir *(Mount St Victoire)*, Pollock *(No. 4)*, Rothko *(No. 3, 1967)* and de Kooning are featured.
The collection of **African art** comprises masks, and ceremonial and royal objects.

**Third Floor** – The **Jarves collection** of early Italian painting (13-16C) includes such jewels as da Fabriano's *Madonna and Child* and Ghirlandaio's *Portrait of a Lady with a Rabbit*. The adjacent galleries, devoted to European art, contain the Medieval collection. Among the Flemish paintings are portraits by Holbein and Hals, an oil sketch by Rubens, Correggio's *Assumption of the Virgin*, and the *Allegory of Intemperance* attributed to Hieronymus Bosch.
The **Garven collection★** of colonial and early 19C Americana is arranged didactically for the university's teaching purposes. Furniture, silver, pewter and ironware are used to illustrate the development of American art forms and their relationship to the society that produced them.
On view in the gallery of American paintings and sculpture from the 19C and 20C are masterpieces by, among others, Eakins, Homer, Church, Cole, Remington, Hopper and O'Keeffe. One section of the gallery displays works of John Trumbull including the original paintings *The Battle of Bunker Hill* and *Signing of the Declaration of Independence*, used as models for copies later produced by Trumbull for the Capitol in Washington DC. Hiram Powers' sculpture *The Greek Slave* is also on display.

**Fourth Floor** – The Asian galleries feature Japanese sculpture and Chinese bronzes, ceramics and paintings spanning the period from 12C BC to the present.

**★★ Yale Center for British Art** – *1080 Chapel St. Open year-round Tue–Sat 10am–5pm, Sun noon–5pm. Closed major holidays.* ♿ 🅿 ☎203-432-2800. In 1966 Paul Mellon, benefactor of the National Gallery in Washington DC, donated to Yale his collection of British art, including 1,300 paintings, 10,000 drawings, 20,000 prints, and 20,000 rare books. Louis Kahn drew the plans for a new building to house the collection, which opened to the public in 1977. Kahn's design allows natural light to enter through numerous skylights and filter down through 3- and 4-story open courts to the display areas.

**The Collection** – The collection, surveying the development of English art during and after the Elizabethan period, includes sporting paintings, town and marine views, portraits and "conversation pieces" (informal group portraits) dating primarily from 1700 to 1850.

The **fourth floor** houses paintings and sculpture that have been installed chronologically to provide a survey of British art from the late 16C through the early 19C. Several rooms on this floor are reserved for the works of **Gainsborough**, **Reynolds**, **Stubbs**, **Turner** and **Constable**. On the **second floor** is a selection of 19C and 20C paintings and sculpture.

**Peabody Museum** – *170 Whitney Ave. Open year-round Tue–Sat 10am–5pm, Sun noon–5pm. Closed major holidays. $4 (free Tue–Fri 3–5pm).* ♿ ☎203-432-5050. Yale's natural history museum showcases a famous collection of **dinosaurs** (1st floor) featuring a horned dinosaur, the first *Stegosaurus* ever mounted, and the fossil of an *Apatosaurus* (67ft long, 35 tons). The 10ft *Archelon* (75 million years old) is the largest turtle in the world. The fossil skeleton of *Deinonychus,* a species discovered in 1964, sports a wicked, sickle-shaped claw. Rudolph Zallinger's mural *The Age of Reptiles* depicts the dinosaurs and plant life that existed 70-350 million years ago.The first floor also houses a collection of mammals, primates and artifacts representing the cultures of Mesoamerica, the Plains Indians and New Guinea. Minerals and rocks, a bird hall and dioramas of North American flora and fauna can be found on the third floor. The second floor is reserved for special exhibits.

**Yale Collection of Musical Instruments [K]** – *15 Hillhouse Ave. Open Sept–Jun Tue–Thu 1–4pm. Closed during academic breaks. $1. A series of concerts is held annually featuring restored instruments from the collection.* ☎*203-432-0822.* The collection consists of more than 800 instruments representative of the traditions of Western European music from the 16C to the 19C.

## ADDITIONAL SIGHTS  *Map p 55*

★ **The Green** – When New Haven was a Puritan colony, the town was laid out as a giant square subdivided into nine smaller squares. The center square, the green, was reserved for the use of the entire community as pastureland, parade ground and burial ground, and has remained the heart of the downtown district over the years. Different architectural styles are represented by the three churches (1812-1815) on the green: **Trinity Church** (Gothic Revival), **Center Church** (Georgian), **United Congregational Church** (Federal).

**Hillhouse Avenue** – Most of the beautiful mansions on this street were built in the 19C by wealthy industrialists and merchants, and are now owned by Yale University. Architectural styles include Federal, Greek Revival, Renaissance Revival and even a Hindu influence.

★ **Ingalls Hockey Rink** – Prospect St. This whale-shaped rink (1957) was designed for Yale by the Finnish architect Eero Saarinen.

**New Haven Colony Historical Society** – *114 Whitney Ave. Open year-round Tue–Fri 10am–5pm, weekends 2–5pm. Closed major holidays. $2.* ♿ ▯ ☎*203-562-4183.* Antique pewter, china and toys dating from the period of the New Haven Colony are among the displays in the society's 11 galleries.

**East Rock Park** – *Follow Orange St. Cross Mill River and turn left, then bear right. The road leads to the summit parking lot. Nov–Apr road to summit open weekends & holidays only, 8am–4pm.* From the summit of this basalt ridge there is a **view**★★ of the entire New Haven area. In the distance stretches Long Island Sound.

## EXCURSIONS

**Shore Line Trolley Museum** – *17 River St in East Haven, 5mi east of New Haven by I-95. Take Exit 51, turn right onto Hemingway Ave, then left onto River St. Open Jun–Aug daily 11am–5pm. May, Sept, Oct weekends 11am–5pm; Apr & Nov Sun only 11am–5pm. Closed Thanksgiving Day, Dec 25. $5. A 3mi trolley excursion operates through the Connecticut shore area between the museum and Short Beach.* ▯ ☎*203-467-6927.* The museum is primarily the work of volunteer trolley buffs who have restored one third of the nearly 100 street, subway and elevated railway cars on the grounds.

**Sleeping Giant State Park** – *6mi from New Haven. Take Whitney Ave (Rte 10) to Hamden and turn right on Mt Carmel Ave. Open year-round daily 8am–dusk.* ▯ *($8/car mid-Apr–Nov weekends & major holidays). Trail maps and information available at ranger headquarters.* ♿ ☎*203-566-2305. Facility information p 251.* The park has picnic facilities and more than 30mi of trails around the Giant. **Tower Path** *(round-trip 1hr 30min)* leads to the highest point in the park where, from a stone tower, there are good **views**★★ of the region.

*In May 1911 novelist Henry James penned his impression of Connecticut to a friend in England: "The very warm heart of 'New England at its best,' such a vast abounding Arcadia of mountains and broad vales and great rivers and large lakes and white villages embowered in prodigious elms and maples. It is extraordinarily beautiful and graceful and idyllic—for America."*

# NEW LONDON

Pop 28,540

Map of Principal Sights p 2   Tourist Office ☎203-444-2206

**CONNECTICUT**

This city, located on a harbor at the mouth of the Thames River, has always depended on the sea for its livelihood. Its deep-water port was a haven for privateers during the Revolution, a fact that led to the British attack on New London and GROTON in 1781. During this assault, led by Benedict Arnold, **Fort Trumbull** *(not open to the public)* and **Fort Griswold** fell to the enemy, and nearly all New London was destroyed by fire. In the mid-19C the city was a principal whaling port. Elegant homes built from the profits of whaling still stand in neighborhoods that have remained residential, despite the development of onshore industries. Home to the US Coast Guard Academy, New London boasts ties with the sea that continue even today. The shipping industry and the US Naval Submarine Base located across the Thames are major contributors to the local economy. Scientists and engineers at the Naval Underwater Systems Center, on the grounds of Fort Trumbull, develop

©Paul Rocheleau

Starr Street

technology related to modern undersea warfare. Some 1,600 men and women attend Connecticut College, a four-year, liberal arts school located near the Coast Guard Academy. Revitalization of the downtown area has included the renovation of several 19C Greek Revival houses on **Starr Street** and the 19C Union Railroad station (designed by H. H. Richardson).

## SIGHTS *4hrs. Map p 59.*

★ **Hempsted Houses** – *Hempstead & Jay Sts. Open mid-May–mid-Oct Tue–Sun 1–5pm. $3. ☎203-443-7949.* Built in 1678, the timber-framed Joshua Hempsted House is a splendid example of 17C American architecture. The walls are insulated with seaweed and pierced with tiny leaded casement windows. Inside, the low-ceilinged rooms contain fine primitive American furnishings. The granite Nathaniel Hempsted House was built by Joshua's grandson in 1759. The interior features an unusual projecting bake oven.

★ **Lyman Allyn Art Museum** – *625 Williams St. Open Jun–Labor Day Tue–Sat 10am–5pm (Wed 9pm), Sun 1–5pm. Mid-Jun–May Tue–Fri & Sun 1–5pm (Wed 9pm), Sat 11am–5pm. Closed major holidays. $3. �&ᐧ203-443-2545.* This small museum established by a bequest of the Allyn family specializes in paintings by Connecticut artists and in the decorative arts of the state. Attractively arranged furnishings, paintings, sculpture and decorative arts, dating from classical civilizations to the present, complement the **American collection** (1680-1920), housed in the Palmer Galleries (1st floor). Particularly noteworthy is the group of dollhouses and dolls on the lower level.

**United States Coast Guard Academy** – *15 Mohegan Ave. Open year-round daily 9am–dusk. &ᐧ203-444-8270 for special events and parade dates.* The academy, a four-year military college that trains officers for the Coast Guard, began in 1876 when the schooner *Dobbin* was chosen to serve as a floating training school, to prepare cadets for the Revenue Marine (which later evolved into the Coast Guard). The *Dobbin* was succeeded by several other ships until the early 20C, when the academy was established at Fort Trumbull. In 1932 the academy moved to its present site beside the Thames.

**Visitor Center** – *Open May–Oct daily 10am–5pm. Apr weekends only 10am–5pm.* Coast Guard history and a video of cadet life *(5min)* are presented.

**Coast Guard Museum** – *In Waesche Hall. Open year-round Mon–Fri 9am–4:30pm, Sat 10am–5pm, Sun noon–5pm. Closed major holidays.* The museum's exhibits deal with the history of the Coast Guard.

**The Waterfront** – The academy's training vessel, the *Eagle*★, is occasionally berthed at the waterfront. German-built, the *Eagle* (1936) is a graceful three-masted square-rigger used for cadet training cruises to Europe and the Caribbean in the summer. *When in port, the Eagle may be visited by guided tour. ☎203-444-8595.*

**Connecticut College Arboretum** – *Williams St. Open year-round daily dawn–dusk. ☎203-439-2140. Map of arboretum available at entrance.* This 425-acre preserve specializes in trees and shrubs native to eastern North America. The main trail *(2mi)* circles a marsh; two optional loops lead to a bog and hemlock forest.

**Ye Towne's Antientest Buriall Place** – *Huntington St. Enter from Hempstead St.* This old burial ground has many early New England slate tombstones carved with winged angels, skull and crossbones, geometric patterns and other designs.

**Whale Oil Row** – *105-119 Huntington St.* These four white mansions with their imposing columns are typical of the Greek Revival residences constructed by wealthy merchants and seamen in the 19C.

**Monte Cristo Cottage** – *325 Pequot Ave. South on Howard St, then turn left on Pequot Ave (in the direction of Ocean Beach). Open mid-Apr–mid-Dec Mon–Fri 1–4pm. Closed major holidays. $3.* The unpretentious 2-story frame dwelling looking out on the Thames was the boyhood summer home of playwright **Eugene O'Neill** (1888-1953) *(p 36)*. The cottage was the setting for his two most autobiographical works: *Long Day's Journey into Night* and *Ah, Wilderness!*
A short *(18min)* film serves as an introduction to the years the O'Neills spent here.

**Ferry to Orient Point, Long Island, NY** – *Departs from New London ferry dock. Jun–Oct daily 7am–9:45pm. Nov–May daily 7am–8:45pm. Closed Dec 25. One-way 1hr 20min. $28 (car & driver). Reservations suggested.* ⚓ ⚐ *Cross Sound Ferry Services.* ☎203-443-5281.

## EXCURSIONS

**Ocean Beach** – *5mi south of New London on Ocean Ave*. This wide sandy beach, edged with a pleasant boardwalk, offers an amusement arcade, miniature golf, archery, swimming and boating.

**Eugene O'Neill Theater Center** – *305 Great Neck Rd in Waterford, 6 mi south of New London. Take Bank St then turn left at Ocean Ave and continue to Rte 213 (Niles Hill Rd). Performances Jun–early Aug. For schedule* ☎203-443-5378. Named in honor of the 20C playwright Eugene O'Neill, the center is devoted to the development of new talent for the American stage. Activities on the center's 10-acre grounds include the annual National Music Theater Conference. The center also sponsors the National Theater Institute and the National Critics Institute.

## NORWALK                                                    Pop 78,331

Map of Principal Sights p 2                    Tourist Office ☎203-854-7825

The spirit of this once lively 19C seaport is alive in **SoNo** (an acronym for South Norwalk) on the Norwalk River, where the restored Victorian buildings along Washington Street between Main and Water Streets house attractive restaurants, shops and galleries. Cruises leave from Hope Dock for the historic 1868 **Sheffield Island Lighthouse** *(late May–mid-Jun weekends & holidays 10am, noon & 2pm; late Jun–Labor Day weekends & holidays 9:30 & 11:30am, 1:30 & 3:30pm; one-way 45min; $9; Norwalk Seaport Association;* ☎203-838-9444*)*.

★ **Maritime Center** – *10 Water St. Open Jul–Labor Day daily 10am–6pm, rest of the year 10am–5pm. Closed major holidays. $7.50. Marine life study cruises Jun–Labor Day, Wed–Sun 1pm. $15.* ✗ ☎203-852-0700. A renovated 19C brick warehouse on the river houses this 2-story complex, which features interactive videos and exhibits on maritime history, demonstrations of boatbuilding, an aquarium with Long Island Sound habitats, and shark and seal tanks as well as an IMAX theater.

**Lockwood-Mathews Mansion Museum** – *295 West Ave. Visit by guided tour (1hr) only, Mar–mid-Dec Tue–Fri 11am–3pm, weekends 1–4pm. Closed major holidays. $5.* ☎203-838-1434. The 3-story turreted, dormered Victorian summer home of LeGrand Lockwood was designed in granite c.1864 with a mansard roof. The 50-room interior, including an art gallery, children's theater and Moorish sitting room, boasts marble floors, and mahogany and walnut woodwork crafted by Italian artisans. The grand staircase alone, with 266 balusters, reportedly cost $50,000.

### EXCURSION

**New Canaan** – *Pop 17,864. 10mi north of Norwalk, via Rte 123*. This choice suburb in Connecticut's Fairfield County has been an art center since the early 20C when artists founded the **Silvermine Guild of Artists** here. The Guild maintains a complex of studios, galleries, classrooms and a photography lab on Silvermine Road *(east of Rte 123)*. Highlighting its program of events is the annual exhibition **The Art of the Northeast** *(p 244)*.

## NORWICH                                                    Pop 37,391

Map of Principal Sights p 2                    Tourist Office ☎203-444-2206

Situated where the Yantic and Shetucket Rivers meet to form the Thames, Norwich has been an important industrial center since the 18C. The city's historic district, radiating out from a prim triangular **green**, has a fine group of early dwellings. The **Rose Arts Festival**, held several days in June at the Chelsea Parade Grounds, features concerts, sporting events, exhibits, live entertainment and an arts and crafts show.

**Leffingwell Inn** – *348 Washington St. Open mid-May–mid-Oct Tue–Sat 10am–3pm, Sun 2–4pm, rest of the year by appointment only. Closed major holidays. $3.* ☎203-889-9440. This dwelling was the site of many political meetings during the Revolution. Restored and converted into a museum, the house contains furnishings, silver and other products made by Norwich craftsmen.

### EXCURSION

**Uncasville** – *5mi south of Norwich by Rte 32*. Named for the Mohegan sachem **Uncas**, the town of Uncasville is still home to members of the Mohegan tribe. In the 17C Uncas made an alliance with the colonists, who agreed to help him and his braves resist any attacks by the powerful Narragansett Indians of Rhode Island. During the last major battle between the two tribes in 1643, Uncas captured and killed Miantonomo, the chief of the Narragansetts.

**CONNECTICUT** *(vertical, right margin)*

**Fort Shantok State Park** – *Fort Shantok Rd off Rte 32. Open year-round daily 8am–dusk. Closed major holidays.* ☎203-848-9876. *Facility information p 251.* The park features an old Indian burial ground and remnants of the fort where the Mohegans were under siege by the Narragansetts.

**Tantaquidgeon Indian Museum** – *Rte 32. Open May–Oct Tue–Sun 10am–4pm.* ♿☎203-848-9145. This small museum was built by John Tantaquidgeon, a descendant of the Mohegan chief Uncas. Items traditionally made and used by the Mohegans, and gifts from other Indian tribes are among the exhibits.

## RIDGEFIELD                                           Pop 6,363

Map of Principal Sights p 2                 Tourist Office ☎203-743-0546

Although Ridgefield lies just an hour's drive from the hustle and bustle of Manhattan, this charming town, with its tree-shaded avenues, shops and mansions, retains a distinctly New England character.

**Keeler Tavern** – *132 Main St. Visit by guided tour (40min) only, Feb–Dec Wed, Sat & Sun 1–4pm. $3.* ☎203-438-5485. The Keeler Tavern operated as an inn from colonial days through the early 20C. During the Battle of Ridgefield, April 27, 1777, a cannonball lodged in the wall post, where it remains to this day. This fact accounts for the tavern's nickname: the Cannonball House.

**Aldrich Museum of Contemporary Art** – *258 Main St. Open year-round Tue–Sun 1–5pm. Closed major holidays. $3.* ☎203-438-4519. Changing exhibits of contemporary art are presented in this handsome Colonial dwelling. The **sculpture garden** displays some 20 works by Sol LeWitt, Tony Smith and other sculptors *(open year-round daily dawn to dusk).*

## RIVERTON                                             Pop 315

Map of Principal Sights p 2                 Tourist Office ☎203-567-4506

During the early 19C this small rural village, situated on a branch of the Farmington River, was known as Hitchcocksville because of its Hitchcock chair factory. The town was renamed Riverton in 1865.

**Hitchcock Chair Factory** – *Rte 20. Factory store open year-round daily 10am–5pm. Closed Easter Sunday, Thanksgiving Day & Dec 25.* ♿☎203-738-0141. Lambert Hitchcock's chair factory, established here in the early 19C, turned out thousands of rush-seated "fancy" hand-stenciled chairs that were sold throughout the country. Restored in 1946, the factory is again producing chairs, tables and chests in the Hitchcock tradition.

**Museum** – *Robertsville Rd, off Rte 20. Open Apr–Dec Fri & Sat 11am–4pm, Sun noon–4pm.* ☎203-738-4950. *Film (15min) "The Hitchcock Story" shown on request.* The museum, arranged in an old granite church not far from the factory, contains hand-painted and decorated furnishings made at the Hitchcock factory.

## SUFFIELD                                             Pop 11,427

Map of Principal Sights p 2                 Tourist Office ☎203-763-2578

The Connecticut River forms the eastern boundary of this small, countrified town established in 1670. Well-preserved houses border Main Street, together with the brick buildings of Suffield Academy, a private preparatory school.
Agriculture has been the principal local activity. Tobacco-growing was the major industry until World War II. Broadleaf tobacco continues to be raised here, though much farmland has been converted to dairies, nurseries and industrial parks.

**Hatheway House** – *55 S. Main St. Open Jul–Aug Wed–Sun 1–4pm. Mid-May–Jun & Sept–mid-Oct Wed & weekends 1–4pm. Holidayfest in Dec. $3.* ♿☎203-668-0055. The house, actually three structures in one, owes its present size to Oliver Phelps, a merchant and land speculator who acquired the property in 1788. Phelps enlarged the main section of the house (c.1760) by adding a single-story structure to the south end. About 1795 Phelps had the Federal-style north wing built. The central section is simple and functional, furnished with William and Mary, and Queen Anne pieces. In contrast, the Federal wing is elegant, decorated with Adamesque ornamentation and fine Hepplewhite, Sheraton and Chippendale furnishings. The original 18C hand-blocked French wallpapers installed in the Federal wing add a special feature to the house.

*For your trip to Canada, New England's northern neighbor, consult the* **Michelin Green Guide to Canada.**

# ★ WETHERSFIELD
Pop 25,651

Map of Principal Sights p 2 · Tourist Office ☎ 203-520-4480

Established in 1694 on a harbor at the head of the Connecticut River, Wethersfield was an important center of trade until the 18C when floods changed the course of the river, leaving only a cove at the original harbor site. This change drastically affected the town's commercial activity, which decreased rapidly until, by the late 18C, farming had replaced trade as the economic mainstay.

Unspoiled by industry throughout the 20C, Wethersfield is a pleasant HARTFORD suburb. Approximately 150 dwellings in the town's picturesque historic district, Old Wethersfield, date from the 17C and 18C. A number of these houses, built by wealthy merchants and shipowners, have been restored.

## ★★ OLD WETHERSFIELD  *3hrs*

**Main Street** – This wide street is lined with attractively restored houses. The 1760 brick **Congregational Meetinghouse** adjoins an early burial ground that contains tombstones dating from the 17C.

★★ **Webb-Deane-Stevens Museum** – *211 Main St. Visit by guided tour (1hr) only, May–Oct Mon, Wed–Sun 10am–4pm. Nov–Apr weekends only 10am–4pm. Closed Jan 1, Thanksgiving Day, Dec 25. $6.* ☎*203-529-0612.* These houses allow a comparison in architectural styles and decorative arts from 1690 to 1840, and of the lifestyles of a wealthy merchant, a politician, and a modest craftsman.

**Webb House** – This elegant Georgian residence (1752), built by the prosperous merchant Joseph Webb Sr, was the scene of a four-day conference in May 1781 between Gen George Washington and the French Count Rochambeau. Plans for the Yorktown campaign, which led ultimately to the defeat of the British in the American Revolution, were discussed by the two military leaders during this time. The house contains a fine collection of period furnishings and decorative arts. Highlights of the tour include the Council Room where Washington and Rochambeau met, and the bedchamber that was specially decorated for General Washington, who lodged at the Webb House during his stay in Wethersfield.

**Deane House** – This house was built in 1766 for Silas Deane, an American diplomat who traveled to France during the Revolution to negotiate arms and equipment for the Continental Army. While abroad, Deane became involved in business deals that aroused suspicions about his loyalty, and he was accused of treason. He returned home and spent the rest of his life attempting, unsuccessfully, to clear his name. The spacious rooms and off-center stairway are unusual for a house of its period.

**Stevens House** – Isaac Stevens was a leather worker who built this house in 1788 for his bride. The modest furniture, woodwork, fabrics and decor offer a pleasing contrast to those of the more richly embellished Webb and Deane Houses.

**Buttolph-Williams House** – *249 Broad St. Visit by guided tour (30min) only, May–Oct Mon, Wed–Sun 10am–4pm. $3; combined ticket with Webb-Deane-Stevens Museum $7.* ⚫ ☎*203-529-0460.* The simple Colonial house (1692) contrasts with the more elegant houses of a later date that border the green.

**Old Academy** – *150 Main St. Open year-round Tue–Fri 10am–4pm, Sat 1–4pm.* ⚫ ☎*203-529-7656.* This handsome brick building (1804) has served as the town hall, library, armory, a female seminary, and is currently the headquarters of the Wethersfield Historical Society. Now a museum, its changing exhibits depict the development of Wethersfield during the last 300 years.

**Cove Warehouse** – *At Cove Park overlooking the cove. Open mid-May–mid-Oct weekends 1–4pm. $1.* Goods that arrived by sea in the 17C were stored in Wethersfield's seven warehouses before they were transported inland. About 1700, floods demolished six of the warehouses, leaving only Cove Warehouse intact. The structure houses an exhibit on the town's maritime trade between 1650 and 1830.

# WOODSTOCK
Pop 6,008

Map of Principal Sights p 2 · Tourist Office ☎ 203-928-1228

Woodstock's village green is set in the sparsely populated northeast section of the state. Facing the green is the summer residence known as Roseland Cottage.

**Roseland Cottage** – *Open Jun–Sept Wed–Sun noon–5pm. $4.* ☎*203-928-4074.* This handsomely landscaped and furnished board-and-batten cottage was built by New York publisher Henry Bowen in 1846. The site became famous in the 19C for the spectacular Independence Day celebrations held here by Mr. Bowen. The festivities included fireworks, dancing and parties and were attended by such distinguished guests as Presidents Grant, Hayes and McKinley.

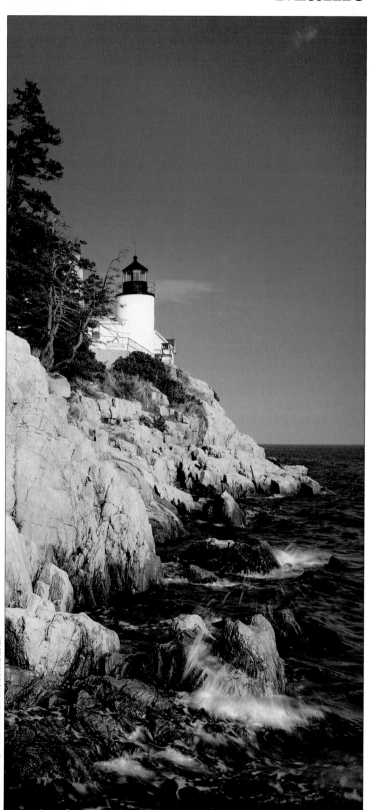

Bass Harbor Head, Acadia National Park / ©Dick Dietrich

# Maine

**Area:** 33,215 sq mi
**Population:** 1,227,928
**Capital:** Augusta
**Nickname:** Pine Tree State
**State Flower:**
White pinecone and tassel

Equal in surface area to the combined size of the other five New England states, Maine is a vast, thickly forested region fringed with a 3,500-mile coastline. The origin of the name Maine is uncertain. Attributed by some historians to the Maine region in western France, the name is believed by others to derive from the term, "the main," used by fishermen to distinguish the mainland from the offshore islands. Maine is also referred to as **DownEast** because of the winds that carry sailing vessels eastward along this section of the coast.

Glaciers sculpted the irregular, deeply indented coastline that characterizes Maine. Moving southeast across the land, then retreating northwest, the ice chiseled out elongated peninsulas and headlands. Offshore, hundreds of islands, the peaks of submerged mountains, dot the water. Pine trees grow on the islands, along the shore and across the interior to the north, giving the state its nickname.

**History** – The Maine coast was explored by the Vikings in the 11C, and several centuries later by European fishermen. In 1604 Pierre du Gua, Sieur de Monts, and Samuel de Champlain established a small colony on an island in the St Croix River from which they set out the following year to found the Acadian territory. An English settlement, the Popham Colony, was established at the mouth of the Kennebec River in 1607; then in 1635 the English monarch Charles I gave the region of Maine to Sir Ferdinando Gorges, appointing him "Lord of New England." From this time on, the coast was the scene of constant battles between the French and the English. In 1677 the Massachusetts Colony bought Maine from the descendants of Sir Gorges and the region remained under the jurisdiction of Massachusetts until 1820, when Maine was granted statehood under the conditions of the Missouri Compromise.

**Economy** – The state of Maine has a diversified economy. In the early days the state's wealth depended upon its forests. Timber was harvested to supply masts for the Royal Navy during the colonial period, when all pine trees 24 inches or greater in diameter belonged to the Crown. In the 19C wooden **shipbuilding** in Maine peaked at Wiscasset, Bath and Searsport, where boatyards turned out four-, five- and six-masted vessels. Today the forests supply important **paper** and **pulp mills** at Jay, Millinocket, Rumford, Westbrook and Woodland.

Fishing, especially **lobstering**, is a major industry; more than 50 percent of the nation's lobster catch comes from Maine. In the many small fishing ports along the coast, thousands of colorful buoys float on the surface of the water, marking the location of traps set by lobstermen. The state leads the US in the sardine-packing industry, producing some 100 million tins of sardines each year. An annual catch of 35,000 metric tons of Atlantic herring nets fishermen $5 million.

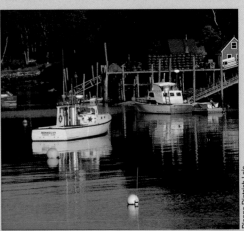

Dianne Dietrich Leis

Textiles, shoes and boots are also Maine-made products. Maine farmers raise the nation's third largest crops of potatoes, as well as 98 percent of the country's blueberries.

# AUGUSTA

Map of Principal Sights p 4                    Tourist Office ☎207-623-4559

Situated on the banks of the Kennebec River, Maine's capital is an attractive industrial and residential city. The river and its adjacent woodlands have been a source
of wealth to Augusta ever since the 17C, when the Pilgrims established a trading
post on its east bank. In the 18C and 19C the Kennebec River served as an important avenue for boat traffic, as well as a source of ice in winter *(p 26)*. Wood cut
from the forests bordering the river also contributed to the region's prosperity.
Government, industry and tourism are Augusta's major businesses. The capital
district, located in the State Street area on the west bank of the Kennebec River, includes the State House, the State Museum and other attractions.

**State House** – *State and Capitol Sts. Open year-round Mon–Fri 9am–5pm.
Closed major holidays. Self-guided walking tour begins on the first floor at the old
museum.* ⚒ & ☎*207-287-2301.* The domed capitol building is best viewed from a
vantage point in the riverside park nearby. Constructed between 1829 and 1832
according to the designs of the eminent Boston architect Charles Bulfinch, the
major portion of the State House was later remodeled and enlarged. Despite this
change, the columned facade and other Bulfinch characteristics were preserved.
The House, Senate and Executive chambers are all located in the State House.

**Blaine House** – *192 State St. Visit by guided tour (20min) only, year-round Tue–
Thu 2–4pm.* ☎*207-289-2121.* Built for a Bath sea captain in the 1830s, this Colonial
mansion was the home of James G. Blaine (1830-1893), congressman, secretary of
state and presidential candidate in 1884. The house has served as the governor's
mansion since 1919.
The tour includes public and family rooms on the main floor.

**Maine State Museum** – *State St. Open year-round Mon–Fri 9am–5pm, Sat
10am–4pm, Sun 1–4pm. Closed major holidays. $2.* & ☎*207-287-2301.* This mod-
ern building houses the State Library and Archives, as well as the State Museum.
Exhibits treat the history, life and environment of Maine and its residents.

**Old Fort Western** – *16 Cony St. Open early Jul–Aug Mon–Fri 10am–4pm, weekends 1–4pm. Late May–Jul 4 daily 1–4pm. Labor Day–mid-Oct weekends only
1–4pm. $4.50.* & ☎*207-626-2385.* This was the site of the trading post built by
the Plymouth Pilgrims in the 17C. In 1754 Fort Western was erected at this riverside
location as a defense against Indian raids. The reconstructed blockhouses and
stockades, and the restored 14-room barracks furnished with antiques appear as
they did during the 18C. The fort was never attacked; for the most part it served as
a supply depot for other garrisons farther up the river.
Today costumed guides re-create the fort's history.

# BANGOR

Map of Principal Sights p 5                    Tourist Office ☎207-947-0307

This tranquil city on the west bank of the Penobscot River faces the Maine woods
in one direction and the sea in the other. Located at the terminus of the log drives
from the north, and near an outlet to the sea, Bangor developed into an international export center for timber in the 19C. Crews of lumberjacks felled trees in the
winter, drove them downriver in the spring, and spent the remainder of their
time—and most of their pay—during the off-season in Bangor. Tough and rowdy,
these expert woodsmen called themselves "the Bangor Tigers." When they were
in town, the taverns, grog shops and brothels in the district dubbed Devil's Half-
Acre seldom had a quiet night or day.
**Paul Bunyan**, a legendary character created by a Michigan newspaperman, typifies
the Bangor Tiger. A gigantic **statue** of Paul Bunyan stands on lower Main Street in
front of the Bangor Civic Center.
Bangor's International Airport serves as a refueling station for airlines flying North
America-Europe routes and as a port-of-entry for flights arriving in the US.

# ★ BATH

Map of Principal Sights p 4                    Tourist Office ☎207-443-9751

Bath has been a shipbuilding center since the 18C, when its coveted location on a
channel to the sea provided the town with advantages over other regional boatbuilding centers. The port once owned a fleet of merchant vessels that sailed
regularly to the West Indies, California and the Far East. Boatyards along the
Kennebec River turned out square-riggers, down-easters *(p 27)*, and some of the
largest schooners ever constructed.
The buildings of the **Maine Maritime Museum** and the graceful old homes on
Washington Street date from this time. The **Bath Iron Works** (BIW), on the west bank
of the Kennebec River, has been building ships since 1893 and is Maine's largest
privately owned employer. The launching of a new tanker, container ship, frigate
or cargo vessel is still a major event at BIW.

## ★★ MAINE MARITIME MUSEUM

*Open year-round daily 9:30am–5pm. Closed Jan 1, Thanksgiving Day, Dec 25. $7. ✗ & ☎207-443-1316. Boat rides (50min) on the Kennebec River ($7 in addition to museum admission) from late Apr–Oct.*

The museum, devoted to preserving Maine's maritime heritage, maintains a historic shipbuilding complex and offers boatbuilding programs that allow apprentices to employ the traditional skills used in constructing wooden sailing craft. Overlooking the Kennebec River, the **Maritime History of Maine** exhibit introduces coastal heritage, seafaring, commerce and shipbuilding. Also on view is an exhibit of Maine's family fleets, as well as changing displays of maritime art and artifacts.

**The Buildings** – In the **Mold Loft** (1917) and **Mill and Joiner Shop** (1899), shipbuilding tools, power machinery, old photographs and illustrated explanations of the making of a wooden ship tell the story of the Percy and Small Shipyard and the great vessels turned out here.

The **Paint and Treenail Shop** (1897), where treenails (wooden pegs used in ship construction), and paints and stains were produced, contains exhibits on the trades related to shipbuilding. Note the re-created 19C shipyard office, and the scale model of Donnell Cordage Co (1843), which originally stood at the south end of Bath, along with its 1000ft-long ropewalk.

In the **Apprenticeshop**, visitors can observe apprentices from the museum's program constructing and restoring wooden boats. On the floor below, there are displays of small craft from the museum's collection.

**Percy and Small Shipyard** – Large wooden schooners were the specialty of the Percy and Small Shipyard (1894-1920). The six-masted, 3,720-ton *Wyoming,* the largest wooden sailing vessel ever to fly the US flag, was built here.

**The Waterfront** – The schooner *Sherman Zwicker* (1942), frequently berthed along the riverbank, was used in the cod and haddock fisheries on the Grand Banks off Newfoundland until 1968. Visitors can board this ship when it is in port. From the boat's deck there is a good view of the lighthouse at Doubling Point, and of the Bath Iron Works, including the BIW's 400ft crane, capable of hoisting a weight of some 220 tons.

A comprehensive exhibit of the state's 200-year lobstering history, **Lobstering and the Maine Coast,** is presented in a reconstructed sail loft that was floated down on a barge from north Bath. Special features include four restored lobster boats and a film *(17min)* about the lobstering industry, written in the 1950s by **E.B. White.**

### EXCURSION

★ **Popham Beach** – *16mi south of Bath on Rte 209.* Situated at the tip of a finger-like peninsula reaching into the ocean, this resort village lies between the Kennebec River and the sea. One of the earliest English settlements in the New World was established at Popham Beach in 1607. The colony lasted only one year, but in that time its residents succeeded in building the first English ship constructed in America, the 30-ton pinnace *Virginia.*

**Fort Popham,** the granite fortress overlooking the point where the Kennebec meets the Atlantic Ocean, was built during the Civil War to prevent Confederate vessels from sailing upriver to Bath.

Nearby, at **Popham Beach State Park,** a broad sandy beach lies on the ocean side of the point *(open mid-Apr–Oct daily 9am–dusk; $2; & ☎207-389-1335; facility information p 251).*

## ★★ BAXTER STATE PARK

*Map of Principal Sights p 5*

Dominated by the state's highest peak, **Mt Katahdin** (5,267ft), Baxter State Park is a densely forested rectangular tract of land (202,064 acres) in the heart of the Maine wilderness. The park is named for **Percival Proctor Baxter** (1876-1969), who devoted the greater part of his life and fortune to acquiring this land, which he ultimately deeded to the people of Maine under the condition that the park be preserved "forever in its natural wild state."

In accordance with Baxter's wishes, the park has remained primarily a wildlife sanctuary for deer, moose, bear and other denizens of the north country. The roads are narrow and unpaved *(speed limit 15-20mph),* camping facilities are primitive, and there are no motels, shops or restaurants within the park boundaries. While only a few scenic attractions can be observed from the road, the park's 175mi trail system, which includes the northern section of the Appalachian Trail, leads to points that afford spectacular views of this remote region. Because of the unique circumstances underlying the establishment of Baxter State Park, the park is administered independently of other state parks. Headquarters are in Millinocket. *For access and orientation, see "Visiting Northern Maine" p 78.*

**Mt Katahdin** – A giant granite monolith, Katahdin (an Indian name meaning "the greatest mountain") has long figured in local Indian mythology. One Abnaki legend tells of Pamola, a deity with the wings and claws of an eagle, the arms and torso of a man, and the enormous head of a moose, who lived on the peak of Mt Katahdin. Whenever he was angry, Pamola cast violent rainstorms, lightning and thunder onto the lands below. To visitors to the park today, Katahdin offers good opportunities for hiking and camping.

Baxter Peak is the highest of Katahdin's four summits, the others being Hamlin Peak, Pamola Peak and South Peak. Observed from the east, the **Great Basin**, a bowl-shaped formation scoured out of the mountain by glacial activity, is Katahdin's most distinguishable feature. Seen from the west, the **Knife Edge**, a narrow, serrated granite ridge that joins Pamola and South Peaks, cuts a jagged profile across the sky.

## VISIT  *1 day*

*Open late May–Labor Day daily 8am–4pm, rest of the year weekdays only 8am–4pm. Closed major holidays. $8 non-resident motor fee. Park map available at entrance. △ ☎207-723-5140. Facility information p 251.* The main entrances to the park lead to the Park Road, the only route through the park; it is not a sightseeing route but does pass several scenic points of interest, such as **Abols Falls** and the **Slide Dam**. *It is necessary to hike to see the other sights and views in the park.*

**Hiking Trails** – *Before starting out, hikers should register and check with the ranger in the area as to weather and trail conditions. Stephen Clark's book,* Baxter Park and Katahdin, *is a comprehensive guide to the park trails. Most trails are in the south section of the park. Baxter's trails are blazed blue; white blazes mark the Appalachian Trail (AT).*

**Sandy Stream Pond Trail** – *Southeast section of the park. 1.5mi. Begin at Roaring Brook Campground.* After .5mi, a short spur to the left leads to Big Rock where there is a good view of Katahdin's Great Basin and Hamlin Peak.

**South Turner Mountain Trail** – *4mi. Begin at Sandy Stream Pond Trail.* After .5mi, where a fork leads left to Russell Pond Trail, take the right fork and follow the blue blazes to the summit. The trail becomes difficult as it ascends the steep boulder-covered slope of the mountain. The view from the summit of Katahdin and the surrounding region is worth the effort.

**Chimney Pond Trail** – *Ascent 3.5mi (2.75 hrs). Begin at Roaring Brook Campground.* Chimney Pond, located on the floor of the Great Basin, is the site of one of the park's many campgrounds.

**Appalachian Trail** – *Southwest section of the park. 1mi hike from Daicey Pond to Big Niagara Falls.* Follow the white-blazed trail. After 1mi you will see **Little Niagara Falls**. Continue a short distance to **Big Niagara Falls**.

**Hunt Trail** – *10.5mi (8-10hrs). Begin at Katahdin Stream Campground. Follow the white blazes.* This is one of the popular trails to the top of Katahdin. Allow a full day for the climb and descent. Only those in excellent physical condition should attempt this long, demanding hike. A pleasant, much shorter hike *(1mi)* on this trail leads to **Katahdin Stream Falls**.

## EXCURSION

**Patten** – *Pop 1,234. 8mi east of the park by the Park Rd, then Rte 159.* This small agricultural community straddles the border between the rich potato fields of Aroostook County and the forests of northern Maine. High-powered diesel trucks hauling wood pulp and logs are a familiar sight on local roads. Lumbering is an important business in Patten, even though the era of lumber camps and river drives has long-since ended.

At the **Lumberman's Museum** *(.5mi west of Patten on Rte 159),* exhibits ranging from crooked knives to steam log-haulers, a sawmill and reconstructed lumber camps tell the story of the lumberjack's life. The 1820 shanty replicates the type shared by as many as a dozen woodsmen during the lumbering season *(open Jul–Aug Mon–Sat 9am–4pm, Sun 11am–4pm; late May–Jun & Sept Tue–Sat 9am–4pm, Sun 11am–4pm; Oct 1–mid-Oct weekends only; $2.50; ☎207-528-2650).*

# BETHEL                                    Pop 2,329

Map of Principal Sights p 4                Tourist Office ☎207-824-2282

Bethel's distinguished inn, prep school and carefully preserved homes situated near the village green, are enhanced by the town's magnificent setting in the White Mountains. Bethel offers opportunities for hunting, fishing, golf, rockhounding in nearby abandoned mines, and excursions into the White Mountains.

## EXCURSIONS

★ **Grafton Notch State Park** – *25mi northwest of Bethel by Rte 26. Open mid-May–mid-Oct daily 9am–dusk. $1. ☎207-824-2912. Facility information p 251.* The road heads through the Bear River Valley and into Grafton Notch State Park, an unspoiled area in the White Mountains. The drive through the park offers views of the notch dominated by **Old Speck Mountain** (4,180ft) to the west, and **Baldpate Mountain** to the east. Several picnic areas near the road are designated.

**Screw Auger Falls** – The falls tumble over slabs of rock and into shallow pools.

**Mother Walker Falls** – *1mi north of Screw Auger Falls.* Old Speck is visible from this small waterfall.

★★ **Evans Notch** – *16mi southwest of Bethel. Follow Rte 2 west for 10mi, then turn left onto Rte 113.* The drive through Evans Notch *(Gilead to North Chatham)* in White Mountain National Forest offers **views★★** of the Cold River Valley, one of the most beautiful valleys in the White Mountains.

---

## ★★ BLUE HILL and DEER ISLE

Map of Principal Sights p 5                    Tourist Office ☎207-348-6124

The quiet, breeze-swept peninsula that reaches from Route 3 down to Stonington seems to have been overlooked by modern civilization. Small, secluded villages and cozy inlets harboring lobster boats nestle in woodlands that hug the water's edge. Views of Penobscot Bay and Mt Desert Island are especially striking on a clear day, when the blue sky frames the dark green spruces.

### CIRCUIT FROM BUCKSPORT
*96mi. 1 day.*

*Leave Bucksport (description p 70) on Rte 1/3 north, then turn right onto Rte 175 south. Continue straight to Rte 166, then Rte 166A.*

★ **Castine** – *Description p 72.*

*Take Rte 166, then Rte 199 to the junction of Rte 175 and follow it south.*

**Reversing Falls** – Five miles south of South Penobscot there is a picnic area where an unusual phenomenon can be seen, a reversing falls. At this point, the waterway is very narrow. When the tide changes, the narrow passage creates a bottleneck, causing the water to rush in (or out, depending upon whether the tide is rising or falling) with such great force that a series of falls is formed. The best view of the reversing falls is from the bridge on Route 175.

Continuing on through North Brooksville and Brooksville, the road begins to climb. Blue Hill is visible to the left. From the **Caterpillar Rest Area** there is a spectacular **panorama★★** of Deer Isle, Penobscot Bay, and Camden Hills and the bay islands.

*At the junction of Rtes 175 and 15, cross the bridge to Little Deer Isle, then continue to Deer Isle. Rte 15 passes through the village of Deer Isle and follows the eastern shore to Stonington.*

★ **Stonington** – Pop 1,252. This tranquil fishing village at the tip of the peninsula typifies the picturesque towns along the coast. Stonington's granite quarries were formerly worked for stone used in the construction of public buildings and monuments throughout the US; today most of the quarries lie abandoned. Hoisting machinery can be seen on the offshore islands. Boats to **Isle au Haut★**, in Acadia National Park *(p 80),* leave from Stonington.

> *Continue along the western shore of the island. A beautiful **view** unfolds upon approaching the town of Sunset. After Sunset take Rte 15 to Little Deer Isle. Cross the bridge, and follow Rte 175 east.*
> *In Sedgewick turn onto Rte 172, which joins Rte 175. Turn right onto Rte 175. Cross two bridges to Blue Hill Falls, a reversing falls similar to the one at North Brooksville (p 68). Return to Rte 172 and continue to Blue Hill.*

**Blue Hill** – Pop 1,941. Named for the hill that dominates the town and yields a hearty annual blueberry harvest, this pretty village is home to many craftsmen, writers and artists. A trail leads to the top of Blue Hill (940ft) where you can look out across Blue Hill Bay to Mt Desert Island.
A summer school for chamber music is held in the village; artist-faculty concerts are presented at Kneisel Hall *(Jul–Aug Fri 8:15pm, Sun 4pm ☎207-374-2811).*

> *Take Rte 15 north.*

The road climbs, passes along the base of Blue Hill, then descends to Rte 3, offering beautiful **views** as it leads on to East Orland.

## ★★ BOOTHBAY HARBOR                                        Pop 2,347

Map of Principal Sights p 5                              Tourist Office ☎207-633-2353

Boothbay Harbor lies at the tip of one of the craggy peninsulas that extend into the sea from the deeply indented, mid-coast section of Maine. Protected headlands sheltering deep natural anchorages make the region a major boating center and a popular summer resort. Small shops line the streets leading down to the wharves, and motels, hotels and inns are found in the snug coves and along the rugged stretches of shore such as **Ocean Point**.
Lobstering is the principal activity of the local fishermen, who can be observed practically year-round gathering shiny, green-brown lobsters from the wooden traps set below the water's surface. Restaurants and lobster wharves feature the fresh-caught delicacy broiled, stuffed, boiled or made into lobster salad.
The popular New England boating event, **Windjammer Days**, takes place at Boothbay Harbor in late June. During the three-day celebration, two- and three-masted schooners parade through the harbor, and residents hold community suppers, a pageant and a street parade.

**Cruising the Bay and Islands** – Boat trips and fishing boat charters are available. Cruises vary from one to several hours in duration. *For information contact Goodtime Excursions at Fisherman's Wharf (Pier 1) ☎207-633-3244.*

## BRUNSWICK                                              Pop 14,683

Map of Principal Sights p 4                              Tourist Office ☎207-725-8797

This attractive community, with its wide avenues, is the home of Bowdoin (BO-din) College. The Bowdoin campus, in the heart of Brunswick, radiates outward from the town's pleasant green, which was laid out by citizens in the early 18C. Shade trees and handsome mansions line Federal Street and other streets nearby.
Construction of a hydroelectric dam began in 1979 in the vicinity of the Androscoggin River falls, the major power source in the 19C for the town's lumbering and textile industries. Small manufacturing plants and the US Naval Air Station are the chief contributors to the local economy today.

**Bowdoin College** – Established in 1794, this fine small college counts among its alumni authors Nathaniel Hawthorne and Henry Wadsworth Longfellow, explorers Adm Robert Peary and Adm Donald MacMillan, and the nation's 14th President, Franklin Pierce. Harriet Beecher Stowe wrote *Uncle Tom's Cabin* while she and her husband, a professor at Bowdoin, lived in Brunswick.
The college is named for James Bowdoin, a former governor of Massachusetts (1785-1787). The Bowdoins were a French family who arrived in Maine in the 17C and rose to prominence during the colonial period. Grateful to their new country, they endowed the college with land, money and old master drawings from their personal art collection.

★ **Bowdoin College Museum of Art** – *Walker Art Building. Open year-round Tue–Sat 10am–5pm, Sun 2–5pm. Closed major holidays & Dec 25–Jan 1.* ♿ ☎207-725-3275. This 19C building was designed by Charles Follen McKim of the prestigious architectural firm, McKim, Mead and White. On the main floor, selections from the museum's group of early American portraits include works by Gilbert Stuart, Robert Feke, John Smibert, Joseph Blackburn and John Singleton Copley. Other galleries contain 19C and 20C American paintings as well as a selection of European works, Greek and Roman antiquities, and Asian and African art. Memorabilia, graphics and paintings by Winslow Homer are displayed annually *(mid-May–mid Aug only).*

**Peary-MacMillan Arctic Museum** – *Open year-round Tue–Sat 10am–5pm, Sun 2–5pm. Closed major holidays.* ✗ ㊡ ☎*207-725-3416*. This museum, dedicated to Admirals Robert Peary and Donald MacMillan, presents the history of polar exploration from the early 1800s through the Arctic expeditions made by Peary, credited with being the first man to reach the North Pole (1909), and his assistant MacMillan.

The major part of the collection consists of clothing, instruments, tools and record books of the Peary and MacMillan expeditions. In the last room there are interesting photos and artifacts related to the Inuit of Greenland and Labrador.

## BUCKSPORT                                           Pop 2,989

Map of Principal Sights p 5                    Tourist Office ☎207-469-6818

This small town lies on the east bank of the Penobscot River at the point where **Verona Island** divides the river. Bucksport's main street, lined with shops and the **Jed Prouty Tavern**, runs parallel to the river. At the northern end of Bucksport, a large paper company employs an innovative technique that prevents the noxious odors associated with papermaking from being released into the air. Across the river, Fort Knox, a massive granite structure, guards the entrance to the Penobscot.

★ **Fort Knox State Park** – *Open May–Oct daily 9am–dusk. $2.* ☎*207-469-7719*. The tense political situation that arose between the US and Great Britain in 1840, as a result of the New England-Canada boundary dispute, led to a decision by the American military to build a fort on this site. Although the dispute was settled before work on the fort began, construction was nevertheless initiated. Named for Gen Henry Knox *(p 89)*, chief of artillery under General Washington during the Revolution, the fort, never completed, served as a military training ground during the Civil War.

The enormous stone fortress, with its archways, buttresses and winding staircases, is a model of 19C American military architecture. From the top of the fort there is a **view** of Bucksport and the Penobscot River.

## ★★ CAMDEN                                           Pop 4,022

Map of Principal Sights p 5                    Tourist Office ☎207-236-4404

Camden's setting at the foot of the Camden Hills, looking out onto the island-speckled waters of Penobscot Bay, is one of the loveliest on the New England coast. The pleasant life-style of Camden's residents is reflected in the attractive village center and waterfront. Restaurants, galleries, and shops decorated with flower-filled window boxes abound in the business district, and nearby streets are lined with large houses. In the harbor sleek yachts are anchored amid the tall two-masted windjammers, sailing vessels that offer vacationers the opportunity to sign on as part of the ship's crew.

Beyond the pastoral setting of the **Camden Public Library** is **Bok Amphitheatre**, where concerts are presented outdoors against the backdrop of the bay. The nearby waterfront park is an ideal place from which to watch the harbor's activity.

Fred Sieb Photography

View of Camden from Mt Battie

** **Camden Hills State Park** – *Rte 1 north of Camden. Open mid-May–mid-Oct daily 9am–dusk $2.* ⚠ ☏*207-236-3109. Facility information p 251.* A road leads to the top of **Mt Battie** (800ft), where there is a view★★★ of the harbor, Penobscot Bay and the bay islands. This scene inspired Maine-born poet Edna St Vincent Millay to write her first volume of verse, *Renascence,* in 1917.

Returning to the center of Camden on Rte 52 affords another good view of the Camden Hills as they slope down to Megunticook Lake.

**Old Conway House** – *From Camden take Rte 1 south 1mi then turn right. The complex is located off Rte 1 on the Camden-Rockport line. Visit by guided tour (1hr) only, Jul–Aug Tue–Fri (call for hours) $2.* ☏*207-236-2257.* This small group of buildings, including an old barn, farmhouse, museum and restored sugarhouse (1820), contains artifacts and memorabilia of Camden and Rockport.

## EXCURSION

**Rockport** – *Pop 2,854. 3mi south of Camden by Rte 1.* This seaside hamlet formerly known for its lime industry, is a picturesque, relaxing spot. Ruins of the lime kilns can be viewed in Marine Park near the harbor.

At the **Artisans School** *(9 Elm St, near Walker Park)* overlooking the harbor, skills used for centuries in building wooden boats are practiced. The smell of fresh cedar shavings fills the loft, where visitors may observe students as they construct dories, peapods, skiffs and other small craft ranging from 8ft to 38ft in length *(open Jul–Aug Mon–Fri 8am–5pm, weekends 10am–5pm; rest of the year Mon–Fri 7am–5pm, weekends 10am–5pm;* ♿ ☏*207-236-6071).*

## ★★ CAMPOBELLO ISLAND (Canada)

Map of Principal Sights p 5

*Campobello Island is part of the Canadian province of New Brunswick. US citizens must present personal identification (such as a birth certificate or voter registration card, and photo identification) at the border. It is advisable to carry proof of citizenship with you. This Canadian time zone is 1hr later than Maine.*
Campobello Island, at the mouth of the Bay of Fundy, is linked to Lubec, Maine by the Franklin Delano Roosevelt Memorial Bridge. An international agreement signed by the US and Canada in 1964 established an international park dedicated to Franklin Delano Roosevelt on Campobello Island.

**A Summer Retreat** – Discovered in the 17C by Samuel de Champlain and Sieur de Monts, the island was named in 1767 for the governor of Nova Scotia, William Campbell—*campo bello* (Italian for "beautiful pasture") calling to mind the island's scenery. In the late 19C the island was again discovered, this time by wealthy Bostonians and New Yorkers, such as the Roosevelts, who bought land and subsequently built summer cottages here. Land developers were quick to use the island's frequent thick fogs to their advantage, advertising that "basking in the fog was as healthy for the body as basking in the sun."

Easily accessible from the mainland, Campobello Island receives many visitors attracted by the international park and the island's wild, unspoiled beauty. In the offshore waters circular **weirs**, composed of nets strung on stakes, trap fish according to an ancient Indian method.

** **Roosevelt Campobello International Park** – *Open late May–early Oct daily 10am–5:50pm.* ♿ ☏*506-752-2922.* **Franklin Delano Roosevelt**, whose four terms as President of the US were unprecedented in the nation's history, spent his early summers at Campobello. He continued to vacation on the island with his wife, Eleanor, and their children until August 1921 when, following a swim in the icy waters of the Bay of Fundy, he was suddenly stricken with polio. Almost completely paralyzed, FDR began a long period of convalescence during which he gradually regained his strength. Unfortunately he remained partially paralyzed for the rest of his life.

Turning his energies toward politics, Franklin was elected governor of New York in 1929, and within four years was elected to the first of four terms he would serve as President. FDR did not return to the island until 1933, 12 years after the onset of his tragic illness. Then, as on the several other occasions when he visited the island before his death (1945), he stayed only for a brief time. The Hammer family donated the Roosevelt cottage and property to the government in 1963, to serve as a park in FDR's memory.

**Visitor Center** – Films are shown as an introduction to Campobello and Roosevelt's life on the island.

★ **Roosevelt Cottage** – The 34-room house facing Eastport across the bay is modestly furnished. Many personal mementos, such as FDR's hat, fishing rod, family photos and letters, recall the vacations the Roosevelts spent at Campobello.

★★ **Drives in the Park** – The vast 2,800-acre park exhibits a variety of magnificent landscapes, including forests, bogs, cliffs, lakes and beaches. The humid, seaside climate favors a dense, rich growth of vegetation. From **Friars Head** *(south of the visitor center turn right at the sign marked Picnic Area)* there is a view west of Lubec and the Maine coast.

A sweeping vista along the shore of **Herring Cove** to **Herring Cove Head** is visible from **Con Robinson's Point** *(follow Glensevern Rd east to the end)*. At **Lower Duck Pond** a pebble beach borders the rocky shore. The island's woodlands, dubbed "fog forests," are often enshrouded in a thick mist.

★ **East Quoddy Head Lighthouse** – *A short distance north of Wilson's Beach, take the gravel road.* The lighthouse and its picturesque surroundings look out on Head Harbor Island.

# ★ CASTINE                                                              Pop 1,161

Map of Principal Sights p 5

The first and most lasting impression one has of Castine is of beautiful tree-lined streets and stately white homes. A stroll along Main Street leads visitors past small shops and down to the waterfront. The large brick buildings in the village belong to the Maine Maritime Academy, owned and operated by the state of Maine.

Each August Castine is the site of the **Retired Skippers Race**. To participate in the regatta, skippers must be long-time Maine residents at least 65 years of age.

**Forts George** and **Madison** and the historical markers found along Castine's streets recount the tumultuous history of this now-peaceful town.

**A Stormy History** – For over 200 years after Castine was established as a trading post by the Plymouth Pilgrims (1629), this vulnerable port on the Penobscot peninsula was the scene of turmoil. Known first as Bagaduce, then as Fort Pentagoet, the town remained in British hands until the Frenchman Baron de St Castine gained control in 1667. Conditions continued to be stormy and Castine, renamed for the Baron, subsequently fell to the Dutch and then to the British.

Although the English were granted control of Castine by the Treaty of Paris (1763), within 13 years England was once again at war—this time with her rebellious colonies in America. A second treaty, signed in Paris in 1783, established the St Croix River as the eastern boundary between the US and Canada and determined Castine's future as an American settlement.

Fort George, built by the British in the 18C, and the American stronghold, Fort Madison (1811), were occupied by the British during the War of 1812.

**Maine Maritime Academy** – Founded in 1941 the academy offers undergraduate and graduate programs in ten fields, with special emphasis on oceanography and marine studies. The **State of Maine**, the academy's 533ft training vessel berthed at the waterfront, can be toured when the ship is in port *(visit by 30min guided tour only, Jul–Aug Mon–Fri 9–11am & 1–4pm; ☎207-326-4311).* Designed originally as a passenger and cargo ship, the vessel has since been used for troop transport in the Korean and Vietnam Wars.

# ★ COBSCOOK BAY

Map of Principal Sights p 5                          Tourist Office ☎207-853-4644

Emptying into **Passamaquoddy Bay**, Cobscook Bay is a natural basin that is almost entirely landlocked. The coastal fishing towns of Eastport and Lubec, separated by less than 3mi of water but nearly 40mi apart by land, stand sentinel over the channels linking the two bay areas. The exceptionally high tides (18-24ft) for which this bay and its neighboring shores are known so impressed the local Indians that they named it *Cobscook*, meaning "boiling waters."

During the 1930s the US and Canada joined forces in the **Passamaquoddy Tidal Power Project** to provide power for local farms and industry by harnessing the energy released by the tides of Passamaquoddy and Cobscook bays. The project called for construction of a dam or series of dams that would link several of the islands to the mainland. Construction began in 1935, but was abandoned after a short time, leaving several thousand workers unemployed and bankrupting the city of Eastport. As a result of the energy crisis of the 1970s and 1980s, interest in the Passamaquoddy Tidal Power Project revived for a time.

## From Lubec to St Croix Island National Monument
*76mi. 1/2 day. Map p 73.*

**Lubec** – Pop 1,853. During the 17C and 18C, this small fishing port was a center for goods smuggled into the US from Canada. Ships authorized to sail to Europe set out from Lubec and returned several days later with cargoes of rum, sugar and other staples. The record-breaking time of these highly profitable round-trip "transatlantic voyages"—in fact only short trips to Canada where goods were available at low prices—was never questioned. By the late 1800s, 20 sardine-packing factories had been established in Lubec, forming the basis of the town's economy. Only two of these factories remain.

*From Lubec the Franklin Delano Roosevelt International Bridge provides access to the International Park on Campobello Island (p 71).*

★ **Quoddy Head State Park** – *6mi south of Lubec. Follow Rte 189 4mi to the gas station and turn left at the sign. Open mid-May–mid-Oct daily 9am–dusk. $1.* ☎*207-733-0911. Facility information p 251.* Red-and-white-striped **Quoddy Head Lighthouse**, marking the easternmost point of the US, is in the park. From the lighthouse there is a view of the island of Grand Manan in New Brunswick, Canada. A coastal **footpath** *(round-trip 1hr 15min)* beginning at the parking lot *(to the right of the lighthouse, arriving from Rte 189)* affords a superb **view** of the sea and the granite ledges.

> *Leave Lubec on Rte 189 heading west. Outside Lubec the road climbs to a point that offers a view of Passamaquoddy Bay and the harbor. At Whiting take Rte 1 north.*

**Cobscook Bay State Park** – *Open mid-May–mid-Oct daily 9am–dusk. $2.* ⚠ ☎*207-726-4412. Facility information p 251.* The park contains campsites located on the shores of Cobscook Bay. Here, tall stands of evergreens, growing out of crevices in the coastal ledges, dominate the island-speckled waters of the bay.

> *Continue on Rte 1. In West Pembroke take the unmarked road on the right (opposite Rte 214) and follow signs for Reversing Falls Park.*

★ **Reversing Falls Park** – This is one of the best places from which to admire Cobscook Bay's pine-covered islands and secluded coves. Twice daily, with the change of tides, the current is so strong in one area that the rushing waters form a .5mi-long falls.

> *Return to Rte 1. Continue through Perry, then take Rte 190 south.*

**Pleasant Point Federal Indian Reservation** – Homes of the Passamaquoddy Indian tribe dot the landscape of this small community. The Passamaquoddys, one of the dozen tribes that originally inhabited Maine, now number about 2,500 throughout the state. They depend primarily on fishing for their livelihood and have constructed a network of weirs to trap fish in the offshore waters. Most of the Indians at Pleasant Point are Catholic, and the celebration of special occasions combines Christian religious rituals with the traditional ceremonies and native costumes of the Passamaquoddy tribe. Between Pleasant Point and Quoddy Village, Route 190 passes over one of the dams constructed as part of the Passamaquoddy Tidal Power Project.

**MAINE**

**Quoddy Village** – This hamlet is enhanced by the absence of industry, crowds and pollution. Spacious dwellings, built in the 1930s to house workers on the tidal project, have been remodeled to provide comfortable, modern living space.

**Eastport** – Pop 1,965. This small community, the easternmost city in the US, is located on Moose Island between the entrances to Cobscook and Passamaquoddy bays. Exceptionally high tides invade the shore at Eastport, making it necessary for the city's wharves to be built on unusually tall piles.
The sardine-canning industry flourished here between 1875 and the 1920s, together with the production of fish meal and pearl essence (a liquid derived from herring scales and used to add iridescence to artificial pearls). Today the aquaculture industry is a principal economic activity. A recent project to develop cargo facilities along the waterfront has once again made Eastport an operational deepwater port and stimulated the city's economy.

*Return to Rte 1 and turn right at Perry.*

**St Croix Island National Monument** – This island off the ruddy shores of the mainland was the site of a colony established in 1604 by a group of 75 men led by Samuel de Champlain and Sieur de Monts. The severe winter resulted in the death of a number of the colonists, and the following year the colony moved across the Bay of Fundy to Nova Scotia. The island was later significant in setting the St Croix River as the boundary line separating the US and Canada.

## COLUMBIA FALLS                                          Pop 552

Map of Principal Sights p 5

Columbia Falls functioned as one of the numerous shipbuilding and lumbering centers on the coast in the 19C. Built in 1818 the **Ruggles House** was one of the finest dwellings in the village. Though modest in size the house boasts a handsome exterior and bright, comfortable rooms. The hand-carved wainscoting, fireplaces and cornices were, according to legend, executed by an Englishman whose hand was guided by an angel. *(Take Rte 1 to sign for Columbia Falls. Turn onto this road and follow it .25mi. Visit by 45min guided tour only, Jun–mid-Oct Mon–Sat 9:30am–4:30pm, Sun 11am–4:30pm; ☎207-483-4637).*

## DAMARISCOTTA                                          Pop 1,811

Map of Principal Sights p 5                    Tourist Office ☎207-563-8340

Situated across the river from Newcastle lies Damariscotta, a pretty seafaring town that offers vacationers a selection of restaurants, shops and motels. The rustic **Chapman-Hall House** (1754), occupied until the 1950s, exemplifies an early Cape Cod dwelling. Antique furnishings and historical exhibits reflect local life-styles between 1750 and 1820 *(on Rte 1; open Jun–Sept Tue–Sun 1–5pm; $1).*

## ELLSWORTH                                          Pop 5,975

Map of Principal Sights p 5                    Tourist Office ☎207-667-2617

Ellsworth, at the same time a traditional coastal village and a small modern city, is graced with the attractive First Congregational Church and Scandinavian-inspired City Hall. The business district, destroyed by fire in 1937, has been rebuilt while older dwellings still occupy the nearby residential areas.

**Black Mansion** – *West Main St. Visit by guided tour (45min) only, Jun–mid-Oct Mon–Sat 10am–5pm. Closed Jul 4. $5. ☎207-667-8671.* The Georgian elegance of this brick mansion is reflected in its harmoniously proportioned columns and balustrades, its tall chimneys and symmetrical single-story wings. There is no entranceway on the street side of the house. The interior contains period furnishings and personal possessions of the house's former residents, the Black family.

## FARMINGTON                                          Pop 7,436

Map of Principal Sights p 4                    Tourist Office ☎207-778-4215

This farming community serves as the shopping center for the vacation areas of the Belgrade Lakes to the south, the Rangeley Lakes *(p 87)* to the west, and the Sugarloaf and Saddleback Mountain ski areas *(ski information p 256)*.
Farmington became known for its famous resident, **Lillian Norton** (1857-1914), the celebrated opera star. Her home has been transformed into a museum, the **Nordica Homestead** (after Norton's stage name, Lillian Nordica), which presents exhibits on her life and career. *(From Farmington Center take Rte 4 north and turn right onto Holley Rd. Visit by 45min guided tour only, Jun–Labor Day Tue–Sun 10am–noon & 1–5pm; $2; ☎207-778-2042).*

# FREEPORT

Map of Principal Sights p 4       Tourist Office ☎207-865-1212

This small town is the home of L. L. Bean, the famous sporting goods mail-order enterprise. The L. L. Bean factory store in the center of Freeport features clothing, foot gear and equipment for hunting, camping, fishing, hiking and canoeing. It is not unusual to see the company's parking lot crowded at 3am or 4am as the store is open 24 hours a day year-round. The popularity of L. L. Bean, and the 120 brand-name factory outlets and stores established in Freeport in the past several years, make the town a favored shopping spot.

**Desert of Maine** – *I-95 Exit 19, then 2mi west on Desert Rd. Visit by guided tour (30min) only, mid-May–mid Oct daily 9am–6pm. $5. △ & ☎207-865-6962.* Once a densely wooded area, these 500 acres are now covered with sand dunes that began to appear in the 18C, after a farmer made a large clearing in the woods to provide his animals with grazing land. As wind and rain caused the soil to wear away, the sandbed, which had lain hidden beneath the earth, was gradually revealed. Over the years the wind has shaped and reshaped the sandy expanse into dunes that now spread across the formerly wooded landscape.

★ **Wolfe's Neck Woods State Park** – *5mi from the center of Freeport. From Rte 1 turn right onto Bow St, then right onto Wolfe's Neck Rd. Open late-May–Labor Day daily 9am–dusk, rest of the year 9am–6pm. $2. & ☎207-865-4465. Facility information p 251.* The beauty and calm of the park's wooded picnic sites and trails overlooking Casco Bay, offer a pleasant diversion from the shop-lined streets of Freeport village. The Casco Bay Trail *(.5mi, 30min)*, which provides close-up views of Googins Island, is especially scenic.

# The KENNEBUNKS

Map of Principal Sights p 4       Tourist Office ☎207-967-0857

Many artists and writers frequent the popular resort villages of the Kennebunk region: **Kennebunk**, **Kennebunkport**, **Kennebunk Beach**, **Goose Rocks**, **Arundel** and **Cape Porpoise**. Kennebunkport is said to be the setting of *Arundel*, a novel by Kenneth Roberts, a native of the region. More recently, the town has gained renown as the site of the summer home of George Bush, 41st President of the US (1989-1993). The magnificent elm trees, white houses and churches in Kennebunk and Kennebunkport date back to the prosperous shipping days of the 19C. Kennebunk contains many year-round homes and businesses. An architectural tour *(below)* of the historical district provides an introduction to the buildings in this village. Kennebunkport's shopping area, Dock Square, harbors a variety of small shops.

**Wedding Cake House** – *In Kennebunk on Rte 9A. The art studio located on the property is the only area open to the public.* According to legend the captain who lived in this house was about to be married when he was unexpectedly called to sea. Although the wedding took place, there was not enough time to bake and decorate a traditional wedding cake. To console his wife the captain promised he would have the house "frosted like a wedding cake" upon his return. His vow resulted in the addition of the lacy gingerbread trim ornamenting the house and barn.

**Brick Store Museum** – *117 Main St in Kennebunk. Open May–mid-Dec Tue–Sat 10am–4:30pm, Jan–Apr Tue–Fri 10am–4:30pm. $3. & ☎207-985-4802.* Formerly a general store, this brick structure has been renovated into a museum including the historic Taylor-Barry House. *An architectural walking tour (1hr 30min) of the Kennebunk Historic District is conducted by museum guides Jun–Sept Wed 10am & Fri 1pm. $2.50. Self-guided tour booklet ($5) available at the museum.*

**Seashore Trolley Museum** – *In Kennebunkport. From Kennebunk take Rte 1 north 3mi to Log Cabin Rd, turn right and continue east about 2mi. Open Jul–Aug daily 10am–5:30pm. May–Jun & Sept–mid-Oct Mon–Fri 11am–3:30pm. $6. ✗ & ☎207-967-2800.* The 3.5mi ride on a restored electric trolley car will be a new experience or a nostalgic one for visitors. Antique trolley cars are on display.

**Cape Porpoise** – *From Kennebunkport, take Rte 9 north 2mi.* The indented shores of Cape Porpoise shelter a fishing village that becomes a pleasant resort during the summer months.

**Goose Rocks Beach** – *From Kennebunkport, take Rte 9 north 4mi. Turn right at the sign for beach. Motels provide guests with beach sticker required for parking.* Salt marsh grasses frame this inviting 2mi sandy beach.

*For visitor information in Maine,*
*plan a stop at the Maine Publicity Bureau*
*(open year-round daily 9am-5pm; closed Jan 1, Easter Sunday, Thanksgiving Day & Dec 25. ☎207-439-1319) on Rte 95/1 north of the New Hampshire line.*

# KITTERY

Shipbuilding, fishing and tourism are the mainstays of this village located just north of the New Hampshire line. Kittery has been associated with shipbuilding ever since the British began constructing warships here in 1647. In 1778 Adm John Paul Jones' ship, the *Ranger*, built in Kittery, carried the news to France of General Burgoyne's surrender and received the first salute ever given an American ship by a foreign power. The Portsmouth Naval Base and Shipyard, established on several Piscataqua River islands in 1800, has been the most important business in Kittery since the 19C. Private boatyards turn out pleasure craft, adding to the town's role as a shipbuilding center. A drive along the tree-shaded road leading to Kittery Point affords glimpses of the river and attractive homes dating from the 18C and 19C.

**Fort McClary Memorial** – *On Rte 103 east of Kittery in Kittery Point. Open late May–Sept 9am–dusk. $1. ☎207-384-5160.* A hexagonal-shaped blockhouse is all that remains of the 17C fort first christened Fort William and afterward renamed for Maj Andrew McClary, who was killed at the Battle of Bunker Hill. The blockhouse is situated in a calm, waterfront park setting.

## EXCURSIONS

★ **Hamilton House** – *9mi west of Kittery by Rte 236 to S. Berwick, turn left opposite junction with Rte 91. Continue to road's end. Bear left, then first right onto Vaughan's Lane. Visit by guided tour (50min) only, Jun–mid-Oct Tue, Thu & weekends noon–5pm. $4. ☎603-436-3205.* This Georgian mansion and its riverside gardens were the setting for much of Sarah Orne Jewett's novel *The Tory Lover*. The house (1785), built for the merchant Jonathan Hamilton, contains hand-carved archways, cornices and molding. Japanned and painted furnishings, and murals of the local countryside adorn the first floor.

**Sarah Orne Jewett House** – *In S. Berwick, 10mi north of Kittery on Rte 236. Same hours & admission as Hamilton House.* This was the home of 19C novelist **Sarah Orne Jewett** (1849-1909). Miss Jewett's novels *The Country of the Pointed Firs* (1896), an expression of her admiration for Maine and its people, and *The Tory Lover*, set in Berwick during the Revolution, are American classics. The house is arranged as it was when the author lived here.

# ★★ MONHEGAN ISLAND

This rocky island, 10mi off the mainland, appears from the distance like a large whale floating on the surface of the ocean. From a closer point, you can see Monhegan's steep cliffs dropping sharply to the sea.

Ledge markings discovered on Manana, the islet across the harbor from Monhegan, are considered by some as evidence that the Vikings landed here in the 11C. Several centuries later Monhegan served as a fishing station for European fishermen.

The island's small year-round population earns its living from fishing and lobstering. A law prohibiting fishermen from trapping lobsters in Monhegan waters between June 25 and January 1 allows Monhegan lobsters to grow bigger and thus to bring a better price. In the summer Monhegan is a haven for artists and

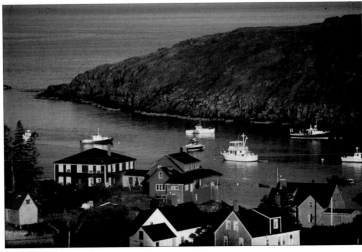

Monhegan harbor at sunrise

tourists. The island's magical beauty and 17mi of trails attract hikers and photographers. *Trails are numbered and can be identified by tiny wooden blocks placed on tree trunks where two or more trails meet. Allow 4hrs for trails below.*

**Burnt Head** – Follow Trail No. 4 to Burnt Head for a **view**★★ of the White Head cliffs.

★★ **White Head** – From Burnt Head follow Trail No. 1, which straddles the ledges and an evergreen forest. White Head's 150ft cliffs are generally blanketed with sea gulls.

**Cathedral Woods** – Trail No. 12 runs along Long Swamp to Cathedral Woods, an inland forest of evergreens towering above lush growths of fern and moss.

★ **Monhegan Lighthouse** – From the top of Lighthouse Hill there is a **panorama** of Monhegan, the harbor and Manana. The lighthouse keeper's house has been transformed into a **museum** that

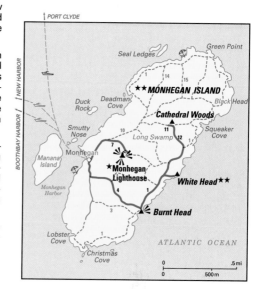

displays photographs, artifacts and prints related to animal, plant and human life on the island *(open Jul–mid-Sept daily 11:30am– 3:30pm)*. There is also an exhibit relating to Ray Phillips (1897-1975), the hermit of Manana, whose house still stands on the island's hillside.

---

# PRACTICAL INFORMATION ............................. Area Code: 207

**Getting There** – From **Portland** to all ferry departure points, I-295 north to I-95 north to Rte 1 north: to **Port Clyde** (81mi), Rte 1 north to Rte 131 south; to **New Harbor** (57mi), Rte 1 north to Rte 130 south to Rte 32; to **Boothbay Harbor** (49mi), Rte 1 north to Rte 27 south.

International and domestic flights to **Portland International Jetport** ☎774-7301. Major rental car agencies *(p 248)*. Closest Amtrak **train** station: South Station, Boston ☎800-872-7245. Greyhound **bus** station: Portland ☎800-231-2222.

*Ferry Schedule 2-3 month advance reservations strongly suggested*

| Departs From: | Schedule | Duration (one-way) | Adult Fare | Company |
|---|---|---|---|---|
| **Port Clyde** | May–Oct, daily; rest of the year weekends only | 1hr 10min | $24 | **Boat Laura B.** ☎372-8848 |
| **New Harbor** | mid-May–mid-Oct | 1hr | $26 | **Hardy Boat Cruises** ☎800-278-3346 |
| **Boothbay Harbor** | Memorial Day–Sept, daily; first 2 weeks Oct weekends only | 1hr 30min | $26 | **Balmy Days Cruises** ☎633-2284 |

**Visitor Information** – Monhegan Island is easily visited by foot or bicycle. No cars or public transportation available on the island; bicycles prohibited on trails. *A Visitor's Guide to Monhegan Island, Maine* can be obtained from the Monhegan Store, PO Box 126, Monhegan ME 04852 ☎594-4126 (please include self-addressed, stamped envelope with request).

**Accommodations** – Lodging directory available *(above)*. Accommodations on Monhegan Island are limited to six inns; advance reservations for rooms required (summer season 3-4 months advance reservations recommended). No camping allowed.

**Recreation** – **Swimming** at Swim Beach only, near the village of Monhegan *(p 252)*. Seventeen miles of **hiking** trails (map available at the Monhegan Store). **Birdwatching** at Lobster Cove. **Harbor seals** usually can be seen at half-tide on Duck Rock.

# MOOSEHEAD LAKE REGION

Map of Principal Sights p 5                    Tourist Office ☎207-695-2702

This remote inland body of water, New England's largest lake (117sq mi), is dotted with hundreds of islands and surrounded by timberlands that reach as far as the Canadian border. Numerous bays and coves indent the lake's 350mi shoreline, making it look from the air like a wide set of antlers.

The region has been a paradise for sportsmen since the 19C. Easy-to-reach ponds and lakes, as well as isolated lakeshore sporting camps *(accessible only by plane)* attract fishermen and hunters. Canoe and raft trips, including those on the Allagash Wilderness Waterway *(p 79),* begin on the shores of Moosehead Lake.

## VISITING NORTHERN MAINE .................................... Area Code: 207

The following information is offered to facilitate access and orientation to this remote area of the state:

**Getting There** – Moosehead Lake area is accessed from Greenville, the Katahdin Region from Millinocket. From **Bangor** to **Greenville** (72mi): Rte 15 north. From **Quebec City** to **Greenville** (219mi): I-73 south to Rte 173 south to Rte 6/15. From **Bangor** to **Millinocket** (71mi): I-95 north to Rte 11 south. From **Quebec City** to **Millinocket** (329mi): I-73 south to Rte 173 south to Rte 201 south to Rte 16 east to Rte 6/16 to Rte 11 north. International & domestic flights to **Bangor International Airport** ☎947-0384. Major rental car agencies *(p 248).* **Train** station (Canadian Via Rail): Greenville ☎800-561-3949. Greyhound **bus** station: Bangor ☎800-231-2222.

**Getting Around** – Public roads in Northern Maine are scarce. Lumber companies maintain private roads, many of which are open to the public and operate like toll roads; 4-wheel drive vehicles recommended. Lumber trucks have right-of-way on logging roads. Many camps are accessible only by seaplane or canoe.

**Seaplanes** – Moosehead Lake area: **Folsom's Air Service** PO Box 507, Moosehead Lake, Greenville ME 04441-0507 ☎695-2821; **Currier's Flying Service** PO Box 351, Greenville Junction ME 04442 ☎695-2778; **Jack's Flying Service** PO Box 584, Greenville ME 04441 ☎695-3020. Katahdin Region: **Katahdin Air Service Inc** PO Box 171, Millinocket ME 04462 ☎723-8378; **Scotty's Flying Service** RR 1 Box 256, Patten ME 04765 ☎528-2626.

**Visitor Information** – Access to designated wilderness areas via **North Maine Woods**, detailed topographic maps provided; PO Box 421, Ashland ME 04732 ☎435-6213. **Allagash Wilderness Waterway:** Maine Department of Conservation, Bureau of Parks & Recreation, State House Station 22, Augusta ME 04333 ☎289-3821. Visitors entering the Allagash Waterway must register at the Telos-Chamberlain entrance, or at the Churchill Dam, Umsaskis Lake or Michaud Farm check points. **Guide Service:** Maine Professional Guides Association, PO Box 591, Ellsworth ME 04605 ☎667-8807.

**Moosehead Lake area** – **Moosehead Vacation & Sportsmen's Assn.** PO Box 366, Rockwood ME 04478 ☎534-7300. **Moosehead Lake Region Chamber of Commerce** visitor center: Main Street. Mailing address: PO Box 581, Greenville ME 04441 ☎695-2702.

**Katahdin Region** – **Katahdin Region Tourism Council** PO Box 502-KB, East Millinocket ME 04430 ☎746-5410. **Millinocket Chamber of Commerce** visitor information kiosk operates seasonally on Rte 11; mailing address: PO Box 5, Millinocket ME 04462 ☎723-4443.

**Accommodations** – Accommodations range from motels, historic inns, and bed and breakfasts concentrated in Greenville and Millinocket. **Sporting camps** located in Greenville, Rockwood and Millinocket. **Camping** at Lily Bay State Park, Baxter State Park *(p 66)* and private campgrounds; reservations required. Camping information: **Maine Forest Service** PO Box 1107, Greenville ME 04441 ☎695-3721. Accommodation information also available from agencies listed above.

John Gerlach/ Dembinsky Photo Assoc.

**Recreation** – **Fishing, ice fishing** and **hunting** bountiful throughout the region (contact game Warden Service for seasons and information PO Box 551, Greenville ME 04441 ☎695-3756). **White-water rafting** throughout area. **Cross-country** rentals and trail maps available in Greenville and Millinocket. **Snowmobiling** on Interstate Trail System, rental and trail information available. Most **supplies** available in Greenville and Millinocket. *Contact organizations listed above for more information regarding recreation in Northern Maine.*

MAINE

**Greenville** – Pop 1,884. Situated at the southern end of Moosehead Lake, Greenville is a resort center, headquarters for two large paper companies and a major outfitting center *(p 78)* for sportsmen heading into the north country. Winter skiing is offered at Squaw Mountain Ski Area outside Greenville. Lily Bay State Park, north of town, has a beach and facilities for camping, boating and picnicking. Lily Bay Road, north of Greenville, provides access to Lily Bay State Park.

**Mt Kineo** – Rising abruptly from the waters of Moosehead Lake, Mt Kineo reaches an altitude of 1,806ft. There is a good view of Kineo from Route 6/15 just north of Rockwood. Kineo was well known among the many tribes who journeyed to this flint mountain to obtain the hard, durable stone needed to make weapons, tools and other implements.

**Allagash Wilderness Waterway** – *74mi north of Greenville.* The 92mi Allagash Wilderness Waterway offers experienced canoeists a magnificent stretch of white water in the heart of a wilderness area. *For access and orientation, see p 78.*

# ★★★ MOUNT DESERT ISLAND

Map of Principal Sights p 5                    Tourist Office ☎207-276-5040

Measuring 108sq mi and cut almost in half by the fjord **Somes Sound**, Mt Desert Island remains an unspoiled region of pink granite mountains, dark forests and freshwater lakes. Pointed evergreens, emerging from rocky ledges that fall away from the shore, recall the description of Mt Desert as "the place where the mountains meet the sea." The major portion of **Acadia National Park** is located here.

The island was once the summer campgrounds of the Penobscot and Passamaquoddy Indians. In September 1604 French explorer **Samuel de Champlain**, and **Sieur de Monts**, grantee of Acadia (the French territory that extended from present-day Montreal to Philadelphia), anchored in what is now **Frenchman Bay**. Champlain's impression of the largest island in the bay as a line of seven or eight mountains with rocky, treeless summits led him to name the island *l'Isle des Monts Deserts.* Nine years later a group of Jesuits established a settlement on this island. Their colony had existed only a month before being destroyed by the British.

View from Cadillac Mountain

Fred Sieb Photography

During the 150 years that followed, the Acadian territory was a constant battlefield between the English and the French. In the late 17C the governor of Canada gave Mt Desert Island to the Frenchman **Antoine de la Mothe Cadillac**, who spent only one summer there before heading west, where he founded the city of Detroit. Following the defeat of the French at Quebec in 1759, English colonists began to settle on the coast in increasingly large numbers. The English dominated the island until after the Revolution, when the boundary between the US and Canada was established by the Treaty of Versailles (1783).

In the mid-19C the area's beauty was discovered by artists. The enthusiasm expressed in their writings and paintings enticed the wealthy to vacation on Mt Desert Island. Elegant summer "cottages" were built, and Bar Harbor developed into a resort community similar to Newport, while Northeast and Southwest Harbors became popular yachting centers.

## PRACTICAL INFORMATION ................................... Area Code: 207

**Getting There** – From **Portland** (127mi): I-95 east to Rte 1 north to Belfast, then Rte 1/3 north to Ellsworth, then Rte 3 south; from **Bangor** (46mi): Rte 1A south to Ellsworth then Rte 3 south. International and domestic flights to **Bangor International Airport** ☎947-0384. Major rental car agencies *(p 248)*. Closest Amtrak **train** station: South Station, Boston ☎800-872-7245. Greyhound **bus** station: Bangor, service to Bar Harbor (Cottage & Kennebunk Sts) late Jun–early Oct ☎800-231-2222.

**Getting Around** – Mt Desert Island is best visited by car, although some sights are accessible by bicycle (rentals available in island towns) and foot. **Shuttle** service between Ellsworth and Mt Desert Island towns (year-round Mon–Fri): Downeast Transportation, PO Box 914, Ellsworth ME 04605 ☎667-5796. Year-round **ferry** service to Cranberry Isles departs from Northeast Harbor (Beal & Bunker, PO Box 33, Cranberry Isles ME 04625 ☎244-3575); to Swans Island from Bass Harbor (Maine State Ferry Service, PO Box 114, Bass Harbor ME 04653 ☎244-3254). Other companies offer periodic crossings from both harbors, contact chambers *(below)*. **Acadia National Park Tours** depart from village green in Bar Harbor mid-May–Oct daily, PO Box 794, Bar Harbor ME 04609 ☎288-9899. **Carriage tours** (one-to-two hours) of the park depart from Wildwood stables mid-Jun–mid-Oct ☎276-3622.

**Visitor Information** – **Bar Harbor Chamber of Commerce** visitor center: 93 Cottage St. Mailing address: PO Box 158, Bar Harbor ME 04609 ☎800-288-5103. **Mt Desert Chamber of Commerce** visitor center: Sea Street Marina, Northeast Harbor (Jun–Oct). Mailing address: PO Box 675, Northeast Harbor ME 04662. **Acadia National Park** visitor center, Hulls Cove entrance open May–Oct; rest of the year park headquarters at Eagle Lake (Rte 233, 3mi west of Bar Harbor). Mailing address: Superintendent, Acadia National Park, Bar Harbor ME 04609 ☎288-3338.

**Accommodations** – Information available from: **Bar Harbor** *(above)*, **Southwest Harbor** (reservation service) ☎244-9264 and **Northeast Harbor** ☎276-5040 chambers of commerce. Accommodations include modest hotels, bed & breakfasts and rental cottages. **Camping** (year-round) in Acadia National Park (reservations for Blackwoods Campground MISTIX, PO Box 85705, San Diego CA 92186 ☎800-356-2267 or 619-452-8787); other campgrounds located near other island towns, contact chambers of commerce *(above)*.

**Recreation** – In Acadia National Park: **swimming** at Echo Lake *(p 83)* and Sand Beach *(p 82)*; **hiking** and **cross-country skiing** (120mi of trails); **biking** restricted to carriage roads (57mi). Fishing licenses and rental equipment available in island towns. Whale-watching *(p 254)* and scenic **cruises** depart from Bar Harbor and Northeast Harbor. Most specialty **shopping** and supplies in Bar Harbor. *Contact the chambers listed above for more information regarding shopping and recreation on Mt Desert Island.*

## ★ BAR HARBOR

Located on Mt Desert Island, Bar Harbor (pop 4,443) is the major gateway to Acadia National Park and a departure point for the ferry to Nova Scotia (☎800-341-7981). Bar Harbor has been accustomed to a heavy influx of tourists ever since the late 19C and early 20C when the town developed into a fashionable summer resort for the wealthy.

Hotels, motels and guest houses line the road approaching the business district; in the center of town there are many fine shops and restaurants. During the winter, numerous lodgings and shops close down and a quiet atmosphere prevails. A large part of the year-round population works at Jackson Laboratory *(p 82)*.

**A Gilded Past** – During the late 19C and early 20C, Bar Harbor was second only to Newport *(p 205)* as a playground of the wealthy. Summer residents arrived by rail and steamship, and spacious Victorian-style hotels provided them with comfortable lodging facing the sea. Affluent families such as the Rockefellers, Astors and Vanderbilts built cottages that became legendary for their magnificence. In one mansion the center of the dining room floor opened to allow the banquet table to descend. The latter then reappeared, completely prepared for the next course! Only a handful of these residences still stand; the remainder were destroyed by a fire that swept Bar Harbor in 1947.

## ★★★ ACADIA NATIONAL PARK

Acadia National Park is located primarily on Mt Desert Island with smaller sections on **Isle au Haut** *(p 82)*, and **Schoodic Peninsula** *(p 82)* across Frenchman Bay.

It was a group of Mt Desert's summer residents that decided to protect the island's natural environment. By 1913 more than 5,000 acres on Mt Desert Island had been set aside as a nature preserve. These lands, donated to the US government in 1916, were declared a national park three years later. In 1929 the park was permanently named Acadia after the historic French territory.

Over one-third of the park's 35,000 acres were donated by John D. Rockefeller Jr, who was also responsible for having 50mi of carriage paths laid out in the eastern end of the island. Thirty-three thousand acres of the park fall on Mt Desert Island. The park's main attraction, Loop Road, parallels a spectacular section of open coast with expansive views, and climbs to the top of Cadillac Mountain. Bordering the temperate and sub-Arctic zones, the park contains a rich variety of flora and fauna. Some 500 species of flowers, shrubs, trees and non-flowering plants grow in the region, and about 300 species of birds have been sighted here over the years.

## ★★★ Loop Road   *Circle drive 29mi. 4hrs. Map above and p 82.*

The many scenic outlooks, turnoffs and parking areas along this coastal road afford vistas ranging from sweeping seascapes to panoramas of pink granite mountains and island-studded waters. *May be fogbound in morning hours.*

> *Begin at the visitor center on Rte 3.*

**Visitor Center** – *Hulls Cove. Open mid-Jun–Sept daily 8am–6pm. May & mid-Oct–Nov 1 daily 8am–4:30pm. Rangers on duty to answer questions about trails & park activities. $7/car (valid 7 days).* ☎207-288-3338. This modern building, rustic in appearance, faces Frenchman Bay.

**★★ Frenchman Bay Overlook** – From the overlook there is an unobstructed **view** to Schoodic Peninsula and across Frenchman Bay. An orientation table aids in identifying the many small, rounded islands in the bay.

The road passes through a forest, by an open meadow and skirts a marsh where beaver dams can be seen. In the early evening you might observe beavers at work.

> *Loop Rd is a one-way road from the Spur Rd entrance to just south of Jordan Pond. After 3mi turn right for Sieur de Monts Spring.*

**Sieur de Monts Spring** – The spring and surrounding area constituted one of the first parcels of land set aside as part of the nature preserve that became Acadia National Park. The spring was named for de Monts, leader of the 1604 expedition to North America.

The **Nature Center** nearby displays exhibits related to the park *(open Jun–mid-Sept daily 9am–5pm; &.)*. In the **Wild Gardens of Acadia**, regional trees, flowers and shrubs are arranged according to their natural habitat: marsh, bog, beach or mountain.

**Abbe Museum [M]** – *Open Jul–Aug daily 9am–5pm. Mid-May–mid-Oct daily 10am–4pm. $2. & ☎207-288-3519.* Dioramas and prehistoric artifacts (Stone Age tools, pottery) in this small pavilion evoke the of life of Maine's natives who inhabited the Frenchman Bay and Blue Hill Bay areas prior to European colonization.

> *Return to Loop Rd.*

To the left are the buildings of **Jackson Laboratory**, internationally known for its role in cancer research. The cliffs of Champlain Mountain loom on the right. There are scenes typical of Acadia: pink granite peaks, tall evergreens and natural roadside rock gardens.

**Sand Beach** – This is the only saltwater beach in the park. Composed of coarse sand, it provides a pleasant swimming spot for those who don't mind the cool water temperatures (50-55°F in season).
A **path** beginning at the upper parking level follows Ocean Drive to the end of Otter Point. This is an enjoyable walk *(2hrs)* along the top of the cliffs.

★ **Thunder Hole** – *Parking on the right.* At high tide the surf breaking on this narrow chasm resembles the roar of thunder.

★★ **Otter Cliffs** – These sheer cliffs, rising 11ft above the ocean, offer **views**★★ along the coast and out to sea.

The road winds around Otter Point and Otter Cove, intersects with the road to Seal Harbor, then follows the shore of **Jordan Pond**, which lies below the cliffs of Penobscot Mountain.
At the northern end of the pond, note the large boulder balanced precariously atop one of the two rounded hills known as **The Bubbles**. From The Bubbles parking area there is a good view of the boulder.

★★★ **Cadillac Mountain** – *Illustration p 79.* The ascent to the top of Cadillac Mountain (1,530ft) affords views of Eagle Lake, Bar Harbor and the islands below. The mountain was named for Antoine de la Mothe Cadillac, the proprietor of Mt Desert Island in the late 17C. Guided trails on the barren summit offer breathtaking **views**★★★ of Frenchman Bay and the park.

> *Return to Loop Rd, then turn right to complete the circle.*

## Other Areas of the Park

★★ **Schoodic Peninsula** – This promontory, jutting out from the mainland east across the bay from Mt Desert, is a kaleidoscope of tall stands of fir trees rimmed by pink granite ledges, and encircled by the blue waters of the bay. Two thousand acres of Acadia National Park are located on the southern tip of this peninsula. From Schoodic Head there are vistas across the bay to Mt Desert Island.

★ **Isle au Haut** – *Map p 68.* Boats depart from Stonington late Jun–mid-Sept Mon–Sat 7, 11am & 4pm, Sun 11:30am. Mid-Apr–mid-Oct Mon–Sat only. Rest of the year Mon–Sat daily 7 & 11am (Tue & Fri additional departure 3pm). One-way 45min. $9 (Sun $11, winter $5). Isle au Haut Co. ☎207-367-5193. The mail boat stops at Isle au Haut Harbor, an anchorage for pleasure craft, and one of the morning boats continues on to Duck Harbor *(late Jun–mid-Sept only)*.
The best way to explore this small island, located south of Stonington, is by taking the hiking trails in Acadia National Park, which occupies two-thirds of the island.

**ADDITIONAL SIGHTS**  *Map p 81*

★★ **Beech Cliff Trail** – *From Somesville take Rte 102 south, turn right, then left onto Beech Cliff Rd to the end of the road.* This easy trail *(round-trip 30min)* leads to the crest of Beech Cliff where there are magnificent **views**★★ reaching from Echo Lake to Acadia Mountain, rising above the opposite shore of Somes Sound.

★ **Bass Harbor Head** – *At the end of Rte 102A.* The Bass Harbor lighthouse towering above the rocky shore of this remote headland *(illustration p 63)* makes a delightful subject for a camera or an artist's paintbrush, especially at sunset.

**Sargent Drive** – *Passenger cars only. Begin at Northeast Harbor.* The road follows the shore of Somes Sound, a deep glacial valley now flooded by the ocean.

**Echo Lake** – Swimming is permitted in this freshwater lake that lies at the foot of Beech Cliff.

**Ship Harbor Nature Trail** – *Rte 102A. To walk the complete loop (1hr), take a right at the first fork, then bear right at the sign for Ship Harbor Loop.* Such natural wonders as a pot-bellied tree, and an exposed root system resembling a tall modernistic sculpture line this trail, which follows the ledges, then enters a spruce forest. Take this walk at high tide when the surf is up.

---

## ★ OGUNQUIT
Pop 974

Map of Principal Sights p 4    Tourist Office ☎207-646-2939

In the Algonquin language, *Ogunquit* means "beautiful place by the sea." The artists who discovered this coastal fishing village undoubtedly agreed with the description, for by the turn of the century, many painters and writers had come to live and work close to Ogunquit's rocky shores. Works by members of the town's present-day artists' colony are exhibited in galleries scattered throughout the village, including the **Ogunquit Art Association Gallery** on Route 1 south of Ogunquit Square, and the rustic **Barn Gallery** on Shore Road. The small, modern **Museum of American Art**, also on Shore Road, overlooks the sea. During the summer a different play is presented every week at the **Ogunquit Playhouse**.

★ **Perkins Cove** – This charming boat haven offers quaint boutiques and craft shops and several seafood restaurants. A footbridge across the entrance to the cove can be raised to allow boats to pass. *Party boats can be hired for deep-sea fishing, or for breakfast, cocktail, and lobstering cruises. For a modest fee, tourists are welcome to join local lobstermen as they set out to gather the day's catch.*

★ **Marginal Way** – *Cherry Lane to Lookout Motel. Turn right, continue to parking area.* This scenic coastal footpath from the center of town leads to Perkins Cove.

### EXCURSION

**Wells** – Pop 8,845. *5mi north of Ogunquit on Rte 1.* Located on the stretch of sandy beach that extends from Kittery to Portland, Wells has been a summer resort since the last century. **Wells Auto Museum** on Route 1 displays antique automobiles as well as motorcycles and bicycles *(open mid-Jun–Sept daily 10am–5pm; late May–mid-Jun & early–mid-Oct weekends only 10am–5pm; $3.50; ⅙ ☎207-646-9064).*

---

## ★★ PEMAQUID POINT

Map of Principal Sights p 5

Carved by glaciers centuries ago, the gnarled ledges at Pemaquid Point are especially spectacular for their pegmatite formations—long, narrow bands of black and white rock, that jut into the sea. The lighthouse, rising on the bluff above, stands guardian over this dramatic section of coastline and is reflected in the shallow pools left by the surf as it rolls back into the ocean. This site is a photographer's dream. Located south of Damariscotta *(p 74)*, this peninsula was one of the first regions on the coast to be settled. The artifacts excavated at the site of Colonial Pemaquid provide evidence that the area was colonized in the 17C. The point was probably a station for European fishermen in the 15C and 16C.

★★ **Pemaquid Point Lighthouse Park** – *Illustration p 84. Open late May–mid-Oct daily 9am–5pm. $1. ⅙ ☎207-677-9068.* From the lighthouse *(closed to the public)* there is a magnificent view of the rocky, splintered coastline.

**Fishermen's Museum** – *Open mid-May–mid-Oct Mon–Sat 10am–5pm, Sun 11am–5pm. Contribution requested. ⅙ ☎207-677-2726.* This small museum, located in the former lighthouse keeper's house, contains photographs, fishing gear and other items related to the life of the fisherman.

**Pemaquid Beach** – *From the lighthouse take Rte 130, then turn left on Snowball Rd (follow sign to beach).* It is unusual to find such a beautiful sandy beach along this rugged section of the coast.

Dan Dempster/Dembinsky Photo Assoc.

Pemaquid Point Lighthouse

★ **Colonial Pemaquid State Historic Site** – *Continue past Pemaquid Beach on Snowball Rd.* Excavations have been conducted in the area near Fort William Henry, a replica of a 17C fort that stood on this spot. The site also includes an archaeological **museum** *(open Jun–Aug daily 9am–5pm; $2;* ✗ Ꮷ ☎*207-677-2423).*

**Christmas Cove** – *13mi west from Colonial Pemaquid. Take Rte 130 to Pemaquid Falls, then turn left onto Rte 129.* Rocky headlands and offshore islands shelter this waterfront settlement. This cove was named by Capt John Smith, who is said to have anchored in this snug harbor on Christmas Eve 1614, during his expedition along the New England coast.

## ★★ PORTLAND                                      Pop 64,358

Map of Principal Sights p 4                    Tourist Office ☎207-772-5800

The largest city in Maine, Portland is located on Casco Bay, known for its picturesque Calendar Islands. The city is the financial, cultural and commercial center of northern New England's major metropolitan area, and an important oil and fishing port. It is also the departure point for the Prince of Fundy Line ferry to Nova Scotia. After having experienced a period of decay during the early 20C, Portland underwent a major economic and cultural rebirth in the 1970s and 1980s.

## PRACTICAL INFORMATION ............................... Area Code: 207

**Getting There** – From **Boston** (109mi): I-93 to I-95 north. Canadian and domestic flights to **Portland International Jetport** ☎774-7301. Taxi service ($7.50 to downtown) and hotel courtesy shuttles. Major rental car agencies *(p 248)*. Closest Amtrak **train** station: South Station, Boston ☎800-872-7245. Greyhound **bus** station: 950 Congress St ☎800-231-2222. **Ferry** service from **Nova Scotia** May–Oct (11hrs): Prince of Fundy, 468 Commercial St, Portland ME 04101 ☎800-341-7540.

**Getting Around** – Public parking lots located throughout the city; 1st hour free at Park & Shop lots, with validation stamp from local businesses. Many sights easily visited by foot. **Greater Portland Transit** bus lines offer transport within Portland and outlying areas ☎774-0351.

**Visitor Information** – **Convention and Visitors Bureau of Greater Portland** visitor center: 305 Commercial St, Portland ME 04101 ☎772-5800.

**Accommodations** – Accommodations include economy and moderate hotels ($50-$130/day) and bed and breakfast ($55-$115/day); information available from Convention and Visitors Bureau *(above)*. Portland **Hostel** (Jun-Aug 20): Portland Hall, 645 Congress St, Portland ME 04101 ☎874-3281. *Average prices for a double room.*

**Recreation** – **Shopping** at Old Port Exchange *(p 85)* and Congress St; concentration of outlet stores (over 125) in Freeport *(p 75)*. Guided **walking tours** and maps of historic areas ($1) from **Greater Portland Landmarks**, 165 State St ☎774-5561. **Hiking** on Eastern Promenade and Back Cove Trail, and Western Promenade. **Biking** on Peaks Island shoreline, rentals available. **Swimming** at Crescent Beach State Park *(p 87)*. *Contact Convention and Visitors Bureau for more information regarding shopping and recreation in Portland.*

**Resurgam: "I shall rise again"** – True to its motto *Resurgam,* Portland has risen like the phoenix from its ashes after being almost entirely destroyed on three different occasions. During the early 17C, the English established a trading post here, and by 1658 the village of Falmouth had sprung up on the site. Abandoned in the 1670s after Indian raids caused the inhabitants to flee, the village was resettled in 1716, and supported itself by its mast trade with England. Falmouth's strong anti-Loyalist sentiments led the British to bombard the town in October 1775, as an example to the other colonies. Following the war, the few hundred colonists who had remained in Falmouth gradually rebuilt the city, and in 1786, ten years after the birth of the nation, renamed it Portland.

The city was the capital of Maine between 1820 and 1832. Mansions lined High and State Streets, and the railroad linking Montreal and Portland was completed in the mid-19C. Portland had grown into a prosperous shipping center by July 4, 1866 when a fire swept through the downtown area, leveling most of the buildings in the business district and destroying one-third of the city. From these ashes rose the city's rich group of Victorian structures.

During recent decades, Portland has experienced an economic revival. The city is responsible for shipping petroleum products to Canada via the Portland pipeline. Renewal of such areas as the Old Port Exchange generated new interest in Portland as a business center in the 1970s. This trend has continued, sparked by the construction of projects including One City Center, the expansion of the Bath Iron Works into Portland, and the development of an 18-acre fishing pier.

## SIGHTS   *1 day. Map p 86.*

The metropolitan area, cutting into Casco Bay, is rimmed with pleasant parks and strolling paths. The Eastern and Western Promenades, both designed by the nation's preeminent landscape architect, Frederick Law Olmsted, offer panoramic views of the bay and the surrounding region. Portland's skyline is best viewed from the walking path around Back Cove.

★★ **Old Port Exchange** – The warehouses, offices and shops in this old waterfront district were run-down and deteriorating rapidly when, in the early 1970s, several persons decided to open a few small restaurants and shops in the area. Their immediate success encouraged other merchants to move into the district and renovate neighboring buildings into attractive specialty shops, professional offices and living space.

A stroll along Middle, Exchange, and Fore Streets will allow you to admire the window displays, art galleries and craft shops and to try some of the dozens of restaurants.The 19C architecture is interesting for its diversity of styles and decorative brickwork, including keystones, cornices and coursing.

**Exchange Street** – Encompassing nos. 103-107, this **block [A]**, is inspired by the Italianate style; the **building [B]** on the corner of Middle and Exchange Streets has a trompe l'œil mural. Several of the windows, though they appear to be a part of the mural, are actually real.

**Middle Street** – The mansard roof reveals the French influence on this elaborately arched and arcaded **block [C]**, which includes nos. 133-141.

**Fore Street** – No. 373, the **Seaman's Club** restaurant **[D]**, displays the Gothic Revival style; the **Mariner's Church [E]**, no. 368, with its tall windows and triangular pediment, illustrates the Greek Revival style. A good example of the Second Empire style, the **Custom House**, no. 312, reflects the maritime wealth of 19C Portland.

★ **Portland Museum of Art** – *7 Congress Sq. Open year-round Tue–Sat 10am–5pm (Thu 9pm), Sun noon–5pm. Closed major holidays. $6. ✗ & ☎207-775-6148.* The museum is the largest and oldest public museum in Maine. Founded in 1882, its original quarters were the McLellan-Sweat House, to which an extension, the L.D.M. Sweat Memorial, was added in 1911. The most recent addition to the complex is the brick and granite Charles Shipman Payson Building (designed by Henry N. Cobb of I. M. Pei and Partners in 1983), which adjoins the earlier structures and now houses the museum's collection. A facade composed of an arresting blend of circles, rectangles and other forms, and an interior boasting gallery spaces illuminated by domed clerestories are noteworthy features of the building.

**The Collections** – The museum's strength is its collection of 19C and 20C American art, and in particular the **State of Maine** collection of paintings, sculpture and prints by artists associated with Maine. Winslow Homer *(Weatherbeaten),* Andrew Wyeth *(Broad Cove Farm, Cushing, Maine),* Edward Hopper *(Pemaquid Light)* and John Marin *(Deer Isle Series: Mark Island Lighthouse)* are among the artists represented who drew their inspiration from the Maine landscape. The collection, which began in 1888 with Benjamin Akers' sculpture *Dead Pearl Diver,* has grown steadily and has been enriched in recent years by the gifts of 17 canvases by Homer and more than 50 works by early 20C artists associated with the Ogunquit art colony.

Several galleries contain sections devoted to American glass, American and English ceramics and the decorative arts. Highlighting the displays are cases of Portland glass, Federal period paintings and furniture, and the Pepperrell collection of silver presented to Maine-born Sir William Pepperrell, leader of the successful siege of the French fortress of Louisbourg in 1745. A regular schedule of changing exhibits of American and international art supplements the permanent collection.

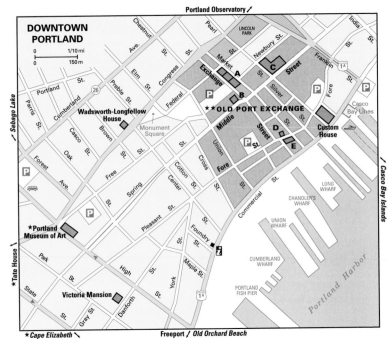

**Victoria Mansion (Morse-Libby House)** – *109 Danforth St. Visit by guided tour (45min) only, Late May–Labor Day Tue–Sat 10am–4pm, Sun 1–5pm. After Labor Day–mid-Oct Fri & Sat 10am–4pm, Sun 1–5pm. Closed major holidays. $4. ☎207-772-4841.* Built by the architect Henry Austin, this brownstone mansion (c.1860) reflects the sumptuous design, decor and furnishings characteristic of the Italianate style. Inside, the lavish decoration includes frescoes, elaborately carved woodwork and stained glass.

**Wadsworth-Longfellow House** – *487 Congress St. Visit by guided tour (45min) only, Jun–Oct Tue–Sat 10am–4pm. $4. ☎207-879-0427.* This brick dwelling, built in 1785, was the childhood home of **Henry Wadsworth Longfellow** *(p 36)*. Longfellow's simple, narrative poems, recounting legends from America's past, won him fame across the nation and abroad. After his death, he was the first American to be memorialized in the Poet's Corner in Westminster Abbey. Furnishings and memorabilia of the poet and his family are on display.

★ **Tate House** – *1270 Westbrook St. Drive west on Congress St, turn right on St John St, then left on Park Ave. At I-295 overpass, continue on Congress St to Westbrook St. Visit by guided tour (1hr) only, Jul–mid-Sept Tue–Sat 10am–4pm, Sun 1–4pm. Closed major holidays. $3. ◻ ☎207-774-9781.* This unusual gambrel-roofed dwelling (1755) located in Stroudwater beside the Fore River, was the home of George Tate, the king's mast agent. Tate's duties included making shipping arrangements for trees selected as masts for Royal Navy ships. All trees higher than 74ft and at least 24in at the base were marked as royal property, not to be felled by colonists. The trees were transported by oxen, and then by ships custom-built to ferry the masts to England. The attractively furnished interior contains fine paneling, cornices, doorways and furniture similar to those in an 18C London townhouse.

**Portland Observatory** – *138 Congress St, northeast of downtown. Open Jul–Aug Sun–Thu 1–5pm, Fri & Sat 10am–5pm. Late May–Jun & Sept–Oct Fri & Sun 1–5pm, Sat 10am–5pm. $1.50. ☎207-774-5561.* Prior to the days of the telephone and telegraph, the observatory was used to signal (with flags) Portlanders that ships were entering the harbor.
From the upper deck there is a beautiful view of Portland and Casco Bay.

## EXCURSIONS

**Casco Bay Islands** – *Departs from Casco Bay Ferry Terminal at Commercial & Franklin Sts. For information & reservations Casco Bay Lines ☎ 207-774-7871.* The Bailey Island Cruise *(round-trip 5hr 45min)* allows for a stop-over at Bailey Island *(Jun 25–Labor Day daily 10am. $13.50. ⧖ ◻).* The **US Mail Boat Cruise** stops at several islands, but passengers are not permitted to disembark *(year-round daily 10am, 2pm; after Labor Day–mid-Jun 2:45pm; round-trip 2hr 45min; $9.25; ⧖ ◻).* As the boat leaves the harbor, note the large storage tanks for the oil pipeline to Montreal, and Fort Gorges, a 19C granite structure.

**Calendar Islands** – These tree-clad islands number about 365, one for each day of the year. From the boat, the houses and shops on heavily populated **Peaks Island** and the beaches of **Long Island** are visible. The population of **Great Chebeague**, the largest of the Calendar Islands (3mi wide and 5mi long), increases from 400 in winter to some 3,000 during the summer. The solitary stone tower on **Mark Island** commemorates shipwrecked sailors; the tower contains food and water and serves as a shelter in the event anyone is shipwrecked in nearby waters. At **Bailey Island** note the granite cribwork bridge constructed to allow the surf to pass freely through the openings.

★ **Cape Elizabeth** – *10mi south of Portland. Take Rte 77 to S. Portland. At the library turn right onto Cottage Rd, which becomes Shore Rd.* Cape Elizabeth's wild and rocky shoreline provides a scenic excursion from Portland.

★ **Portland Head Light** – *Take Shore Rd north to the lighthouse, which is located at Fort Williams.* This was the first lighthouse built on the east coast after the Revolution. In an effort to reduce construction costs, builders used materials from the local shores and fields. The 300,000-candlepower electric light is visible 16mi offshore. From the deck of the tower there is a **view★** of Casco Bay.

**Two Lights** – This tiny community is named for the two lighthouses standing side by side on this section of the Cape. Nearby is **Two Lights State Park★** *(open year-round 9am–dusk; ☎207-799-5871; facility information p 251).*

**Crescent Beach State Park** – *Open late May–mid-Oct 9am–dusk.* ⚑ ♿ ☎207-767-3625. *Facility information p 251.* The park has one of the finest sand beaches in Maine.

**Freeport** – *20mi north of Portland by Rte 1 or Rte 295 (I-95). Description p 75.*

**Old Orchard Beach** – *12mi southwest of Portland by Rte 1.* Americans and Canadians have been summering at this first stretch of salt-water beach south of Montreal for more than 100 years. Motels, cottages, trailer parks and restaurants front the broad, 7mi-long beach.

**Sebago Lake** – *20mi north of Portland by Rte 302.* Portlanders who enjoy swimming, boating and fishing favor Sebago Lake, the second largest inland body of water in Maine after Moosehead Lake *(p 78).* **Sebago Lake State Park** *(25mi from Portland by Rte 302)* bordering the lake, has picnic areas, campsites and a sandy beach *(open May–mid-Oct 9am–dusk; $2.50; ☎207-693-6611; facility information p 251).*

## ★ RANGELEY LAKES REGION

Map of Principal Sights p 4                    Tourist Office ☎207-864-5571

Nestled in the mountains of western Maine, this region contains an abundance of lakes and ponds, the largest being the lakes of the Rangeley chain. Spectacular mountain and lake panoramas unfold along Routes 4 and 17, and for those who prefer the solitude of the woods, there are trails leading to quiet brooks and mountain tops. Scenic turnoffs on Route 17, south of Oquossoc, afford **views★★★** of the area's largest lakes. There are also rewarding views from Route 4 between Oquossoc and the village of **Rangeley**.

**Activities** – Possibilities for warm-weather activities include tennis, golf, swimming, canoeing, mountain climbing and fishing, especially for trout and salmon in the spring. Ski areas have been developed at **Saddleback** and **Sugarloaf Mountains**.

**Rangeley Lake State Park** – *From Rte 4 or 17, take Southshore Dr and follow signs to park. Open mid-May–Sept daily 9am–dusk. $2.* △ ♿ ☎207-864-3858 *(seasonal). Facility information p 251.* This park on the south shore of Rangeley Lake includes a beach area with boat ramps, docks and secluded campsites.

★★ **Eustis Ridge** – *26mi north of Rangeley by Rte 16. Turn left onto Rte 27. After 3mi turn left onto the unmarked road.* From this vantage point there is a **view** of the region. Route 27 continues to the Canadian border through unspoiled countryside.

★ **Mt Blue State Park** – *31mi southeast of Rangeley by Rte 4, then Rte 142. Open mid-May–Oct 1 daily 9am–dusk. $2.* △ ☎207-585-2347. *Facility information p 251.* This 1,273-acre park on the shores of **Lake Webb★** offers varied recreation in a pretty setting. From the **State Park Beach Road** there are mountain and lake vistas.

## ROCKLAND                                      Pop 7,972

Map of Principal Sights p 5                    Tourist Office ☎207-596-0376

Visitors heading north on Route 1 to the towns and islands of Penobscot Bay frequently pass through Rockland, a busy modern seaport and one of the leading exporters of lobsters in the world today. Light industry, commerce and tourism are also major activities.

During the summer Rockland is the home port of a fleet of windjammers. The **Lobster Festival**, held the first weekend in August, offers a good opportunity to savor fresh seafood caught along this area of the coast.

**Farnsworth Art Museum** – *19 Elm St. Open Jun–Sept Mon–Sat 10am–5pm, Sun 1–5pm (rest of the year closed Mon). $5.* ♿ ☎207-596-6457. Highlights of this collection of 19C and 20C American paintings include works by Fitz Hugh Lane and a large group of Wyeth family paintings. The New England landscape inspired many works by Andrew Wyeth, who has summered in Maine.

## EXCURSIONS

**Owl's Head** – *4mi south of Rockland*. This tiny community is known for its lighthouse, **Owl's Head Lighthouse**, perched atop a 100ft cliff.

**Owl's Head Transportation Museum** – *2mi south of Rockland by Rte 73. On grounds adjacent to Knox County Airport. Open Apr–Oct daily 10am–5pm, rest of the year Mon–Fri 10am–4pm, weekends 10am–3pm. Closed Jan 1, Thanksgiving Day, Dec 25. $4.* ☁ ☎207-594-4418. The museum's collection of working antique airplanes, automobiles and bicycles dates from the early 20C. Demonstrations of automobiles and airplanes from the collection are held at special summer and fall events on the museum grounds. *Call for events schedule.*

**Vinalhaven and North Haven Island Ferries** – *Depart from Rockland: to Vinalhaven Apr–Oct daily 7am–5pm, rest of the year daily 7am–3:15pm; one-way 1hr 15min; $6; to North Haven year-round daily 9:30am, 1:30 & 4:30pm; one-way 1hr; $6; Maine State Ferry Service* ☎207-596-2202. This boat cruises among the serene tree-clad islands in Penobscot Bay, the region that is the setting of Sarah Orne Jewett's novel, *The Country of the Pointed Firs.*
Residents of **Vinalhaven** earn their living largely from lobstering. Lobster boats anchor in quiet inlets, and fishing sheds, with their stacks of lobster traps and brightly painted buoys, are found throughout the island. Several of Vinalhaven's abandoned granite quarries provide a place to swim in the summer. From the northern end of the island there is a view across the water to **North Haven**, a small quiet island with many summer residents.

## SABBATHDAY LAKE

*Map of Principal Sights p 4*

This hilly lakeside property is the site of the Sabbathday Lake Shaker Village, the last active Shaker community in America. Founded in the 18C by Shaker missionaries, the settlement continued to exist throughout the 19C and 20C, a period when most other Shaker villages became extinct. Although there are less than a dozen Shakers now living here, the principles of Shakerism, "hands to work and hearts to God," and a strong devotion to the Shaker religion continue to guide their lives.

**Shaker Village and Museum** – *I-95 to Exit 11, then Rte 26 north 8mi. Visit by guided tour (1hr 15min) only, late May–mid-Oct Mon–Sat 10am–4:30pm. $4.* ☎207-926-4597. The Shakers occupy a number of these buildings, most of which can be viewed only from the outside. The **Brick Dwelling House**, with its granite trim and delicate wooden porch, appears elegant when contrasted with the simple white clapboard structures found throughout the village. The museum in the **Meeting House** (1794) contains examples of Shaker furniture, clothing, fancy goods and other Shaker industries and inventions *(p 148).*

## EXCURSION

**Poland Spring** – *3mi north of Sabbathday Lake by Rte 26*. This mountain and lake hamlet became famous in the 19C, after a man who had been seriously ill drank from the spring on Ricker's Hill and quickly regained his health. A small factory was established to bottle the water, and a lavish hotel complex, including the Poland Spring House, developed near the spring. The resort, which burned down in 1975, catered to businessmen and dignitaries who came "to take the waters." Poland Spring water is still bottled at a factory on Ricker's Hill and sold in stores and supermarkets around the world. From the hill it is possible to look out onto the mountains in the southern part of the state.

## SEARSPORT                                    Pop 2,603

*Map of Principal Sights p 5*                Tourist Office ☎207-548-6510

Located near the head of Penobscot Bay, this seafaring town was a boatbuilding center and the home of more than ten percent of the nation's deep-water shipmasters in the 19C. Searsport captains sailed the trade routes to the other side of the world, making the name of their hometown one of the most familiar in the ports of the Orient, Africa, Europe and the Caribbean. The beautiful dwellings built for these seamen still line the streets of Searsport near the waterfront. The second busiest harbor in the state, Searsport also serves as a major export center for the potato crop raised to the north in Aroostook County.

★ **Penobscot Marine Museum** – *Church St. Open late May–mid-Oct Mon–Sat 9:30am–5pm, Sun 1–5pm. $5.* ☁ ☎207-548-2529. The museum's rich collection of marine paintings, models and artifacts illustrating the era of sail and trade is arranged in a group of buildings that includes several restored sea captains' homes, the former Town Hall, and the Phillips Memorial Library and adjoining Douglas and Margaret Carver Memorial Gallery. In the **Fowler-True-Ross House** (1820) there are wall hangings, furniture, tableware and paintings that Searsport captains brought back to New England. Products of Chinese artisans were admired for their fine craftsmanship and often adorned almost every room in a sea captain's home. The barn attached to the **Nickels-Colcord-Duncan House** features an exhibit on Penobscot Bay fisheries and a display of small craft. The old **Town Hall** contains ship models, half-models, shipbuilding tools, Oriental trade objects and a permanent exhibit on the large wooden ships built in Maine in the 19C (p 27).

The first floor of the **Captain Merithew House** (c.1850) contains an exhibit about the people and ports of Penobscot Bay. Rooms on the second floor feature paintings by Thomas and James Buttersworth, ship models, watercolors and ostrich eggs skillfully etched with whaling scenes, among other items.

# THOMASTON                                        Pop 2,445

Map of Principal Sights p 4                    Tourist Office ☎207-596-0376

This yachting center, a village of attractive old homes and churches, is the site of Maine State Prison. Adjacent to the prison, on Route 1, is a showroom where woodenware made by the inmates is sold. Dragon Products, a cement plant located outside the village center, employs a large number of Thomaston's residents.

**Montpelier** – On Rte 1 south. Visit by guided tour (45min) only, late May–Sept 1 Wed–Sun 9am–5:30pm. $2.50. ☎207-596-2253. This stately white mansion replicates the original residence built in 1794 by Gen **Henry Knox**, an aide to General Washington during the Revolution. In the winter of 1775–1776, General Knox led an expedition that carried cannon and supplies from Fort Ticonderoga to Boston. This equipment was used against the British the following spring (p 97). Later appointed as the nation's first secretary of war, Knox was a wealthy landowner when he resigned his government post and settled in Thomaston.

The Federal-style mansion contains graceful oval rooms, a freestanding staircase flanking an arched doorway, and antique furnishings including Knox family pieces and a mirrored bookcase reportedly owned by Marie Antoinette.

# ★★ WISCASSET                                     Pop 3,339

Map of Principal Sights p 4

An appealing town with broad tree-lined streets, Georgian mansions, antique shops and restaurants, Wiscasset was once the home of wealthy merchants and shipmasters and America's busiest international port north of Boston. Wiscasset's shipyards, built on the banks of the Sheepscot River, turned out clipper ships that carried lumber and ice to the West Indies and returned laden with the staples necessary for daily living. The deteriorating hulks of two schooners once active along the Atlantic coast, **Luther Little** and **Hesperus**, lie on the west bank of the river. Situated midway between Wiscasset and the mouth of the Sheepscot River, the Maine Yankee Atomic Power Co has been in operation since 1972.

★★ **Musical Wonder House** – 18 High St. Open mid-May–mid-Oct daily 10am–6pm. ☎207-882-7163. This Georgian dwelling contains a superb collection of some 500 19C and 20C antique mechanical instruments, including player pianos, gramophones and music boxes, all in working order. Constructed primarily to reproduce melodies by means of metal discs or cylinders, these machines, enclosed in hand-crafted boxes or cabinets, were highly treasured by their owners as works of art. The Regina Orchestral Corona, which changes discs automatically; the Harpe Aeolienne music box; the Emerald polyphon with its hand-tuned silver bells; and the Regina Sublima drum table, a Louis XV-style table decorated with hand-painted scenes, all play tunes as rich as their names imply.

**Lincoln County Museum and Old Jail** – Federal St. Visit by guided tour (30min) only, Jul–Aug Tue–Sun 11am–4:30pm. Closed Jul 4. $2. ☎207-882-6817. This grim jail (1809), with its granite walls up to 41in thick, was built when the whipping post and other forms of public punishment were no longer effective in dealing with problems arising in the rapidly growing villages on the coast. About 40 prisoners could be housed in the cells on the original two floors; the third floor was added later to accommodate debtors and the insane.

**Nickels-Sortwell House** – Corner of Main and Federal Sts. Visit by guided tour (50min) only, Jun–Sept Wed–Sun noon–5pm. $4. ☎207-882-6218. This Federal-style mansion (1807) with its well-proportioned facade and entry fronts Main Street. Built by a Wiscasset shipmaster, the house contains period furnishings.

## EXCURSION

**Fort Edgecomb** – 1mi southeast of Wiscasset. Take Rte 1 across the Sheepscot River, then turn right. Open late May–Labor Day daily 9am–5pm. $1. Picnic area on the grounds. ☎207-596-2253. This small fort was built during the War of 1812 to protect Wiscasset. The wooden octagonal-shaped blockhouse commands a view of the river and Westport Island.

# ★ YORK

Map of Principal Sights p 4       Tourist Office ☎207-363-4422

The town of York includes several communities: historic **York Village**, dating from colonial times; **York Harbor**, a fashionable resort at the mouth of York River; **York Beach**, a beachfront amusement and swimming area; and **Cape Neddick**.

## HISTORICAL NOTES

In 1624 the Pilgrims established a trading post at Agamenticus, the present-day site of York. The small settlement that grew up around the trading post was chosen by **Sir Ferdinando Gorges**, the proprietor of Maine, as the capital of his vast New World territory. In 1641 Sir Gorges gave the village a city charter and renamed it Gorgeana in his honor. Gorges' dreams of developing "the main" (later Maine) were never realized; the Massachusetts Bay Company assumed control of this section of the coast in 1652, and reorganized Gorgeana as the town of York. Although York was completely destroyed by a raiding party during the French and Indian Wars, the town had developed into a busy port and become the county seat by the dawn of the American Revolution. Since the 19C York residents have preserved the early colonial charm of their town.

## ★★ COLONIAL YORK  *1/2 day*

A group of early structures flanks the village green. To one side stands the 18C **church** with its cock weathervane, and the **Town Hall**, which served for a time as the York County courthouse. Nearby are the Emerson-Wilcox House, an 18C schoolhouse, the old cemetery, Jefferds Tavern, and rising from the top of a small hill, the Old Gaol, an 18C jail. *Open mid-Jun–Sept 29 Tue–Sat 10am–5pm, Sun 1–5pm; $6 (payable at Jefferds Tavern);* & ☎*207-363-4974.*

★ **Old Gaol Museum** – Originally a stone dungeon, built in 1720 to serve the entire province of Maine, this jail was enlarged soon after to include several cells and provide living quarters for the jailer and his family. Small openings cut in the thick stone walls allow shards of sunlight to enter the cool, damp cells.

**Emerson-Wilcox House** – Built in 1740 as a private dwelling, this large house served over the years as a tailor shop, tavern, and post office. The tavern catered to travelers on the Post Road, as well as to local residents and the occupants of the Old Gaol. The interior contains some interesting period furnishings.

★ **Old Burying Ground** – Surrounded by a low stone wall, this cemetery is interesting for its 17C tombstones. Note the grave covered with a large horizontal stone, placed there, according to legend, to stop a "witch" from leaving the tomb. In actuality, the spouse of the deceased placed the block to protect the grave from wandering cattle.

★ **Jefferds Tavern and Schoolhouse** – This tavern built in Wells *(p 83)* in 1750, served as a wayside station on the York-Kennebunk stage route. The large, cozy tap room contains plank floors and a wooden bar. Rooms on the floor above were set aside for women and children, who ordinarily did not congregate downstairs with the men.

Now used as an orientation center, the one-room schoolhouse features an exhibit on early schooling in Maine.

> *Follow Lindsay Rd to Sewall's Bridge beside the York River.*

Nearby are the John Hancock Warehouse, the George Marshall Store (a craft shop), and fishermen's sheds covered with lobster buoys. The inviting red colonial dwelling beside the river was the home of **Elizabeth Perkins** (1879-1952) one of York's prominent residents.

**John Hancock Warehouse** – This is one of several coastal warehouses owned by John Hancock, Revolutionary War patriot, signer of the Declaration of Independence and prosperous merchant.

## ADDITIONAL SIGHTS

**York Harbor** – This landlocked boating center is a haven for small craft. Beautiful homes grace the harbor's tree-covered shores. The **Sayward-Wheeler House** contains family heirlooms of a prosperous trader and his descendants *(79 Barrell Lane Ext, visit by 50min guided tour only, Jun–mid-Oct Wed–Sun noon–4; $4; 207-436-3205).*

The coastal road leads to **Long Beach**, a 2mi stretch of beach bordered by summer cottages.

★ **Nubble Light** – *Leave Rte 1A and take Nubble Rd on the right to the tip of Cape Neddick.* From the shore there is a magnificent view of Nubble Lighthouse and the island it occupies; the Isles of Shoals lie in the distance.

**York Beach** – This summer resort on the shores of Short Sands Beach offers an assortment of busy concession stands, eating places and souvenir shops. Several hotels built during the last century stand near the beach like a group of distinguished dowagers proudly surveying their waterfront domain.

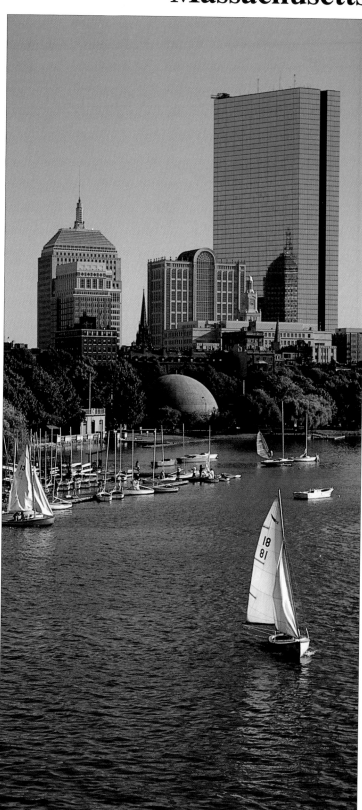

# Massachusetts

**Area:** 8,093sq mi
**Population:** 6,016,425
**Capital:** Boston
**Nickname:** Bay State
**State Flower:** Mayflower

**E**xtending from the Atlantic Ocean to the border of New York state, Massachusetts provides a cross section of the region's varied topography. The tree-covered Berkshire Hills in the west slope gradually down to the fertile meadows of the Connecticut Valley in the center of the state. Miles of sandy beach lie south of Boston, while to the north the coast is irregular and rocky. The state is rectangular in shape, except for the southeast section that juts into the ocean, adding hundreds of miles to the Massachusetts coastline.

**Birthplace of American Independence** – New England's earliest permanent settlements were in Massachusetts. In search of religious freedom, the Pilgrims established Plymouth Colony in 1620, followed within ten years by the Puritans, who founded Boston. As the population expanded and prospered, Parliament's taxation policies placed an increasing financial burden on the colonists. Angered by England's policy of "taxation without representation," and inspired by the oratory of **Samuel Adams**, **James Otis** and **John Hancock**, the colonists reacted to the passage of the **Stamp Act** in 1765 by staging the **Boston Tea Party**, and later with the **Boston Massacre**. These events proved to be merely the prelude to the confrontations at Lexington and Concord, and the ensuing battle for American independence.

**Economy** – For two centuries Massachusetts earned its living from the sea by fishing, whaling and trade. Great fortunes were made in the China Trade, and when maritime commerce declined in the 19C, this wealth provided the capital needed for the shift to industrialization.

With the advantages of an abundance of waterpower and the increasing waves of immigration that provided a large labor force, the Berkshires, the southern section of the coast and the Merrimack Valley were soon dotted with many small industrial centers, or "mill towns." Massachusetts developed into a prominent manufacturer of textiles and leather goods. By 1850 **Lowell** *(p 151)*, the first planned industrial city in the nation, was the world's leading producer of textiles. In the 20C these industries migrated to the South and were supplanted by the manufacture of electronics, machine tools and electrical equipment. Today Massachusetts' most important source of revenue is its **"brain power,"** represented by the state's excellent educational institutions and technological and financial services industries.

Massachusetts continues to lead the New England states in commercial fishing, with Gloucester and New Bedford ranking among the nation's major ports. Agriculturally, the Bay State's **cranberry crop**, cultivated in the regions of Cape Cod and Plymouth, is the nation's largest.

John Lazenby (f/STOP PICTURES)

Cranberry harvest in Carver

# ★★★ The BERKSHIRES

Map p 94                                    Tourist Office ☎413-443-9186

In westernmost Massachusetts lies a valley watered by the streams of the Housatonic and bordered by the foothills of the Taconic and Hoosac Ranges. This region,
the Berkshires, is a mix of small 19C mill towns and comfortable residential communities that blend gracefully with their surroundings.
Many New Yorkers and Bostonians have second homes in the Berkshires. Attractive in summer for its refreshing climate and cultural offerings, in the fall for its
splendid foliage, and in the winter for skiing, this versatile region also offers hiking, fishing, golf and other sports.

**The Mohegans** – The Mohegans once lived on the banks of the Hudson River
and journeyed to the Housatonic Valley, "the place beyond the mountains" as
they called it, to hunt. In time, reduced in number by disease and warfare, they
abandoned the lowlands for the thickly wooded hills where they lived peacefully
until the arrival of the colonists in the 18C. Devoted to Christianizing the Indians,
the colonists established Stockbridge (p 172) in 1734 as an Indian mission on land
granted for this purpose by the General Court.
To the north lived the **Mohawks**, enemies of the Mohegans and the French, and
allies of the British. One of the major routes traveled by pioneers migrating to the
Midwest from the eastern colonies followed an old Indian trail (p 155) blazed by
the Mohawks through the Appalachian Mountains to the Great Lakes.

**From Agriculture to Industry** – The early settlers farmed the land, but after the
Revolution, many farms were abandoned as their owners moved westward to the
fertile plains region. In New England the migration westward was accompanied by
a transition from farming to industry. The Berkshires developed into a major manufacturing center, and **mill towns**, small factory communities such as North Adams,
Pittsfield, Dalton and Lee, with their monotone rows of brick mill buildings, sprang
up throughout the region. The railroad followed, linking the valley towns to the
rest of the state after the construction of the Hoosac Tunnel in 1875 (p 155).

**The Grand Estates** – Favorable descriptions of the Berkshires, written in the
mid-19C by Nathaniel Hawthorne, Henry Ward Beecher and others, attracted
wealthy families to summer here. These families built the handsome residences
that still punctuate the countryside outside Great Barrington, Lee, Lenox and
STOCKBRIDGE. At the beginning of the 20C, Lenox alone could count 75 of these
magnificent properties including Tanglewood (p 95) and the estate of Andrew
Carnegie, the richest man in the Berkshires.
Increased taxes, spiraling costs and the Depression brought an end to the luxuries
of the era, and most of the estates were abandoned, or sold and converted into
schools or resorts. A growing number of former estates are now operated as year-
round inns.

---

## TOURING THE BERKSHIRES

Allow several days to follow the excursions described below and to attend at
least one of the music or dance festivals held in the summer. Included among
these events are the **Tanglewood Music Festival** (☎413-637-1600 summer, 617-266-
1492 year-round) and the **South Mountain Concert Festival** (☎413-442-2106). The
**Jacob's Pillow Dance Festival** brings together international performers of ballet,
modern dance and mime (Jul–Aug ☎413-243-0745). See Calendar of Events
pp 244-245. Summer theater is offered at the **Berkshire Playhouse** in Stockbridge
and at the **Williamstown Theater** in WILLIAMSTOWN. Classical Shake-spearean theater
is presented in Lenox at **The Mount**, once the summer home of novelist Edith
Wharton (1862-1937).
In winter, there is skiing at **Butternut Basin, Brodie Mountain** and **Otis Ridge**.
The map (p 94) covers only the southern part of the Berkshires. For attractions
in the northern part of the region, see **Mt Greylock** (p 156) and **Williamstown**
(p 177). For information on festivals and lodging in the Berkshires ☎413-443-
9186, or 800-237-5747 (US and Canada).

**One-day Itinerary in the Berkshires** – From the south, take Route 7. Stop in
**Stockbridge** (p 172), and follow the itinerary between Stockbridge and Lenox
(p 95). Visit the **Hancock Shaker Village** (p 148) outside of Pittsfield, then the **Clark
Art Institute** in Williamstown.

---

## ★★ GREAT BARRINGTON AND THE SURROUNDING REGION

**Great Barrington** – Pop 7,725. Great Barrington is the commercial center for the
many vacation homes on the outskirts of this pleasant town. The Great Barrington
Rapids, once the site of Mohegan camps, were the major power source for local
mills in the 18C. It was here, on the banks of the Housatonic, that the inventor
William Stanley demonstrated for the first time the use of alternating current. On
March 20, 1886, Great Barrington became one of the first cities in the world to
have its streets and homes lit by electricity.

**Bartholomew's Cobble** – *11mi south of Great Barrington. Take Rte 7 south, then Rte 7A to Ashley Falls; take Rannapo Rd, then Weatogue Rd. Open Apr–Oct daily 9am–5pm. $3.* ☎413-229-8600. This natural rock garden covered with a variety of trees, wildflowers and ferns, rises above the Housatonic River. The **Ledges Trail** through the Cobble *(round-trip 45min)* follows the river. At station 17, cross the road and continue on Hulburt's Hill Trail to an open pasture on Miles Mountain (1,050ft) with a view of the Housatonic Valley.

★ **Bash Bish Falls** – *16mi southwest of Great Barrington. Follow Rte 23 west to South Egremont, then Mt Washington Rd, East St, West St and Bash Bish Falls Rd. From the parking area, a steep trail marked with blue triangles and white blazes leads to the falls. Continuing on the same road 1mi there is another parking area; from there, a longer, but easier, path leads to the falls.* These steep

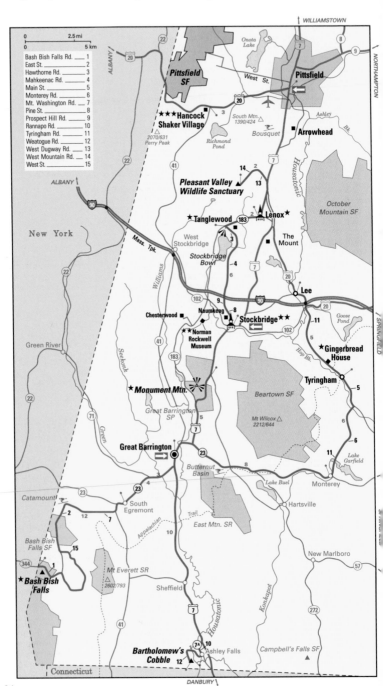

| | |
|---|---|
| Bash Bish Falls Rd. | 1 |
| East St. | 2 |
| Hawthorne Rd. | 3 |
| Mahkeenac Rd. | 4 |
| Main St. | 5 |
| Monterey Rd. | 6 |
| Mt. Washington Rd. | 7 |
| Pine St. | 8 |
| Prospect Hill Rd. | 9 |
| Rannapo Rd. | 10 |
| Tyringham Rd. | 11 |
| Weatogue Rd. | 12 |
| West Dugway Rd. | 13 |
| West Mountain Rd. | 14 |
| West St. | 15 |

*slopes can become icy and dangerous in fall, winter and spring. Open year-round daily 8am–8pm. ☎413-528-0330. Bash Bish brook flows over a 275ft gorge, creating a 50ft waterfall and natural pool in this forest setting.*

★ **Monument Mountain** – *4.5mi north of Great Barrington on Rte 7. From the parking area on the west side of Rte 7, two trails lead to the summit. The easier trail, the Indian Monument Trail (ascent 1hr), begins to the left, 600yds south along the highway, and enters the woods, where a sign points right to Indian Monument (a cairn about 100yds off the trail). Turn right and continue, always selecting the right spur. The second, more difficult trail (ascent 45min) begins to the right of the parking area and is blazed with round white markers.*

From the rocky summit, named Squaw Peak for an Indian maiden who leaped to her death from this point, the visitor can behold a **panorama★** of the Berkshires. A cairn at the base of the mountain is said to mark the grave of the Indian maiden *(see directions above).*

## ★ TYRINGHAM VALLEY

*From Great Barrington take Rte 23 to Monterey, then turn left onto Tyringham Rd, which becomes Monterey Rd.*

**Tyringham** – Pop 369. This charming valley town was the site of a community of Shakers in the 19C. The valley's scenic landscape attracted many artists, including Henry Kitson, sculptor of the Lexington *Minuteman (p 150)*, at the beginning of the century. Kitson's former studio, the picturesque **Gingerbread House★**, is the home of Tyringham Art Galleries *(open late May–mid-Oct daily 10am-5pm; $1; ☎413-243-0654).*

*Continue on Main St, then Tyringham Rd to Rte 20.*

**Lee** – Pop 5,849. In the mid-19C five paper factories operated in this mill town. During the same period, rich marble deposits were discovered beneath a section of land that had been considered worthless because it was too poor to farm. Lee marble was quarried and used in the construction of the Capitol in Washington DC and in other public buildings, making the name of this small town famous.

## ★★★ FROM STOCKBRIDGE TO LENOX

★★ **Stockbridge** – *Description p 172.*

*In Stockbridge take Pine St opposite the Red Lion Inn. Turn left onto Prospect St (Mahkeenac Rd), and drive along the lakeshore of Stockbridge Bowl; continue on Hawthorne Rd. At the junction of Hawthorne Rd and Rte 183 there is a good view of the lake.*

★ **Tanglewood** – Tanglewood is the summer home of the Boston Symphony Orchestra and the site of one of the nation's most famous musical events, the **Tanglewood Music Festival** *(p 93)*. More than 300,000 music lovers attend every year. The festival was inaugurated in 1934 with concerts by the New York Philharmonic Symphony. In 1936 the New York Philharmonic was replaced by the Boston Symphony Orchestra, which has presented the summer series of concerts ever since. Tanglewood, formerly the residence of the Tappan family, was given to the Berkshire Festival Society in 1937 to serve as the festival's permanent home. Buildings on the 500 acres include the main house, the 5,000-seat Koussevitzky Music Shed, designed by Eliel Saarinen, and the 1,180-seat Seiji Ozawa Hall, opened in 1994. From the gardens there is a **view** of the waterbody called **Stockbridge Bowl** and **Hawthorne Cottage** *(not open to the public)*, a replica of the dwelling where Nathaniel Hawthorne lived for 18 months while writing *The House of the Seven Gables* (1851) *(p 168)*.

*Take Rte 183 to Lenox.*

★ **Lenox** – Pop 5,069. Surrounded by estates that have been transformed into schools and resorts, Lenox, with its inviting inns and restaurants, is a delightful place to stay.

*Take Rte 7 north and turn left opposite the Quality Inn onto West Dugway Rd; then bear left at the fork on West Mountain Rd.*

**Pleasant Valley Wildlife Sanctuary** – *3mi from Lenox. Open year-round Tues–Sun dawn to dusk. $3. ☎413-637-0320.* The refuge has 7mi of trails that lead through fields and woodlands revealing vegetation typical of the region. A beaver colony occupies the string of ponds in the valley, and their dams are visible.

## PITTSFIELD AREA

**Pittsfield** – Pop 48,622. Pittsfield is a commercial center and the capital of the Berkshires. Martin Marietta is the city's largest employer, providing some 1900 jobs. The **Berkshire Museum**, which includes a small aquarium, exhibits fine European and American paintings and sculpture, and history and science displays *(39 South St; open Jul–Aug Mon–Sat 10am–5pm, Sun 1–5pm; rest of the year Tue–Sat 10am–5pm, Sun 1-5pm; closed major holidays; $3; ☎413-443-7171).*

**Pittsfield State Forest** – *Entrance on Cascade St, 3mi from the Park Square rotary; take West St, turn right on Churchill St, then left on Cascade St. Open year-round daily 8am–8pm. $2/car.* △ ⅙ ☎413-442-8992. This area offers year-round opportunities for hiking, skiing and other activities.

**Arrowhead** – *780 Holmes Rd. From Park Square, drive east on East St; turn right onto Elm St, then right onto Holmes Rd. Visit by guided tour (1hr) only, late May–Labor Day daily 10am–4:30pm. After Labor Day–Oct Mon, Fri–Sun 10am–4:30pm. Rest of the year by appointment only. $4.50.* ☎413-442-1793. Arrowhead, the home of Herman Melville, is being restored to reflect the atmosphere of the era when he lived here (1850-1863). Melville wrote a number of his most important works at Arrowhead including his masterpiece, *Moby-Dick*. The kitchen with its huge fireplace bearing an inscription from Melville's *I and My Chimney*, the upstairs study with its view of Mt Greylock and the remaining rooms all contain furnishings owned by the Berkshire County Historical Society, which maintains the house.

★★★ **Hancock Shaker Village** – *3mi west of Pittsfield by Rte 20. Description p 148.*

---

# ★★★ BOSTON                                     574,283

Map of Principal Sights p 3                    Tourist Office ☎617-536-4100

Massachusetts' historical capital city has earned a reputation as one of the nation's most appealing urban centers. The "Hub," as Bostonians refer to their hometown, is the "cradle of American independence," a renowned center of learning and culture, and the administrative and financial nexus of New England. Its proximity to CAMBRIDGE, home of Harvard and the Massachusetts Institute of Technology, has contributed to Boston's role as a cultural mecca.
Boston is New England's largest city. The combined populations of the metropolitan area total 4.7 million. Over half a million people representing diverse ethnic cultures reside within the 46sq mi of the city proper. While offering the advantages of a modern metropolis, Boston has retained a pleasant human scale, evident in its historic neighborhoods such as Beacon Hill, the Back Bay and the North End.

## HISTORICAL NOTES

**European Settlement** – In 1630 about 1,000 Puritans led by **John Winthrop** arrived on the coast of Massachusetts to establish a settlement for the Massachusetts Bay Company. Disenchanted with the living conditions in SALEM and CHARLESTOWN, they set their sights on the peninsula the Indians named Shawmut, then inhabited by an eccentric Anglican clergyman, **Reverend William Blackstone**. The Englishman welcomed the Puritans, who proceeded to establish a permanent settlement on the small peninsula. When the Puritans tried to make Blackstone a member of their church, he sold them his remaining 50 acres and left for the more peaceful atmosphere of Rhode Island.
The new colony, known as Trimountain because of its hilly topography, was soon renamed Boston after the town in Lincolnshire from which many of the Puritans hailed. Under the firm guidance of Governor Winthrop, the settlement developed as a theocratic society where church and state were one. A rigid moral code was enforced and a pillory was built on the Common to punish offenders, among them

Bird's-eye view of Boston in 1850

the carpenter whose price for constructing the pillory was deemed too high. Because of its maritime commerce and shipbuilding, Boston rapidly became the largest town in the British colonies—a distinction it held until the mid-18C.

**Cradle of American Independence** – In an attempt to replenish the Crown's coffers in the wake of the costly French and Indian Wars, the British Parliament voted to enforce high taxes and harsh trade regulations against the American colonies. This policy enraged the colonists, who, as British citizens, claimed that their rights to representation were being denied. Following the passage of the **Stamp Act** (1765), a tax on publications and official documents in Massachusetts, public reaction became violent. Mobs roamed the streets, the governor's mansion was burned and a boycott was organized. Although Parliament repealed the Stamp Act the following year, renewed demonstrations erupted in 1767 with the passage of the **Townshend Acts**, which regulated customs duties. England responded immediately by sending troops to enforce British law. The colonists, especially those who were forced to lodge and feed soldiers, grew increasingly hostile. Steadily mounting tensions eventually exploded into clashes between Bostonians and the British.

The **Boston Massacre** was the first of these clashes. On March 5, 1770, a group of Bostonians gathered near the State House to protest recent events. When a British officer answered the insults of a member of the crowd with the butt of his musket, the crowd became abusive and the guard was called out. Several Redcoats, provoked by the civilians, loaded their weapons and fired, killing five men. Political activist **Samuel Adams** seized on this incident to rally the citizens to his cause.

Three years later the **Boston Tea Party** further aggravated the situation. By 1773 Parliament had repealed all the Townshend Acts except the tax on tea, which gave the East India Company a monopoly to sell tea in the colonies. This tax so angered colonists that in November 1773, Bostonians refused to allow the captains of three of the company's tea-laden ships to unload their cargo. At a well-attended meeting held December 16, 1773 in the Old South Meeting House, an attempt was made to resolve the issue. When British compromise was not forthcoming, Samuel Adams concluded with his famed cue: "This meeting can do nothing more to save the country." Thereupon 90 Bostonians disguised as Indians fled the building with a war cry, trailed by a large crowd, and proceeded to board the ships and dump the tea into the harbor. In retaliation England closed the port of Boston and invoked punitive measures that served only to further unite the colonists against the British. Colonial militia were organized and began training on village greens.

**The Ride of Paul Revere** – In April 1775 Gen Thomas Gage dispatched 800 British soldiers to the outlying towns of CONCORD and LEXINGTON to seize the colonists' stash of arms and arrest patriot leaders **John Hancock** and Samuel Adams. The patriots, forewarned by their network of spies, were prepared. According to a prearranged plan, the night the British began to march to Concord the sexton of Old North Church (*p 112*) signaled the direction they took by hanging two lanterns in the steeple. In the meantime Paul Revere safely crossed the river to Charlestown and set out to Lexington on horseback to warn Hancock and Adams. Thanks to the legendary ride by Revere, William Dawes and Dr Samuel Prescott, the militia was ready when the British arrived at Lexington, and later at Concord.

**The Siege of Boston and the Battle of Bunker Hill** – Following events at Lexington and Concord, the British retreated to Boston, where they were surrounded by rebel forces. While the British eyed the strategic heights around Boston, colonial leaders, informed of the British plan to fortify Bunker Hill in Charlestown, hastened to occupy nearby Breed's Hill before the arrival of the British. On June 17, 1775, when the British awoke and discovered an American redoubt had been built on Breed's Hill during the night, a force of 5,000 soldiers was sent out to capture the site. Although the colonists' position was defended by only 1,500 militiamen, the British failed in their first two attempts to secure the fort. They then set fire to Charlestown and launched the third and final attack against the rebels. Colonial leader William Prescott, aware that his men were low on ammunition, gave his famous order: "Don't fire until you see the whites of their eyes!"

The British succeeded in capturing the fort, but in doing so, they lost over ten percent of all the British officers killed during the Revolution. Though it took place on Breed's Hill, this struggle is known under the misnomer, the Battle of Bunker Hill.

**The British Evacuation** – During the early months of 1776, the supplies captured by the colonists at Fort Ticonderoga (*p 225*) were hauled across New England to Boston. American artillery began to bombard Boston on March 2, and when, by March 5, the colonists had fortified Dorchester Heights to the south with the cannon from the fort, the British were forced to accept a compromise. The colonial troops peacefully reclaimed Boston, and British General Howe and his men were permitted to evacuate the city unharmed. Soon after, General Washington made a triumphant entry into Boston, which saw little subsequent war activity as the theater of operations shifted to New York, Pennsylvania and the southern colonies.

## URBAN DEVELOPMENT

Modern Boston is the product of transformations wrought by two centuries of prodigious landfill projects. Familiar place names such as Back Bay, the South End and Dock Square recall features of the area's original 783-acre landmass, which has increased almost fourfold through landfill alone since the early 19C.

**19C: "Cutting Down the Hills to Fill the Bays"** – The Puritans who settled Shawmut found an irregularly shaped peninsula joined to the mainland by a natural causeway (the "neck") stretching along a section of present-day Washington Street. On the western side rose a three-peaked ridge (Trimountain) dominated by Beacon Hill. Extending south of Beacon Hill, the tract purchased from Reverend Blackstone was designated as "Common Field," and remains parkland to this day as the Boston Common.

The eastern shore facing the harbor was indented by Town or East Cove, which divided the residential North End from commercial and public sectors that burgeoned in the vicinity of the harbor, the original South End.

Over the course of the 19C, Boston's population increased dramatically, rising from 18,000 in 1790 to 54,000 in 1825. By the turn of the century, it totaled over half a million. The pressing need for more living space prompted a flurry of landfill projects that forever transformed the city's topography. These ambitious programs, characterized by noted historian Walter Muir Whitehill as "cutting down the hills to fill the bays," involved

Land reclaimed since early 19C

hauling colossal quantities of earth into the waters around the city, thus transforming the spindly peninsula into an extension of the mainland. The filling in of the waters on either side of the narrow neck was crucial to the city's growth, for it enabled a network of railroad lines to penetrate the downtown area.

Boston's great 19C transformation began with the development of the Beacon Hill district in the early 19C *(p 104)*. In the following decades the areas on the peninsula's east and south sides were filled in, leading to the expansion of the waterfront area *(p 112)* and the creation of the residential district now called the South End *(p 125)*. The century's most spectacular landfill project took place in the insalubrious Back Bay on the neck's north side. This 40-year project *(p 113)* increased the city's land by 450 acres and resulted in one of the nation's finest planned residential districts. After the Great Fire of 1872 leveled 776 buildings downtown, many residents and churches resettled in the fashionable Back Bay, precipitating the development of the downtown as a commercial district. Landfill projects continued to increase the city's area throughout the 19C and into the present century, particularly around Charlestown and East Boston, site of Logan International Airport.

The city's system of public parks, parkways and tree-shaded malls, designed in the 19C by the nation's premier landscape architect **Frederick Law Olmsted**, encircles the city with a nearly continuous swath of greenery. The so-called **Emerald Necklace** begins at the Common and stretches southwest along the Public Garden, Commonwealth Avenue, the Fenway, Jamaica Park, the Arborway, Arnold Arboretum and Franklin Park.

**The New Boston** – By the mid-20C Boston was deteriorating. Rising property taxes, the exodus of businesses to the suburbs or out of state and the general population decline had taken their toll. Faced with problems associated with urban blight, the city reacted by establishing the **Boston Redevelopment Authority** in 1957. Under the leadership of **Edward Logue**, BRA inaugurated a program aimed at "revitalizing" one-fourth of the city. The plan generated much controversy since it mandated the bulldozing of entire neighborhoods, including Scollay Square and the adjacent Jewish and Italian enclave known as the West End.

The architect **I. M. Pei**, who had trained at the Massachusetts Institute of Technology, was among the experts called upon in the 1960s to draw up designs for the new **Government Center** on the site of Scollay Square, Boston's bawdy entertainment district. This $260 million project called for an enormous brick-paved expanse showcasing the award-winning City Hall building *(p 110)* alongside several contemporary structures of varying architectural merit and a 19C commercial building (the Sears Crescent). In the following decades Pei further contributed to reshaping Boston's built environment by executing such important commissions as the John Hancock Tower *(p 115)*, the Kennedy Library *(p 123)*, and the West Wing of the Museum of Fine Arts *(p 118)*.

A major renewal project of the 1960s, the mixed-use Prudential Center *(p 118)* created controversy, largely because it failed to create a human scale compatible with surrounding Back Bay neighborhoods. More successful was the 1970s renovation of the Faneuil Hall Marketplace *(p 111)*, which dramatically revived the ambience of downtown Boston by injecting new vitality into the city's historic heart.

In the 1980s the **Financial District**, long established in the vicinity of Federal and Congress Streets, began expanding in the direction of the rejuvenated harbor district. The waterfront's redevelopment *(p 112)*, which was boosted by the rehabilitation of the adjacent Faneuil Hall area, has reestablished Boston's historic link to the sea. In the near future this area will be further enhanced with the dismantling of the unsightly, traffic-clogged Central Artery that has long severed the waterfront and the North End from the downtown proper. The $7.7 billion Central Artery-Tunnel project, begun in the early 1990s, calls for the construction of an underground highway beneath the site of the current expressway as well as a new harbor tunnel to provide more efficient access to the airport. Upon its completion around the year 2005, this ambitious public works program is expected to alleviate Boston's infamous traffic snarls and create over 150 acres of new parkland.

## BOSTON TODAY

**Bostonians** – Reflecting various waves of immigration, Boston's population is quite diverse. The "proper Bostonian," or **Brahmin** descends from New England's early Puritan settlers who shared a common language and culture, and whose close-knit society set Boston apart by the 19C as the city where "the Lowells talk only to the Cabots, and the Cabots talk only to God." Stereotyped as refined, conservative and Harvard educated, the proper Bostonian today represents an ever-decreasing percentage of the city's population.

Boston's large **Irish** population began arriving by the thousands in the wake of the 1840s potato famine. Penniless yet hardworking, the Irish integrated into mainstream American life, and many succeeded in rising to positions in local and federal government. One of Boston's most famous Irish-Americans was former US president John Fitzgerald Kennedy.

Towards the end the century, many **Italian** immigrants, particularly from southern Italy, settled in Boston. The Italians eventually replaced the Irish and Jewish populations in the North End *(p 111)* and the now-destroyed West End.

The **African-American** community, once concentrated on Beacon Hill *(p 104)*, represents a large presence in Roxbury and the adjacent neighborhoods of Dorchester and Mattapan. Boston is home to one of the oldest black communities in the US. The first blacks were brought to colonial Boston as slaves from the West Indies in 1638, just eight years after the colony's establishment. A growing number of freed blacks settled in the North End, and many of them worked as barbers, sailors, laborers and coachmen and served in the Revolution, including **Crispus Attucks**, an assassinated hero of the Boston Massacre. In the 1780s the slave trade was legally abolished in Massachusetts—a reflection of the state's staunch abolitionist stand. In the 19C, with the dedication of the African Meeting House *(p 106)* on Beacon Hill, the black community moved to the north slope of the Hill in search of improved living conditions. Better housing, job opportunities and schools led blacks to gradually move out to Cambridge, the Back Bay and the South End.

Boston's rapidly growing **Hispanic** population has settled in pockets such as the South End, Jamaica Plain and East Boston. It is estimated that these and other minority groups, such as Asians, now make up about one-third of the city's population. In the 1970s and 1980s, Boston became a national testing ground for controversial busing policies. In an attempt to provide quality education for students of all socio-economic classes and particularly blacks, the federal government attempted with limited success to integrate the city's public schools.

Each year the area's colleges and universities draw a new influx of students and professors from across the country and abroad. The large **student population**, estimated in recent years at over 200,000, lends great diversity to the area's social and cultural fabric. Students reside on and around the numerous urban and suburban campuses scattered throughout the area, and they constitute a particularly strong presence in large sections of Cambridge, Brookline and Allston-Brighton.

**Economy** – Since the days of the Bay Colony, shipping and trade have been the mainstays of Boston's economy. Following a period of decline in the early 20C, modernization of the port's services and of the 25mi of docking space in the 1950s and 1960s increased the amount of cargo the port could handle. Today, however, Boston is not among the 20 top-ranking ports in the country.

A similar surge of growth was experienced in the business sector, particularly in the insurance industry. Insurance giants Prudential and John Hancock have established a towering presence in the Back Bay through the construction of the area's two tallest skyscrapers. Boston financiers, guardians of the Yankee fortunes made in shipping and industry, continue to generate a large share of New England's economic activity from their offices in the Financial District.

Industrially, a new era was born in the 1950s with the construction of Route 128, a circumferential highway outside the downtown area, and the emergence along this highway of about 700 research and development firms. Boston is a recognized world leader in this field; its universities are training grounds for scientists and research specialists, especially in electronics and computer technology. Boston is also a world leader in health care; the city's medical facilities, notably **Massachusetts General Hospital**, are internationally recognized centers of research and treatment. The nationwide recession of the 1980s dealt a serious blow to Boston's economy as evidenced by skyrocketing unemployment and a sagging real-estate market. Signs of recovery are apparent in the 1990s.

**A Cultural Hub** – *For the locations of theaters and concert halls see map below.* By the 19C Boston had become a gathering place for intellectuals and writers, earning the sobriquet "the Athens of America." Well-heeled and cultivated Bostonians traveled extensively, returning home with treasures that initiated the collections of the Museum of Fine Arts *(p 118)*, the Isabella Stewart Gardner Museum *(p 121)* and the museums of Harvard University *(p 132)*. In 1881 philanthropist Henry Lee Higginson founded the **Boston Symphony Orchestra**. Today the BSO and the **Boston Pops**, with its repertoire of lighter music, perform seasonally in Symphony Hall. In the summer the Pops presents free concerts on the Charles River Esplanade *(p 117)*. The heart of the **Theater District** lies in the area near Tremont and Stuart Streets. Boston is a testing ground for Broadway productions. The Colonial Theater, the Shubert Theater and the Wilbur Theater present musicals and comedies. Dramas are staged at the Charles Playhouse and at numerous university theaters. Performances by the **Boston Ballet Company** occur seasonally at the Wang Center.

**Education** – A principal concern of the Puritans was the establishment of a sound educational system. Ever since the founding of Boston Public Latin School (c.1630), the first public school in America, and Harvard College (1636), the first college in the colonies, Boston has remained a leader in the field of education. The metropolitan area's roster of some 68 colleges and universities includes Harvard, Massachusetts Institute of Technology, Radcliffe, Boston University, New England Conservatory of Music, Boston College, Brandeis University, Tufts University and Wellesley College.

| Theaters and Concert Halls | | | |
|---|---|---|---|
| Boston Center for the Arts | FZ, 1 | 539 Tremont St. | 426-7700 |
| Boston Ballet (Wang Ctr.) | FZ, 7 | 270 Tremont St. | 695-6955 |
| Boston Lyric Opera | FZ, | 219 Tremont St. | 248-8660 |
| Charles Playhouse | FZ, 2 | 76 Warrenton St. | 426-6912 |
| Colonial Theater | FZ, 3 | 106 Boylston St. | 426-9366 |
| Emerson Majestic Theater | FZ, 7 | 219 Tremont St. | 578-8727 |
| Hatch Memorial Shell | FZ | Charles River Esplanade | 266-1492 |
| NE Conservatory of Music | EZ | 290 Huntington Ave. | 536-2412 |
| Shubert Theater | FZ, 4 | 265 Tremont St. | 426-4520 |
| Symphony Hall | EZ | 301 Massachusetts Ave. | 266-1492 |
| Wang Center | FZ, 5 | 270 Tremont St. | 482-9393 |
| Wilbur Theater | FZ, 6 | 246 Tremont St. | 426-9366 |

# PRACTICAL INFORMATION ................................... Area Code: 617

## Getting There

**By Air** – International and domestic flights to **Logan International Airport**, 2mi northeast of downtown ☎800-235-6426 (ground transport information). Taxi service to downtown ($10-$15); commercial shuttles ($8); major rental car agencies *(p 248)*. MBTA Blue Line service from airport. Airport Water Shuttle (between Logan and Rowes Wharf) ☎800-235-6486 or 330-8680.

**By Bus and Train** – Greyhound **bus:** South Station ☎800-231-2222; Peter Pan: 555 Atlantic Ave ☎426-7838. Amtrak **train:** South Station ☎800-872-7245; suburban trains North and South Stations ☎722-3200.

## Getting Around

**By Public Transportation** – **Subway and buses** *(p 103)*. Commuter **ferry** service between Long Wharf and Charlestown Navy Yard *(schedule p 124)*, Boston Harbor Cruises ☎227-4321.

**Sightseeing** – **Old Towne Trolley Tours** (daily year-round; no service Thanksgiving Day, Dec 25; $16) offers 1hr 30min narrated tours of the city; visitors can board at major attractions along the route ☎269-7150. **Cruises:** departures from Long Wharf - **Bay State Cruise Co, Inc** ☎723-7800, **Boston Harbor Cruises** ☎227-4321, **Schooner Liberty Tall Ship** ☎742-0333; departures from Rowes Wharf - **Spirit of Boston Harbor Cruises** ☎457-1450 and **whale-watching cruises** *(p 254)*.

**By Car** – Use of public transportation or walking is strongly encouraged within the city as roads are often congested and street parking may be difficult. Parking garages generally charge $5-$15/day. Some facilities give "early-bird" discounts (25-50%) before 10:30am. Construction of the Central Artery/Tunnel Project will divert traffic for the next few years; for information on road closures and detours ☎228-4636.

## By Taxi

| | ☎ | | ☎ |
|---|---|---|---|
| Boston Cab | 536-5010 | Checker Taxi | 536-7000 |
| Red Cab | 734-5000 | Red & White Cab | 742-9090 |
| Town Taxi | 536-5000 | | |

## General Information

**Visitor Information** – **Greater Boston Convention and Visitors Bureau:** ground floor **Prudential Center** (open Mon–Fri 8:30am–6pm, Sat 10am–6pm, Sun 11:30am–6pm), **Boston Common** Tremont & West Sts (open Mon–Sat 8:30am–5pm, Sun 9am–5pm). Mailing address: PO Box 490, Boston MA 02199 ☎800-888-5515 or 536-4100. **National Park Service** visitor center: 15 State St (open daily 9am–5pm).

## Useful Numbers ☎

| | |
|---|---|
| Police/Ambulance/Fire | 911 |
| Police (non-emergency) | 343-4240 |
| Dental Emergency (24hrs) | 508-651-3521 |
| Medical Emergency Inn-House Doctor (24hrs) | 431-5959 |
| Phillips Drug Co (daily 7am–midnight) | 523-1028 |
| Main Post Office 25 Dorchester Ave (24hrs) | 654-5327 |
| Weather | 936-1234 |

**Accommodations** – Reservation services: **Citywide Reservation Services** 25 Huntington Ave, Suite 607, Boston MA 02116-5713 ☎267-7424; **Host Homes of Boston**, PO Box 117, Waban Branch, Boston MA 02168 ☎244-1308; **Bed and Breakfast Cambridge & Greater Boston**, PO Box 665, Cambridge MA 02140 ☎800-888-0178 or 576-1430. *Boston Travel Planner* available (free) from the Convention and Visitors Bureau *(above)*. Accommodations range from elegant downtown hotels ($195-$260/day) to budget motels ($90-$130/day). Most bed and breakfasts are in residential areas of the city ($40-$75/day). *Average prices for a double room.*

**Local Press** – Daily news: *Boston Globe* (am), Thursday entertainment section; *Boston Herald* (am). Weekly entertainment: *Boston Phoenix.*

**Entertainment** – Consult the arts and entertainment sections of local newspapers for schedule of cultural events and addresses of principal theaters *(listing p 101)*. Tickets for local events: **Bostix Ticket Booth** (Faneuil Hall Marketplace) offers half-price tickets for selected events on the day of the performance (purchases must be made in person, cash only) ☎723-8915 or **Ticketmaster** ☎931-2000.

## Shopping in Boston

| IN THIS AREA... | YOU WILL FIND... |
|---|---|

**Downtown** — **Downtown Crossing** – major department stores including Jordan Marsh, Filene's and Filene's Basement (renowned for its great bargains). **Faneuil Hall Marketplace** *(p 111)* – lively cluster of specialty shops and eateries in a historic setting. **Haymarket** *(p 111)* – outdoor farmers market.

**Back Bay** *(p 113)* — **Copley Place** *(p 118)* – boutiques, restaurants, Neiman-Marcus department store. **Prudential Center** *(p 118)* – apparel and specialty stores, Lord & Taylor and Saks Fifth Avenue department stores. **Newbury Street** *(p 115)* – antique shops, galleries and boutiques.

**Beacon Hill** *(p 104)* — **Charles Street** *(p 106)* – antique shops and galleries.

**Cambridge** *(p 129)* — **Harvard Square** *(p 129)* – trendy shops, records stores, boutiques. **Cambridgeside Galleria** – over 100 apparel and specialty stores.

**Foreign Exchange Offices** – *p 246.* BayBank currency exchange office located in terminal E, Logan International Airport (Mon–Fri 8am–9:30pm, Sat 11:30am–9:30pm) ☎800-788-5000.

**Sports** – Tickets for major sporting events can be purchased at the venue, or through Ticketmaster outlets *(Entertainment p 102)*. The 26-mile Boston Marathon, run every year from Hopkinton to the Back Bay, takes place on Patriot's Day (3rd Mon in Apr).

| SPORT | TEAM | SEASON | VENUE |
|---|---|---|---|
| Major League Baseball | Red Sox | Apr–Oct | Fenway Park |
| Professional Football | New England Patriots | Sept–Dec | Schaefer Stadium (Foxboro) |
| Professional Basketball | Celtics | Nov–May | Boston Garden |
| Professional Hockey | Bruins | Sept–Apr | Boston Garden |

## Subway and Buses

The Massachusetts Bay Transportation Authority (MBTA) operates underground and surface transportation in the greater Boston area. Stations are indicated by the ⓣ symbol at street level. Most MBTA lines operate Mon–Sat 5:15–12:30am, Sun 6–12:30am. **Subway** fare $.85, **bus** fare $.60, exact fare required. MBTA Visitor Passports are good for 3 ($9) or 7 ($18) days of unlimited travel on all MBTA subway and local bus lines, available at some stations and hotels. Subway maps are available at the main stations; MBTA system maps ($2.50) can be purchased at the Globe Corner Bookstore at 1 School St. *For route & sales information ☎722-3200.*

MBTA designated main stops are shown.

## ** ① BEACON HILL  *Map p 107*

Historically the home of Boston Brahmins and the city's early black community, the "Hill" preserves an ethereal Old-World ambience undisturbed by the bustle of the surrounding metropolis.

**Historical Notes** – Today's Beacon Hill is the only remnant of the three peaks comprising the Trimountain ridge *(p 96)*. Its name derives from the primitive beacon that the Puritans raised on its summit in 1634 to warn of invasion. From 1795 to 1798 preeminent architect Charles Bulfinch oversaw the erection of his golden-domed State House on the Hill's southern slope. Construction of this grand building spurred Bulfinch, Harrison Gray Otis *(p 107)* and their business associates to create an elegant residential district on a nearby tract purchased from painter John Singleton Copley. From 1799 until the mid-19C, these developers transformed the entire face of the Trimountain area: Beacon Hill's summit was lowered 60ft and the two neighboring peaks were leveled, creating abundant landfill for the surrounding marshlands; the present street system was laid out and the charming enclave of English-style brick residences that we know as Beacon Hill came into being.

The sunny south slope, between Pinckney Street and the Common *(p 108)*, became the bastion of Boston's affluent society and the center of its respected intellectual and artistic community, whose members included Daniel Webster, Julia Ward Howe and the Alcotts *(p 143)*. The more modest north slope, spilling into Cambridge Street, became the center of Boston's black community in the 19C *(p 106)*, many of whom worked for the well-to-do on the Hill. Today Beacon Hill reigns as one of Boston's most desirable addresses. A stroll along its serene streets lined with gas lamps and brick facades transports the visitor to a bygone era.

**An Architectural Showcase** – Created almost entirely in the first half of the 19C, Beacon Hill constitutes a living museum of the period's architectural heritage, showcasing the works of the city's leading 19C architects. The work of Charles Bulfinch is well represented by the State House and some 15 Federal-style town houses found primarily on the fashionable south slope. Houses designed in this area by architects Asher Benjamin and Alexander Parris reflect the Greek Revival style in vogue in the 1820s.

The Hill's streetscape is noteworthy for its extraordinary visual unity, resulting from the predominant use of brick, a uniform 3-4 story building height, and harmonious blending of flat and bowed facades. Quaint service lanes are lined with former stables and servants quarters, while intimate cul-de-sacs evoke a sense of mystery. The Hill's designation as a historic district in 1955 and the determination of residents to safeguard its precious architectural heritage have been instrumental in the preservation of this urban jewel. *Beacon Hill's private gardens are revealed to the public in May by special tour. For information:* ☎617-227-4392.

Acorn Street, Beacon Hill

**Walking Tour**  *2hrs (not including guided tours).* Ⓣ *Park St.*
*Visitors are advised to exercise caution in inclement weather as brick sidewalks can be very slippery.*

> *Begin at the corner of Park and Tremont Sts and walk uphill on Park St.*

Gently sloping Park Street provides a pleasant approach to the gold-domed State House crowning **Beacon Street★**. Writer Oliver Wendell Holmes dubbed Beacon, "the sunny street that holds the sifted few." The row of stately edifices forming the Hill's southern facade offers coveted views of the Common. Beyond the Common, this fashionable thoroughfare stretches west into Back Bay *(p 113)* and points beyond.

> *Turn right on Beacon St.*

★ **Boston Athenaeum** – *10 1/2 Beacon St. First two floors open to the public year-round Mon–Fri 9am–5pm (& Oct–May Sat 9–4pm). The entire building may be visited by guided tour (1hr) only, Tue & Thu 3pm. One-day advance reservation required.* ☎617-227-0270. This venerable Boston institution was established in 1807 as one of the nation's first private lending libraries. Later in the century numerous important works from the Athenaeum's art trove formed the core of Boston's Museum of Fine Arts' *(p 118)* world-class collection. The library's present home on Beacon Hill was built in the 1840s to accommodate its growing holdings, which today total some 750,000 volumes and works of art. Walking through the hallowed reading rooms packed with leather-bound volumes and fine sculptures, paintings and prints, visitors are ushered into a rarefied atmosphere of tradition and erudition. Works by Gilbert Stuart, Thomas Sully and Jean-Antoine Houdon highlight the collection. The art gallery *(2nd floor)* features changing exhibits from the collection. Several rooms and terraces provide lovely **views** of the Old Granary Burying Ground.

★★ **State House** – *Corner of Park and Beacon Sts. Open year-round Mon–Fri 10am–4pm. Closed major holidays.* ✕ ⅙ ☎617-727-3676. The golden dome of Massachusetts' capitol building dominates Beacon Hill, enduring as a cherished Boston landmark for nearly two centuries. Completed in 1798 by Charles Bulfinch, the original brick edifice, fronted by a projecting portico, was extended in 1895 and 1916 by large additions to its sides and rear. Most of the original ornamentation and design of the interior spaces specified by Bulfinch have been left intact.

Statues on the front lawn depict Anne Hutchinson (west wing), banished from the 17C colony for her theological views; Mary Dyer (east wing), hanged for her Quaker beliefs; orator Daniel Webster (left), and Horace Mann (right), a pioneer in American education.

The main entrance of the State House leads into **Doric Hall**, named for its rows of Doric columns. In the 19C addition the **Senate Staircase Hall**, with its marble walls and floors, displays paintings immortalizing Paul Revere's ride, James Otis' oratory against the Writs of Assistance, and the Boston Tea Party. Paintings in the **Hall of Flags**, which was built to house a collection of Civil War battle flags, portray the Pilgrims on the Mayflower, John Eliot preaching to the Indians, and the scene at Concord Bridge April 19, 1775.

The main staircase leads to the **Third Floor Hall**, dominated by Daniel Chester French's statue of Governor Wolcott. The Senate Chamber, Senate Reception Room, Governor's Office and House Chamber occupy this floor. Before leaving the domed House Chamber, note the **Sacred Cod**, a gilded, carved-wood symbol of the fish that supported Massachusetts' early fishing industry.

Upon exiting the State House, cross Beacon Street to admire the **Shaw Civil War Monument★ [A]**, a bronze relief by Augustus Saint-Gaudens that honors Col Robert Gould Shaw and the 54th Massachusetts Colored Infantry, the Union's first regiment of free black volunteers. Shaw was killed in 1863 during the Union assault on Fort Wagner in South Carolina.

> *Continue walking down Beacon St.*

Among the street's noteworthy buildings are the exclusive Somerset Club at **nos. 42-43**, a double-bowed granite structure whose right half is attributed to Alexander Parris (1819) and **no. 45** (1808), the last of three houses that Bulfinch designed and built for Harrison Gray Otis on Beacon Hill.

> *Cross Spruce St.*

The handsome pair of bowfronted Greek Revival houses at **nos. 54-55** are attributed to Asher Benjamin, architect of the Charles Street Meeting House and the Old West Church *(both described later on the tour)*. The state chapter of the National Society of Colonial Dames occupies no. 55.

> *Return to the corner of Beacon and Spruce Sts, turn up Spruce and take a right on Chestnut St.*

As you pass narrow Branch Street on the left, note the modest buildings that once housed servants.

★ **Chestnut Street** – This picturesque street presents a fine assortment of houses reflecting architectural styles dating from 1800 to 1830. **No. 29A** (1800, Charles Bulfinch) features distinctive purple glass in its bowfront. Other examples of the

Hill's famed 18C purple window panes—resulting from the glass' manganese dioxide content—may still be seen in a few other dwellings on the Hill (including 63-64 Beacon St). The graceful trio at nos. 13-17, known as the **Swan Houses** (c.1805), further evidences Bulfinch's preference for a restrained Federal style.

*Continue one block up Chestnut St, turn left on Walnut St and continue one block to Mt Vernon St.*

★★ **Mt Vernon Street** – Qualified by writer Henry James as "the only respectable street in America," this gracious thoroughfare boasts some of the Hill's finest residences. At no. 55 stands the **Nichols House Museum [M¹]** *(visit by 30min guided tour only May–Oct Tue–Sat noon–5pm; rest of the year Mon, Wed, Sat noon–5pm; closed Jan & major holidays; $4; ☎617-227-6993)*, the Hill's only residence open to the public. Designed by Bulfinch in 1804, the house preserves the possessions and spirit of a colorful Beacon Hill lady.

On the way downhill, pause to admire the freestanding edifice at **no. 85** (1802) set back some 30ft from the street line. Faced with slender pilasters and topped by a wooden balustrade and an octagonal tower, this handsome residence was the second of three mansions Bulfinch designed for Harrison Gray Otis. Bulfinch also conceived the neighboring mansions at nos. 87 and 89.

★★ **Louisburg Square** – Named in honor of the victorious siege of the French fortress at Louisbourg (Nova Scotia) led by the Massachusetts militia in 1745, this select enclave epitomizes Beacon Hill's refined life-style. The appearance of the elegant Greek Revival bowfronted row houses and the small private park have changed little since their creation in the 1830s and 1840s. Writer Louisa May Alcott lived in no. 10 from 1880 until her death eight years later. Christmas Eve caroling on the square is a cherished Bostonian tradition.

*Leave the square via Willow St, and turn right onto Acorn St.*

★ **Acorn Street** – *Illustration p 104*. This romantic cobblestone passage is the most photographed street on the Hill.

*At the end of Acorn St, turn right on West Cedar St, then left on Mt Vernon St to Charles St.*

★ **Charles Street** – Antique shops, art galleries and coffee shops line the Hill's bustling commercial thoroughfare. At the corner of Mt Vernon Street stands the **Charles Street Meeting House** (c.1807) designed by Asher Benjamin. This popular forum for 19C abolitionists William Lloyd Garrison, Frederick Douglass and Sojourner Truth was converted into offices in the 1980s.

*Continue one block on Charles St and turn right on Pinckney St.*

**Pinckney Street** – This lovely, sloping street was the dividing line between the affluent neighborhood on the sunny south slope and the more modest community on the north slope.

*Turn left on West Cedar St. After one block, go right on Revere St.*

**Revere Street** – The street's left side is interrupted by a series of intimate private courts: **Bellingham Place, Sentry Hill Place** and **Rollins Place**. At Rollins Place the white "house" at the end of the court is not a house at all, but rather a decorative wall at the head of a drop.

*Walk back to Anderson St and turn left.*

The imposing brick edifice (1824) crowning the corner of Pinckney and Anderson Streets **(no. 65)** formerly housed the Phillips Grammar School (1844-1861), the city's first racially mixed school.

*Continue uphill on Pinckney St.*

The small clapboard house at **no. 5**, built for two black men in the 1790s, is one of the Hill's oldest surviving structures.

*Turn left onto Joy St.*

**Joy Street** – This long street descends the north slope of the Hill, the center of Boston's historic black community from the late 18C to the 19C.

**Smith Court** – This small cul-de-sac was the heart of the black community following the Revolution. Many of its residents worked for wealthy families who lived on the elite south slope. At no. 46 Joy Street stands the **Abiel Smith School** (1830s), an elegant pedimented structure that housed the city's first black school. Behind the school stands the nation's oldest remaining black church, the **African Meeting House★** *(open year-round daily 10am–4pm; closed major holidays)*. Built in 1806 by black Baptists disenchanted with the discrimination encountered in the white churches, this handsome brick edifice provided a forum for supporters of the anti-slavery movement.

For most of the 20C, the building served as a synagogue. Today it is preserved as a privately owned historic site managed by the National Park Service. The lower floor houses the Museum of Afro-American History, a small showplace for exhibits on themes relating to New England's black community. The meetinghouse proper occupies the upper floor. *For more information on Beacon Hill's African-American history, obtain the free brochure describing the Black Heritage Trail, which identifies 14 historically significant sites (most of which are included on the present walking tour) from the Boston African-American National Historic Site, 46 Joy St.* ☎617-742-5415.

*At the foot of Joy St, cross busy Cambridge St.*

★ **Harrison Gray Otis House** – *141 Cambridge St. Visit by guided tour (45min) only, year-round Tue–Fri noon–5pm, Sat 10am–5pm. Closed major holidays. $4.* ☎*617-227-3956.* The house (1796) was the creation of two men who permanently influenced Boston's urban landscape: architect Charles Bulfinch and Harrison Gray Otis, lawyer, speculator and politician. The first of three houses Bulfinch designed for Otis on Beacon Hill, this Federal-style dwelling reflects the refined taste of the

upper classes during the early years of the Republic. A second-story Palladian window softens the facade. Exquisite period furniture, ornate moldings, hand-blocked borders, and a freestanding staircase adorn the interior.
The house serves both as a museum and as the headquarters of the Society for the Preservation of New England Antiquities (1910), which operates over 30 house museums in five states *(p 254)*.

**Old West Church** – Complimenting its Federal-style neighbor, the Otis House, this handsome structure with its strong vertical lines was designed by Asher Benjamin in 1806. In 1775 British troops razed the original meetinghouse that stood on this site when they suspected the patriots of using its steeple to signal American troops.

For an abrupt return to the 20C, glance across Staniford Street at the State Health, Education and Welfare Service Center (1970, Paul Rudolph), a sprawling concrete complex that replaced six blocks of tenement buildings in the bulldozed West End district *(p 99)*. The facade on Staniford and Merrimac Streets features a dramatic exterior staircase.

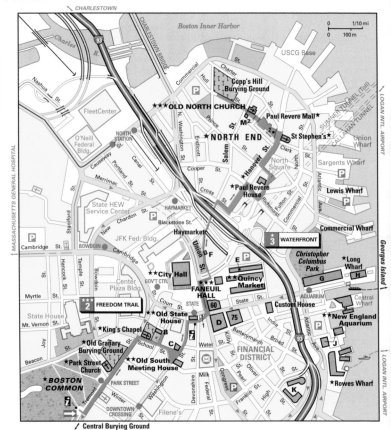

★★★ ② **THE FREEDOM TRAIL** *1 day. Map above.* ☏ *Park St.*

The following walk includes most of the historical monuments along the Boston section of the Freedom Trail, a popular itinerary linking major Revolutionary and other sites of the Boston National Historical Park *(for Freedom Trail sights in Charlestown, see p 124)*. The route is indicated on the pavement by red brick or a painted red line.

> *Begin at the visitor center on the Common at Tremont and West Sts (open year-round Mon–Sat 8am–5pm, Sun 9am–5pm ☏617-536-4100).*

## Downtown

★ **Boston Common** – *Map p 107.* This 50-acre park in the heart of the city has belonged to the people of Boston since the 1630s, when Reverend Blackstone sold the tract to the Puritans. Designated by these early Bostonians as "Common Field" forever reserved for public use, this Boston landmark has served over the centuries as pasture land, military training ground, public execution site, rallying ground and concert venue.

Lacking a formal landscape scheme, the park's hilly terrain is crisscrossed by tree-lined paths linking downtown to Beacon Hill and the Back Bay. The **Central Burying Ground** (1756), fronting Boylston Street, contains the unmarked grave of preeminent early American portraitist Gilbert Stuart *(p 33)*.

> *Proceed to the corner of Tremont and Park Sts and follow the Freedom Trail red line for the rest of the tour.*

★ **Park Street Church** – *Open Jul–Aug Tue–Sat 9:30am–3:30pm.* The graceful, 217ft wooden steeple of this brick edifice (1809, Peter Banner), inspired by the work of English architect Christopher Wren, is one of Boston's loveliest landmarks. The church carillon chimes the melodies of familiar hymns on the hour. William Lloyd Garrison delivered his first anti-slavery speech in this meetinghouse in 1829, and *America* was sung for the first time here on July 4, 1831.

★ **Old Granary Burying Ground** – Named for the 17C granary that once stood nearby, this burial ground contains the remains of the great Revolutionary War orators James Otis and Samuel Adams, as well as Paul Revere, and Crispus Attucks, who was killed in the Boston Massacre. An obelisk in the center of the cemetery honors Benjamin Franklin's parents.

★ **King's Chapel** – *Corner of Tremont and School Sts. Open mid-Jun–Labor Day Mon–Sat 10am–4pm. Mid-Mar–early Jun & mid-Sept–Oct Mon, Fri, Sat 10am–4pm. Contribution requested.* ☎617-523-1749. New England's first Anglican church, this massive granite edifice (1754, Peter Harrison) replaced the original wooden chapel built on the site in the 1680s. The central tower was wrapped in a wooden Ionic colonnade in the 1780s, but never received its steeple due to lack of funds. Only nine years after the British evacuation of Boston, the structure was reborn as the first Unitarian Church in America. Enter the church to admire its outstanding Georgian **interior**. The adjoining **burying ground**, Boston's oldest, is the final resting place of John Winthrop (the colony's first governor) and John Alden (son of Priscilla and John).

**Old City Hall** [B] – *45 School St.* Constructed on the site of America's first public school (c.1630), this stately granite building (1865) is Boston's finest example of the Second Empire style. Its architect, Arthur Gilman, is also credited with planning the Back Bay *(p 113)*. The structure was converted to commercial use in the late 1960s following completion of the present City Hall *(p 110)*. A statue of Benjamin Franklin, who was born nearby, graces the left side of the forecourt.

**Old Corner Bookstore** [C] – *Corner of Washington and School Sts.* This restored 18C brick commercial building, now operating as a bookstore specializing in Boston-related publications, has figured prominently in Boston's publishing world. Over the centuries it has housed the publisher of New England literati Longfellow, Emerson and Hawthorne as well as the offices of the *Atlantic Monthly* and the *Boston Globe*.

★★ **Old South Meeting House** – *Washington and Milk Sts. Open Apr–Oct daily 9:30am–5pm; rest of the year Mon–Fri 10am–4pm, Sat 5pm. $2.50.* ☎617-482-6439. Noted orators Samuel Adams and James Otis led many of the protest meetings held at Old South prior to the Revolution. The momentous rally that took place on the evening of December 16, 1773, gave rise to the Boston Tea Party *(p 97)*.
Sporting a plain brick facade and a tower surmounted by a wooden steeple, the edifice was inspired by the designs of Christopher Wren. Its expansive interior was transformed into a riding stable by the British during the siege of Boston *(p 97)*.
The story of the structure's history is told through interpretive displays, artifacts and recordings of passionate speeches and private conversations that are audible at various points throughout the interior.

★★ **Old State House** – *Washington and State Sts. Open year-round daily 9:30am–5pm. Closed major holidays. $3.* ☎617-720-1713. Boston's oldest public building (1713) was the British government headquarters in the colonies until the Revolution and the site of several crucial events. In 1770 the Boston Massacre *(p 97)* erupted on this site. On July 4, 1776, the colonies declared their independence in Philadelphia. Two weeks later the Declaration of Independence was read from the balcony, inciting the crowds to topple and burn the lion and unicorn—symbols of the British Crown—perched on the building's gables (reproductions now adorn the building). The Massachusetts government met in this building until the new State House was completed in 1798; the Old State House was later converted into shops and subsequently housed the city government. In 1881 The Bostonian Society was founded to maintain the site as a museum devoted to Boston's history.

Inside, two floors accessed by a spiral staircase feature excellent exhibits on the city, past and present. The historic balcony can be seen from the Council Chamber.

Old State House

Peter Vanderwarker

To the rear of the State House, note the circle of cobblestones embedded in the traffic island in the busy intersection of Congress and State Streets, marking the actual Boston Massacre **site [1]**. This vantage point affords a dizzying look at several of the skyscrapers dwarfing the Old State House. Standing sentinel over State Street are two noteworthy 20C towers: on the left, **60 State Street** (1977, Skidmore, Owings and Merrill) and on the right, **Stock Exchange Place [D]** (1984, Peabody and Stearns), which integrates part of the existing granite structure. Almost hidden behind Stock Exchange Place is Boston's most exuberant modern tower: **75 State Street★** (1988, Skidmore, Owings and Merrill), distinguished by upper stories boldly adorned in multi-colored granite and over 3,500sq ft of gold leaf. Farther down State Street rises the tower of another enduring Boston landmark, the **Custom House** (base: 1840s, A. B. Young; tower: 1910s, Peabody and Stearns).

After negotiating the intersection of Congress and State Streets, turn around to admire the east facade of the Old State House against the dramatic backdrop of a looming black metal tower (One Boston Place).

★★ **City Hall** – *Open year-round Mon–Fri 8am–4pm. Closed major holidays.* ☎617-635-4000. On the left emerges the rear of City Hall *(best viewed from the plaza reached via the stairs flanking the building)*. Rising from its brick base, this top-heavy concrete pile has remained one of Boston's controversial architectural statements since its completion in 1968. The nationally acclaimed edifice by Kallman, McKinnell and Knowles recalls the works of the influential modernist Le Corbusier and helped to bring the so-called Brutalist style to prominence in the US. The architecturally minded will enjoy exploring the vast public spaces on the lower floors. City council meetings may be observed from the 5th-floor galleries *(Wed 4pm)*.

★★★ **Faneuil Hall** – *Dock Sq, main entrance facing Quincy Market. Open year-round daily 9am–5pm. Closed Jan 1, Thanksgiving Day, Dec 25.* ☎617-242-5675. Presented to Boston in 1742 by wealthy merchant Peter Faneuil, this revered landmark served as the city's town meeting hall throughout the Revolutionary period. Among the noted American leaders who have addressed groups assembled here over the years are Samuel Adams, Wendell Phillips, Susan B. Anthony and John F. Kennedy. Damaged by fire in 1762, the building was reconstructed according to the original plans drawn by John Smibert. In 1806 a major renovation supervised by Charles Bulfinch doubled the building's size.

Faneuil Hall's cupola is crowned with the grasshopper weathervane commissioned by Peter Faneuil in 1742. Modeled after the gilded bronze weathervanes that top the Royal Exchange in London, the grasshopper has symbolized the Port of Boston since the 18C. A statue of Samuel Adams stands fronts the building.

A staircase leads up to the large meeting hall, where George P. A. Healy's painting *Daniel Webster's Second Reply to Hayne* covers the front wall. The **Ancient and Honorable Artillery Company**, America's oldest military organization, maintains a museum of historical arms, uniforms, flags and paintings on the floor above *(open year-round Mon–Fri 9am–5pm;* ☎617-227-1638).

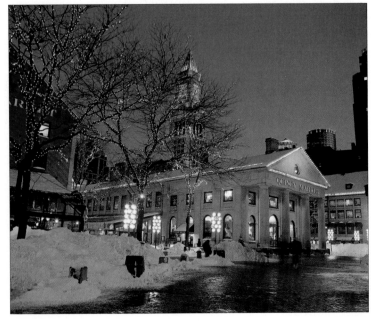

Faneuil Hall Marketplace

**★★ Quincy Market** – *Behind Faneuil Hall.* The lively Faneuil Hall Marketplace complex, known as Quincy Market after its principal edifice, exemplifies the successful revitalization of a formerly blighted urban area. Run-down market buildings and warehouses have been restored, and the renewed commercial complex has become one of the most popular sections of the city. Bostonians and tourists alike flock day and night to its numerous restaurants, outdoor cafes, specialty and craft shops.

The heart of the development consists of three granite buildings built in 1825 by Alexander Parris. The centerpiece, Quincy Market proper, is a long arcade in the Greek Revival style. Glass enclosures from the 1970s restoration flank its sides and contain dozens of small shops and eateries. The North and South Street buildings adjoining Quincy Market house more elegant stores. In North Market is the popular family-style restaurant **Durgin Park [E]**.

**Union Street** – During the late 18C this street was lined with taverns and pubs. The Duke of Orleans, later King Louis-Philippe of France, lived for several months on the second floor of the venerable institution **Ye Olde Union Oyster House [F]** (still in operation as a restaurant), where he gave French lessons to earn his keep.

> *Cross Blackstone St to Haymarket, site of a colorful farmers market on weekends, and continue through the pedestrian tunnel and into the North End.*

## ★ North End

Severed from the rest of the city by an elevated expressway, this colorful district has been continuously inhabited since 1630. Throughout the 17C and 18C, the North End reigned as Boston's principal residential district and included a community of free blacks. Irish and Jewish immigrants who settled here in the 19C eventually moved on, replaced by Southern Italian immigrants, who have maintained a strong presence here. Rooftop gardens; shops bulging with fresh meats, poultry and vegetables; and restaurants and cafes that serve home-cooked pasta, pizza, pastries and espresso crowd **Hanover★** and **Salem Streets**, the main thoroughfares. The local community continues to celebrate numerous saints' days throughout the year *(schedules of feasts are posted in storefronts and churches)*. These lively events feature religious processions, outdoor entertainment and an abundance of street food.

**★ Paul Revere House** – *19 North Sq. Open Apr–Dec daily 9:30am– 5:15pm (Nov–Dec & early Apr 4:15pm). Jan–Mar Tue–Sun 9:30am–4:15pm. Closed Jan 1, Thanksgiving Day, Dec 25. $2.50. ☎617-523-2338.* This 2 1/2-story wooden clapboard house is the only extant 17C structure in downtown Boston. The dwelling was already 90 years old when the silversmith Paul Revere bought it in 1770. This house was the starting point of Revere's historic ride to Lexington on April 18, 1775 *(p 150)*. Furnishings include items owned by the Revere family.

**★ St Stephen's Church** – *Hanover and Clark Sts. Open year-round daily 7am–dusk.* Skillfully positioned at a bend on Hanover Street and aligned with the Paul Revere Mall across the street, this former Congregational meetinghouse, built in 1806, was renamed in the 1860s by the Catholic diocese of Boston, which purchased it to meet the spiritual needs of the North End's immigrant population. Of the five churches designed by Charles Bulfinch in Boston, St Stephens is the only one still standing. The well-preserved stark interior is flanked with a delicate colonnade supporting a balcony.

**★ Paul Revere Mall** – Linking St Stephen's and the Old North Church, this intimate brick plaza succeeds as one of Boston's finest public spaces. Beyond Cyrus Dallin's equestrian **statue [2]** of Paul Revere looms the spire of the Old North Church. A series of bronze plaques set into the side walls traces the role of the North End's residents in Boston's history.

© Joanne Devereaux

Paul Revere Mall

★★★**Old North Church (Christ Church)** – *Entrance at 193 Salem St. Open year-round daily 9am–5pm. Closed Thanksgiving Day.* ☎*617-523-6676.* It was here, on the evening of April 18, 1775, that the sexton displayed two lanterns in the steeple to signal the departure of the British from Boston by boat, on their way to Lexington and Concord. A century later this church was immortalized by Longfellow in his poem *Paul Revere's Ride.* Built in 1723 Old North was surmounted by a spire that was destroyed and replaced twice following violent storms. The present spire dates from 1954. Inside, the box pews, the large windows and the pulpit, from which President Gerald Ford initiated the celebration of the nation's Bicentennial, are characteristic features of New England's colonial churches. The four wooden cherubim near the organ were among the bounty captured from a French vessel. Replicas of the famous lantern can be seen in the **museum [M²]** adjacent to the church.

**Copp's Hill Burying Ground** – *Open year-round daily 8am–6pm (late fall & winter 3pm).* ☎617-635-4505. This cemetery contains the graves of noted Bostonians, including three generations of the prominent Mather family: Increase Mather (1639-1723), minister and Harvard president; Cotton Mather (1663-1728), churchman and writer; and his son, The Reverend Samuel Mather (1706-1785). *The Mather plots are located in northeast corner near Charter St gate.* Also interred here are the remains of hundreds of black Bostonians who settled in the North End in the 18C.

> *Return to Hanover St to taste some Italian specialties or simply take in the local color. Note that the red line of the Freedom Trail continues to Charlestown (sights in Charlestown are described on p 124).*

★ ③ **THE WATERFRONT** *2 hrs. Map p 108.* ⊤ *Aquarium.*

During Boston's long period of maritime prosperity, sailing ships brimming with exotic cargoes frequented the busy harbor. To accommodate the port's burgeoning shipping industry, the original harborfront was dramatically transformed in the first half of the 19C via a landfill project that added over 100 acres. After 1900 Boston's shipping activities sharply declined, precipitating the deterioration of the waterfront area. The construction of two traffic arteries (Atlantic Avenue in the 1860s and the elevated Central Artery in the 1950s) severed the area from the rest of the city.

Long-awaited rehabilitation of this historic area did not begin in earnest until the 1960s. Renovation of several wharf buildings injected new commercial and residential activity, and the 1970s Quincy Market restoration created a crucial link between the downtown and **Christopher Columbus Park** (1976), a popular harborside promenade extending from Commercial to Long Wharf. A flurry of new residential and hotel complexes in the 1970s and 1980s significantly enhanced the waterfront's cachet while adding new texture to Boston's skyline. The waterfront's historic link to the downtown will at last be re-established in the 21C when an underground expressway replaces the unsightly Central Artery.

**Sights**

**Commercial Wharf and Lewis Wharf** – Constructed in the 1830s, the granite buildings on these wharves were renovated (1960s) into modern harborfront offices and luxury apartments.

★ **Long Wharf** – The original wharf (1710) stretched like a monumental avenue from the Custom House Tower some 2000ft into the harbor to service large craft unable to anchor closer ashore. Over the centuries Long Wharf's length was halved and its row of shops and warehouses demolished. The low-scale profile of the brick **Marriott Hotel Long Wharf [G]** (1982, Cossutta and Assocs.) harmonizes well with the traditional architecture of the waterfront. The granite **Custom House Block [H]** (1837, Isaiah Rogers), occupying a fine site on the wharf's edge, has been converted into a mixed-use commercial and residential complex.

Long Wharf is the docking point for boats offering sightseeing cruises of the harbor and its islands, as well as a water shuttle *(p 124)* to the Charlestown Navy Yard.

**Cruises** – Sightseeing cruises and excursion boats (Provincetown, Nantasket) that depart from the waterfront *(p 102)* are a wonderful way to see the harbor and view the Boston skyline.

**Georges Island** – *Depart from Long Wharf late May–Labor Day daily 10am–4pm (Sat & Sun 5pm); mid-Sept–early Oct Wed–Sun 10am–4pm. Round-trip 45min. $6.* ⚹ ⅙ *Bay State Cruise Co.* ☎617-723-7800. This 28-acre island, inhabited during colonial times and later fortified due to its strategic location, is a public recreation site with picnic areas at water's edge. Dominating the island is well-preserved Fort Warren, used during the Civil War to incarcerate some 2,000 Confederate military prisoners. Among those held were James Mason and John Slidell, Confederates who figured prominently in the **Trent Affair**. The two had embarked for England aboard the British steamer *Trent* to solicit funds for the Confederate cause. Enroute, they were taken prisoner by the Union. The Union's disregard for diplomatic convention so incensed Britain that it threatened to join the war on the Confederate side. The Union, however, bent to British demands and released the men.

The fort's observation tower offers **views** of the Boston skyline and the many islands and islets composing the Boston Harbor Islands State Park. *Free water taxis run from Georges Island to several nearby islands during the summer season.*

**Whale-Watching Cruises** – Several cruises are available *(p 254).*

★★ **New England Aquarium** – *Central Wharf. Open Jul–Labor Day Mon–Fri 9am–6pm (Wed & Thu 8pm), weekends 9am–7pm. Rest of the year Mon–Fri 9am–5pm (Thu 8pm), weekends 9am–6pm. $8.50.* ✕ ☎617-973-5200. The interior of the aquarium, illuminated mainly by the light from displays and exhibit tanks, creates the illusion of being underwater. Over 70 exhibits of fishes and animals are arranged according to the type of environment in which they live: temperate, fresh, cold and tropical waters. Sea horses, primitive fish, flashlight fish, penguins and an electric eel number among the more unusual animals.

A 4-story, 187,000-gallon **ocean tank** containing a re-creation of a Caribbean coral reef dominates the center of the aquarium. As visitors descend the ramp encircling this glass-enclosed world, they can watch sharks, sea turtles, moray eels and the many species of fish that inhabit the tank. In the Edge of the Sea Tidepool (third level) youngsters are invited to handle crabs, sea stars and urchins. Shows featuring California sea lions take place on the **Discovery**, a vessel berthed next to the aquarium.

★ **Rowes Wharf** – From the harbor this sprawling multi-use complex (1987, Skidmore, Owings and Merrill) functions as a dramatic waterfront facade for the downtown area. The brick complex, comprising the luxury Boston Harbor Hotel, residences and offices, was designed to harmonize with its surroundings, as evidenced by its three wharf-like extensions and the maximum 15-story height. The monumental entrance arch offers views of the harbor and waterfront access. Note the delightful airport water-shuttle *(p 102)* pavilion capped by an attractive dome.

Immediately to the north and east of the wharf loom two ensembles—both by eminent contemporary architects—that contrast markedly with the scale and style of the waterfront's traditional architecture: **Harbor Towers [J]** (1971, I.M. Pei and Partners), a pair of 40-story concrete blocks, and **International Place [K]** (1987, Burgee and Johnson), a 2.6-acre complex dominated by a graceless cylindrical tower.

**Tea Party Ship** – *Map p 101* **[FZ]**. *Congress St Bridge. Open Mar–Nov daily 9am–5pm. Closed Thanksgiving Day. $6.* ☎617-338-1773. A full-size replica of the brig *Beaver*, one of the original tea ships that was boarded by marauding "Indians" on December 16, 1773, is berthed at the pier on Congress Street. The museum alongside the ship features pictures, documents, a model of 18C Boston and a video *(12min)* that illustrate the Boston Tea Party and events leading to the Revolution.

## ★★ ④ BACK BAY  *Map p 116*

Hailed by architectural critic Lewis Mumford as "the outstanding achievement in American urban planning for the 19C," fashionable Back Bay presents contrasting faces. Its well-preserved historic district of 19C town houses lies in the shadow of a bustling high-rise sector that exemplifies the best and the worst of 20C planning.

**Historical Notes** – Back Bay was once an expanse of mud flats submerged at high tide by the Charles River estuary. In the early 19C construction of a 1.5mi tidal mill dam along present-day Beacon Street disrupted the area's natural drainage, creating acres of foul swampland. By mid-century this threat to public health and the need for additional housing provided the impetus for the most ambitious of Boston's landfill projects. From 1857 to the 1890s, more than 450 acres—contained within the present-day boundaries of the Charles River, the Public Garden, Huntington and Massachusetts Avenues—were reclaimed. For over 30 years, 3500 carloads of earth a day from gravel pits 9mi away were dumped into the swamp.

Architect Arthur Gilman's master plan called for five east-west axes, the grandest being Commonwealth Avenue, a wide Parisian-style boulevard divided by a central planted mall. To the north Copley Square functioned as the principal public space and a grand setting for prominent civic institutions. Stately rows of 4-5 story mansions and town houses, punctuated by towering churches sprung up along the rectilinear streets.

Back Bay's early residential architecture reflects contemporary French tastes, as evidenced by the omnipresent mansard roof, the controlled building height and a unified streetscape. As construction progressed architects adopted the period's prevailing revival styles (Gothic, Chateauesque, Richardsonian Romanesque, Italian Renaissance, Georgian) as exemplified in buildings erected after the 1870s in the area west of Dartmouth Street.

Back Bay's east end near the Public Garden, boasting tony boutiques, watering holes and the area's finest residences, has a decidedly upscale flavor. The Kenmore Square area attracts a mixed crowd of students and young urban dwellers to its funky shops, bookstores and the Tower Records megastore *(360 Newbury St)*. Art enthusiasts will enjoy gallery hopping along Newbury Street and viewing a show at the Institute of Contemporary Art *(p 123)*. The riverfront Esplanade *(p 117)* to the north functions as a playground and outdoor entertainment forum.

BOSTON

South of the fast-paced Boylston Street corridor, Back Bay takes on a dramatically different appearance. Monumental redevelopment schemes of varying quality, such as the Prudential Center, Copley Place and the Christian Science Center, create a decidedly 20C scale and flavor. Here, buildings of cement and steel offer a striking counterpoint to the low-scale brick universe of the 19C residential streets.

## Walking Tour    *1/2 day. Ⓣ Copley.*

★★ **Copley Square** – Named for painter John Singleton Copley, Back Bay's principal public square showcases some of the city's most celebrated architectural treasures. The former railroad yard was transformed into the Back Bay's civic center in the 1870s and 80s with the construction of Boston's finest 19C public buildings. Today the square's east end is dominated by the contrasting silhouettes of massive Trinity Church and soaring John Hancock Tower. To the south rises the sober limestone facade of posh Copley Plaza Hotel (1912), designed in Renaissance Revival style by Henry J. Hardenbergh, architect of New York's Plaza Hotel. The handsome 19C facade of the Boston Public Library graces the west side, while the New Old South Church, in the northwest corner, adds exoticism to the ensemble.

★★★ **Trinity Church** – *Open year-round daily 8am–6pm.* ☎617/536-0944. Recognized as the masterpiece of architect Henry H. Richardson, this imposing granite and sandstone pile (1877) initiated the popular style known as Richardsonian Romanesque in America. Richardson studied at the Ecole des Beaux-Arts in Paris, where he was impressed by the power and richness of the Romanesque style. His successful designs for Trinity Church reveal this influence. A massive central tower, inspired by one of the towers of the Old Cathedral in Salamanca, Spain, dominates the church; the west porch, influenced by the church of St-Trophime in Arles, France, is carved with statues and friezes representing biblical figures.

Richardson chose John La Farge to oversee the decoration inside. The lavishly painted walls, murals, paneled ceilings and small lunettes above the high, tower windows, are among the best works executed by La Farge. Intricately carved scenes depicting the life of Christ and the figures of past preachers adorn the pulpit, dedicated in 1916. The richly decorated chancel, designed in 1938, appears to be illuminated solely by light reflecting from the metal leaf that covers the ceiling.

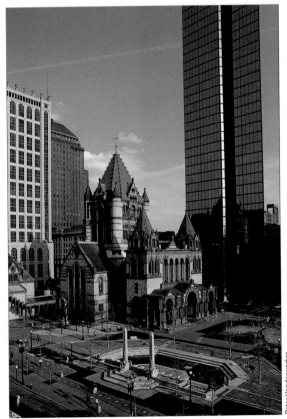

Trinity Church plaza

★★ **John Hancock Tower** – *Enter on St. James Ave.* This striking 60-story slab, sheathed in 10,344 units of .5in-thick tempered glass, was designed by I. M. Pei. Since completion, Hancock Tower (1975) has reigned as New England's tallest skyscraper. The unusual rhomboid shape creates a variety of profiles, depending on one's vantage point. From the opposite side of Boylston Street, the tower appears one dimensional. From other angles it is a gigantic mirror reflecting the sky and its venerable neighbors, notably Trinity Church and the old John Hancock Building (1947), whose pyramidal summit is topped by a functioning weather beacon.

**The Observatory** – *Open year-round Mon–Sat 9am–10pm, Sun 10am–10pm. (Nov–Apr Sun noon–10pm). Closed Thanksgiving Day, Dec 25. $3.50.* ⏱ 🅿 ☎617-247-1977. From the 60th floor sweeping **views**★★★ of the city and its environs unfold. Touch screens allow visitors to zoom in and identify landmarks. An insightful commentary on Boston's history is narrated by eminent architectural historian Walter Muir Whitehill and a topographic map is used to recount the city's exciting Revolutionary times in a presentation entitled "Boston 1775" *(16min).*

★★ **Boston Public Library** – *Dartmouth St entrance on Copley Sq. Open year-round Mon–Fri 9am–9pm, Sat 9am–5pm, Sun1–5pm. Closed major holidays & Sun mid-Jun–mid-Sept.* ☎617/536-5400. Widely considered the exemplar of Renaissance Revival style, this handsome building (1895, McKim, Mead and White) influenced countless public edifices in the US for over half a century. The granite facade sports elaborate wrought-iron lanterns, relief panels by Augustus Saint-Gaudens, and an elegant row of second-story arched windows. Daniel Chester French, sculptor of the seated Lincoln on the Mall in Washington DC, crafted the bronze doors dominating the vestibule. Beyond, the **grand entry,** with its two-tiered monumental staircase, is faced with yellow Siena marble and features romantic mural paintings *(The Muses)* by French artist Puvis de Chavannes. Pause on the landing to view the peaceful **courtyard** *(accessible from ground floor),* a popular haven for readers and lunchers. Visitors may wander through the cavernous rooms on the upper floors to admire murals executed by Edwin Abbey *(Quest of the Holy Grail; delivery room, 2nd floor)* and John Singer Sargent *(Judaism and Christianity; 3rd floor corridor). Visibility of 2nd- and 3rd-floor murals may be hampered by poor lighting.*

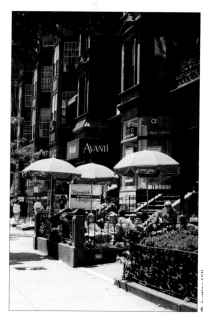

Newberry Street

© Justine Hill

Fronting Boylston Street, the stark granite addition to the library was designed by renowned architect Philip Johnson as a contemporary complement to the venerable McKim, Mead and White edifice.

Across Boylston Street rises the picturesque **New Old South Church** (1874, Cummings and Sears), replete with a lofty bell tower, a Venetian-style cupola and a profusion of Italian Gothic detailing. The Boston Marathon ends at this church.

> *Turn right on Exeter St and right on Newbury St.*

★ **Newbury Street** – Originally a quiet residential street, Newbury now reigns as the city's most exclusive shopping district. Converted town houses sport glass storefronts showcasing the city's finest boutiques, antique shops, specialty stores and cafes. The block between Exeter and Dartmouth Streets boasts a cluster of art galleries and a lively street scene, making it one of Back Bay's most pleasant pockets. Anchoring the corner of Newbury and Exeter, the fortress-like **Exeter Street Theatre Building [L]** (1884, Hartwell and W. C. Richardson)—originally the First Spiritualist Temple and, later, a popular movie house—clearly shows the influence of H. H. Richardson's nearby Trinity Church. The intersection at Newbury and Dartmouth, engulfed in a steady flow of vehicle and foot traffic, offers numerous visual delights: the former **Boston Arts Club [N]** (1881, W. R. Emerson), whose graceful hexagonal corner turret plays off the looming tower and cupola of the adjacent New Old South Church; the former **Hotel Victoria** (1886) with its Moorish window detailing; and a humorous trompe-l'œil **mural [3]** crowded with prominent Boston "personalities" *(wall facing parking lot).*

> *Turn left on Dartmouth St and continue to Commonwealth Ave.*

**★★ Commonwealth Avenue** – Inspired by the grand boulevards laid out in late 19C Paris under Napoléon III, this 200ft-wide thoroughfare was reputedly the address of choice for Boston's new rich. Today "Comm Ave" as it is known locally, retains much of its former grandeur and still connotes elegant living.

On the southwest corner *(no. 160)* extends the sprawling **Vendome** (1871, W. G. Preston), once Back Bay's most luxurious hotel and temporary home to such celebrities as Oscar Wilde, Mark Twain, Sarah Bernhardt and Ulysses S. Grant. This Second Empire behemoth, with regrettable upper-story transformations, was converted into condominiums in the 1970s. Facing the Vendome from its corner lot across the mall *(306 Dartmouth St)*, the outwardly restrained **Ames-Webster Mansion** (1872-1882) *(not open to the public)* preserves a lavish reception room considered by many as the Back Bay's most impressive interior space.

*Cross to the planted mall and continue east one block.*

Commonwealth Avenue's pleasant **mall**, lined with elm trees and punctuated by commemorative statues, offers a good vantage point to view a characteristic sampling of Back Bay houses on either side of the wide avenue.

Just before reaching the next corner, glance to the right for a view of **First Baptist Church★** (1872), a pivotal work by H.H. Richardson. The **frieze** adorning the upper portion of the bell tower is attributed to Frédéric-Auguste Bartholdi, designer of the Statue of Liberty. Note the trumpeting angels and figures representing the Sacraments, whose faces are reputedly modeled after well-known contemporaries such as Longfellow, Emerson and Hawthorne.

*Turn left on Clarendon St and right on Marlborough St.*

**Marlborough Street** – The most tranquil of Back Bay's five east-west axes, this generously shaded residential street lined with brick sidewalks and gas lamps exudes a romantic 19C ambience. At the end of the block on the right, note the bold concrete **First and Second Church** (1971, Paul Rudolph), which incorporates the tower and other remnants from the original 19C church that burned in 1968.

*Turn left on Berkeley St and right on Beacon St.*

**★ Beacon Street** – Favored by Boston's old rich in the 19C, this distinguished thoroughfare is flanked by grand town houses, many converted to colleges and cultural institutions. North-side residences are prized for their views of the Charles River. The **Gibson House** (*no. 137*), built in 1859, has retained its Victorian flavor and offers a rare glimpse into the tastes and lifestyle of an affluent Back Bay family *(visit by 1hr guided tour only, May–Oct Wed–Sun 1–3pm; rest of the year weekends only; closed major holidays; $4; ☎617-267-6338).*

*Continue to the corner of Beacon and Arlington Sts.*

At this point TV fans will enjoy making a detour to the nearby Bull and Finch Pub *(84 Beacon St; map p 107)* to glimpse the familiar stone and brick facade popularized in the successful television series **"Cheers."**
Near the corner of Beacon and Arlington Streets, the serpentine Fiedler footbridge leads to the Charles River **Esplanade★** *(map p 107).* Landscaped in the early 1930s, this delightful waterfront park extending over 10mi attracts joggers, rollerbladers, cyclists, picnickers and sailing enthusiasts. Outdoor performances given at the **Hatch Memorial Shell** are popular summertime events.

*Return to the corner of Beacon and Arlington Sts. Continue on Arlington St.*

**Arlington Street** – This elegant thoroughfare fronting the Public Garden boasts some of the Back Bay's earliest structures, such as the sandstone Second Empire mansion at **no. 12** (1860, Arthur Gilman), where society matron Mrs Montgomery Sears entertained leading artists of the day. On the other side of Commonwealth Avenue rises the 1981 addition to the venerable Ritz-Carlton Hotel.

*Cross to the Public Garden.*

★★ **Public Garden** – *Map p 107.* Entering from the Arlington Street gate, the eye is drawn to the equestrian **statue [4]** of George Washington (1878, Thomas Ball), which extends its gaze along the perfectly aligned Commonwealth Avenue. This 24-acre rectangular park, bounded by a handsome cast-iron fence, was reclaimed from swampy Back Bay in the 1830s for the purpose of creating a botanical garden. Today the popular retreat charms visitors with its flowering parterres, tree-lined footpaths and commemorative statuary. First launched in the 1870s, the beloved **swan boats** ply the tranquil waters of an artificial pond traversed by a whimsical suspension bridge and bordered with weeping willows. The "Make Way for Ducklings" statue grouping in the northeast section re-creates the title characters of Robert McCloskey's classic children's book.

Dianne Dietrich Leis

*Continue to the corner of Arlington and Boylston Sts.*

Standing sentinel over this heavily trafficked intersection is the sandstone **Arlington Street Church,** (Arthur Gilman). Begun in 1859, it holds the distinction of being the first building erected in the Back Bay. The church's Unitarian congregation takes pride in its long tradition of social and political activism.

*Turn right onto Boylston St.*

**Boylston Street** – Returning to this much-transformed 19C thoroughfare, the visitor is struck by the abrupt change in scale created by the imposing 20C buildings that line its south side. The festive **Berkeley Building★** (1905, Codman and Despredelle), a white terra-cotta and glass extravaganza topped by an obelisk-studded parapet, enlivens the corner lot at no. 420. Across the street at **234 Berkeley Street** stands the French-style stone and brick edifice (1863, W. G. Preston) that originally housed the Museum of Natural History. A glance north toward Newbury Street will reveal the massive Gothic Revival **Church of the Covenant** (1867, Upjohn), whose 236ft tower prevails as a familiar landmark.
The block between Berkeley and Clarendon Streets accommodates an oddly matched pair of high rises designed by prominent post-Modern architects: **222 Berkeley Street** (1991, Robert Stern) playfully refers to Boston architectural tradition (note for example the miniature State House dome capping the Boylston Street entrance); the more ostentatious **500 Boylston Street★** (1988, Burgee and Johnson), crowned with an oversized fanlight element and a row of urns, now figures as a prominent element of the Boston skyline.

From the corner of Boylston and Clarendon, pause to admire the striking **view★** of the glass Hancock tower mirroring the deconstructed forms of the Old Hancock and Trinity Church.

## Additional Sights in Back Bay

**Copley Place** – *Access via the Westin Hotel on southwest corner of Copley Sq.* Occupying an irregularly shaped site between the Back Bay and the South End, this controversial 9.5-acre, $500 million multi-use complex (1984, Architects Collaborative) comprises two luxury hotels (Westin and Marriott), four office buildings, an upscale mall (Neiman-Marcus and 100 shops and restaurants), apartments, a multi-screen cinema and a 1500-car garage.

Glass-covered pedestrian bridges link the complex to the Prudential Center and to the Westin Hotel, whose undistinguished facade closes the southwest corner of Copley Square.

**Prudential Center** – *Access from Boylston St.* One of Boston's major urban renewal projects of the 1960s, this 32-acre complex (Luckman and Assocs.) built at a cost of $150 million has been widely criticized for its uninspired architecture and alienating public spaces. The center was built over the railroad freight yards that long divided the Back Bay from the South End. Clustered around the 52-story **Prudential Tower**, "the Pru" comprises apartment high rises, the Sheraton Boston Hotel, a convention center, shops including major department stores (Lord and Taylor, Saks Fifth Avenue), restaurants and parking facilities. A long-awaited renovation begun in the 1980s has succeeded in infusing new life into the complex: an attractive shopping mall (over 50 shops and eateries) now interconnects the various buildings, and the entire complex is linked with the surrounding streets and with the tony Copley Place by means of sleek arcades and bridges. The enlarged **Hynes Convention Center** sports a handsome colonnade on its Boylston Street facade. **Skywalk**, an observation deck on the 50th floor of the tower, offers good *views* of the surroundings *(access from lower mall: at information desk turn right, then right again to glass doors for tower elevators; open year-round Mon–Sat 10am–10pm, Sun noon–10pm; closed Dec 25; $2; ☎617-859-0648).*

★★ **Christian Science Center** – *From Prudential Center, take Huntington Ave exit.* This stunning ensemble houses the world headquarters of the Christian Science Church. The Christian Science religion was founded in 1866 by Mary Baker Eddy following a serious injury from which she quickly recovered after meditating on a Gospel account of one of Jesus' healings. Mrs Eddy believed she had discovered the science of man's true relation with God, and that through the practice of Christian Science the individual could learn to overcome the ills that challenge mankind. After a decade of studying the Bible, she published *Science and Health with Key to the Scriptures*, the textbook of Christian Science. In 1879 Mrs Eddy and her students established the Church of Christ Scientist, which was reorganized as the First Church of Christ Scientist (The Mother Church) in 1892. The Christian Science Publishing Society was later founded to help carry the religion's word around the globe.

Today church members gather weekly to attend services during which passages from the Bible, and texts written by Mrs Eddy are read. *The Christian Science Monitor*, an international daily newspaper published by the Church of Christ Scientist since 1908, has correspondents around the globe and is highly respected for its objective news coverage.

**Visit** – *Open year-round Tue–Fri 10am–4pm, Sat noon–4pm, Sun 11:30am–2pm. Closed Sat Nov–May & major holidays. ☎617-450-3790.* Facing Massachusetts Avenue the grandiose **Mother Church Extension** (1904) features Renaissance-inspired elements such as the expansive entrance portico and a central dome rising 108ft. The Romanesque-style Mother Church (1894), with its rough granite facade and bell tower, is connected to the rear of the Extension. The interior is adorned with mosaics and stenciled frescoes. Enter the Publishing Society building (1933) to experience the **Mapparium [M3]**, a 30ft walk-through glass-paneled globe that represents the worldwide scope of the church in the 1930s *(open year-round Tue–Fri 9:30am–4pm, Sat noon–4pm; closed Sat Nov–May).*

The original complex was expanded in the 1970s by a group of architects led by **I.M. Pei**. The result is an extraordinary urban space infused with an elegant monumentality rarely found in 20C urbanism. Three bold concrete structures—the 26-story Administration Building, the porticoed Broadcasting Center and the fan-shaped Sunday School—stand like abstract sculptures around an enormous **reflecting pool** (670ft by 100ft). The graceful rolling of the water over the pool's rounded granite edges creates the illusion of boundlessness.

## THE MUSEUMS

★★★ **Museum of Fine Arts** – *Map p 100* [EZ]. *465 Huntington Ave, ⓣ Museum. Open year-round Tue–Sun 10am–4:45pm (9:45pm Wed–Fri). Closed Thanksgiving Day, Dec 24 & 25. $8. ▫ ╳ ⓰ ☎617-267-9300.* One of the country's leading museums, the Museum of Fine Arts (MFA) houses a comprehensive collection of holdings organized into eight distinct departments: Asiatic; Ancient Egyptian, Nubian and Near Eastern; Classical; European Decorative Arts and Sculpture; American Decorative Arts and Sculpture; Paintings; Contemporary Art; and Prints, Drawings and Photographs. The original building contains the bulk of the collections, while the newer West Wing displays 20C art and special exhibits.

## MUSEUM OF FINE ARTS

In the 19C Bostonians traveled abroad extensively and returned with art treasures for their private collections. These collections, together with works from the Boston Athenaeum *(p 105)* and Harvard University, formed the core of the museum's holdings in its early years. Officially opened in 1876 in Copley Square, the museum's first building proved inadequate by the turn of the century. More spacious quarters were provided with the construction of the present Neoclassical building (1909, Guy Lowell) with its impressive portal, columns and domes, in the Back Bay Fens. The need for expansion brought about the addition of the **West Wing** (1981). Sleek and modern in character, the 3-story granite structure designed by I. M. Pei and Partners features a 225ft galleria capped by a barrel-vaulted glass roof. The newer facility houses visitor services and gallery space for 20C art and traveling exhibits. *Throughout the galleries are specially commissioned sculpted seats, designed as functional works of art. Note that they are labelled: "Please be seated." Specific works mentioned on pp 120-121 may not be on display, given the museum's rotation policy. It is advisable to inquire in advance as to their exhibit status.*

★★★**Asiatic Department** – The Japanese and Chinese collections are exceptional. Works gathered by **Edward Morse, Ernest Fenollosa** and **Sturgis Bigelow** during their travels across Japan in the late 19C form the core collection. Displays also include selections from the distinguished **Hoyt Collection** of Chinese and Korean ceramics.

Japanese art began to develop in the 6C, when Buddhism arrived in Japan through Korea. Painting was a preferred medium. The MFA boasts fine examples of Japanese painting (13C-18C), including rare screens and handscrolls, such as the renowned *The Burning of the Sanjo Palace* (Heiji Monogatari Emaki), which portrays the violence of the Japanese civil wars. The decorative 17C screen *The Gay Quarters of Kyoto* presents a detailed record of the dress and activities of the times. Buddhism dominated sculpture as well; many of the museum's representations of Buddhas are displayed in a temple setting.

Highlighting the Chinese art section is an extensive collection of ceramics from the Neolithic (3rd millenium BC) through the Yuan dynasties. Two statues are interesting for their contrasting demeanor: a graceful limestone **Bodhisattva** (6C), and the magnificent polychromed wooden statue of **Kuan Yin** (12C), with its casual pose.

The galleries are also graced by a collection of rare **Korean celadons**, painted screens and statuary depicting the Buddhist mystical traditions of Tibet and Nepal and outstanding paintings, sculpture and glassware from India and the **Islamic cultures**.

On the museum grounds the **Japanese Garden** Tenshin-En exemplifies Karesansui-style garden art, in which the placement of large stones, plants and raked pebbles suggests natural scenes and forces.

★★ **Ancient Egyptian, Nubian and Near Eastern** – The bulk of the MFA's superb collection of Egyptian art, spanning 4,000 years of Egyptian civilization, came to the museum as a result of a 40-year MFA/Harvard expedition to Egypt and the Sudan beginning in 1905. Excavations conducted by the expedition at Giza yielded **Old Kingdom** treasures (2778-2360 BC) rivaled only by the Egyptian Museum in Cairo. Among the many pieces of sculpture excavated from the tombs and temples of the Fourth Dynasty is **King Mycerinus** and his queen **Kha-merer-hebty II**, one of the oldest extant statues portraying a couple. Dating from the same period is the realistic portrait bust of **Prince Ankh-haf**.

The expedition's digs at El Bersheh and in the Sudan produced treasures from the more recent Twelfth Dynasty: the well-preserved paintings on the coffins of **Prince Djehutynekht and his wife**, the black granite statue of **Lady Sennuwy**, painted wooden servant models designed to serve the dead in eternity, and Meroitic jewelry from Meroë, capital of the former Kushite (Ethiopia) civilization. In the **Near Eastern** section, note the collection of cylindrical **seals** that were skillfully carved by Mesopotamian craftsmen.

★★ **Classical Department** – The cameos, coins, bronzes and collection of Greek vases (5C BC) were gathered by **Edward Perry Warren**, curator of the department in the late 19C and early 20C. Under his guidance the department acquired the major portion of its holdings, which include Bronze Age ceramics and Minoan seal stones; a three-sided marble bas-relief from the Greek Isle of Thasos, and the ivory and gold statue of the **Minoan Snake Goddess or Priestess** (1600-1500 BC).

★★ **American Art** – The American collection is represented primarily by paintings, furnishings and silver. Portraiture dominated American painting in the 17C, as is illustrated by the portrait of *Robert Gibbs*, painted by an unknown artist. Prominent among the 18C portraitists were Gilbert Stuart *(p 33)*, whose paintings of George and Martha Washington (the *Athenaeum Portraits*) are exhibited alternately at the National Portrait Gallery in Washington DC and at the MFA, and John Singleton Copley *(p 33)*, who painted wealthy and noted Bostonians of his day (*Samuel Adams* and *Paul Revere*).

In the 19C painters turned their attention to nature, and in particular to the sea. The adventure, excitement and beauty of the sea were portrayed on canvas by Fitz Hugh Lane *(Boston Harbor; Owl's Head, Penobscot Bay, Maine)*, Albert Pinkham Ryder, and Winslow Homer *(Fog Warning; Lookout–"All's Well")*. During the same era John Singer Sargent and Mary Cassatt *(At the Opera)*, who was influenced by the Impressionists, lived abroad. Sargent's *The Daughters of Edward Darley Boit* was inspired by *Las Meninas* of Velázquez.

Works by Georgia O'Keeffe *(White Rose with Larkspur No. 2)*, Joseph Stella *(Old Brooklyn Bridge)* and Jackson Pollock, a number of canvases by noted color field artist Morris Louis and contemporary exhibits showcase mid- to late-20C art.

Among the MFA's collection of **American Decorative Arts** is a large and representative group of furniture made by the early American craftsmen of Boston, New York, Newport and Philadelphia. Many pieces are from the rich **M. and M. Karolik Collection**. The museum's extensive collection of early American silver includes the historic **Liberty Bowl** (1768) made by Paul Revere and dedicated to the members of the Massachusetts legislature who refused to rescind a letter to the colonies protesting against the Crown.

**European Decorative Arts** – Period rooms, including an English Tudor paneled room (15C), a French Louis XVI salon and the Hamilton Palace Room fill these galleries. Note the medieval statues carved from wood and ivory, and the enamels.

On the first floor, in a special suite of rooms, is the **Forsyth Wickes Collection** of 18C French furnishings, porcelain, paintings, watercolors and sculpture. The graceful red-and-gold-laquered writing desk was made for Queen Marie Antoinette.

Courtesy Museum of Fine Arts, Boston

*The Daughters of Edward Darley Boit* (1882) by John Singer Sargent

★★ **European Painting** – Principal European schools from the Middle Ages to the present are represented. A Catalonian chapel with 12C apse frescoe and 15C paintings is interesting for its Romanesque decoration. From the Flemish school note *St Luke Painting the Virgin* (15C) by Rogier Van der Weyden. Nearby galleries display Tiepolo's *Time Unveiling Truth,* a powerful and symbolic analogy, and portraits by Rembrandt. The section devoted to the Spanish school contains paintings by Goya, El Greco *(Fray Felix),* Velázquez and Zurbarán *(Saint Francis).*

Bostonians' preference for the Romantics (Delacroix), realists (Courbet), the Barbizon school (Corot), Impressionists and post-Impressionists brought a distinguished group of 19C French paintings to the MFA. Among the masters represented are: Renoir *(Bal à Bougival),* Monet *(La Japonaise; Haystacks; Rouen Cathedral),* Degas *(Carriage at the Races),* Manet *(Execution of Maximillian; The Street Singer),* Van Gogh *(The Postman Joseph Roulin),* Cézanne *(Madame Cézanne in a Red Armchair).* Gauguin's *D'où venons-nous? Que sommes-nous? Où allons-nous?* (Where do we come from? What are we? Where are we going?) treats the eternal questions regarding mankind's life and destiny. Millet's sympathetic rendering of the peasant is illustrated in *The Sower* and in his many other works exhibited in the museum.

More recent paintings by **20C artists**, including Picasso and Frida Kahlo, are displayed in a first-floor gallery. Picasso's strong anti-war sentiments are expressed in his bold, vibrantly colored *Rape of the Sabine Women.*

★★★ **Isabella Stewart Gardner Museum** – *Map p 100* [EZ]. *280 The Fenway.* Ⓣ *Museum. Open year-round Tue–Sun 11am–5pm. Closed Jan 1, Thanksgiving Day, Dec 25. $7. Guided tours (1hr) available Fri 2:30pm. Concerts Sept–May weekends 1:30pm.* ✗ & *☎617-566-1401.* Isabella Stewart Gardner, born in New York City in 1840, became a Bostonian when she married financier Jack Lowell Gardner. Daring and vivacious, Mrs Gardner was a free spirit whose actions were often frowned upon by other members of Boston's staid society. Art and music were her life-long delights, and in 1899 she initiated the construction of **Fenway Court** to house her fabulous art collection, part of which she gathered in Europe, and part of which was acquired in the US by her agents.

The galleries of Fenway Court, permanently arranged by Mrs Gardner herself, contain furnishings, textiles, paintings and sculpture from her collections. Nothing has been changed since her death; the galleries, opening onto flower gardens in the courtyard, create an impression of continual summer.

**Ground Floor** – In the **Spanish Cloister** ceramic tiles from a 17C Mexican church cover the walls, enhancing John Singer Sargent's dramatic painting, *El Jaleo.*

The **Courtyard**, with its refreshing gardens, Venetian window frames and balconies abrim with fresh flowers, provides a graceful haven in the city. Classical sculptures surround an ancient Roman mosaic pavement (2C) from the town of Livia. In the **small galleries** off the courtyard is an exhibit of 19C and 20C French and American paintings, including portraits by Degas and Manet, and landscapes by Whistler, Matisse and Sargent. The Yellow Room houses *The Terrace of St Tropez,* the first canvas by Henri Matisse ever to enter an American museum.

**Second Floor** – The room of **early Italian paintings** contains Simone Martini's altarpiece *Madonna and Child with Four Saints,* two allegorical panels by Pesellino, Fra Angelico's *Death and Assumption of the Virgin* and Gentile Bellini's delicately executed *Turkish Artist.* The fresco of Hercules is the only fresco by Piero della Francesca outside of Italy.

The **Raphael Room** exhibits two of the Italian painter's works: a portrait of *Count Tommaso Inghirami* and a *Pietà.* The *Annunciation* exemplifies the technique of linear perspective developed in the 15C. Other works in the room include Botticelli's *Tragedy of Lucretia* and Giovanni Bellini's *Madonna and Child.*

Adjacent to the Raphael Room, in the **Short Gallery,** is Anders Zorn's spirited painting of Mrs Gardner at the Palazzo Barbaros in Venice.

Courtyard, Isabella Stewart Gardner Museum

John Kennard/Isabella Stewart Gardner Museum

*Continue through the Little Salon, decorated with 18C Venetian paneling and 17C tapestries, to the Tapestry Room.*

The **Tapestry Room** is the setting for concerts held at Fenway Court. On an easel sits *Santa Engracia* by Bermejo (15C Spain). There are also lovely 16C tapestries. Rubens' masterful portrayal of *Thomas Howard, Earl of Arundel,* and works by Hans Holbein and Anthony Van Dyck *(Lady with a Rose)* grace the **Dutch Room.**

**Third Floor** – From the **Veronese Room** with its Spanish and Venetian tooled and painted leather wall coverings, enter the **Titian Room,** which contains one of Titian's masterpieces, the sensual *Rape of Europa,* painted for Philip II of Spain.
In the **Long Gallery** the life-size terra-cotta statue of the *Virgin Adoring the Child,* attributed to Matteo Civitali, provides a beautiful example of Renaissance sculpture. On the wall above a large sideboard hangs Botticelli's *Madonna and Child of the Eucharist* (1410, the "Chigi Madonna"), which hung in the Chigi palace in Rome until the 19C. *A Lady of Fashion,* by Uccello, is characteristic of portrait art in 15C Florence.
The **Gothic Room** contains a full-length portrait of *Mrs. Gardner* (1888) painted by her friend John Singer Sargent. Nearby is a small panel entitled *The Presentation of the Infant Jesus in the Temple,* which has been attributed to Giotto, the master of the 14C Florentine school.

★★ **Children's Museum** – *Map p 101* [**FZ M⁴**]. *300 Congress St at Museum Wharf.* ⊤ *South Station. Open late May–Labor Day daily 10am–5pm (Fri 9pm), rest of the year closed Mon. Closed Jan 1, Thanksgiving Day, Dec 25. $7 ($1 Fri 5–9pm).* ⌖ ☎*617-426-8855.* This museum, conceived exclusively for children, will delight adults as well. Four floors of interactive exhibits include Teen Tokyo, where visitors can ride a Japanese subway car; Science Playground, where children can experiment with physics; and TV & ME, where youngsters can see themselves on television. Playspace welcomes toddlers and preschoolers.

★★ **Boston Museum of Science** – *Map p 101* [**FY**]. *Msgr O'Brien Hwy (Rte 28).* ⊤ *Science Park. Open year-round daily 9am–5pm (Fri 9pm). Closed Thanksgiving Day & Dec 25. $7.* ⌖⌖⌖ ☎*617-723-2500.* Located in a modern building beside the Charles River, the museum invites children and adults to explore the world of science and technology. The kaleidoscopic array of push-button displays and life-size models allows visitors to participate in activities ranging from playing with lightning produced by a Van de Graaff generator to pretending to fly through the cosmos in models of American spacecraft. Visitors can also watch new chicks hatch, hear dinosaurs roar, and peer through the world's largest magnifying glass. The **Charles Hayden Planetarium** presents programs that explore the world of stars, galaxies, pulsars, clusters, quasars and other phenomena of outer space. There are usually two or more programs daily, in addition to laser shows *(call for schedule)*.

★ **Computer Museum** – *Map p 101* [FZ **M⁴**]. *300 Congress St at Museum Wharf.* Ⓣ *South Station. Open mid-Jun–Labor Day daily 10am–6pm, rest of the year Tue–Sun 10am–5pm. Closed Jan 1, Thanksgiving Day, Dec 25. $7.* Ⓐ ☎*617-423-6758.* Computer-literate or not, visitors to the museum will marvel at the wonders of high technology housed here. A gigantic 2-story **Walk-Through Computer** bares the insides of one of these machines and explains in comprehensive, and comprehensible, detail how it works. In **Tools and Toys: The Amazing Personal Computer**, visitors can test-drive PC's themselves, trying out graphics programs or entering the virtual reality of a test flight. The **People and Computers** gallery traces the incredible advances made in technology, from the unwieldy early behemoths of the 1940s to the portable home computers of today. In **Robots and Smart Machines** banks of computers prove that these intelligent machines can hear, see, and even be used to create life.

**Institute of Contemporary of Art** – *Map p 116. 955 Boylston St.* Ⓣ *Hynes/ICA. Open year-round Wed–Sun noon–5pm (Wed, Thu 9pm). Closed major holidays. $5 (free admission Wed & Thu 5–9pm).* Ⓔ ☎*617-266-5152.* This Richardsonian building, which once housed a police station, has been renovated into modern gallery space. The institute presents several multimedia programs that explore the trends and themes in American and international contemporary art. Documentaries complementing the exhibits are shown in the ICA theater.

★ **Museum at the John Fitzgerald Kennedy Library** – *Map p 127. Columbia Point in Dorchester, near the University of Massachusetts.* Ⓣ *JFK/U Mass, .5mi from the museum; free shuttle bus available. Open year-round daily 9am–5pm. Closed Jan 1, Thanksgiving Day, Dec 25. $6.* ✕ Ⓐ Ⓔ ☎*617-929-4523.* This sleek, white concrete and glass structure, a monument to the late President John F. Kennedy, was designed by architect I. M. Pei. The building's neat, sharp lines seem to point across the harbor to the impressive view of the Boston skyline. Approximately one-third of the library building is reserved for the **contemplation pavilion**, a 9-story gray glass pavilion that contains simply an American flag, a bench and quotations from President Kennedy on the wall.

The tour begins with a film *(17min)* on the early life of JFK. In a series of exhibit bays, personal memorabilia and historic videos trace the life and accomplishments of John Kennedy. The archives on the upper floors house thousands of photos, tapes and taped interviews with people who knew Kennedy.

Fred Sieb Photography

John F. Kennedy Library

## ★ CHARLESTOWN   *Map p 101* [FY]

Located on a hill across the Charles River, Charlestown is easily recognized by its tall stone obelisk, the Bunker Hill Monument. The *USS Constitution* sits in its permanent berth at a wharf in the Navy Yard. Charlestown's colonial dwellings were destroyed by the British during the Battle of Bunker Hill, and replaced following the Revolution by the rows of Federal-style houses that line the streets leading to the monument. A large-scale renovation program begun in the 1980s transformed the Navy Yard into a waterfront complex containing luxury apartments, offices and marinas. *Ferries depart from Boston's Long Wharf to Pier 4 in the Charlestown Navy Yard year-round Mon–Fri 6:30am–8pm, Sat 10am–6pm. $1 (one-way). &. Boston Harbor Cruises.* ☎617-227-4321.

**Bunker Hill Monument** – *Open year-round daily 9am–5pm.* ☎*617-242-5601.* This 221ft granite obelisk, designed by Solomon Willard, marks the site of the American redoubt during the Battle of Bunker Hill *(p 97)*. The observatory, reached by a 294-step winding stairway, offers a **view★** of Charlestown, Boston and the harbor.

**Bunker Hill Pavilion** – *Open Jun–Aug daily 9:30am–5pm; Apr–May & Sept–Nov daily 9:30am–4pm. Closed Thanksgiving Day. $3.* & ▣ ☎617-241-7575. The historic Battle of Bunker Hill, as seen by an American militiaman and a British soldier, is presented in a multimedia program entitled "Whites of their Eyes" *(30min, shown continuously).*

**Charlestown Navy Yard** – Construction of the US Naval Shipyard at Charlestown in 1800 made this city a shipbuilding center. Thirty of the yard's 130 acres, including the site of the *USS Constitution* and its museum, were designated a part of the Boston National Historic Park after the yard was closed in 1974.

*Visitor Center* – *Open Jun–Aug daily 9am–6pm, rest of the year daily 9am–5pm.* & ☎617-242-5601. Information on the Navy Yard, the Freedom Trail and the Boston National Historic Park is available here. Park rangers conduct free tours of the Navy Yard *(call for schedule)*. Berthed a short distance from the *USS Constitution* is the **USS Cassin Young**, a World War II destroyer similar to the type built here in the 1930s and 40s *(open year-round daily 10am–5pm, weather permitting; for guided tours, apply on ship)*.

★★ **The USS Constitution** – *Visit by guided tour (25min) only, year-round daily 9:30am–3:50pm. Self-guided tours daily year-round 3:50pm–dusk.* & ☎617-242-5670. The *USS Constitution*, the pride of the American fleet, is the oldest commissioned warship afloat. Authorized by Congress in 1794, this 44-gun frigate designed by Joshua Humphreys and Josiah Fox was constructed from timbers provided by states from Georgia to Maine. Within four years after being built, the *Constitution* sailed to the Mediterranean at the head of the American Fleet, to participate in the Tripolitan War, which ended the payment of tribute by American shipping to the Barbary pirates. Distinguished for the role she played in the war, the *Constitution* nevertheless won her greatest victories during the War of 1812 against the British: capturing the *HMS Guerrière* and the *Java* in 1812, and simultaneously seizing the *Cyane* and the *Levante* three years later. It was during the battle with the *Guerrière*, when enemy fire seemed to bounce off her planking without causing damage, that the *Constitution* was given her nickname *"Old Ironsides."* By 1830, after having survived 40 military engagements, the *Constitution* was declared unseaworthy and destined for the scrap heap. Oliver Wendell Holmes's poem *Old Ironsides* aroused such strong popular sentiment in favor of the ship that funds were appropriated to rebuild it. Reconstructed in 1905, 1913 and 1973, the ship has retained only 18 percent of her original timbers.

**USS Constitution Museum** [M⁵] – *Pier 1. Open Jun–Labor Day daily 10am–5:30pm; Mar–May & mid-Sept–Nov 5pm; Dec–Feb 3pm. Closed major holidays. $4.* ✗ & ☎617-426-1812. Exhibits in the granite building (designed by Alexander Parris) trace the history of *Old Ironsides* from 1794 to the present.

---

*Sailing vessels are distinguished by the type of sail and the number of masts they carry. A sloop is a one-masted, fore-and-aft-rigged vessel. A schooner carries two or more masts; all its sails are fore-and-aft rigged.*

---

## BROOKLINE   *Map p 126*

The affluent suburb of Brookline (pop 51,860) was the birthplace of **John Fitzgerald Kennedy** (1917-1963), the 35th President of the US. Ever since 1870 Boston has made six attempts, unsuccessfully, to annex Brookline, one of the largest towns in Massachusetts and a pleasant residential community, located only 4mi to the southwest from the center of the city's downtown area.

**John Fitzgerald Kennedy National Historic Site** – *83 Beals St. Visit by guided tour (30min) only, year-round Wed–Sun 10am–4:30pm. Closed Jan 1, Thanksgiving Day, Dec 25. $1.* ▣ ☎617-566-7937. Joseph and Rose Kennedy lived in this modest wooden house from 1914 to 1921, a period during which four of their children, including John, were born. The house is restored to its 1917 appearance.

## ADDITIONAL SIGHTS

★ **South End** – *Map p 116.* Situated literally and figuratively on the other side of the tracks with respect to upscale Back Bay, the long-neglected South End is on its way to becoming one of Boston's most vibrant inner-city neighborhoods. This English-style community of bowfronted brick row houses developed between the 1840s and 1870s in the newly reclaimed area along the "neck" connecting Boston's original peninsula to the mainland. After a short period of popularity, the district fell into decline, and by the end of the century, shabby rooming houses and derelict apartments abounded, inhabited largely by transients and immigrants.

In recent decades pockets of the South End have undergone gentrification, attracting businesses and cultural institutions, such as the **Boston Center for the Arts** *(541 Tremont St)*, housed in the landmark Cyclorama Building (1884). Very much in transition, the South End remains a socially and culturally mixed neighborhood. The vicinity of Tremont and Clarendon Streets best exemplifies the rejuvenation, with its meticulously restored row houses, fashionable restaurants and specialty shops. Intimate **Union Park**, the finest of the South End's remaining oval-shaped residential parks, is bordered by handsome row houses with high stoops sporting fanciful cast-iron and brownstone balustrades.

**Chinatown** – *Map p 101* [FZ]. Alive with distinctive dialects, scents and traditions, this small ethnic enclave functions as the cultural and commercial hub for New England's Chinese and Chinese-American communities. Street signs displaying oriental calligraphy, pagoda-roofed telephone booths, markets overflowing with exotic foods, shops stocked with jade and porcelain and tempting eateries enliven this otherwise bleak commercial area wedged between the Theater District, the downtown shopping zone and the Massachusetts Turnpike. Beach Street, Chinatown's main thoroughfare, is spanned by a monumental **gateway** *(at Hudson St)*. Nearby **Tyler Street** boasts numerous popular restaurants serving oriental fare.

The month-long celebration of the Chinese New Year, beginning in late January or early February, is Chinatown's major annual festival. Chinese residents traditionally hold a colorful parade on the first Sunday of their New Year.

**Bay Village** – *Map p 101* [FZ]. This quaint residential enclave, tucked away in the shadow of the Park Square area and the sometimes-seedy Theater District, rose on reclaimed mud flats between 1825 and 1840 as a speculative venture. Many of the 2-story brick row houses along Church, Melrose and Fayette Streets have been lovingly restored to their 19C appearance.

**Franklin Park Zoo** – *Map p 126. Intersection of Blue Hill Ave and Columbia Rd. From Boston take Rte 1 south to Rte 203, then follow the signs. Open year-round daily 9am–4:30pm (Sat & Sun 5pm). Closed Jan 1, Thanksgiving Day, Dec 25. $5.* ✕ ⏁ ▯ *☎617-442-2002.* Franklin Park is part of Boston's Emerald Necklace of parks. Principal attractions of the zoo include A Bird's World, housing naturalistic bird environments; a free-flight outdoor aviary *(open summer only);* the children's petting zoo, featuring informal demonstrations; and the Range, showcasing antelope, horses and other hoofed animals. The **African Tropical Forest Pavilion★** provides a sensory and educational foray into one of the planet's environmentally threatened areas. The humid climate, dense vegetation and native animal sounds give visitors a taste of life in the rain forest of equatorial Africa.

**Arnold Arboretum of Harvard University** – *Map p 126. Near the Zoo, at The Arborway, Jamaica Plain. Open year-round daily dawn–dusk. ☎617-524-1718.* This 265-acre arboretum is an outdoor research-educational facility administered by Harvard University and the Department of Parks. Founded in 1872 the arboretum has evolved into a living museum of approximately 7,000 species of ornamental trees and shrubs. It is especially beautiful in May and June when the delicate scents of blooming lilacs, azaleas, rhododendrons and magnolias fill the air.

**Suggested walks:** Jamaica Plain Gate to pond area *(15min);* pond area to Bonsai House *(10min);* Bonsai House to Bussey Hill *(15min),* where there is a panorama of the arboretum.

## EXCURSIONS

★★ **Cambridge** – *Description p 129.*

★★ **Lexington** – *11mi northwest of Boston. Description p 150.*

★★ **Concord** – *17mi northwest of Boston. Description p 143.*

**Medford** – *Map p 126. Pop 57,407.* This residential suburb north of Boston is the home of **Tufts University**.

**Isaac Royall House** – *15 George St. Visit by guided tour (45min) only, May–Oct Tue–Thu & Sat–Sun 2–5pm. $3. ☎617-396-9032. The house has no interior lighting and may be dark on overcast days.* This gracious 3-story mansion exemplifies the Georgian architectural style in vogue during the colonial period. The residence was built by wealthy British merchant Isaac Royall Sr, who moved his household (including 27 slaves) here from the West Indies in 1732. When his Loyalist son Isaac Jr fled to Halifax in the early days of the Revolution, the house was con-

# GREATER BOSTON

▶ Golf course

NEWBURYPORT / PORTSMOUTH (NH) / GLOUCESTER

BEVERLY

Elliott St.

Andover St.

MASSACHUSETTS

Main St.

Pillings Pond

Summer

Lynnfield

Suntaug Lake

Newburyport Tpk.

PEABODY

North St.

Bridge St.

SALEM

MARBLEHEAD
Lee Mansion

Fort Sewall

Washington St.

Abbot Hall

Pleasant St.

Marblehead Neck

Water St.

Walden Pond

Spring Pond

Highland Ave.

Loring

Lafayette St.

Atlantic Ave.

Breakheart Reservation

Lynn Woods Reservation
Breeds Pond

Broadway

Eastern Ave.

Paradise St.

Swampscott

Humphrey St.

Falls

Main St.

Bennett St.

Central St.

Saugus Iron Works ★

SAUGUS

LYNN

Western

Saugus River

Nahant Bay

MELROSE

Hwy.

Pines

Tpk.

River

Salem

Shore Rd.

Nahant

Eastern Ave.

Squire

Rd.

North

BROAD SOUND

MASSACHUSETTS

REVERE

Lea-Burbank Hwy.

BAY

EVERETT

107

Revere Beach Pkwy.

CHELSEA

Boston Expwy.

Winthrop

Northeast

LOGAN INTERNATIONAL

Inner Harbor

Tunnel to open late 1995
(commercial traffic only)

Harbor Islands

Georges Island

Dorchester Bay

University of Mass. (Boston)

Museum at the
J. F. K. Library ★

South Bay

Hancock St.

Granite Ave.

HINGHAM BAY

Nantasket Beach

Hull Ave.

QUINCY BAY

Adams St.

Adams NHS ★

QUINCY

Southern Artery

★ World's End

G. Washington Blvd.

Broad Cove Rd.

Rockland St.

United First
Parish Church

Washington St.

Quincy

Bridge St.

Weymouth Fore River

Lincoln St.

Otis

Summer

HINGHAM

★ Old Ship Church

East St.

Chief Justice
Cushing Hwy.

BRAINTREE

Ave.

WEYMOUTH

Washington

Union St.

Whitmans Pond

Main St.

Wompatuck State Park

Great Pond

St.

0    2 mi
0  3 km

PLYMOUTH ∼ CAPE COD

fiscated and served as the headquarters for Gen John Stark *(p 191)* before the 1776 British evacuation. Inside, some of the original 18C woodwork has been preserved. Rooms are appointed with lovely period pieces, including a fine collection of 18C clocks. The 2-story slave quarters beside the mansion is reputedly the only structure of its kind remaining in the northern US.

**Saugus** – *Map p 127*. Pop 25,549. The buildings of the Saugus Iron Works, which operated in this small town north of Boston in the 17C, were reconstructed in 1954 to appear as they did during the colonial period, when they housed one of New England's earliest industries.

★ **Saugus Iron Works** – *244 Central St. Open year-round daily 9am–5pm (Nov–Mar 4pm). Closed Jan 1, Thanksgiving Day, Dec 25.* & ☎617-233-0050. In 1646, encouraged by the government's interest in developing the natural resources of the colonies, John Winthrop, Jr, the son of the governor of Massachusetts, established the first ironworks in America at Hammersmith (Saugus). Despite the advanced techniques used and the skill of the workers, the operation was a financial failure, and within 30 years it ceased to function. By this time, however, many workers had been trained, and the Saugus works had provided the impetus for the development of the iron industry in America.

**Museum** – Artifacts excavated at this site, including items turned out by the early iron works and a 550-pound hammerhead used in the original forge, are on display.

**Iron Works House** – This dwelling, the only surviving 17C structure on site, is a good example of early Colonial architecture in America. Casement windows, batten doors, steep gables and the second-story overhang decorated with pendants underscore the medieval character of this style.

Other buildings include the **furnace**, where the ore was transformed into liquid and cast into bars; the **forge**, with its fires and large waterwheels; the **rolling and slitting mill**, where the iron bars were flattened and cut into nail rods; and the **Iron House**, where iron products were stored before being shipped downriver to Boston or Lynn.

**Waltham** – *Map p 126*. Pop 57,878. Located on Boston's peripheral Route 128, this industrial center is a leading producer of electronic equipment.

★ **Gore Place** – *52 Gore St. Visit by guided tour (1hr) only, mid-Apr–mid-Nov Tue–Sat 10am–5pm, Sun 2–5pm. Closed major holidays; grounds open rest of the year. $4.* ☎617-894-2798. This elegant Federal-style estate, located 9mi west of Boston, was the country residence of US senator and Massachusetts Gov Christopher Gore (1758-1827). Attributed to French architect J-G Legrand, the house features spacious oval-shaped rooms, marble floors and an impressive spiral staircase—all well-suited to the lavish entertaining for which the Gores were renowned. The finely proportioned rooms are appointed with distinctive period pieces and portraits by eminent early American artists such as Copley, Stuart and Trumbull.

**Brandeis University** – *415 South St*. Named for former Supreme Court Justice Louis D. Brandeis, this was the first Jewish-sponsored, nonsectarian university established in the US (1948). A strong commitment to the liberal arts underlies the program of study at Brandeis, where 3,600 students of all faiths are enrolled in 32 undergraduate and 20 graduate programs.

A harmonious, contemporary design unifies the more than 95 modern buildings on the 235-acre campus. The three chapels (Jewish, Protestant and Catholic) designed by **Max Abramowitz** exemplify this influence. The **Rose Art Museum** contains exhibits of contemporary paintings and sculpture, including works by Willem de Kooning, Robert Rauchenberg and Andy Warhol *(open year-round Fri–Wed 1–5pm, Thu 1–9pm; closed Jan 1, Dec 25;* & ☎617-736-3434). Plays are presented in the **Spingold Theater Arts Center**.

**Weston** – *15mi west of Boston*. Pop 10,200. Pleasant, attractively landscaped homes line the streets of this growing Boston suburb.

**Cardinal Spellman Philatelic Museum** – *235 Wellesley St. Open year-round Tue–Thu 9am–4pm, Sun 1–5pm. Closed major holidays.* ☎617-894-6735. This brick building, located on the Regis College campus, is home to the Cardinal Spellman philatelic collection and other famous collections, including four million stamps from around the world. The museum library contains over 40,000 volumes.

**South Sudbury** – *21mi west of Boston*. Pop 14,358. The **Wayside Inn** *(20mi west of Boston on the Old Post Rd–Rte 20;* ☎508-443-1776) *(illustration p 249)* was made famous by Longfellow's *Tales of a Wayside Inn*. Overnight guests are welcome at the inn, which also serves meals and allows visitors to tour the rooms, including the Longfellow Parlor, where the clock, etched panes of glass and other memorable objects described in Longfellow's poems have been preserved.

**Dedham** – *Map p 126*. Pop 23,782. In April 1920, this quiet community became known nationwide when the controversial murder trial of Nicola Sacco and Bartolomeo Vanzetti took place here.

**Fairbanks House** – *511 East St at Eastern Ave. Visit by guided tour (40min) only, May–Oct, Tue–Sat 9am–5pm, Sun 1–5pm. $5.* ☎617-326-1170. This early wooden dwelling, built in 1636, was enlarged on several occasions as the owner's family and fortune increased. Furniture, textiles and other family possessions are on view.

**Sharon** – *18mi south of Boston.* Pop 15,517. This pleasing community is one of the more than 90 cities and towns that make up the Boston Metropolitan Area.

**Kendall Whaling Museum** – *27 Everett St. 1mi north of the village center. Open year-round Tue–Sat 10am–5pm. $2.* & ☎617-784-5642. Although this museum is small, its fascinating collection of artwork, artifacts and other whaling memorabilia make the trip worthwhile. International in flavor, it displays British, Dutch, American and Japanese **paintings★** that illustrate several centuries of whaling including the "factory ship" era of the 20C. Equally impressive is the extensive collection of **scrimshaw★**, especially the scrimshaw violin. In addition to whaling implements and tools, ship models, Inuit whaling gear and the museum's seal-hunting collection, small craft are on exhibit: an Inuit kayak, and a whaleboat used aboard the *John R. Manta* (the last American sailing whaler).

## ★★★ CAMBRIDGE                                        Pop 95,802

Map of Principal Sights p 4                    Tourist Office ☎617-497-1630

Located on the Charles River across from Boston, Cambridge is the world-renowned home of Harvard University and the Massachusetts Institute of Technology (MIT). The city consists of a maze of university buildings, commercial streets and residential neighborhoods.

Massachusetts Avenue, the state's longest thoroughfare, extends the length of Cambridge from Harvard Bridge, past MIT and through the city's center, **Harvard Square**, with its lively coffee shops, restaurants and theaters. Between Harvard Square and the Common lie quiet streets lined with colonial dwellings. **Memorial Drive** borders the Charles River, affording views of central Boston.

### HISTORICAL NOTES

**From New Towne to Cambridge** – In 1630 New Towne, the small settlement across the river from Boston, was chosen as the capital of the Bay Colony. Fortifications were built to protect the town, and six years later, when the Puritans voted to establish a college to train young men for the ministry, New Towne was selected as the site. Leaders of the Bay Colony agreed to give the college a sum of money equal to the total colony tax. In 1638, recognizing the close bond between the college and the colony, they changed the name of New Towne to Cambridge, after the English university town.

The school was called Harvard, in honor of the Charlestown pastor **John Harvard**, who died later that year, leaving half his estate and library to the college.

**Literary Cambridge** – Cambridge developed as a publishing center in the 17C, when the first printing press in the colonies was established here by the widow of an English pastor and her assistants, the Daye brothers. A Bible in an Indian language, an almanac and the *Bay Psalm Book* were among the first works printed.

Charles River and Harvard University

Joe Wrinn/Harvard University

As the seat of Harvard College, Cambridge became the home of many leading educators and scholars of the day. By the mid-19C the city had developed into a center of progressive thought, attracting a circle of prominent writers, reformers and intellectuals to live, study or teach in Cambridge. Among the more famous figures associated with Cambridge are Henry Wadsworth Longfellow, Oliver Wendell Holmes, Margaret Fuller and Dorothea Dix.

**Cambridge and the Revolution** – Following the events at Lexington and Concord, the patriots established their military headquarters in Cambridge. Harvard buildings and private homes, abandoned by fleeing Tories, were transformed into hospitals and barracks. On July 3, 1775, George Washington took command of the Continental Army on Cambridge Common, and during the months that followed, he lived in the Vassal House (Longfellow National Historic Site) on Tory Row (now Brattle Street, p 133).

**City of the Future** – The development of modern technologies by Harvard and MIT have made the city a vital research center. The majority of the seminal research on computer processing was carried out by international scientists working in Cambridge. Since World War II, research and development industries have flourished in Cambridge and have played a key role in the growth of the industrial parks on Route 128.

## ★★★HARVARD UNIVERSITY   1 day. Map p 132. ⊕ Harvard.

**Harvard College** – Harvard, the first college established in America, has been one of the nation's most prominent educational institutions since it was founded in 1636 to train young men for the leadership of church, state and trade. Its enrollment grew from 12 students to its current total of over 18,000 degree candidates. The school's affiliation with Congregationalism declined as new and more liberal programs and policies were adopted; its affiliation with the Commonwealth of Massachusetts ended in 1865, when Harvard became a private institution.

**Harvard University** – Harvard developed as a modern university in the 19C, as other professional schools were added to the original college: Medicine (1782), Divinity (1816), Law (1817), School of Dental Medicine (1867) and Arts and Sciences (1872). Renowned teachers such as **James Russell Lowell, William James, Louis Agassiz** and **Henry Wadsworth Longfellow** introduced new fields of study into the curriculum. Harvard continued to expand in the early 20C as new laboratories, lecture halls, museums and libraries were built.

Harvard's superior academic traditions, extensive course offerings, distinguished faculty and devotion to research have made it one of the world's leading institutions of higher learning. The university library houses more than 12 million volumes, and the Fogg Art Museum (p 132) is a world-class university art museum. Harvard is closely associated with research facilities such as the Astrophysical Observatory of the Smithsonian Institution and engages scholars to study and resolve global problems relating to government, health and education.

Harvard's $6 billion endowment, the largest of any university in the world, is shared by the undergraduate college and ten graduate schools: Divinity, Law, Dental Medicine, Medical, Arts and Sciences, Business Administration, Education, Public Health, Design, and the John F. Kennedy School of Government. As a member of the **Ivy League**, a group of prestigious East Coast colleges that also includes Yale (p 53), Dartmouth (p 184) and Princeton, Harvard does not award athletic scholarships or academic credit for physical education courses, but it does sponsor 40 varsity athletic teams. The university's rowing crews, practicing on the Charles River, are a familiar sight to local residents.

**Harvard Men and Harvard Women** – Some 6,600 undergraduate students attend Harvard and **Radcliffe** (p 133). Women were first admitted to the Harvard community in 1879, when Radcliffe was founded to provide women with equal access to a Harvard education. Today, Harvard's undergraduate program is completely coeducational. Students live in one of 13 Harvard Houses, often lovely Georgian-style buildings that surround courtyards.

### The Campus   Map p 132

Harvard is a city within a city with 500 buildings, including more than 100 libraries, nine museums and dozens of laboratories on 380 acres of land, primarily in Cambridge. A variety of architectural works, from Colonial residences to public buildings by prominent 20C figures, such as Gropius (Harkness Commons and the Graduate Center, 1950 map p 132 **[L]**), Le Corbusier (Carpenter Center of Visual Arts p 131), and James Stirling (Sackler Museum p 133), reflect Harvard's role as a cultural hub.

*Begin at Harvard Information Center in Holyoke Center.*

★★ **Harvard Yard** – From Massachusetts Avenue, note the **Wadsworth House [A]**, a clapboard dwelling (1726) that was the residence of Harvard presidents until 1849. The Yard is the oldest part of the university. Administration buildings, dormitories and Holden Chapel, Harvard's first official chapel, are located here. To the left is **Massachusetts Hall [B]** (1720), the oldest Harvard building still standing; across from

Massachusetts Hall, Harvard University

it sits **Harvard Hall [C]** (1766). Beyond Harvard Hall is **Holden Chapel [D]**, ornamented with the blue and white Holden coat of arms. **University Hall [E]** (1815), a granite building designed by Charles Bulfinch, occupies the other side of the Yard. Daniel Chester French's **statue of John Harvard [1]** stands in front of University Hall. Because of the plaque on the statue that reads: "John Harvard, founder 1638," the statue is known as the "statue of the three lies": the college was founded in 1636, John Harvard was the school's benefactor not its founder, and the figure portrays a student who attended Harvard in 1882.

To the rear of University Hall stands **Memorial Church [F]**, dedicated to Harvard men killed in the world wars. Opposite rises the **Widener Memorial Library [G]**, with its imposing stairway. Inside, visitors can admire the Renaissance-style octagonal rotunda. Named for Harry Widener, a former Harvard student who lost his life in the *Titanic* tragedy, Widener Memorial is the largest university library in the world. Nearby is the modern **Pusey Library [H]** where the Harvard University archives are stored; the **Houghton Library [J]** possesses Harvard's rare books and manuscripts. Pass in front of the Romanesque facade of **Sever Hall [K]**, the work of H.H. Richardson, and leave the Yard.

*Turn left onto Quincy St.*

The concrete and glass **Carpenter Center of Visual Arts** (1963), the only structure in North America designed by modern architecture pioneer Le Corbusier, features a dramatic entrance ramp and his signature sun screens; nearby is the **Fogg Art Museum** *(p 132)* and just beyond is the **Sackler Museum** *(p 133)*, a contemporary L-shaped orange brick structure. Continue on to **Gund Hall** (the Graduate School of Design) with its modernistic glass-enclosed stairway. Across the way, **Memorial Hall**, a massive Victorian building topped with a square tower and pyramidal roofs, houses the Sanders Theater.

*Turn left onto Kirkland St. Pass Adolphus Busch Hall, then the striking Science Center, completed in 1973 by Jackson, Sert and Assocs. Cross the Yard.*

### The Harvard Houses   *Map p 132*

Many Harvard students live in the elegant Georgian residences found between the Charles River and Massachusetts Avenue: **Adams House, Quincy House** and **Lowell House**. These houses, most of which are brick, share a similar design and have broad grassy courtyards, provide a small-college atmosphere to the sprawling university community. During the warmer months, students use the yards to prepare for class, study for exams, or perhaps toss a frisbee.

*From Massachusetts Ave turn right onto Linden St. You will pass Adams House. Cross Mt Auburn St.*

From the intersection of Linden and Mt Auburn Streets, you can see a building that resembles a Flemish castle. This structure houses the offices of the **Lampoon**, a satirical magazine published by Harvard students.

*Continue on Holyoke Pl.*

Opposite rises the blue cupola of **Lowell House**; for a glimpse of the elegance that typifies the Harvard Houses, glance into its yard.

*Continue on Holyoke St, then cross the yard opposite. Turn right on Memorial Dr. The buildings of the Business School, on the Boston side of the Charles River, come into view. To reach Harvard Square, follow J.F. Kennedy St. On the way pass Eliot House and the "Garage," a complex of boutiques.*

## The Museums *Map below*

**★★ Harvard Museums of Cultural and Natural History** – *Entrances on Divinity Ave and 24 Oxford St. Open year-round Mon–Sat 9am–4:30pm, Sun 1–4:30pm. Closed Jan 1, Jul 4, Thanksgiving Day, Dec 25. $4. & ☎617-495-3045.*
Grouped under one roof, these four museums serve as the repository for the myriad specimens and artifacts comprising Harvard's outstanding research collections. Many of the galleries, dimly lit and packed with simple glass and wooden display cases, have retained the old-fashioned charm of a 19C exhibition hall. Don't be fooled by the no-frills presentation; the collections merit an attentive visit. *Begin your visit of the Peabody Museum at the Divinity Ave entrance.*

**★ Peabody Museum of Archaeology and Ethnology** – Founded in 1866 by George Peabody, this large museum displays objects and works of art brought back from early 20C Harvard-sponsored expeditions.The ground floor contains a delightful museum shop and an exhibit that explores the evolution of North American cultures to the present day. The third-floor exhibit, containing original artifacts and plaster casts of pre-Columbian monuments, interprets Latin America's archaeological heritage and the impact of European contact. The Victorian-style **Oceania** exhibit *(4th floor)* reveals a variety of exquisitely crafted artifacts from the Pacific Rim.*The other museums are accessible from the 3rd-floor gallery.*

**Mineralogical and Geological Museum** – Among the numerous minerals, gemstones and meteorites featured in the three galleries, do not miss the eye-catching giant gypsum crystals from Mexico.

**Botanical Museum** – The world-renowned collection of **Blashka Glass Flowers★★** occupies the museum's two galleries. Crafted in Germany by Leopold and Rudolph Blashka between 1877 and 1936, these hand-blown glass models accurately represent more than 780 species of flowering plants and are prized for their scientific and aesthetic value.

**Museum of Comparative Zoology** – Some of the rare finds on view in the fossil collections are: the 25,000-year-old Harvard mastodon, unearthed in New Jersey; a *Paleosaurus*, one of the oldest fossil dinosaurs (180 million years old); and a *Kronosaurus* (120 million years old), perhaps the largest marine reptile to have ever lived. In the adjacent galleries, scores of large glass cases enclose specimens of animals from around the globe. Note in particular the impressive North American bird collection representing 650 species.

**★ Fogg Art Museum** – *32 Quincy St. Open year-round daily 10am–5pm. Closed major holidays. $5 (includes admission to Sackler Museum). & ☎617-495-9400.*
On entering the museum, take a moment to admire the Italian Renaissance-style

courtyard. Exhibits on two levels surrounding the courtyard span all periods of Western art from the Middle Ages to the present and include notable examples of **Italian Renaissance** painting, Impressionist and post-Impressionist painting and sculpture, and classical art.

A corridor on the second floor leads to the **Busch-Reisinger Museum★**, specializing in the art of 20C German-speaking Europe. Its renowned collection, displayed on a rotating basis in six galleries, boasts works by Expressionists such as Max Beckmann and members of the Die Brücke and Der Blaue Reiter (Kandinsky, Klee, Feininger) groups.

★ **Sackler Museum** – 485 Broadway. Same hours as Fogg Museum. A dramatic post-Modern building designed by James Stirling (1985) houses this companion museum to the Fogg. The Sackler focuses on Ancient, Near Eastern and Far Eastern Art. Asian ceramics, sculpture, Japanese prints and a noteworthy group of Chinese **bronzes** and **jades** highlight the collection. In addition, temporary exhibits on a variety of subjects are presented in the ground-floor galleries.

★ **HISTORIC CAMBRIDGE**  2hrs. Map p 132.

**Cambridge Common** – The Common was the town center for more than 300 years, and was the site of General Washington's main camp from 1775 to 1776. According to tradition Washington took command of the Continental Army under the "Washington Elm" that grew on the Common until the 1920s. A plaque [2] and scion of the elm mark the spot where the tree once stood on the Garden Street side of the green.

**Christ Church** – Zero Garden St. Open year-round Mon 1pm–dusk, Tue–Sun dawn–dusk. & ☎617-876-0200. The oldest church in Cambridge, this gray wooden structure, designed in 1760 by Peter Harrison, is notable for its lovely Georgian interior. Abandoned at the beginning of the Revolution, the church was later used as a barracks for American troops.

**Radcliffe College** – Named for Ann Radcliffe, a Harvard benefactor, Radcliffe College was established in 1879 to provide women access to a Harvard education. In 1894 Radcliffe became officially associated with Harvard. The relationship between Harvard and Radcliffe continues to evolve. In 1975 the admissions offices of both colleges were joined, quotas for women were abolished and equal admission standards were established for women and men. Today Radcliffe students are Harvard students; they receive Harvard degrees that bear the seals of both institutions. In the **Radcliffe Yard** there are several buildings to note. The Federal-style **Fay House** is the first structure acquired by Radcliffe; the **Gymnasium** now houses the Murray Research Center and the Radcliffe Dance Center. Part of the original yard, the **Agassiz House** contains a theater where playwrights Eugene O'Neill and David Mamet premiered their early works. A building at the far end of the Yard houses the **Schlesinger Library**, the most extensive library of women's studies in the country, and the **Bunting Institute**, a multidisciplinary center for women scholars and artists. Before exiting the yard and turning onto Mason Street, observe the First Church (19C) surmounted by a gilded cock weathervane made in the 17C by Deacon Shem Drowne, the artisan who crafted the grasshopper atop Faneuil Hall (p 110).

★ **Brattle Street** – Loyalists to the British Crown, wealthy Tories, built homes here in the 18C, thus the name Tory Row. The stately residences now lining Brattle Street date primarily from the 19C. Note **no. 101** (Hastings House) and **nos. 113** and **115** (these two structures belonged to Longfellow's daughters).

★ **Longfellow National Historic Site** – 105 Brattle St. Visit by guided tour (40min) only, late May–mid Oct Wed–Sun 10am–4:30pm. $2. ☎617-876-4491. This Georgian dwelling, built in 1759 by the Loyalist John Vassall, served as the headquarters of General Washington during the siege of Boston. In the 19C, **Henry Wadsworth Longfellow** lived in the house between 1837 and 1882, the period during which he wrote Evangeline (1847) and The Song of Hiawatha (1855). The Poet's Study contains a chair made from the wood of the "spreading chestnut tree." Opposite the house, **Longfellow Park** extends down to the river.

Returning to Harvard Square by Brattle Street, you will pass in front of the **Loeb Drama Center** (no. 64), Harvard's modern theater.

★ **MASSACHUSETTS INSTITUTE OF TECHNOLOGY**
Map p 100. Ⓣ Kendall Center/MIT.

Founded during the 19C in Boston's Copley Square, the Massachusetts Institute of Technology was at first known as Boston Tech. By 1916 the school had outgrown its Copley Square site, and moved to its new location in Cambridge, accompanied by three days of parades, speeches and celebrations.

The school was established as the Massachusetts Institute of Technology in 1861 by **William Barton Rogers**, a natural scientist, who stressed the practical application of knowledge as the institute's principal goal. Guided through its early years by Rogers, MIT continued to pursue its original goal in the 20C and is today a leader in modern research and development, with schools of Engineering, Science, Architecture and Planning, Management, and Humanities and Social Science. The international character of the institute is reflected in its enrollment of some 9,700 students from 50 states and 101 foreign countries, who benefit from MIT's sophisticated teaching methods and modern equipment. Scientific works published by MIT are diffused to centers of learning and cities around the world.

**East Campus** – *To the right of Massachusetts Ave, arriving from Harvard Bridge.* The Neoclassical buildings along Massachusetts Avenue were designed by Welles Bosworth as part of the institute's new campus in 1916. A low dome tops the **Rogers Building** (no. 77). Part of the MIT Museum, the **Hart Nautical Collections** (*entrance at 77 Massachusetts Ave; open year-round daily 9am–8pm; ☎617-253- 4444*) display ship models that demonstrate the evolution of shipbuilding. Contemporary art exhibits are held at the **List Visual Arts Center** on the main floor of the Wiesner Building (*open Sept–Jun Tue–Fri noon–6pm, Wed 8pm, weekends 1–5pm; ☎617-253-4680*). Between the Hayden Memorial Library and the Earth Sciences Center looms Alexander Calder's stabile *La Grande Voile (The Big Sail).* Nearby stands *Transparent Horizon*, a black steel sculpture by Louise Nevelson.

**West Campus** – *To the left of Massachusetts Ave, arriving from Harvard Bridge.* The smooth-surfaced, modern Student Center houses the Tech **Coop**, the student union and restaurants. **Kresge Auditorium★** and the **MIT Chapel★** were designed by Eero Saarinen in 1956. Note the auditorium's triangular shell roof, which rests essentially on three points. The interfaith chapel, a cylindrical brick structure, is topped with an aluminum sculpture by Theodore Roszak. Inside the chapel, light enters from above, illuminating the mobile over the altar. Water in the moat casts reflections on the interior walls, creating a continual play of light and shadows. Also noteworthy is **Baker House**, a dormitory designed in 1947 by Finnish architect Alvar Aalto.

> *"After God had carried us safe to New England and we had...provided necessaries for our livelihood...one of the next things we...looked after was to advance learning and perpetuate it to posterity...."*
>
> From *New England's First Fruits* (1643)

# ★★ CAPE ANN

Map of Principal Sights p 3                    Tourist Office ☎508-283-1601

Salty sea air, exhilarating and clear, pervades the fishing villages, coastal estates and harbors of this rocky island north of Boston. The cape was explored in 1604 by Champlain, then in 1614 by Capt John Smith, who mapped and named the area in honor of Queen Anne, wife of James I of England. A small colony was established in 1623 at Gloucester by a group of Englishmen who had come "to praise God and catch fish." Their descendants were the generations of Cape-born sailors who have made the region one of the world's largest fishing centers.

Bostonians frequent Cape Ann, seeking out its maritime atmosphere, art galleries and fine seafood restaurants. Browsing in the shops and enjoying the area's ruggedly beautiful scenery are among the popular pastimes. **Whale-watching cruises** *(p 254)* offer visitors the opportunity to observe these great mammals in their summer feeding grounds just off the coast. Camera buffs delight in the magnificent natural light, which strikes the rocky shores and transforms the landscape into a changing spectrum of color and shadows throughout the day.

## ★★ TOUR OF CAPE ANN   *32mi. 1/2day. Map p 135.*

The itinerary follows Routes 127 and 127A around Cape Ann, passing through quaint fishing villages and offering views of the coast and the ocean.

**Magnolia** – This former fishing village developed into a summer resort in the 19C. Many of Magnolia's large comfortable dwellings, built as vacation homes during that era, are now year-round residences. Shore Road follows the coast, presenting views of the modest harbor and, in the distance, the Boston skyline.

*From Shore Rd turn left onto Lexington Ave, then right onto Norman Ave, which becomes Hesperus Ave.*

★ **Hammond Castle Museum** – *80 Hesperus Ave, about 1mi northeast of town center. Open Jun–Labor Day daily 10am–5pm (Sat 4pm, Sun 6pm). Nov–May weekends only 10am–5pm. Closed major holidays. $5.50. ☎508-283-2080.* This stone castle, inspired by castles built in the Middle Ages, overlooks Gloucester Harbor. Completed in 1929 by the inventor John Hays Hammond Jr, the castle contains his collection of medieval furnishings, paintings and sculpture. The Great Hall houses an 8,200-pipe organ Hammond constructed over a period of 20 years. From the museum, you can look down onto Norman's Woe, the treacherous rocks that are the setting of Longfellow's poem *Wreck of the Hesperus.*

*Return to Hesperus Ave, which leads to Rte 127 (Western Ave).*

Drive by **Stage Fort Park**, site of the settlement established in 1623, then cross the drawbridge that links the Cape to the mainland. To the right is Leonard Craske's statue the **Gloucester Fisherman★ [A]**, a tribute to the thousands of Gloucestermen who have died at sea.

**Gloucester** – Pop 28,716. Gloucester, the oldest seaport in the nation, is one of the world's leading fishing ports. Its fleet of schooners, which once sailed between Virginia and Newfoundland in search of cod, halibut and mackerel, was immortalized by Rudyard Kipling in his novel *Captains Courageous*. Still a principal provider of fish, with its fleet of about 250 boats, Gloucester is also a distribution center for the industry. At the seafood processing plants near the waterfront, the catch of fishermen from New England, Canada, Iceland, Greenland and Scandinavia is cured, packaged and prepared for shipping to cities across the nation.

The fishermen, many of whom are of Portuguese or Italian descent, remain devoted to their traditions, and especially to the annual **Blessing of the Fleet**, which takes place during the last weekend in June on the feast of St Peter.

*Enter Gloucester by Rte 127 (Rogers St).*

Crowning a knoll above a small park stands the austere stone house of noted 19C maritime artist Fitz Hugh Lane *(grounds only open year-round daily dawn–dusk)*. Views from the knoll sweep across the harbor.

*Turn left on Manuel E. Lewis St, left on Main St and right on Pleasant St.*

★ **Cape Ann Historical Museum [B]** – *27 Pleasant St. Open Mar–Jan Tue–Sat 10am–5pm. $3.50. & ☎508-283-0455.* The museum is dedicated to the seafaring and artistic traditions of Cape Ann. Galleries trace the history of the fisheries and maritime industries here and highlight works of 19C and 20C artists attracted to the Cape's light and landscape. Among the museum's holdings are works by Maurice Prendergast and John Sloan as well as the nation's largest collection of **seascapes★** by 19C American marine painter **Fitz Hugh Lane** (1804-1865). His paintings of Gloucester Harbor and of local scenes are admired for their warm, luminous colors, attention to detail and serene atmosphere.

*Return to Rte 127 (Rogers St) by Prospect St.*

You will pass the Portuguese-inspired **Our Lady of Good Voyage Church** surmounted by two blue cupolas.

*Follow Rte 127 north to East Main St and bear right.*

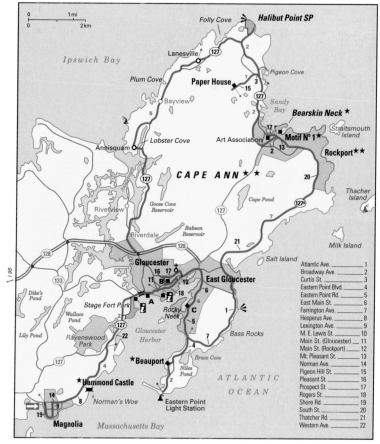

**East Gloucester** – Among East Main Street's restaurants and art galleries is the **North Shore Arts Association [C]**, located in a weathered red barn *(197 East Main St; open Jun–Sept Mon–Sat 10am–5pm, Sun 1–5pm; ☎508-283-1857)*. The Association features the work of local artists. Opposite is **Rocky Neck**, which has been the site of an artists' colony since the 19C and is replete with small galleries.

*Follow Eastern Point Rd to Eastern Point (private). Visitors to Beauport are permitted access via the private road.*

★ **Beauport** – *Eastern Point Blvd, in Eastern Point. Visit by guided tour (1hr) only, mid-Sept–mid-Oct Mon–Fri 10am–4pm, weekends 1–4pm. Mid-May–early Sept Mon–Fri 10am–4pm. Closed Memorial Day, Jul 4, Labor Day. $5. ☎508-283-0800.* Overlooking Gloucester Harbor and the distant Boston skyline, this 40-room summer residence of architect-decorator Henry Davis Sleeper (1873-1934) contains an imaginative mix of period styles and decors. Sleeper wished to create in each room a different mood and character. Thus beneath the varied roofline of chimneys, turrets, spiral flues and towers, he designed a colonial Paul Revere Room, an Indian Room, a Byron Room and a China Trade Room, among others. His creations here made him one of the most celebrated decorators of his day.

At the tip of Eastern Point is **Eastern Point Light Station**, dominating a long, granite breakwater at the entrance to Gloucester Harbor.

*Return along Eastern Point Blvd to the entrance of the private road, then turn right onto Farrington Ave and left onto Atlantic Rd.*

The drive along Atlantic Road affords a good **view** of the coast, and, across the water, of the twin lights on Thacher Island.

*Return to Rte 127A (Thatcher Rd), which skirts beaches, occasional salt marshes and rocky, wooded areas. Thatcher Rd becomes South St as you approach the town of Rockport.*

★★ **Rockport** – Pop 7,482. *During tourist season, downtown parking is difficult to find. A free shuttle bus operates every 15min between the parking lot outside of town and the town center (parking fee $5 weekends & holidays).* This tranquil fishing village, which developed as an artists' colony in the 1920s, enjoyed its industrial heyday in the 19C, when granite quarried from its shores was shipped to ports as far away as South America. Rockport's art galleries and shops, found in the vicinity of Main Street, as well as the village's charming character and coastal setting, attract many visitors.

The village is especially picturesque in the late afternoon, when the setting sun illuminates the sea, the granite ledges, the boats anchored offshore and the red fishing shed **Motif No. 1★**, named for the many paintings it has inspired. The shed is accessible from **Bearskin Neck★**, a small promontory where old fishing sheds have been converted into shops. Narrow walkways lead to the end of the neck, a good vantage point from which to

Motif No. 1, Rockport

observe the rocky shore and the harbor. On Main Street (no. 12), the **Rockport Art Association** exhibits the works of regional artists. A public, oceanside pathway passes through private lawns and leads to Garden, North and South Beaches.

*Leave Rockport on Mt Pleasant St, then turn right onto Broadway Ave, which leads into Rte 127 (Railroad Ave and Granite St). Just before Pigeon Cove turn left onto Curtis St, then left onto Pigeon Hill St.*

**Paper House** – *52 Pigeon Hill St. Open Jul–Labor Day daily 10am–5pm. $1. ☎508-546-2629.* The walls and furnishings are constructed almost entirely of newspapers. It took Elis F. Stenman and his family 20 years to complete the project.

*Return to Rte 127; continue north for almost 1mi and turn right on Gott Ave.*

**Halibut Point State Park** – *Open May–Oct daily 8am–8pm, rest of year dawn–dusk. $2/car.* ☎508-546-2997. *Facility information p 251.* From the parking lot, numerous self-guided trails wind through the woods and past granite quarries *(guided quarry walk in Jul & Aug Sat 10am)* to the northern tip of Pigeon Cove. Vantage points on the rocky shore provide extensive **views★** across Ipswich Bay to the south, and as far as Maine to the north. The Halibut Point State Park headquarters incorporates a concrete World War II watchtower.

*Continue on Rte 127.*

The coastal region between Pigeon Cove and **Annisquam** is a succession of charming villages and rocky inlets: **Folly Cove, Lanesville, Plum Cove** and **Lobster Cove.** After Annisquam, Route 127 joins Route 128 in Riverdale.

# ★★★ CAPE COD

Map of Principal Sights p 3                          Tourist Office ☎508-362-3225

This large, bent arm of the mainland is fringed with 300mi of sandy, often wild and desolate beaches. The product of a fascinating geological and human past, Cape Cod has been a favorite resort since the development of the automobile.

Despite the strips of motels, fast food places, souvenir shops and clusters of condominiums found in or near the old fishing ports, the Cape has managed to preserve its natural beauty and seafaring charm. Small colonial and fishing villages dot the North Shore (the Bay Side); to the east, miles of windswept dunes are protected in the Cape Cod National Seashore (CCNS). Acres of low-lying cranberry bogs and salt marshes, pine and scrub oak forests, and dozens of lakes, ponds and small, gray-shingled "Cape Cod" houses offer a pleasing relief to the sandy landscape of this peculiar Atlantic peninsula.

A large number of craftspeople live on Cape Cod. The hundreds of shops found on the roadside feature their handmade specialties: glassware, leather goods, candles, wooden decoys, fabric and pottery.

## PRACTICAL INFORMATION ............................ Area Code: 508

**Getting There** – From **Boston** to **Sagamore Bridge** (56mi): I-93 south to Rte 3 south, continue on Rte 6. International and domestic flights to **Logan International Airport** (Boston) or **T. F. Green State Airport** (Providence) ☎401-737-4000. Major rental car agencies *(p 248).* Closest Amtrak **train** station: Boston ☎800-872-7245. Greyhound **bus** station: Hyannis ☎800-231-2222. **Ferry** service from Boston to Provincetown: Jun–Labor Day daily, Memorial Day–end of Jun & after Labor Day–mid-Oct weekends only; 3hrs; $29; Bay State Cruises ☎617-723-7800. Year-round **shuttle** service between Logan Airport (Boston), Plymouth and Provincetown; Plymouth & Brockton Street Bus Co (Hyannis) ☎775-5524.

**Getting Around** – Cape Cod is easily visited by car or bicycle. Bicycle rentals in most island towns; car rentals in Hyannis. Cape Cod Railroad excursions (1hr 45min) depart from Hyannis station May–Oct ☎771-3788.

**Visitor Information** – **Cape Cod Chamber of Commerce** visitor center: junction of Rtes 6 and 132; kiosks operate seasonally at Sagamore and Bourne Bridges. Mailing address: Hyannis MA 02601 ☎362-3225.

**Accommodations** – Reservation services: **Bed & Breakfast Cape Cod,** Box 341, W. Hyannisport MA 02672-0341 ☎775-2772; **Golden Slumber Accommodations,** 640 Boulevard, Revere MA 02151 ☎800-892-3231, **Taylor-Made Reservations** ☎401-848-0300. *Cape Cod Resort Directory* available from **Cape Cod Chamber of Commerce** *(above).* Accommodations include economy and moderate hotels ($50-$125/day) and bed & breakfasts ($70-$100/day). *Average prices for a double room.*

**Rental cottages** and **campgrounds** throughout the island; contact the Chamber of Commerce. **American Youth Hostel:** The Outermost Hostel, 28-30A Winslow St, PO Box 491, Provincetown MA 02657 ☎487-4378.

**Recreation** – Salt and freshwater **beaches** located throughout island. Most beaches are town-owned. Waters on the Atlantic Ocean are cooler than waters along the South Shore. Unlike the calmer waters of Cape Cod Bay, the ocean has a strong undertow. A parking fee ($5-$8) is usually charged at public beaches in the summer. Ask the local tourist office or your lodging's staff about beach fees and regulations, which vary from town to town.

**Bicycle** trail maps (including 19.6mi Cape Cod Rail Trail from South Dennis to Eastham) available at visitor information centers in Eastham and Provincetown. Public **golf** courses in Brewster, Falmouth, Dennis and Mashpee. Excellent **bird-watching** along the eastern peninsula.

Specialty **shopping** and supplies are available in most island towns. *Contact Chamber of Commerce for more information regarding shopping and recreation on Cape Cod.*

MASSACHUSETTS

**A Glacial Past** – During the last Ice Age, the Laurentide ice sheet extended southward from the Labrador peninsula across New England. Its glaciers terminated along a line running westward across Long Island to New York and on to Ohio and the Great Lakes. MARTHA'S VINEYARD and NANTUCKET are remnants of eroded and submerged terminal moraines, extensive arched ridges of unsorted earth and rocks deposited in front of the glaciers. As temperatures rose and the ice melted, the glaciers retreated northward leaving behind a series of recessional moraines. At the end of the Ice Age, the rising sea flooded the land around the upstanding morainic debris, creating the peninsula now known as Cape Cod.

Wind and sea have also played a significant part in shaping the Cape. Marine erosion created the tall cliffs of the Outer Cape; ocean currents, carrying sand northward, formed the Province Lands sector of PROVINCETOWN, the sandy hook at the tip of Cape Cod.

**Cape of the Cod** – Cape Cod was named by explorer **Bartholomew Gosnold**, who landed here in 1602 and was impressed by the cod-filled waters that surrounded the peninsula. Eighteen years later, in 1620, the *Mayflower*, en route to its original destination in Virginia, anchored at the present site of Provincetown, and the Pilgrims spent five weeks exploring the region before continuing on to PLYMOUTH.

The earliest permanent settlements on the Cape were established around 1630 with fishing and farming as the mainstays. In the 18C whaling grew into a principal industry on the Cape, as vessels sailed out of Barnstable, Truro, Wellfleet and Provincetown to hunt. The rocky, treacherous shoals, a challenge to even the most expert seamen, posed a great danger to all shipping in these waters. Traces of several of the hundreds of vessels that sank off the Cape before the construction of the canal *(p 143)*, are occasionally revealed on the beach during low tide; as the tide rushes in, they are again hidden by the shifting sands.

Cape Cod National Seashore

**The Cape Islands** – The Cape Islands, **Martha's Vineyard** *(p 153)*, **Nantucket** *(p 156)* and the **Elizabeth Islands**, lie to the south. Purchased by Englishman Thomas Mayhew in 1642, the islands developed into whaling centers in the 18C and 19C and remained unspoiled by industry into the 20C. Bordered by magnificent beaches bathed by the warm Gulf Stream waters, the islands today are devoted primarily to tourism.

**Cranberry Bogs** – Half of the nation's cranberries come from southern Massachusetts and Cape Cod, where natural conditions such as marshy areas and sandy bogs lend themselves to the production of this small red berry *(illustration p 92)*. Named by Dutch settlers for the likeness of its flower's stamen to a crane's beak, the cranberry is used to make juice, baked goods and jellies.

Widespread cultivation of this fruit was begun in the early 19C, when a local resident, Henry Hall, discovered that the berries thrive best when covered with a layer of sand. Each spring sand was spread over the plants, and the berries were harvested in the fall. The process remains basically unchanged, although it is now mechanized. Festivals are held each fall on the Cape and in nearby areas to celebrate the harvest of the cranberry crop from the region's bogs.

## ★★ THE NORTH SHORE  *30mi. 1 day. Map pp 140-141.*

Route 6A follows the North Shore, (also known as the **Bay Side** because it fronts Cape Cod Bay), passing through tiny villages that were prosperous 19C ports.

*From the intersection with Rte 6, take Rte 6A east for .5mi.*

**Pairpoint Glass Works** – *851 Sandwich Rd (Rte 6A), in Sagamore. Glassblowing demonstrations Apr–Jan Mon–Fri 9am–4:30pm. ₺ ☎800-899-0953.* At America's oldest glassworks, visitors may observe skilled glassblowers as they produce, then decorate, pieces of Pairpoint crystal according to the methods traditionally employed in the production of handmade glassware through the 19C.

*From Rte 6A bear right onto Rte 130, then turn right onto Pine St.*

## ★★ Heritage Plantation – *On Pine St. Description p 171.*

## ★ Sandwich – *Rte 6A. Description p 170.*

Cranberry bogs, then sand dunes and salt marshes are visible as Route 6A nears Barnstable. Beyond the dunes lies **Sandy Neck**, a 7mi strip of land that protects Barnstable Harbor. At one time, whalers boiled down whale blubber in cauldrons that lined the shores of **Sandy Neck Beach**, a popular swimming area.

**Barnstable** – Pop 40,949. Pleasure craft have largely replaced the fishing and whaling boats that once filled Barnstable's harbor. A road on the left *(follow the Barnstable Harbor sign)* leads to the water's edge. The Custom House has been transformed into the **Donald G. Trayser Museum**, which contains memorabilia and artifacts related to Barnstable's maritime past *(open mid-Jun–Sept Tue–Sun 1:30–4:30pm; contribution requested; ₺ ☎508-362-3021).*

**Yarmouth Port** – Pop 21,174. The beautiful sea captains' homes on Main Street are reminiscent of Yarmouth's era as a busy port. The **Winslow-Crocker House** (c.1780), fronting Route 6A, may be visited *(visit by 1hr guided tour only, Jun–mid-Oct Tue, Thu, Sat–Sun noon–4pm; closed major holidays; $4; ☎508-362-4385).*

**Dennis** – Pop 13,864. Musicals, dramas and comedies are presented at the **Cape Playhouse**, a well-known summer theater. From **Scargo Hill Tower** *(from Rte 6A turn right after the cemetery, then left onto Scargo Hill Rd)* there is a **view** that extends from Plymouth to Provincetown.

## ★ Brewster – Pop 8,440. Extending 8mi along Cape Cod Bay, this charming resort town, first settled in the mid-17C, has preserved many of the stately residences built by prosperous sea captains in the 19C. The town's eight public beaches *(accessible from various points along Main St/Rte 6A)* are noteworthy for the 2mi garnet-tinted flats that are uncovered at low tide.

**Sydenstricker Glass Factory [A]** – *On Rte 6A in West Brewster. Demonstrations year-round Tue–Sat 2–4pm. ☎508-385-3272.* The owner of this glassworks has developed an original technique in glassmaking. Two sheets of glass are used to make each item; one of the sheets is decorated, then joined to the second according to the principles used in the enameling process. The factory also produces tableware and other items.

**Cape Cod Museum of Natural History [B]** – *869 Main St. Open year-round daily 9:30am–4:30pm. Closed major holidays. $4. ☎508-896-3867.* This learning center featuring interactive exhibits on the fauna and geology of the Cape appeals to visitors of all ages. Three **nature trails** crisscrossing the museum's 80-acre property allow exploration of typical Cape Cod landscapes, such as saltmarshes, cranberry bogs and a pristine beach. Tours of Monomoy Island *(p 142)* are also conducted by museum naturalists.

**New England Fire and History Museum [C]** – *1439 Main St. Open late May–mid-Sept Mon–Fri 10am–4pm, weekends noon–4pm. $4.50. ₺ ☎508-896-5711.* Five buildings contain equipment and memorabilia that tell the story of the important role played by the firefighters and their volunteer companies throughout the nation's history. A diorama vividly illustrates the Great Chicago Fire of 1871. A blacksmith shop and 19C apothecary are among the buildings on the green.

**Stoney Brook Mill [D]** – *1mi from Rte 6A. Turn right onto Stoney Brook Rd. Open Jul–Aug Thu–Sat 2–5pm.* The old gristmill still grinds corn into cornmeal. From April through mid-May, the stream that runs beside the mill is the scene of an exciting natural phenomenon: a herring run. During this period, alewives (fish 10in-13in long) swim upstream to freshwater ponds and lakes to spawn. They then return downstream with their newborn fingerlings, following an instinct similar to that of the salmon.

**Nickerson State Park** – *On Rte 6A. Open mid-Apr–mid-Oct daily 8am–8pm (Jul–Aug 24hrs/day). ⚠ ₺ ☎508-896-3491. Facility information p 251.* Picnic grounds, bicycle rentals and a small store are located in the park, the former estate of pioneer railroad-builder Roland Nickerson. Swimming is permitted in Flax Pond, and boat rentals are available.

**Orleans** – Pop 5,838. Orleans is the first town on the Cape where you will see ocean beaches. **Nauset Beach**, about 10mi long, protects Nauset Harbor, Pleasant Bay, Orleans and Chatham from the violent storms called northeasters that pound this section of the coast.

## ★★★ CAPE COD NATIONAL SEASHORE   *Map p 141*

In 1961 the eastern coast of Cape Cod, with its fragile dunes, cliffs, marshes and woodlands, became a federally protected area: the Cape Cod National Seashore (CCNS). Since that time bicycle trails, nature trails and dune trails for over-sand vehicles (dune buggies, four-wheel drive vehicles and jeeps) have been created, allowing visitors to enjoy the magnificent landscape. A visitor center is located at each end of the 27,000-acre seashore, and lifeguard services are available at the CCNS beaches: **Coast Guard Beach, Nauset Light Beach, Marconi Beach, Head of the Meadow Beach, Race Point Beach** and **Herring Cove Beach** *($5 parking fee is charged at all CCNS beaches).*

★ **Salt Pond Visitor Center** – *On Rte 6 in Eastham. Open late Jun–mid-Sept daily 9am–8pm. Late Sept–mid-Oct daily 9am–6pm. Jan & Feb weekends only 9am–4:30pm. Closed major holidays.* ♿ ☎508-255-3421. Rangers at the center provide literature and information regarding seashore regulations, trails, facilities and programs. A large room contains exhibits on Cape Cod's history, geography, natural history and architecture.

**Nauset Marsh Trail** – *1mi (30min). Access near the visitor center.* Beautiful views of the pond and marshes can be seen from the trail.

**Fort Hill Trail** – *1.5mi. To reach the Fort Hill parking lot from Rte 6 take Governor Prince Rd.* The trail leaves from Penniman House and leads through open fields that afford expansive views of the marshes.

**Marconi Station** – The area was named for **Guglielmo Marconi**, the Italian physicist who established the transatlantic wireless station that operated here between 1901 and 1917. The first formal transmission from this station was a communication between President Theodore Roosevelt and King Edward VII on January 19, 1903. Scattered remnants of the station remain; other sections have been destroyed by shore erosion, which is especially evident along the cliffs and beach here.

*The* 🏊 *symbol designates beaches where swimming is permitted (p 252).*

Gov. Prince Rd. _____ 1
Pine St. _____ 2
Scargo Hill Rd. _____ 3
Shore Rd. _____ 4
Stony Brook Rd. _____ 5
Trowbridge Rd. _____ 6

★ **Atlantic White Cedar Swamp Trail** – *1.25mi. The trailhead is located at Marconi Station parking lot.* The trail reveals various aspects of the vegetation on Cape Cod as it leads through the low brush, where beach grasses prevent erosion, then passes into an area of scrub oaks and pitch pines. The trail continues through a white cedar swamp before opening out onto the road that formerly led to the wireless station.

**Pilgrim Spring Trail** – *.5mi from the interpretive shelter near the Pilgrim Heights parking lot.* The trail leads through a section of scrub pines and brush to the site of a spring where the Pilgrims are believed to have first found drinking water in 1620.

★ **Province Lands Visitor Center** – *Race Point Rd outside of Provincetown. Open Jul 4–Labor Day daily 9am–6pm. Apr–early Jul & mid-Sept–Nov daily 9am–4:30pm.* ᵴ ☎508-487-1256. In addition to presenting interpretive exhibits and films on the area's geography, flora and fauna, the center offers a rich program of nature walks and lectures. The observation deck atop the contemporary wooden building offers a fine **panorama★** of the dunes.
After visiting the center, follow the road to **Race Point Beach**, an expansive stretch of coast graced by the picturesque silhouette of the former lifesaving station *(open to the public)* relocated here from its original site in Chatham.

**Beech Forest Trail** – *1.5mi. Access from Beech Forest parking lot.* The trail passes through a beech forest threatened at certain spots by the advancing dunes. A pond that is filling in (one day it will become a bog) can be seen from the trail.

★★ **Provincetown** – *Description p 164.*

## SOUTH SHORE  *Map pp 140–141*

Route 28 runs along the South Shore through Hyannis and Dennis Port, the major shopping centers of the Cape. Extremely commercial and tourist-oriented, with its motels, shops and restaurants, this section of the Cape also has a number of pretty villages including Chatham, Harwich and Falmouth.

★ **Chatham** – Pop 6,579. Protected by the sandy offshore barrier of Nauset Beach, Chatham remains an active port. Fishing boats depart daily from the **Fish Pier** *(off Shore Rd)* and return in the late afternoon. Farther on, Shore Road leads to **Chatham Lighthouse**, which affords a good view of Pleasant Bay and Nauset Beach.

**Chatham Railroad Museum** – *Depot Rd. Open mid-Jun–mid-Sept Tue–Sat 10am–4pm.* ᵴ. Located in Chatham's former Victorian-style railroad depot, the museum contains locomotive models, schedules, posters, the original ticket office and other exhibits that evoke the history of railroading.

**Monomoy Island** – *Access by boat only. Ferry & tour information* ☎508-945-0594. Because of the island's importance as a stop-over for birds in the Atlantic Flyway, it has been established as Monomoy National Wildlife Refuge *(open year-round daily dawn–dusk).*

**Harwich Port** – Picturesque **Wychmere Harbor** is visible from Route 28.

**Harwich** – Pop 10,275. *On Rte 39.* The white-columned buildings in the center of Harwich include the **Brooks Free Library** and the **Harwich Community Museum at Brooks Academy** *(open Jun–Sept Thu–Sun 1–4pm;* ᵴ ☎508-432-8089). Harwich is a leading producer of cranberries.

**Hyannis** – Pop 11,258. Situated midway on the South Shore, this town is the major shopping center for the Cape. Hyannis, with its regularly scheduled airline and island ferry services *(pp 153 and 157)*, is also an important gateway to Cape Cod. The small **John F. Kennedy Museum** displays photos primarily of the family's vacations on the Cape *(397 Main St; open mid-Apr–Dec Mon–Sat 10am–4pm, Sun 1–4pm; rest of the year Thu–Sat 10am–4pm; closed major holidays; $1;* ☎508-790-3077).

**Hyannis Port** – This fashionable waterfront resort is the site of the Kennedy family's summer compound. *(The compound is not visible from the road, nor is it open to the public.)* The **John F. Kennedy Memorial**, a bronze medallion set in a fieldstone wall, is located on Ocean Street. **Craigville Beach** *(off Rte 28)* is a pleasant place to swim and sunbathe.

**Mashpee** – Pop 7,884. *On Rte 130.* The Wampanoag Indians were already living on the Cape when the English settlers arrived. In the 17C the Reverend Richard Bourne appealed to the Massachusetts legislature to set aside land for the Indians. In response, they gave the large tract of land known as Mashpee Plantation to the natives. In the 19C this parcel of land became the town of Mashpee. The **Old Indian Meeting House**, built in 1684, is the oldest meetinghouse on the Cape *(Meetinghouse Rd, off Rte 28; open Jun–Labor Day Wed 10am–4pm & Fri 10am–3pm;* ☎508-477-1536).

★ **Falmouth** – Pop 27,960. Despite its development as a tourist town, Falmouth has retained a quaint 19C atmosphere in its village center. Lovely old homes stand near the green.

**Woods Hole** – This former whaling port is a world center for the study of oceanography and marine life. Two private laboratories are located here: the **Marine Biological Laboratory**, where approximately 400 scientists conduct research in the field of marine flora and fauna *(visit by 90min guided tour only, Jun–Aug Mon–Fri 1 & 2:30pm; 2-week advance reservation recommended; ☎508-548-3705)* and the **Woods Hole Oceanographic Institution**, the largest independent marine research laboratory in the US. The latter institution studies all aspects of ocean science from the sea floor to the atmosphere and maintains a small visitor center *(15 School St; open mid-May–Oct Tue–Sat 10am–4:30pm, Sun noon–4:30pm; rest of the year hours vary; $1; ☎508-289-3378)*. In September 1985, Woods Hole marine geologist Dr. Robert Ballard led the team of French and American scientists who discovered the wreck of the *Titanic* off the coast of Newfoundland.

In addition, the US Geological Survey's **Branch of Atlantic Marine Geology** and the **National Marine Fisheries Service**, both federal facilities, are part of the center. The **Aquarium**, used by the Fisheries Service in its research, may be visited *(open mid-Jun–mid-Sept daily 10am–4pm, rest of the year Mon–Fri; ಓ ☎508-548-7684)*.

**Cruises** – *Boats to Martha's Vineyard depart from the Steamship Authority Pier in Woods Hole (p 153).*

## CAPE COD CANAL  *Map p 140*

Dug between 1909 and 1914, the Cape Cod Canal separates Cape Cod from the rest of Massachusetts. The **Sagamore** and **Bourne Bridges** (for automobiles) and a railroad bridge that resembles London's Tower Bridge constitute the Cape's only links to the mainland. The 544ft central span of the railroad bridge can be lowered in less than 3min to allow a train to cross the canal. *Cruises (2-3hrs) on the canal depart from Onset Bay Pier May–mid-Oct daily 10am & 1:30pm mid-Jun–early Sept Mon–Sat 10am, 1:30 & 4pm. $6.50–$12. ✗ ಓ ☎508-295-3883.*

**Aptucxet Trading Post Museum** [E]– *24 Aptucxet Rd in Bourne Village. From the rotary on the Cape Cod side of Bourne Bridge, follow the sign for Mashpee, then Shore Rd. Turn right onto Aptucxet Rd and follow the signs. Open Jul–Aug Mon–Sat 10am–5pm, Sun 2–5pm. May–Jun & Sept–mid-Oct Tue–Sat 10am–5pm, Sun 2–5pm  (open Mon holidays). $2. ಓ ☎508-759-9487.* The Pilgrims established this trading post in 1627 to promote trade with both the Dutch from New Amsterdam and the Wampanoag Indians. Furs, sugar, tobacco and cloth were bought and sold here, using wampum, or currency, that the Indians made from shells.

The present building was reconstructed in 1930 on the foundations of the former trading post. Inside there are examples of the goods bartered. An ancient Rune Stone found in Bourne bears an inscription translated as: "God Gives Us Light Abundantly." A saltworks, similar to those used by early Cape settlers to evaporate salt from seawater, has been built near the canal.

# ★★ CONCORD                                      Pop 17,076

Map of Principal Sights p 2                    Tourist Office ☎508-921-3120

A quiet, refined colonial town, with beautiful homes tucked amid the rustic landscape, Concord is a desirable place to live. Named in the 17C for the "concord" of peace established between the Indians and the settlers, this small town was the site, 150 years later, of a confrontation between American patriots and British soldiers that changed the course of American history forever. On April 19, 1775, following a skirmish with colonists at LEXINGTON, the British marched to Concord. At the **Old North Bridge**, the untrained, poorly equipped farmers—called **"minutemen"** because of their readiness to take up arms to fight the British at a minute's notice—stood their ground against the Redcoats, thus triggering the American Revolution *(for an account of the events leading up to April 19, see p 150)*.

Concord has a distinguished literary past, having been the home, in the 19C, of intellectuals and writers including Ralph Waldo Emerson, Nathaniel Hawthorne, Henry David Thoreau and Bronson Alcott.

**Transcendentalism** – Ralph Waldo Emerson (1803-1882), a native of Concord, popularized transcendentalism (a philosophical movement characterized by the belief that God exists in both man and nature) and expressed his philosophical ideas in his *Essays on Nature*, a series of lectures he delivered across the US. Other writers and thinkers, attracted by the liberal ideas and the return-to-nature philosphy inherent in transcendentalism, came to Concord to live near Emerson. Among them was **Henry David Thoreau** (1817-1868), who built a cabin in the woods near Walden Pond *(p 144)*, where he lived from 1845 to 1847. Thoreau's book *Walden* recounts the author's personal experiences during this period.

**Nathaniel Hawthorne, Margaret Fuller** and others founded Brook Farm, an experimental community near West Roxbury that was envisioned as a retreat from Victorian society, and a return to a simple life. **Amos Bronson Alcott**, a proponent of transcendentalism, established his School of Philosophy adjacent to Orchard House, where his daughter **Louisa May Alcott** penned an account of her childhood in *Little Women*. Admirers come to Concord to tour the literary shrines associated with these eminent writers: Emerson House; the Wayside, where Hawthorne lived for several years; the Alcotts' Orchard House and School of Philosophy; and Sleepy Hollow Cemetery *(p 144)*, where many of them have been laid to rest.

## SIGHTS 2hrs. Map below.

★ **Minute Man National Historical Park** – This park was established to commemorate events that took place April 19, 1775 along Battle Road *(Rte 2A between Lexington and Concord)* and in Lexington, Lincoln and Concord. The 750-acre park is essentially a contiguous strip of land 4mi long, stretching over the three townships, with additional separate sections in Concord.

**Battle Road Visitor Center** – *Off Rte 2A in Lexington. Open Apr–Oct daily 9am– 5:30pm, rest of year call for hours.* & ☎508-369-6993. A film *(22min)* introduces visitors to the events of April 19, which occurred in the surrounding area.

★★ **North Bridge Unit** – A replica of the **Old North Bridge**★ [1] marks the place where colonial farmers advanced on the British and fired the "shot heard 'round the world." Emerson immortalized the old "rude bridge" in his poem *Concord Hymn*. Brief interpretive talks are held at the North Bridge Apr–Oct, weather permitting. Nearby, Daniel Chester French's famous statue of the **Minute Man** honors the patriots who resisted the British at Concord. The **North Bridge Visitor Center** has exhibits and provides information regarding ranger talks and other special programs *(up the road from the North Bridge; open Apr–Oct daily 9am–5:30pm; closed Jan 1 & Dec 25;* &*).*

As you leave, on the right is the **Old Manse** where Ralph Waldo Emerson, and later Nathaniel Hawthorne, lived *(visit by 40min guided tour only, mid-Apr–Oct Mon, Wed–Sat 10am–5pm, Sun 1–5pm.* ☎508-369-3909).

**The Wayside** – *455 Lexington Rd. Visit by guided tour (30min) only, Apr–Oct Mon, Tue, Fri–Sun 11am–4pm. Closed major holidays. $3.* ☎508-369-6993. In 1775 this was the residence of Concord's muster master, whose job it was to gather the colonial troops together in the event of a British attack. In the next century, The Wayside was the home of Nathaniel Hawthorne (who named the house), Margaret Sydney (author of *Five Little Peppers and How They Grew*), and Bronson Alcott, who at one time hoped to establish a community similar to Brook Farm *(p 143)* here.

★ **Concord Museum** – *Lexington Rd and Cambridge Tpk. Open Apr–Dec Mon–Fri 10am–5pm, Sun 1–5pm, rest of year Mon–Fri 11am–4pm, Sun 1–4pm. Closed Jan 1, Easter Sunday, Dec 25. $6.* & ☎508-369-9609. This extensive collection provides visitors with an excellent survey of trends in American decorative arts from the 17C to the 19C. Cummings E. Davis, a Concord merchant, amassed the collection in the mid-19C, mostly from local sources. Now arranged in 15 galleries, many of which feature authentic period pieces, the collection also depicts the development and prosperity of early Concord. One of the lanterns hung in the steeple of the Old North Church to signal Paul Revere on April 18, 1775, a diorama of the battle at Old North Bridge, and objects used by Thoreau at Walden Pond are displayed.

**Orchard House and School of Philosophy** – *399 Lexington Rd. Visit by guided tour (45min) only, Apr–Oct Mon–Fri 10am–4:30pm, Sun 1–4:30pm; rest of the year Mon–Fri 11am–3pm, Sat 10am-4:30pm, Sun 1–4:30pm. Closed Jan 1–15, Easter Sunday, Thanksgiving Day, Dec 25. $4.50.* ☎508-369-4118. Orchard House was the home of the Alcott family from 1858 to 1877, the period during which Louisa May Alcott wrote her autobiographical novel *Little Women* (1868). The **School of Philosophy**, built on the hillside, was operated by her father, Bronson Alcott, until the end of the 19C. It is now used for special programs that are open to the public.

**Ralph Waldo Emerson House** – *28 Cambridge Tpk at Rte 2A. Visit by guided tour (30min) only, mid-Apr–Oct Thu–Sun 10am–5pm, Sun 2–5pm. $3.50.* ☎508-369-2236. The house is furnished as it was during the years that the New England writer and philosopher Ralph Waldo Emerson lived here (1835-1882).

**Walden Pond Reservation** – *1.5mi south of Concord center on Rte 126 (Walden St).* Henry David Thoreau *(p 36)* built his cabin on the shore of this lake. A cairn marking the site of the cabin can be reached from the parking lot by following trail signs to a granite post where the trail turns right before reaching the site *(15min).*

**Sleepy Hollow Cemetery** – *From Concord center turn right onto Rte 62. Enter the cemetery through the second gate on the left. Follow signs for Author's Ridge. Open year-round daily dawn–dusk, weather permitting.* ☎508-371-6299. A short climb from the parking lot leads to **Author's Ridge**, where the Alcotts, Hawthorne, Emerson and Margaret Sydney are buried.

## EXCURSION

**Lincoln** – Pop 7,666. *5mi southeast of Concord via Rte 126.* This affluent residential town with a decidedly rural charm traces its origins to the mid-17C.

**Codman House** – *Codman Rd. Visit by guided tour (1hr) only, Jun–mid-Oct Wed–Sun noon–4pm. Closed major holidays. $4. ☎617-259-8843.* This enchanting estate, nestled in a bucolic setting, preserves the legacy of the family who resided here for five generations. Built in 1749 by a gentleman farmer, the house was acquired in the 1790s by the Codman family, who transformed the original Georgian structure. The initimate interior reflects changing tastes of the members of this family over the centuries: Georgian woodwork, Victorian paneling, 20C stuffed chairs. The walls of several rooms are hung with paintings from the family's collection of 18C European art.
A romantic Italianate **garden** (c. 1920), filled with decorative statuary and a long pool dotted with water lilies, graces a quiet corner of the estate.

**Gropius House** – *68 Baker Bridge Rd. Open Jun–mid-Oct Fri–Sun noon–4pm, Nov–May first full weekend of each month only noon–4pm. Closed major holidays. $5. ☎617-259-8843.* Walter Gropius (1883-1969), founder of the influential German school of art and architecture, the Bauhaus, and Director of Harvard School of Architecture, designed this International-style house for his family in collaboration with Marcel Breuer in 1938.
Gropius' characteristic industrial aesthetic predominates throughout, as evidenced in the use of ribbon windows, large unadorned surfaces and glass brick. The freeflowing space within extends outdoors by means of large window surfaces and terraces. The interior, which contains furniture and accessories created at the Bauhaus as well as family mementos, evokes a sense of order and tranquility.

★ **DeCordova Museum and Sculpture Park** – *Sandy Pond Rd. Open year-round Tue–Fri 10am–5pm, weekends noon–5pm. $4. Free admission to the sculpture park. Galleries closed for renovation until late 1996. ☎617-259-8355.* Opened in 1950 on a lush lakeside estate bequeathed by Boston businessman Julian de Cordova, this museum is devoted to promoting appreciation for contemporary art by Americans, with particular emphasis on New England artists. The 35-acre sculpture park provides a sylvan setting for a rotating selection of monumental works by nationally and internationally acclaimed artists. *Concerts are held in summer in the outdoor amphitheater.*


## ★★ DEERFIELD   Pop 5,018

Map of Principal Sights p 2   Tourist Office ☎413-665-7333

Deerfield's mile-long main street (referred to locally as "The Street"), with its 18C and 19C dwellings and shops, provides a picture of a wealthy early American farming community. The **Brick Church** (1824) and several buildings of **Deerfield Academy** stand on the grassy **common** near the post office—a replica of a Puritan meetinghouse. A little farther down the street is the **Deerfield Inn** (1884).

**A Frontier Town** – Deerfield was not always the tranquil town it appears to be today. Incorporated in 1672, Deerfield was abandoned three years later after the massacre at Bloody Brook, and again in 1704 when the village was burned down during Queen Anne's War. A peace treaty signed in 1735 encouraged the settlers to return, and during the following century the village grew into one of New England's most prosperous agricultural centers.

**Architecture and Preservation** – The restoration of Deerfield's colonial and Federal structures, begun in 1848, was the first project of its kind in the US. Painstakingly renovated and redecorated, these large structures reflect the prosperity of their early owners. Many of the dwellings are topped with gambrel roofs, and adorned with richly carved entranceways characteristic of the Connecticut Valley style. The interiors are equally luxurious and elegant.

## ★★ HISTORIC DEERFIELD   1 day
*Open year-round daily 9:30am–4:30pm. Closed Thanksgiving Day, Dec 24 & 25. $10. A visitor orientation film is shown at the Hall Tavern. ✗ & ☎413-774-5581.*

Thirteen buildings are open to the public. Special collections include: the **Helen Geier Flynt Textile Museum**, the **Henry Needham Flynt Silver and Metalware Collection**, and the George A. Cluett Collection of American Furniture.

★★ **Ashley House** – The house (1730) is typical of the dwellings that were built in the Connecticut Valley in the 18C. The interior contains richly carved woodwork and beautiful furnishings. This house was the home of Parson Jonathan Ashley, a devoted Tory who, despite threats from the townspeople to bar him from the church, persisted in his loyalty to the Crown during the Revolution.

★ **Wright House** – The light and airy Federal dwelling (1824) has American paintings, porcelains and the fine Cluett collection of Federal and Chippendale furniture.

★ **Asa Stebbins House** – The Stebbins House (1810), with its distinctive arched doorway, was the first Deerfield residence to have a dining room. A splendid collection of wall coverings, including 19C French wallpaper illustrating Captain Cook's voyages to the South Seas, decorates the interior of the house.

★ **Hall Tavern** – This former tavern (1760) is now the site of Historic Deerfield's visitor center. The building contains many rooms decorated with 17C and 18C New England furniture. The ballroom is embellished with stenciled designs.

**Frary House** – This late 18C dwelling was later enlarged to serve as a tavern. Inside is a ballroom with a fiddlers' gallery, and rooms filled with country antiques, pewter and ceramics.

© Paul Rocheleau

Door of the Dwight House

**Wells-Thorn House** – The house's kitchen (1717) retains its early primitive characteristics while the refined paneling, furnishings and the use of color in the rooms built later (1751) reflect the refined tastes of its well-to-do owner.

**Dwight House** – The facade of this dwelling (1725) is ornamented with a handsomely carved doorway, a feature typical of Connecticut Valley architecture.

**Memorial Hall** – This brick building houses the museum of the **Pocumtuck Valley Memorial Association**, a memorial to the Pocumtuck Indians and the settlers of Deerfield. Among the exhibits is the door from the original Indian House, the only dwelling not destroyed in the 1704 raid.

## FALL RIVER

Pop 92,703

Map of Principal Sights p 3               Tourist Office ☎508-997-1250

The site of the famous 1892 trial of Lizzie Borden, who was accused of murdering her parents with an axe, Fall River was a major textile center in the 19C and early 20C. During the same period, luxuriant steamships of the **Fall River Line** linked New York to BOSTON, and carried the wealthy to their summer cottages in NEWPORT.
Fall River was hard hit by the Depression, then by the migration of the textile mills to the South and the development of synthetic fibers. Despite these setbacks, textiles and clothing have remained among the city's most important products.

### ★★ BATTLESHIP COVE

*Access from Rte 195 east, Exit 5. Open Jun–Sept daily 9am–5pm (Jul–Aug 7pm). Closed Jan 1, Thanksgiving Day, Dec 25. $8. ☎508-678-1100.*

**Ships** – In 1965 the battleship *USS Massachusetts* was moored at Fall River to serve as a permanent memorial to the 13,000 Massachusetts men and women who gave their lives in service to their country during World War II. In recent decades, several other naval ships have joined the *Massachusetts* as exhibits at this outdoor naval museum.

**PT Boat 796** – The ferocious shark painted on the hull symbolizes the threat these modest-sized boats posed to the enemy. PT boat memorabilia is displayed.

**Submarine Lionfish** – This World War II submarine carried 20 torpedoes and an 80-member crew. The vessel's sophisticated operating equipment, once considered classified, can be seen in the control room.

**Destroyer USS Joseph P. Kennedy** – The ship was named for the eldest of the four Kennedy brothers who was killed on a volunteer mission in World War II. A typical World War II destroyer, the *Kennedy* carried a crew of 275.

MASSACHUSETTS

**Battleship USS Massachusetts** – Remarkable for its enormous size and the large crew required for its operation (2,300 men), the *Massachusetts* logged 225,000 miles in wartime service between 1942 and 1945, and was the first and last battleship to fire her 16in guns against the enemy (off the coast of North Africa in 1942).

Below deck, sections of the ship have been set aside for an exhibit devoted to aviation, and for the Memorial Room honoring the Massachusetts men and women killed in World War II. Narrow corridors lead visitors past the barbershop, laundry and other service areas that were indispensable aboard a large ship.

**Fall River Heritage State Park Visitor Center** – *Take the pedestrian bridge at Battleship Cove. Open year-round daily 10am–4pm.* ✗ & ☎508-675-5759. *A slide show (30min) relating the history of the city's textile industry is shown daily.* This brick riverside building has the appearance of a 19C New England mill. From the tower, visitors are treated to a sweeping view of the entire Mt Hope Bay region.

**Marine Museum** – *70 Water St. Open year-round Wed–Fri 9am–4pm, weekends noon–4pm (Jul–Aug 5pm). $3.* & ☎508-674-3533. The museum's photographs, marine paintings, prints and ship models bear witness to the region's maritime past and the Fall River Line. Accurately constructed ship models, such as the 28ft model of the *Titanic* and the 13ft 9in model of the *Puritan*, and photographs of the plush Victorian interiors found on the Fall River steamers, suggest the luxury and comfort enjoyed by Fall River Line passengers.

*Developed in Europe, small, fast PT (Patrol, Torpedo) boats
first served the US Navy in World War II.
Destroyers, among the fastest ships in the Navy,
were originally designed to protect the fleet's battleships
from enemy torpedo boats. Because of their tactical flexibility,
destroyers are now used offensively as well as defensively.*

## ★★ FRUITLANDS MUSEUMS

Map of Principal Sights p 2

In 1843 the philosopher of Concord, Bronson Alcott *(p 143)*, the English reformer **Charles Lane** and their followers attempted to establish a Utopian community on the 18C farm known as Fruitlands. Idealistic and reacting to the materialism of the times, they became vegetarians, wore only linen clothing and spent most of their time outdoors. Their return to nature lasted but a few months, as disillusioned members of the community left Fruitlands one by one.

Fruitlands, the farm that was for a brief while their home, tops a hill that dominates the Nashua Valley. The farmhouse has been transformed into a museum of transcendentalism; other museums on the grounds treat varied aspects of early American culture. From the restaurant there is a **view** of the region, including Mts Monadnock and Wachusett.

**VISIT** *2hrs*
*The farm is located on Prospect Hill Rd in Harvard. From Rte 2 (Exit 38A), take Rte 110/111 toward Harvard, then take the first right on Old Shirley Rd. Follow the signs. Open mid-May–mid-Oct Tue–Sun 10am–5pm. $6.* ✗ & ☎508-456-3924.

**Fruitlands** – The museum of transcendentalism *(p 143)* is arranged in this 18C farmhouse. The museum exhibits mementoes belonging to Emerson, Thoreau and Alcott, the philosophers and writers of the period.

**Shaker Museum** – This simple Shaker building (1794) was moved to Fruitlands after the Harvard Shaker Community, founded in the late 18C, was disbanded in 1919. The structure contains Shaker products and furnishings.

**Indian Museum** – Two statues by Philip Sears, *The Dreamer* and *He Who Shoots the Stars,* flank the entrance to the building, inviting visitors to enter and view the superb collection of North American Indian artifacts.

**Picture Gallery** – The primitive portraits and landscape paintings hanging in this building are representative of America's 19C itinerant portraitists and the artists of the **Hudson River school** (Cole, Bierstadt).

# ★★★ HANCOCK SHAKER VILLAGE

Map p 94

The Hancock Shaker Village, an active Shaker community between 1790 and 1980, is today a museum village that relates the history of this sect, which for more than two centuries has practiced a form of communal living.

**Origin of the Shakers** – In the mid-18C, a group of Quakers in Manchester, England were called the "Shaking Quakers" because of the dances they performed during their religious services. Later they became known simply as the Shakers. In 1774 Shaker **Ann Lee**, an English textile worker who considered herself to be the second incarnation of Christ, emigrated to America to avoid persecution for her religious beliefs. Settling in New York, Lee—known to the other members of her sect as Mother Ann—and her followers dedicated themselves to preaching the beliefs of the Shaker religion. They attracted new members wherever they went, and by the mid-19C, the Shaker movement had reached its peak, with a total of 19 communities in the US. The number of Shaker communities has steadily declined since the end of the 19C, although the Shaker experience in communal living never ceases to fascinate people from all walks of life.

**The Shaker Community** – Life in the community was based on the principles of community property, equality of the sexes, celibacy, separation from the outside world and public confession of sin. Men and women lived in families of 30 to 100 people who shared responsibilities equally with the Elders and Eldresses (two men and women from the village who served as the group's spiritual leaders). Duties in the field, shops and kitchen were divided among the members, and all activities in the community were governed by a rigid time schedule.

Because Shakers lived a celibate life, converts, called New Believers, were important to the community's continued existence. New Believers came both from Shaker society and from the outside world as well, since orphans adopted by the group often became permanent members of the community.

**Shaker Industries** – Guided by the words of Mother Ann, "Do all your work as though you had 1,000 years to live, and as though you were going to die tomorrow," the Shakers became known for the products they made. Originally invented solely for the use of Shakers, these items were in time marketed across the country as the sect grew dependent on the outside world for certain goods. Although the garden and seed industry was the Shakers' specialty, the Shaker label on brooms, furniture and other items guaranteed the highest quality.

Gathering room, Brick Dwelling

**Architecture** – Shaker architecture exemplified simplicity, purity and functionalism. Buildings were designed to serve a specific purpose and were constructed from materials best suited to that purpose. The order and peace that guided the religious life of the Shakers inspired the designs of their buildings. Spacious, light and airy, the Brick Dwelling boasted 100 large doors, 245 cupboard doors, 369 drawers, and 95 windows with 3,194 panes of glass. Shaker innovations, such as the pegboard, sliding cupboard and low-back chair, reflect the functionalism of the products crafted by members of this sect.

## VISIT *3hrs*

*At the junction of Rtes 20 and 41, 9mi north of the Massachusetts Tpk (Exit1). Open late May–late Oct daily 9:30am–5pm. Visit by guided tour (1hr 30min) only, Apr–late May & late Oct–Nov 10am–3pm. Closed Thanksgiving Day. $10. ✗ ☎413-443-0188. A slide-show orientation (10min), and two documentary films (18min & 1hr) on the Shakers are presented.*

From the visitor center, pass the **garden tool shed** then the **herb garden**. On the other side of Route 20 you will find the Shaker **cemetery**, the **school** and **ministry shop**.

**Poultry House** – This former poultry house contains exhibits of Shaker life, industry and religion.

★★ **Brick Dwelling** – The community dining room, kitchens and retiring rooms were located in this structure, which also houses displays of pharmaceutical, infirmary and sewing artifacts from buildings that are no longer standing.

**The Shops** – In these shops the Brothers made tinware, brooms, oval boxes and clocks; the Sisters dried herbs, wove cloth and made dairy products. Today artisans work here, reproducing Shaker crafts.

★★★ **The Round Stone Barn** – Built in 1826, the barn is a masterpiece of Shaker architecture and functionalism. Wagons entered the third level and emptied their hay into the central haymow. On the middle level, stables radiated out from the central manger, making it easy for one person to feed the entire herd. Manure pits were located on the lower level.
Nearby, the **Tan House** served as a blacksmith shop, cider room and tannery and now functions as a cabinetmaker's workshop. The **Ice House** and the **Hired Men's Shop** are also located close to the barn.

**Trustees Office and Store** – Official community business was conducted in this building, which also housed the Shaker Fancy Goods Store.

**The Meeting House** – The Shakers met here every Sunday for their religious services. Neatness and symmetry characterize the overall design of the structure; the meeting room, a large open hall, provided ample space for dancing. The offices and living quarters of the community's spiritual leaders occupied the second floor.

**Laundry and Machine Shop** – The machines in this large building were at one time activated by a turbine that was powered by water flowing from a mountain reservoir to the north of the village. A herb and seed room and the laundry fill other sections of this building.

## HINGHAM
Pop 19,821

Map p 127 | Tourist Office ☎617-826-3136

Hingham is a lovely old settlement on Massachusetts' South Shore. This BOSTON suburb is graced with tree-shaded streets lined with 18C and 19C dwellings, including the **Old Ordinary**, now a museum devoted to local history.

★ **Old Ship Church** – *90 Main St. Open Jun–Aug Tues–Sun noon–4pm. Closed major holidays.* ☎617-749-1679. Built by ships' carpenters in 1681, Old Ship Church is the last remaining Puritan meetinghouse in the US. Inside, the finely crafted pulpit, galleries, columns, paneling and box pews remain unpainted, and the interior glows with the rich tones of natural wood. The church probably received its popular name, Old Ship, owing to the curved ceiling timbers that give the roof the appearance of an inverted ship's hull.

★ **World's End** – *Follow Rte 3A to the Hingham Harbor rotary, then take Summer St east .5mi. Turn left onto Martin's Lane and continue .75mi to sign for World's End. Open year-round daily 9am–5pm (May–Aug 8pm). $3.50.* ☎617-749-8956. Trail access to the left of the parking lot. From the entrance bear left onto the wide gravel road; always take the left fork (round-trip 1hr 30min). This quiet peninsula lies only 14 mi from Boston. Gentle hillsides are covered with grassy meadows, shaded paths and wildflowers. The trail leads past Pine Hill, Planters Hill and then over the Bar (a narrow neck of land) before arriving at the "world's end," the tip of the peninsula, where there are views of Boston and Nantasket Beach.

## IPSWICH
Pop 11,873

Map of Principal Sights p 3 | Tourist Office ☎508-921-4990

This small colonial town, bordered by white sandy beaches and woodlands, attracts many artists and tourists. The popularity of Ipswich has given rise to the concentration of restaurants and shops in the center of town, and the gastronomically famous **Ipswich clam** is a regional favorite. Restored 17C and 18C dwellings line the streets of Ipswich, enhancing its centuries-old charm.

**Whipple House** – *1 S. Village Green. Visit by guided tour (50min) only, May–mid-Oct Wed–Sat 10am–4pm, Sun 1–4pm. $3.* ☎508-356-2811. This handsome dwelling, built by John Whipple around 1655, provides evidence of the comfort and refinement that graced the lives of many early New Englanders. The spacious rooms are decorated with enormous fireplaces and period furnishings.

★ **Richard T. Crane Beach Reservation** – *From Rte 1A south of Ipswich, take Rte 133 east toward Essex. Turn left on Northgate Rd. At the end of Northgate Rd, turn right on Argilla Rd. The road ends at Crane Beach. Open year-round daily 8am–dusk. $3-$12/car (rates vary seasonally).* ☎508-356-4354. This sandy beach stretches for several miles along the coast. The dunes beyond the beach are covered with a pitch pine forest and a red maple swamp. The best way to explore the area is by following the **Pine Hollow Trail** *(45min; access to the right of the parking lot)*. During the summer concerts are presented at the mansion on **Castle Hill**, the former residence of the Crane family *(for concert information ☎508-356-4351)*.

## EXCURSION

**Topsfield** – Pop 5,754. *7mi southwest of Ipswich by Topsfield Rd. From the center of Ipswich take Market St to Topsfield Rd.* Topsfield was a prosperous farming village until the 19C, when it became a residential community.

**Parson Capen House** – *1 Howlett St, facing the green. Open mid-Jun–mid-Sept Wed, Fri & Sun 1–4pm. Closed major holidays. $1.* ☎508-887-3998. The pitched roof, central chimney, overhanging stories and hanging pendants of this Elizabethan dwelling (1683) reflect the trend towards English building traditions in American Colonial architecture.

## ★★ LEXINGTON                                              Pop 28,974

Map of Principal Sights p 2                        Tourist Office ☎617-862-1450

This serene residential community has been historically inseparable, in the minds of most Americans, from the town of Concord *(p 143)* since April 19, 1775 when British and colonial troops clashed at Lexington and at Concord, triggering the events that exploded into the American Revolution. The Revolutionary War sites and monuments preserved here allow visitors to retrace, step-by-step, the incidents that occurred on that day, over 200 years ago, as the British marched from Boston to Lexington and on to Concord.

**April 19, 1775** – Tensions between the colonists and the British increased steadily following the passage of the Stamp Act in 1765. In 1774 the colonists established their own legislative body, the Provincial Congress, with John Hancock as its president. Within a year, the Congress had created a militia and stockpiled arms in Concord for the colonial troops. England reacted swiftly by dispatching troops to Boston and closing the city's port. In an attempt to put an end to the rebels' activity, General Gage, the leader of the British troops in Boston, decided to march on Concord and seize the weapons hidden there *(p 97)*.

Forewarned of the British soldiers' approach by Paul Revere and his riders, 77 minutemen who had spent the night of April 18 at **Buckman Tavern** in Lexington awaiting the enemy, moved toward the **green** where their leader, Captain Parker, advised them: "Stand your ground and don't fire unless fired upon, but if they mean to have a war, let it begin here!" At about 5 o'clock in the morning, the British began to arrive, and Parker, realizing that his men were greatly outnumbered, gave the order to disperse. He was too late; a shot rang out and during the skirmish that followed, eight minutemen were killed and ten others lay wounded. The British commander ordered his men to regroup and march on to Concord.

In Concord, the minutemen who had arrived from nearby villages observed from a hilltop as British soldiers began to search for the supplies. Aware that fires were burning in the town below, and fearful that the British would raze Concord, the patriots descended to the **Old North Bridge**, where they found themselves confronted by the enemy. There, a battle ensued until the British, weary and reduced in numbers, began their retreat to Boston along the Battle Road. Snipers firing from the woods added to the day's British casualties; before nightfall another skirmish between the two forces took place at **Meriam's Corner**.

**SIGHTS**  4hrs. Map p 151.

★★ **The Lexington Green** – The first confrontation between the British soldiers and the minutemen on April 19 took place on this triangular park. Henry Kitson's statue of **The Minuteman [1]** represents the leader of the Lexington militia, Captain Parker. Seven of the colonists killed here that day are buried beneath the **Revolutionary Monument [2]**.

★ **Buckman Tavern** – *1 Bedford St. Visit by guided tour (30min) only, Apr–Oct Mon–Fri 10am–5pm, Sun 1–5pm. $3. Combination ticket ($7) available for Buckman Tavern, Hancock-Clarke House & Munroe Tavern.* ☎617-862-1703. The minutemen gathered here on the evening of April 18 to await the arrival of the British troops. Following the battle between the British and the militia on the green, the minutemen who had been wounded were carried to Buckman Tavern, where they were given medical care. Restored to its original 18C appearance, the tavern comprises a bar, bedchambers, ballroom, separate rooms set aside for women, and an attic where, for a few pennies a night, drovers were permitted to sleep.

★ **Minute Man National Historical Park** – *Off Rte 2A west of Lexington Green. Description p 144.*

**Old Burying Ground** – In the old cemetery behind the church there are well-preserved examples of grave markers dating from the 17C.

**Hancock-Clarke House** – *36 Hancock St. Visit by guided tour (30min) only, Apr–Oct Mon–Fri 10am–5pm, Sun 1–5pm. $3. ☎617-862-1703.* Samuel Adams and John Hancock were at this house (1698) the evening of April 18 when Paul Revere rode into Lexington to warn them to flee.

**Munroe Tavern** – *1332 Massachusetts Ave. Visit by guided tour (30min) only, Apr–Oct Mon–Fri 10am–5pm, Sun 1–5pm. $3.☎617-862-1703.* This 17C tavern served as the headquarters and hospital for the British troops during their retreat from Concord to Boston on April 19.

**Museum of Our National Heritage** – *Rte 2A and Massachusetts Ave. Open year-round daily 10am–5pm (Sun noon–5pm). Closed Jan 1, Thanksgiving Day, Dec 24, 25, 31. ☎617-861-6559.* This contemporary brick and glass building contains a museum and library of American history. Changing exhibits feature the growth and development of the nation from its founding to the present. Weekend programs include films, concerts and special events.

# LOWELL
Pop 103,439

*Map of Principal Sights p 2*

Tourist Office ☎508-459-6150

In the early 19C New England merchant Francis Cabot Lowell (1775-1817) developed a modified version of the English power loom with a view to establishing America's first planned industrial community. The Boston Manufacturing Co, founded by Lowell and a group of investors, began their experiment in Waltham on the banks of the Charles River west of Boston. After Lowell's death, the group selected the present site because of its proximity to a larger power source: **Pawtucket Falls**, a 1mi stretch of the Merrimack River that drops some 32ft in elevation. The new mill town, appropriately named Lowell, soon boasted blocks of brick factories, company-owned dwellings, warehouses, stores, churches and 5.6mi of canals required to transport the water from the falls to the turbines.

Incorporated as a town in 1826, Lowell quickly rose to prominence as the nation's largest cotton textile producer. Initially the city's labor force consisted of young Yankee women from the farms of New England, but by the mid 19C, the so-called "mill girls" were replaced by Irish and French-Canadian immigrants willing to accept lower wages. Successive waves of newcomers from other European countries followed. The early chapters of America's labor history unfolded in the mills of Lowell, where strikes and social unrest periodically disrupted production. A number of factors, including increased competition from Southern mills, and the development of steam as an alternative energy source, contributed to the city's decline in the late 19C. The crash of 1929 sounded the death knell for Lowell.

The revitalization of Lowell's economy in the late 1970s is attributed to the concerted efforts of preservationists and the influx of modern industries, such as Wang Labs, Raytheon and other major employers. Local and state bodies, in collaboration with the Federal Government, restored many of Lowell's 19C buildings and its canal system to preserve the city's unique industrial heritage. This successful restoration project has served as a model for similar sights around the US.

Lowell is the birthplace of three famous personalities in the arts: painter **James Abbott McNeill Whistler** *(birthplace/museum at 243 Worthen St, one block from visitor center)*, writer Jack Kerouac and screen star Bette Davis.

★★ **Lowell National Historical Park** – *Begin your visit at the visitor center to obtain a free map, daily schedule of tours and opening hours of sights mentioned below.* ☎508-970-5000. Established in 1978 the park comprises a group of buildings, canals and walkways scattered throughout Lowell's downtown district. The **visitor center** *(246 Market St; open Jun–Sept daily 8:30am–5pm, rest of the year 9am–5pm; closed Jan 1, Thanksgiving Day, Dec 25. &.)*, located in a renovated mill complex, offers an introduction to Lowell's history through a slide presentation *(20min)* and display panels. Restored vintage **trolleys** *(free boarding)*, running continuously around the downtown area, allow visitors to tour the attractions at leisure.

MASSACHUSETTS

Canal tours explore the remarkable man-made water network that channeled the waters of the Pawtucket Falls to the mill turbines *(depart from the visitor center daily Jun–Labor Day; $3; advance reservations recommended)*.

★ **Boott Cotton Mills** – *Open daily 9am-5pm. $3.* &. Wedged between the Eastern Canal and the Merrimack River, this imposing industrial complex graced by a central bell tower, houses the park's main exhibit. The first floor **weave room** equipped with 88 operating power looms *(earplugs provided at entrance)* re-creates the jarring atmosphere of a 1920s textile mill. The second floor features a series of exhibits focused on America's Industrial Revolution, Lowell's history, textile production and technology and labor relations. Recorded oral histories of former mill workers provide poignant testimony to the grim realities of mill life.

**Additional Sights** – Located in an authentic boardinghouse across the street from the Boott Mills, the Working People Exhibit offers insight into the lives of factory workers: from the "mill girls" to 20C immigrants. St Anne's Church (1825), the Gothic Revival structure fronting Merrimack Street near the Merrimack Canal, was conceived as a religious center for the mill community. The state-administered Waterpower Exhibit *(25 Shattuck St; hours vary)* traces the evolution of man's exploitation of waterpower. The enlightening tour of the Suffolk Mill *(visit by guided tour only)* includes a close look at an operating 19C turbine and a power loom. Fronting the long facade of the Massachusetts Mills, Eastern Canal Park contains an elegant group of marble monoliths inscribed with quotations from the works of native son and Beat generation writer **Jack Kerouac (1922-1969)**. *A handout locating sights associated with Kerouac is available at the visitor center.*

**Museum of American Textile History** – *Scheduled opening 1996. 491 Dutton St. ☎508-686-0191.* Located in North Andover since 1960, this museum will be moved to the historic 160,000sq ft Kitson building *(currently under restoration)*. The permanent exhibit will include tools, illustrations and machines, which trace changes that occurred as automation replaced traditional methods of cloth-making.

## EXCURSION

**Andover** – *Pop 29,151. 11mi northeast of Lowell by Rte 495 (Exit 41), then Rte 28.* This small colonial village is home to the select preparatory school, **Phillips Academy** (1778). The focal point of the village is the academy's spacious green and attractively designed buildings: Bulfinch Hall, the Andover Inn, the Archaeological Museum and the **Addison Gallery of American Art**, which has a noteworthy collection of American paintings and sculpture *(open year-round Tue–Sat 10am–5pm, Sun 1–5pm; closed Aug & major holidays. & ☎508-749-4015).*

★ **MARBLEHEAD**  Pop 19,971

Map p 127  Tourist Office ☎508-921-4990

Prior to the Revolution, this small fishing port had grown into a flourishing trade center. Marblehead vessels returned home with great wealth, and their owners and captains spent freely in building the Colonial and Georgian homes that line the narrow, winding streets of Old Marblehead. Losses suffered during the war, competition from other ports and the gale of 1846, which destroyed ten Marblehead ships and killed 65 men, caused the inhabitants to turn to industry, such as shoe manufacturing, to earn their living.

The sea again became the source of prosperity for Marblehead when, in the late 19C and early 20C, the town developed into a resort and boating center because of its magnificent harbor. Today Marblehead continues to be one of the major yachting centers on the East Coast. In season the sail and motor pleasure craft that crowd the harbor is especially impressive when viewed from **Fort Sewall** *(at the end of Front St)*, **Crocker Park** *(off Front St)*, or from the lighthouse on **Marblehead Neck**, a select residential area.

**Jeremiah Lee Mansion** – *161 Washington St. Visit by guided tour (1hr) only, mid-May–mid-Oct Mon–Sat 10am–4pm, Sun 1–4pm. $4. ☎617-631-1069.* The wood blocks composing the exterior of this dignified 16-room Georgian dwelling, built in 1768 for the successful merchant Jeremiah Lee, have been refinished with a mixture of paint and sand to resemble stone.

Inside, the immense entrance hall, with its grandiose proportions, highly polished mahogany woodwork and English mural wallpapers, makes this house one of the most memorable of the period in New England. In several rooms wallpaper hand-painted in the style of the 18C Italian artist Giovanni Pannini depicts classical ruins and fishing scenes. The house contains 18C and 19C furniture, silver, ceramics and textiles. An upstairs room displays a group of brightly colored primitive paintings by the Marblehead artist John Frost, formerly a Grand Banks fisherman.

**Abbot Hall** – *Town Hall. Open year-round daily (hours vary); Nov–May 29 closed weekends. Contribution requested. & ☎617-631-0000.* The familiar patriotic canvas, **The Spirit of '76**, painted by A.M. Willard to celebrate the nation's centennial, hangs in the Selectman's Room. The picture was given to the town by Gen John Devereux, whose son was the model for the drummer boy in the painting.

# ★★ MARTHA'S VINEYARD

Map of Principal Sights p 3       Tourist Office ☎ 508-693-0085

When Bartholomew Gosnold landed on this island in 1602, he found an abundance of wild grapes growing here. He thus named this land Martha's Vineyard, in honor of his daughter Martha. No longer covered with wild grapes, this triangular-shaped island, 5mi south of CAPE COD, is blessed with a landscape that resembles the Cape. Here, undulating heaths spotted with ponds and lakes give way to forests of oak and pine, seaside cliffs and broad beaches. The towns on the Vineyard are small fishing villages and summer resorts, each with its own history and character.

## PRACTICAL INFORMATION .................................. Area Code: 508

**Getting There** – From **Boston** to **New Bedford** (64mi): I-93 south to Rte 24 west to Rte 140 east. From **Boston** to Sagamore Bridge, **Cape Cod** (56mi): I-93 south to Rte 3 south; to **Hyannis** (17mi): Rte 6 west to Rte 132 west; to **Falmouth** (20mi): Rte 6 west to Rte 28 east (continue on Woods Hole Rd to Woods Hole).
International and domestic flights to **Logan International Airport** (Boston) or **T. F. Green State Airport** (Providence) ☎401-737-4000. Major rental car agencies *(p 248)*. Amtrak **train** station: Providence, RI ☎800-872-7245. **Bus** stations - Greyhound: Hyannis ☎800-231-2222; Bonanza: Woods Hole ☎800-556-3815.

| Ferry | Schedule | Duration (one-way) | Adult Fare | Company |
|---|---|---|---|---|
| **Falmouth to Oak Bluffs** | Memorial Day–Columbus Day, daily | 40min | $9 | **Island Commuter Corp** ☎548-4800 |
| **Falmouth to Edgartown** | mid-May–mid-Oct, daily | 45min | $22 | **Falmouth Ferry Service** ☎548-9400 |
| **Hyannis to Oak Bluffs** | May–Oct, daily | 1hr 45min | $22 | **Hy-Line** ☎778-2600 |
| **Woods Hole to Vineyard Haven** | year-round, daily | 45min | $9.50 | **Steamship Authority** ☎477-8600 |
| **Woods Hole to Oak Bluffs** | May–Sept, daily | 45min | $9.50 | **Steamship Authority** ☎477-8600 |
| **Nantucket to Oak Bluffs** | Jun–mid-Sept, daily | 2hr 15min | $22 | **Hy-Line** ☎693-0112 |
| **New Bedford to Vineyard Haven** | mid-May–mid-Oct, daily | 1hr 45min | $8.50 | **Martha's Vineyard Ferry** ☎997-1688 |

**Getting Around** – Streets in Martha's Vineyard are often congested and parking may be difficult (especially in July and August); bicycle or public transportation recommended. Shuttle service between main island towns of Vineyard Haven, Oak Bluffs and Edgartown Memorial Day–mid-Oct daily, Martha's Vineyard Transportation Services ☎693-1589. Bicycle and car rentals available in main island towns.

**Visitor Information** – **Martha's Vineyard Chamber of Commerce** visitor center on Beach Rd, mailing address: PO Box 1698, Vineyard Haven MA 02568 ☎693-0085.

**Accommodations** – Reservation services: **About the Beach** PO Box 269, Oak Bluffs MA 02557 ☎693-1718, **Destinnations** PO Box 1173, Osterville MA 02655 ☎800-333-4667, **House Guest Cape Cod & The Islands** PO Box 1881, Orleans MA 02653 ☎896-7053, **Martha's Vineyard & Nantucket Reservations** PO Box 1322, Vineyard Haven MA 02568 ☎693-7200. Lodging directory available from Chamber of Commerce *(above)*. Accommodations include economy and moderate hotels, bed and breakfasts and rental cottages. **Camping**: Vineyard Haven. **American Youth Hostel**: Edgartown-West Tisbury Rd, mailing address: PO Box 3158, West Tisbury MA 02576 ☎ 693-2665.

**Recreation** – Southern **beaches** offer heavy surf, northern and eastern beaches are more protected *(p 252)*. **Boat rentals** in main island towns, windsurfing equipment rentals in Vineyard Haven. Paved **biking** trails throughout island. Most specialty **shopping** and supplies in main island towns.
*Contact Chamber of Commerce for more information regarding shopping and recreation on Martha's Vineyard.*

**VISIT**   *1 day. Map p 154.*

**Vineyard Haven** – Gift and coffee shops border Main St.

★ **Oak Bluffs** – Pop 2,804. In the 1830s, the Methodists of Edgartown began to meet regularly in an oak grove at the northern end of town. Each summer the group attracted a larger number of followers who spent three months in a tent camp situated a short distance from the place where religious services were held.
By the 1850s, more than 12,000 persons were attending the annual services at Cottage City (as the encampment came to be known), and by the end of the 19C, the city had been renamed Oak Bluffs for the oak grove where the first revival meetings were held. At about the same time, small wooden cottages were built to replace the tents that stood near the Tabernacle, the center of religious worship.

MASSACHUSETTS

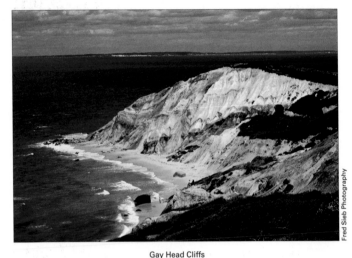

Fred Sieb Photography

Gay Head Cliffs

★★ **Trinity Park and Gingerbread Cottages** – *Leave the car near the harbor and follow Central Ave to Cottage City.* Small ornate Victorian "gingerbread" houses, colorfully painted and decorated with lacy wooden trim resembling cake frosting, ring the Tabernacle, a beautiful example of ironwork architecture.

★ **Edgartown** – Pop 3,062. Most of Edgartown's large, handsome dwellings were built in the 1820s and 1830s when the town was an important whaling center. A number of these homes line North Water Street and face Edgartown Harbor, once dominated by a fleet of whaling vessels and now filled with modern pleasure craft. Opposite Edgartown is **Chappaquiddick Island**, where private homes and unspoiled natural areas are sheltered by thick woodlands. The ferry, *On Time,* so-called as an ironic reference to its irregular schedule, provides service between Edgartown and Chappaquiddick.

**Vineyard Museum of the Dukes County Historical Society** – *Open Jul 5–mid-Oct Mon–Sat, 10am–4:30pm, Sun noon–4:30pm. $5.* ☎508-627-4441. The skill of the ships' carpenters who built the Thomas Cooke House (1765) is reflected in its fine interior wood paneling and trim. Artifacts related to whaling, including a picture of Capt

Valentine Pease, (master of the *Acushnet* on which Herman Melville sailed) on whom Melville based his character of Captain Ahab in *Moby-Dick,* offer glimpses of the era of whaling.

**Katama Beach** – This sandy stretch of beach linking Chappaquiddick to the main island, extends the entire length of the south shore.

Drive across the island, heading west, through oak and pine forests. As the road approaches Gay Head, it climbs above Menemsha and Squibnocket Ponds where alewives spawn in the spring, permitting a **view** of Menemsha.

** **Gay Head Cliffs** – These 60ft cliffs, composed of striated layers of clay, display a rainbow of color: blue, tan, gray, red, white and orange. Dating back 100 million years, the cliffs contain fossils of prehistoric camels, wild horses and ancient whales. Erosion of the cliffs often causes the inshore waters to turn a reddish color. Gay Head's predominantly Indian population uses the clay to make the decorative pottery they sell.

**Menemsha** – With its picturesque lobster traps and weathered fishing sheds, this tiny waterfront village is a favorite subject of photographers.

## ** MOHAWK TRAIL

Map of Principal Sights p 2                    Tourist Office ☎413-664-6256

The scenic 63mi stretch of Route 2 through northwestern Massachusetts, running from Millers Falls to the New York border, is known as the Mohawk Trail. Following an old Indian path along the banks of the Deerfield and Cold Rivers, through the Connecticut Valley and into the Berkshire Hills, this trail was used by the Mohawks as an invasion route during the French and Indian War. It passes through tiny mountaintop hamlets, sheer river gorges and dense forests. Views from the highway and off-road overlooks are spectacular in foliage season.

### From Greenfield to Williamstown   *67mi. 3hrs.*

**Greenfield** – Pop 14,016. This small agricultural town at the eastern end of the Mohawk Trail is named for its fertile green valley.

*Follow Rte 2. After 6mi the road rises, affording views into the valley. Continue to the intersection of the road to Shelburne Falls (13.5mi after Greenfield).*

* **Shelburne Falls** – Pop 2,012. This quiet mountain village is located beside the falls of the Deerfield River. Glacial potholes, ground out of granite during the last Ice Age, can be seen on the riverbank near Salmon Falls *(Deerfield Ave).*

**Bridge of Flowers** – *On the south side of the bridge over the Deerfield River.* Originally used by trolleys, this bridge has been transformed into a 400ft-long path of flower beds above the Deerfield River.

*Return to Rte 2.*

Two miles past Charlemont the road enters **Mohawk Trail State Forest**. At the entrance to the forest stands a statue of an Indian brave entitled **Hail to the Sunrise**. This bronze sculpture was created as a memorial to the five Indian tribes who once lived along the Mohawk Trail.

The road continues through a mountainous and rugged section of Route 2. Between Florida and North Adams there are good views to the north of Mt Monadnock and Mt Greylock.

From **Whitcomb Summit** the Green Mountains stretch into the distance; from **Western Summit** the Hoosac Valley is visible. **Hairpin Curve** offers broad **views★★** across the Hoosac and Berkshire Valleys to the Taconic Range.

*Just before North Adams turn right onto Rte 8 north, then turn left after .5mi.*

* **Natural Bridge State Park** – *Open Jul–Aug daily 10am–6pm. Late May–Jun & Sept–mid-Oct daily 8am–4:30pm. $2 per car.* ☎413-663-6312. *Facility information p 251.* The white marble natural bridge that gives the park its name rises 60ft above the churning waters of a narrow 475ft-long chasm. Glaciers sculpted and polished this marble, which was formed primarily from seashells deposited about 550 million years ago.

**North Adams** – Pop 16,797. North Adams' large brick mill buildings provide wistful reminders of the city's past as a leading industrial center in western Massachusetts. The mills attracted thousands of Canadians and Italians to settle in the area. In 1875, with the opening of the **Hoosac Tunnel** linking Massachusetts to the West, North Adams also grew into a bustling railroad center. Manufacturing and light industry continue to support the economy today.

**Western Gateway Heritage State Park** – *Rte 8 south.* Occupying the restored buildings of the city's old freight yard, this urban park preserves the history of North Adams' heyday as a manufacturing and railroad boom town. In the **visitor center**, displays tell the story of the Hoosac Tunnel, one of the major engineering feats of the 19C *(open year-round daily 10am–5pm; closed Jan 1, Easter Sunday, Dec 25; $1;* ✗ & ☎413-663-8059).

Built over a period of 25 years (1851-1875), the 4.8mi tunnel through Hoosac Mountain marked the first use of nitroglycerin as a blasting agent, and was the longest tunnel in the nation when it was completed. Its glory has always been overshadowed by the fact that almost 200 workers lost their lives during the tunnel's construction.

*Return to Rte 2 west, then 1mi after North Adams center turn left onto Notch Rd. Follow the sign for Mt Greylock Reservation. The road rises through wooded areas to the summit.*

★★★ **Mt Greylock** – Located between the Taconic and Hoosac Ranges, Mt Greylock (3,491ft) is the highest point in Massachusetts. The mountain was named for chief Grey Lock whose tribe once hunted on these lands. From the War Memorial Tower at the summit there is a magnificent **view★★★** of the entire region including the Berkshire Valley, the Taconic Range and nearby Vermont and New York.

*Descend to North Adams and continue on Rte 2 west.*

★★ **Williamstown** – *Description p 177.*

# ★★★ NANTUCKET Pop 3,069

Map of Principal Sights p 3 Tourist Office ☎508-228-1700

Lying 30mi south of CAPE COD, Nantucket is a triangular patch of land 14mi long and 3.5mi wide that Herman Melville described in *Moby-Dick* as "a mere hillock and elbow of sand." The flat relief, sandy soil, rounded ponds and tree-studded moors are evidence of the island's glacial origins and underlying moraine *(p 138)*. The island of Nantucket—an Indian word meaning "distant land"—includes the village of the same name, situated on a magnificent harbor protected by a long, narrow barrier of sandy beach. The history of the island is interwoven with that of its famous port, which was the world capital of the whaling industry in the early 19C.

Nicknamed "the little gray lady in the sea" by early sailors because of its weathered gray cottages covered with pink roses in the summer, Nantucket was spared the industrialization of the 19C. With its comfortable old homes, wharfside structures and cobblestone streets, Nantucket today reigns as one of the most charming, well-preserved towns on the East Coast.

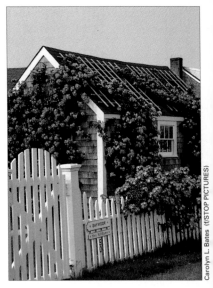

A Nantucket cottage

Carolyn L. Bates (f/STOP PICTURES)

**The Rise and Fall of Whaling** – In the 17C the Indians taught the settlers how to harpoon whales that passed close to shore. As hunting depleted the whale population in the Atlantic Ocean, Nantucketers sought their prey in the unexploited waters of the Pacific. For almost 100 years, between 1740 and the 1830s, Nantucket reigned as the preeminent whaling port. Merchants and shipowners grew rich by selling as many as 30,000 barrels a year of precious whale oil in London and other major cities. With their wealth whalers built the magnificent homes that stand on Main Street near the wharves.

Then came the decline. A sandbar stretching across the mouth of Nantucket harbor prohibited the entrance of the large whaleships that were being constructed in the early 19C, and the island's whaling industry gradually migrated to the deepwater port of New Bedford *(p 159)*. During that period the island tragically lost much of its population to a great fire in 1846, to the California Gold Rush and to the discovery of oil in Pennsylvania, events which ultimately brought Nantucket's golden era to a close.

**Nantucketers** – The difficult life led by seamen and their wives, and the Quaker religion many of them practiced, contributed to the simple, austere and strong character for which Nantucketers are known. **Peter Foulger**, the grandfather of Benjamin Franklin, and **Maria Mitchell**, the first American woman astronomer, were both from Nantucket.

## PRACTICAL INFORMATION .............................. Area Code: 508

**Getting There** – From **Boston** to **Hyannis** (74mi): I-93 south to Rtes 3 & 6 south to Rte 132 east. International and domestic flights to **Logan International Airport** (Boston) or **T.F. Green State Airport** (Providence) ☎401-737-4000. Major rental car agencies *(p 248)*. Closest Amtrak **train** station: Providence, RI ☎800-872-7245. Greyhound **bus** station: Hyannis ☎800-231-2222.

**Ferry Schedule**

| Departs From | Schedule | Duration (one-way) | Adult Fare | Company |
|---|---|---|---|---|
| Hyannis | year-round, daily | 2hrs 15min | $10 | **Steamship Authority** ☎477-8600 |
| Harwich Port | mid-May–mid-Oct | 1hr 45min | $29 | **Freedom Cruise Line** ☎ 432-8999 |
| Hyannis | May–Oct, daily | 1hrs 50min | $11 | **Hy-Line** ☎778-2600 |
| Martha's Vineyard | Jun–mid-Sept, daily | 2hrs 15min | $11 | |

**Getting Around** – Nantucket is best visited on foot or bicycle as streets are often congested and parking may be difficult (especially May–Sept). Bicycle and moped rentals available. Steamship Authority ferries offer automotive transport ($180 round-trip, reservations suggested).

**Visitor Information** – **Nantucket Island Chamber of Commerce** visitor center: 48 Main St, Nantucket MA 02554-3595 ☎228-1700, **Nantucket Visitor Services:** 25 Federal St, Nantucket MA 02554; kiosks throughout island operate seasonally ☎228-0925.

**Accommodations** – Reservation services: **Nantucket Accommodations** PO Box 217, Nantucket MA 02554 ☎228-9559; **Destinnations** ☎800-333-4667; **House Guests Cape Cod & the Islands** ☎800-666-4678; **Nantucket & Martha's Vineyard Reservations** PO Box 1322, Lagoon Pond Rd, Vineyard Haven MA 02568 ☎693-7200. Accommodations directory available from Nantucket Island Chamber of Commerce *(above)*. Accommodations range from hotels and inns ($85-$300/day) to bed & breakfasts ($90-$150/day). **American Youth Hostel** 31 Western Ave, Nantucket MA 02554 ☎228-0433. Camping prohibited on island. *Average prices for a double room.*

**Recreation** – **Swimming** at all island beaches, **surfing** at South Shore beaches. **Bicycle** and **hiking** paths throughout island. Most specialty **shopping** and supplies center of the town of Nantucket.

A less well-known, yet splendid example of the determination of Nantucketers was the wife of Capt Charles Grant. Tired of spending years alone at home while Grant was at sea, Nancy Grant joined her husband on a whaling voyage in 1849, and spent the better part of the next 32 years sailing with him.

★★★ THE CENTER   *1 day. Map p 158.*
*The Nantucket Historical Association sells a combination pass ($8) to the historic houses and museums it administers. The pass may be purchased at any of the sights.* ☎508-228-1894.

★★★ **Main Street** – Shaded by venerable elms, paved with cobblestones and lined with captains' homes, shops and art galleries, Main Street has preserved its colonial atmosphere. During the summer it is a delightful place for a leisurely stroll.

★ **Straight Wharf** – This wharf at the head of Main Street and its old fishing sheds have been transformed into modern marinas and shops, art galleries and restaurants. Yachts and other pleasure craft tie up here in summer.

★ **Hadwen House–Satler Memorial** – *Main and Pleasant Sts. Visit by guided tour (30min) only, Jun–mid-Oct daily 10am–5pm. $2.* This impressive dwelling, with its Neoclassical pediment and columns, was built in 1845 for the whale oil merchant, William Hadwen. The house and its rich decor bear witness to the life of luxury led by its owner. Large, well-lit rooms contain beautiful furnishings and numerous other treasures.
Opposite the Hawden House stand the identical **Three Bricks**, dwellings built by a wealthy merchant for his three sons.

★ **Whaling Museum** – *Broad St. Open Jun–mid-Oct daily 10am–5pm. May & late Oct–Dec weekends only 11am–3pm. $4. &.* The building, once a factory where candles were made from whale oil, contains fine collections of scrimshaw, harpoons, models and paintings. Workshops have been reproduced, illustrating the trades and crafts related to the whaling industry: a blacksmith shop, sail loft and cooper's shop. There is an interesting model of the **Camel**, a type of floating dry dock that was used from 1840 to 1850 to assist the new and larger vessels to enter the shallow waters of Nantucket Harbor.

**Congregational Church** – *Centre St. Open mid-Jun–Sept daily 10am–4pm. $1.50.* The original Old Vestry (1725) now functions as a rear chapel to the present structure (1834). The interior seems larger than it is because of the trompe l'œil paintings on the front wall and ceiling. Nantucket history is presented in displays on the tower landing. The tower itself affords a **panorama**★ of the town and island.

**The Oldest House** – *Sunset Hill. Visit by guided tour (20min) only Jun–mid-Oct daily 10am–5pm. $3.* A narrow, gravel road outside town leads to the oldest house on the island, the **Jethro Coffin House**. Built in 1686 for Jethro Coffin and his wife, this wooden saltbox, with its casement windows and large central chimney, typifies 17C Colonial architecture. The horseshoe design, fashioned in brick on the chimney, was intended as a special charm to protect the residents from witches.

**Old Gaol** – *Vestal St. Open Jun–mid-Oct daily 10am–5pm.* The old pillory in the courtyard recalls the severity of early justice. Inside, the four stone prison cells appear as they did in the early 19C.

**Old Mill** – *Mill Hill. Visit by guided tour (20min) only Jun–mid-Oct daily 10am–5pm. $2.* Corn is still ground at this old windmill (1746) that operates with its original machinery and grinding stones.

## ADDITIONAL SIGHTS

★ **Siasconset** – Islanders call this village "Sconset." Fishermen who came here during the 17C to fish for cod built the sheds that were later converted into the gray **cottages**★ of Siasconset. Discovered at the end of the 19C by artists in search of unspoiled natural scenery, the area rapidly grew into a fashionable resort as handsome dwellings were built on the land surrounding the small shanties. Between 1881 and 1918, a railroad linked Siasconset to the center of Nantucket.

**Sankaty Head Lighthouse** – The lighthouse is a short walking distance from the shore road, which affords views of the ocean on one side, and of cranberry bogs and rolling moors on the other side. The road between Quidnet and Nantucket offers a succession of scenic landscapes.

**Surfside Beach** – A road *(Surfside Rd)* and bicycle path lead to the south shore, where visitors can swim at Surfside Beach.

**Madaket** – A paved road leads through the moors to Madaket Beach on the western end of the island. The afternoon is the best time to enjoy Madaket's white sandy stretches and refreshing surf.

---

## ★ NEW BEDFORD     Pop 99,922

Map of Principal Sights p 3     Tourist Office ☎ 508-997-1250

New Bedford, the whaling capital of the world during the mid-19C, still depends on income gained from fishing and manufacturing. The smell of saltwater pervades this old New England port city, located one hour south of BOSTON. Cobblestone streets lead down to the waterfront, where ship's supplies and antiques are sold. Once the anchorage of majestic whaling ships, the wharves are now crowded with modern fishing craft. Follow one of these streets up from the waterfront to Johnny Cake Hill to discover memories of New Bedford's illustrious whaling days, which are well preserved in the Whaling Museum and the Seamen's Bethel, or mariner's chapel.

**Whaling's Golden Age** – New Bedford's 30-year reign as the world capital of the whaling industry began in 1765 when Joseph Rotch, a Nantucketer who had established the whaling industry on his island, came to this fishing village. Rotch's efforts formed the foundation of New Bedford's burgeoning whaling trade. By the late 1830s New Bedford had surpassed NANTUCKET as the center of the industry. In 1840 Herman Melville described the influence that whaling exerted on the quality of life in New Bedford: "All these brave houses and flowery gardens came from the Atlantic, Pacific and Indian Oceans, one and all they were harpooned and dragged up hither from the bottom of the sea."
Sperm whale oil and bone indeed formed the basis of the city's wealth. Factories worked day and night converting the oil into candles; whalebone, destined to be transformed into corset stays, umbrellas and walking sticks, was set out along the piers to dry. New Bedford's glory days peaked in the 1850s, when 80 percent of America's whaleships sailed from this town, and more than 10,000 men—about half the town's population—participated in whaling.

**The Decline** – Although the discovery of petroleum in Pennsylvania brought about a decline in the demand for whale oil, the fatal blow to New Bedford's principal industry was also due, in large part, to the reduction in the size of its fleet: 39 vessels were lost in the Stone Fleet episode *(p 26)*, and an additional 32 ships were abandoned after they became icebound in the Arctic Ocean in 1861. Similar disasters diminished the size of the fleet even further until, by the end of the 19C, almost all New Bedford's capital had shifted from whaling to manufacturing.

### SIGHTS *3hrs*

★★ **New Bedford Whaling Museum** – *18 Johnny Cake Hill. From I-95 Exit 15, follow the signs to downtown New Bedford. Turn right on Elm St, then left on Bethel St. Open year-round Mon–Sat 9am–5pm, Sun 1–5pm (Jul–Aug Sun 11am–5pm), closed Jan 1, Thanksgiving Day, Dec 25. $4.50. ☎508-997-0046.* The museum's collections, which relate to the history of whaling, are among the finest in the world. On the ground floor, in the section reserved for **scrimshaw** *(p 35)*, note the sleigh and bird cage carved out of whale bone. A large hall contains the half-scale model of the fully rigged whaling bark **Lagoda★★**. Formerly a trade ship, the *Lagoda* made 12 whaling voyages out of New Bedford in the 1800s. Visitors may climb aboard the model vessel, which is the largest of its kind in the world, to examine the elaborate rigging and the tryworks.
The collection of marine engravings, whale hunt illustrations, oils and watercolors, includes ship portraits and seascapes by 19C artists Benjamin Russell and **William Bradford**, as well as a series of panels painted by Charles Raleigh in the 1870s. A separate gallery displays sections from the vast **panorama★** by **Benjamin Russell** and **Caleb Purrington**, entitled *Whaling Voyage 'Round the World.*
More than 1,000 logbooks, with their simple, and often humorous illustrations, give vivid accounts of life aboard a whaling ship. On the floor above, a cooperage, sail loft and rigging loft have been reconstructed to demonstrate trades that supported the whaling industry.

**Seamen's Bethel** – *15 Johnny Cake Hill. Open mid-May–Labor Day Mon–Sat 10am–4pm, Sun 1–4pm; rest of the year Mon–Fri 11am–1pm, Sat 1–4pm, Sun 1–4pm. Closed Jan 1, Thanksgiving Day, Dec 25. Contribution requested. ☎508-992-3295.* This chapel (1832), described in Herman Melville's classic novel *Moby-*

*Dick,* was a necessary stop for the mariner who was about to embark on a perilous whaling voyage. Still used for services today, the chapel contains a pulpit shaped to resemble the hull of a whaleship.

**Lightship New Bedford** – *The lightship (not open to the public) is adjacent to, and part of, the Coast Guard Exhibit at the State Pier.* This vessel was one of the dozens of lightships that once guarded the waters where it was considered too dangerous to erect lighthouses.

## ★ NEWBURYPORT                                                  Pop 16,317

Map of Principal Sights p 3                          Tourist Office ☎508-459-6150

This small city at the mouth of the Merrimack River was the home of a large fleet of merchant vessels in the 18C and 19C. The dignified Federal mansions built on **High Street** by sea captains, and the charming lanes reaching from Bartlett Mall to the restored **Market Square District★** evoke Newburyport's heyday as a bustling ship-building port and trading center.

Down by the waterfront, historic structures mark the site of the 19C boatyards that produced some of the finest clippers ever to sail the seas.

### SIGHTS

★ **High Street** – Ornamented with carved porches and columns, the houses represent the major styles of early American architecture: late Georgian, Federal and Greek Revival. **Frog Pond** and **Bartlett Mall**, fronting High Street, provide the setting for the **Court House** (1800) designed by Charles Bulfinch and remodeled 53 years later.

**Cushing House** – *No. 98. Visit by guided tour (45min) only, May–Oct Tue–Fri 10am–4pm, Sat 10am–2pm. $3. ☎508-462-2681.* This brick mansion (c.1808) was home to three generations of the Cushing family. The dwelling's most famous occupant, Caleb Cushing, was the first US envoy to China in 1842. Furnishings that Cushing acquired in the Orient, a small group of early American folk paintings, and a collection of silver, clocks and needlework are among the exhibits.

**Custom House** – *25 Water St. Open Apr–Dec 22 Mon–Sat 10am–4pm, Sun 1–4pm. $3. ☎508-462-8681.* Designed by Robert Mills, architect of the Washington Monument in the nation's capital, this granite structure once welcomed mariners returning from long sea voyages. Today it contains the **Museum of the Maritime History of the Merrimack Valley** featuring exhibits on shipbuilding, the Coast Guard and foreign imports.

### EXCURSIONS

★★ **Plum Island – Parker River National Wildlife Refuge** – *3mi from Newburyport by Water St, then Plum Island Tpk. Open year-round daily dawn–dusk. Refuge Beach closed Apr–Jun. $5. Refuge closes when parking capacity is reached. Parking available in the small lots off the road that leads through the refuge. Certain lots provide access to observation towers, trails & beach. Camping prohibited. ☎508-465-5753.* The southern two-thirds of this island has been designated as a haven for waterfowl in the Atlantic Flyway. Opportunities for bird watching abound (more than 270 species have been sighted), especially during the spring and fall migrations. The observation towers offer **panoramas** of the island's 4,650 acres of dunes, marshlands and oceanfront beach. From Hellcat Trail and Pines Trail, you can see the marshes.

**Haverhill** – Pop 51,418. Industry continues to be important to this community, a major center for the production of shoes in the 19C.

**John Greenleaf Whittier Birthplace** – *305 Whittier Rd. 13mi from Newburyport by Rte 1 north, then Rte 110 west. Open year-round Tue–Sat 10am–5pm, Sun 1–5pm; rest of the year 1–5pm (Sat 10am–5pm). Closed major holidays. $2. ☎508-373-3979.* The 19C Quaker poet and abolitionist John Greenleaf Whittier was born in this rustic farmhouse. Whittier's poem *Snow-bound* describes the writing desk and fireplace in this restored dwelling.

## ★ PIONEER VALLEY

Map of Principal Sights p 2                          Tourist Office ☎413-665-7333

The fertile Connecticut River Valley, extending north to south through the center of Massachusetts, was one of the major axes settled by pioneers during the 17C. The valley remained the western frontier of New England until the 18C, as the colonists did not dare risk crossing the Berkshire Mountains and venturing into the Hudson Valley, the domain of the Dutch.

**Unusual Relief of a Fertile Valley** – The broad, gentle farmlands that reach from one end of the valley to the other are framed against a backdrop of dramatic rocky ledges and craggy, volcanic **basalt ridges**. These asymmetrical ridges rise abruptly from the valley floor, forming sheer, steep drops on the west side and gentle slopes on the east, because of the way the basalt split. Vantage points along these ridges command beautiful views of the valley and the Connecticut River. Vegetables and tobacco are raised in the valley's fertile soil; netted coverings distinguish the fields where tobacco grows.

**Valley of the Dinosaurs** – Less dramatic in appearance than the basalt ridges, but of great geological interest, are the finer-grained sedimentary rocks containing the tracks of dinosaurs that roamed the CONNECTICUT VALLEY approximately 200 million years ago. These footprints, pressed into the mud on the valley floor and baked by the sun, were later covered and preserved by additional layers of mud. Eventually, they became layers of sedimentary rocks, primarily sandstone and shale. Today these rocks reveal the fascinating story of the region's prehistoric past. The creatures that once roamed this area were small, about the size of a man, according to the size of their footprints. Dinosaurs did not attain their mammoth size until about 100 million years later.

Dinosaur tracks can be seen at the Pratt Museum at Amherst College, in their original formation in Rocky Hill *(p 48)*, and at various other locations.

**A Center of Education** – More than 60,000 students attend the numerous schools, colleges and the university in the Pioneer Valley. Five of these institutions have joined together to form a consortium, sharing such projects as a radio station and a bus system, as well as departments and courses.

The consortium includes: the **University of Massachusetts** at Amherst, a sprawling campus with tall modern towers, where 26,000 students attend classes; **Amherst College**, established in 1821; innovative **Hampshire College**, established in 1971 by the other members of the consortium; **Smith College** at Northampton, one of the most select colleges in the nation for women, founded in 1875 by Sophia Smith; and **Mt Holyoke College**, across the river in South Hadley, established in 1837 as the first women's college in the US. The poet **Emily Dickinson** was a student at Mt Holyoke before she settled in Amherst, where she lived the remainder of her reclusive life.

## SIGHTS

★★ **Deerfield** – *Description p 145.*

★ **Quabbin Reservoir** – *Access from Rte 9; 2mi from Belchertown. Drive on Windsor Dam then follow the signs for Quabbin Hill Tower.* Construction of the 28sq mi reservoir (storage capacity: 412 billion gals) that serves the BOSTON region was accomplished by damming the Swift River and flooding four of the valley towns. The many islands that stud Quabbin's vast water reserves (*Quabbin* in the Nipmuck language means "a lot of water") were created by hilltops jutting out of the submerged area. Impressive **views★★** are available from **Enfield Lookout** and from the **observation tower** on Quabbin Hill. The reservoir offers opportunities for fishing, hiking, picnicking and scenic shore drives *(swimming and hunting prohibited).*

**Mt Sugarloaf State Reservation** – *Follow the signs from Rte 116.* From the top of this basalt ridge there is an expansive **view★★** of the Connecticut River as it meanders through open farmlands. Small towns fleck the valley landscape.

**Mt Tom State Reservation** – *From Holyoke take Rte 141 north 3mi. Open year-round Mon–Fri 8am–dusk, weekends 9am–dusk. $2/car (mid-May–Labor Day & weekends Sept–Oct)* ☎413-527-4805. Easthampton and Northampton can be seen in the valley below the access road to this 1,800-acre recreation area, which includes some 30mi of hiking trails.

The summit of Mt Tom commands a view of the curved arm of the Connecticut River, made famous by Thomas Cole's painting *The Oxbow* (Metropolitan Museum of Art), and Northampton and the Berkshire Hills beyond. The slopes of Mt Tom provide a venue for skiing in winter; a water park is in operation during the summer *(open Jun–early Sept daily 10am–8pm; $14.95;* ☎413-536-0516).

**Northampton** – Pop 29,289. Northampton has grown from a remote frontier town into a bustling commercial center. The **Smith College Museum of Art**, on Elm Street, owns a collection noted for its American and French works of the 19C and 20C *(open Aug Tues–Sun noon–4pm; rest of the year hours vary.* ☎413-585-2760).

**Skinner State Park** – *From Rte 47 follow the signs for the Summit House. Open May–Oct Mon–Fri 8am–dusk, weekends 10am–dusk, weather permitting. $2/car (weekends & holidays only)* ☎413-586-0350. *Facility information p 251.* The old summit hotel *(open Jun–Oct weekend afternoons only)*, built on a basalt ridge, offers a **view★** of the valley. The towers of the University of Massachusetts in Amherst are visible in the distance.

*Cross-references to sights described in this guide are indicated by* SMALL CAPITALS. *Consult the index (p 258) for the appropriate page number.*

## ★★ PLYMOUTH — Pop 45,608

Map of Principal Sights p 3 — Tourist Office ☎617-826-3136

Pilgrims landed here in 1620 to establish Plymouth Colony, the first permanent settlement in New England. The long voyage of their ship, the *Mayflower*, the hardships they endured, and the eventual success of Plymouth Colony form part of the cherished story related in Plymouth's historic monuments and sites.

The town itself, modern and attractive, is a residential and industrial community with hilly streets sloping down to the harbor. From **Burial Hill**, where an old cemetery contains gravestones dating back to the Plymouth Colony, there are views that reach beyond the town and out to sea. The **Town Brook**, close to the place where the Pilgrims built their first homes, runs through a lovely public park, **Brewster Gardens**.

**A Colony Off Course** – During the 16C a group of Puritans known as **Separatists** attempted to reform the Church of England. In 1607, to avoid persecution by the authorities, members of the group emigrated from Scrooby, England, to Holland.

Plimoth Plantation

They remained there until, impressed by favorable accounts of the New World, they decided to emigrate to America. Early in September 1620, 102 passengers, including 35 Separatists, boarded the *Mayflower* at Plymouth, England, and set sail for the Virginia Colony in North America. Diverted north by a storm, the settlers landed two months later on the shores of CAPE COD. They spent five weeks in the region before again setting sail for Virginia. Detoured a second time by strong winds, the Pilgrims headed for the bay that had been charted six years earlier by Capt John Smith; on the shores of this bay they established Plymouth Colony.

**The First Winter** – The harsh weather and a scarcity of food left almost half the colony dead by the end of the first winter. Burials were held at night on **Cole's Hill**, and graves were left unmarked to conceal the settlers' dwindling numbers from the neighboring Wampanoag tribe. The spring brought hope to the settlement along with a group of Indians who befriended the Pilgrims and taught them how to raise crops and to hunt and fish. After the harvest that fall, members of Plymouth Colony joined with the Indians in a three-day feast, the first American **Thanksgiving celebration**, in gratitude for their blessings.

**Pilgrims' Progress** – Every Friday in August and on Thanksgiving Day, modern Plymouth residents dress as Pilgrims and take part in a Sabbath procession up Leyden Street to Burial Hill, where a religious service is held.

### HISTORIC DISTRICT — 1 day. Map p 163.

*Begin at the visitor center at 225 Water St (open Jul–Sept daily 9am–9pm, Apr–Jun 8am–5pm, Oct–Dec 9am–6pm; ☎800-872-1620).*

★★ **Mayflower II** – *Berthed at the State Pier. Open Apr–Nov daily 9am–5pm (Jul–Aug 7pm). $5.75. ☎508-746-1622.* The *Mayflower II*, built in England (1955-1957), is a full-scale replica of the type of ship that brought the Pilgrims to Plymouth in 1620.

★ **Plymouth Rock** – *On the beach at Water St.* This boulder set at the harbor's edge has traditionally been regarded as the stepping stone used by the *Mayflower* passengers when they disembarked at Plymouth. The boulder is sheltered by a multi-columned granite structure. Opposite is **The Pilgrim Mother [1]**, a fountain honoring the women of the *Mayflower*.

**Plymouth National Wax Museum [M¹]** – *16 Carver St. Open Jul–Aug daily 9am–9pm. Mar–May & Nov 9am–5pm. Jun, Sept & Oct 9am–7pm. Also open first weekend in Dec 10am–4pm. $5.* ☎508-746-6468. Located on **Cole's Hill** *(p 162)*, the museum contains 26 life-size dioramas which, enhanced by realistic soundtracks, depict the Pilgrim story from the emigration of the Separatists to Holland in 1607, to the first Thanksgiving celebration in 1621. In front of the museum stands a statue of **Massasoit [2]**, chief of the Indians who helped the Pilgrims to survive that first spring.

★ **Mayflower Society Museum [M²]** – *4 Winslow St. Visit by guided tour (45min) only, Jul–Aug daily 10am–4:15pm; end of May–Jun & mid-Sept–mid-Oct weekends only 10am–4:15pm; open Thanksgiving weekend 10am–4:15pm. $2.50.* ☎508-746-2590. Built during the Colonial period and enlarged in the 19C, the house is a graceful blend of Colonial and Victorian architectural features. Attractive roof railings and the multi-paned cupola add harmonious relief to the white brick exterior.

Inside, a flying stairway joins the original rooms with later sections of the house. Among the antiques found throughout the house is a rare set of biblical fireplace tiles in the drawing room.

**Spooner House** – *27 North St. Visit by guided tour (30min) only, Jul–Aug Tues–Sun noon–4:30pm. Mid-May–Jun & Sept–mid-Oct Wed–Sat noon–4:30pm. Closed major holidays. $2.50.* ☎508-746-0012. This quaint mid-18C dwelling preserves many of the furnishings belonging to members of the Spooner family, who owned the house for over 200 years.

**Richard Sparrow House [A]** – *42 Summer St. Open mid-May–Dec 24 Thu–Tues 10am–5pm. $1.* ☎508-747-1240. The oldest dwelling (1640) in Plymouth contains 18C furnishings. Pottery-making is demonstrated on site.

**Pilgrim John Howland House [B]** – *33 Sandwich St. Visit by guided tour (45min) only, late May–mid-Oct daily 10am–4:30pm. Thanksgiving Day weekend 10am–3pm. $ 2.50.* ☎508-746-9590. This is the only house remaining in Plymouth where Pilgrims are known to have lived.

★ **Pilgrim Hall Museum** – *75 Court St. Open Feb–Dec daily 9:30am–4:30pm (closes at noon Dec 24 & 31). Closed Dec 25. $5.* ☎508-746-1620. Built as a memorial to the Pilgrims and the Plymouth Colony, this austere granite structure (1824), designed by Alexander Parris, contains original Pilgrim furnishings and artifacts, including chairs owned by Governors Bradford and Carver; the cradle of Peregine White, who was born on the *Mayflower;* Bibles belonging to John Alden and Governor Bradford; and a sampler made by Lora Standish, daughter of Myles Standish.

**National Forefathers' Monument** – *Allerton St off Rte 44.* Representing the virtue Faith, this large monument (36ft) honors the Pilgrims and their small colony.

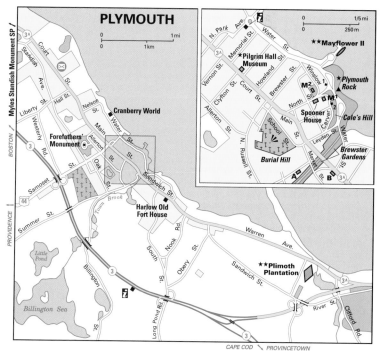

## ADDITIONAL SIGHTS  *Map p 163*

★★ **Plimoth Plantation** – *Illustration p 162. 3mi south on Rte 3 from the center of Plymouth, Exit 4. Open Apr–Nov daily 9am–5pm, rest of the year by appointment only. $18.50 (includes visit to the Mayflower II).* ✗ ☎*508-746-1622.* The plantation is a reproduction of the Pilgrims' village as it appeared in 1627. (The spelling of "Plimoth" was adopted from Governor Bradford's early journals by the museum curators.) Buildings, paths and gardens have been constructed to resemble those that once stood on the site of modern Plymouth's business district.

The **Fort/Meetinghouse**, at the entrance to the plantation, offers a good vantage point from which to view the entire village, with its neat rows of thatched-roof cottages similar to those inhabited by the Alden, Carver, Bradford and Standish families. Rooms inside the houses are decorated with reproductions of 17C English furnishings. Throughout the village, costumed guides portray specific Pilgrim settlers, sharing experiences with visitors while performing tasks such as gardening, cooking, and harvesting crops according to the methods used in the early colony.

A path leads to **Hobbamock's Wampanoag Indian Homesite**, where the culture of this native Indian group is interpreted by staff members engaged in raising crops, drying food, weaving and other chores traditionally performed by the Wampanoag people. The campsite includes examples of the *wetus*, domed dwellings once built as shelters by the Wampanoag.

**Harlow Old Fort House** – *114 Sandwich St. Visit by guided tour (45min) only, Jul–Aug Tue–Sun noon–4:30pm. Late May–Jun & Sept–mid–Oct Wed–Sat noon–4:30pm. Closed major holidays. $2.50.* ☎*508-746-0012.* The framework of this house (1677) contains timbers of a 17C fort that originally stood on Burial Hill.

**Cranberry World Visitor Center** – *From Rte 3, take Rte 44 east .75mi. Cross Rte 3A and continue on Rte 44 to the waterfront rotary, then bear left. Open May–Nov daily 9:30am–5pm.* ♿ ☎*508-747-2350.* A leading producer of cranberries, the Ocean Spray cranberry cooperative sponsors this historical and educational exhibit in Plymouth. The visitor center features exhibits, antiques and outdoor bogs.

## EXCURSION

**Myles Standish Monument State Park** – *In Duxbury, 8mi from Plymouth by Rte 3A to Crescent St. Turn right, and enter through the gate at left. Open year-round daily 8am–4pm. Closed Jan 1, Thanksgiving Day, Dec 25.* ☎*508-866-2526.* The Standish monument, a gigantic figure of Pilgrim leader Myles Standish, overlooks the bay and offers a **view**★★ of Plymouth, Cape Cod Bay and PROVINCETOWN.

> *"To think of landing here [at Plymouth] on the 22nd of December without a shelter and three thousand miles from what once was a beloved home. The idea as I stood upon the burying place which is high and overlooks the harbour made me shiver."*
>
> —Charles Francis Adams, *Diary*, 14 September 1835

★★ # PROVINCETOWN                           Pop 3,561

Map of Principal Sights p 3                          Tourist Office ☎ 508-362-3225

As Route 6 heads north through the Province Lands sector of the Cape Cod National Seashore, Provincetown Harbor is visible to the left; in the distance a tall, solitary monument resembling an Italian bell tower appears. Motels and bungalows stand like sentries along the road, guarding the sandy stretches that lead into Provincetown, or "P-town," as it is called. Extending to the tip of Cape Cod, the town combines elements of a fishing village, artist's colony and resort.

During the summer, the arrival of large numbers of tourists swell the population of the town from 3,500 to 75,000. Crowds weave in and out of the shops, galleries and eating places that line the narrow streets. **Commercial Street**★, the main thoroughfare in town, becomes almost impassable. Visitors and residents alike find the nearby beaches of the CCNS—**Herring Cove Beach**, **Race Point Beach** *(map p 141)*—a refreshing contrast to the hustle and bustle that characterize the center of town at this time of year *(in summer, shuttle buses run hourly along Bradford St and to Herring Cove Beach).* Nature lovers will appreciate the nature walks and lectures organized by the **Center for Coastal Studies (CCS)**, a research organization devoted to conservation of the marine habitat *(*☎*508-487-3622).*

**From the Mayflower to Whaling Port** – When the *Mayflower* was blown off course and arrived at this end of the Cape in November 1620, the Pilgrims saw only stark, endless stretches of sand. The settlers spent five weeks exploring this region, and aware that this area was not within the bounds of their charter, drew up the **Mayflower Compact** to serve as their instrument of government. Then they reset their sails for a voyage that ended a few days later at Plymouth *(p 162)*.

By the 18C, less than 100 years after the Pilgrims landed on the Cape, Provincetown had grown into the third largest whaling center after Nantucket and New Bedford. In the mid-19C, 75 wharves could be counted along its shores, and the beaches were covered with fish flakes, or racks for drying fish, and saltworks, wooden structures used to filter salt from seawater. Provincetown vessels recruited seamen in the Azores and Cape Verde Islands, a factor that accounts for the town's large Portuguese population and the traditions they have preserved. Other Provincetowners found fortune closer to home. Villians known as mooncussers erected lights along the shore to lure unwitting ships into dangerous shoals where they ran aground. They then boarded the vessels, killed the crew and stole the valuable cargo. The place where these rogues gathered was nicknamed "Helltown" and was cautiously avoided by the village's more respectable citizens.

**Provincetown of the Artists** – At the beginning of the 20C, Provincetown's wild natural beauty attracted artists and writers to its shores. In 1901 Charles W. Hawthorne founded the **Cape Cod School of Art** here, followed 15 years later by the establishment of the **Provincetown Players**, a group of playwrights and actors rebelling against the rigid criteria of the Broadway stage. Eugene O'Neill's *(p 36)* career as a playwright was launched at Provincetown in 1916 when his first play, *Bound East for Cardiff*, was produced at the Wharf Theatre. At about the same time, the town became a prestigious artist's colony where writers and dramatists such as O'Neill, John Dos Passos, Sinclair Lewis and Tennessee Williams gathered. Over the ensuing decades, the town has hosted art world celebrities such as Robert Motherwell and Mark Rothko. Today the numerous galleries along Commercial Street, the **Provincetown Art Association** and the **Provincetown Theater Company** carry out the cultural and artistic traditions so closely associated with the town's character. *For a listing of current art shows, consult the free gallery guide available from the visitor center at MacMillan Wharf and from major galleries.*

## SIGHTS   *4hrs. Map below.*

**MacMillan Wharf** – *At the end of Standish St. Public parking lot on the wharf.* Late in the afternoon, fishing boats, announced by the procession of seagulls that greets them, return to the wharf where their fresh catches are unloaded and shipped to markets in Boston and New York. On the last Sunday in June, the **Blessing of the Fleet**, a colorful and impressive Portuguese tradition, takes place in the harbor. This lively pier is also the departure point for **whale-watching cruises** *(p 254)*, a popular local attraction *(obtain schedules from the visitor center).*

**Provincetown Heritage Museum** – *Commercial & Center Sts. Open mid-Jun–mid-Oct daily 10am–6pm. $3. ☎508-487-7098.* Housed in a gleaming white Neoclassical edifice (1860) originally built as a Methodist church, the town's small history museum presents multiple aspects of Provincetown's varied past through artifacts, photos and re-created 19C interiors. The second floor is dominated by the 66ft *Rose Dorothea*, a half-scale model of a fishing schooner that plied the Grand Banks in the early 20C.

★ **Pilgrim Monument and Provincetown Museum** – *Winslow St. Open mid-Apr–Oct daily 9am-5pm (Jul–Aug 7pm). Nov & Mar–early Apr daily 10am–4pm. $5. �& ☎508-487-1310.* The small museum, located near the base of the tower, features a fascinating temporary exhibit on the shipwrecked 18C pirate ship *Whydah* discovered off the coast of nearby Wellfleet in 1984. Visitors can observe conservation experts at work on original salvaged artifacts. The permanent collection of documents and objects, including a model of the *Mayflower*, illustrates the town's rich history.

The monument, inspired by the 14C bell tower in the Tuscan hilltown of Siena, was erected in 1910 to commemorate the 1620 landing of the Pilgrims at Provincetown. The observation deck atop this 253ft granite structure affords sweeping **views★★** of the entire Cape *(116 steps and 60 ramps; 15min climb).*

★★ **Dunes Tour** – *Apr–Oct daily 10am–sunset. 1hr 15min. Commentary. $9. Art's Dune Tours. ☎508-487-1950.* This tour by vehicle is a magnificent way to explore the spectacular Provincetown Dunes of the Cape Cod National Seashore, both of which are constantly being reshaped by the winds.

# QUINCY
Pop 84,985

Map of Principal Sights p 3　　　　　　　　　Tourist Office ☎617-826-3136

This large community of the state's South Shore was prominent during its early days as the home of the Adams family, which gave the nation its second and sixth presidents: **John Adams** and **John Quincy Adams**. In the 19C Quincy's granite quarries and shipyards attracted laborers from Finland, Greece, Ireland, Italy and Eastern Europe. Today their descendants form the basis of the town's ethnically diverse population. Quincy shipyards produced the only seven-masted schooner *(Thomas W. Lawson)* ever built, as well as the first atomic-powered surface ship produced in the 20C. This Boston suburb remains a hub of industrial and commercial activity.

**The Adams** – John Adams (1735-1826), a spokesman for the revolution against England's colonial policies, was among the men who drafted the Declaration of Independence. Beginning in 1778, his diplomatic posts took him to France, Scotland and England, where he was instrumental in negotiating the Treaty of Paris (1783) to end the Revolution. He served as Vice President under George Washington, then as President from 1796 to 1801. After his defeat in 1801, John Adams retired to his home in Quincy. By incredible coincidence, John Adams and Thomas Jefferson, who also helped draft the Declaration of Independence, died on the same day—July 4, 1826—50 years to the day that the historic document was signed.

John Quincy Adams (1767-1848), who followed in the steps of his father, studied law before beginning a diplomatic career, serving at various times as ambassador to Prussia, the Netherlands, Russia and Great Britain. In 1824 he was elected President of the United States, an office he held until 1829. Having lost the election in 1828, Adams retired to his hometown. His election to Congress two years later began a 17-year career in the legislature for this devoted statesman.

## SIGHTS　*2hrs. Map p 127.*

**John Adams and John Quincy Adams Birthplaces** – *1250 Hancock St. Visit by guided tour (55min) only, mid-Apr–mid-Nov daily 9am–5pm. $2. ☎617-770-1175.* These modest Colonial saltboxes *(p 28),* where John Adams and John Quincy Adams were born, contain memorabilia and period furnishings.

★ **Adams National Historic Site** – *135 Adams St. Same hours as above.* In 1787 John Adams and his wife, Abigail, bought this house, referred to by the Adams family as the "Old House." Each of the four successive generations of Adams who lived here added their own mementoes and furnishings to the house, which explains the diversity of styles. Especially noteworthy is the study where John Adams died, the rich mahogany in the Panelled Room, and the Long Room, which is furnished with elegant French pieces. The Stone Library contains the Adams family collection of 12,000 volumes.

**United First Parish Church** – *1306 Hancock St. Open mid-Apr–mid-Nov Mon–Fri 9am–5pm, Sun 1–5pm. $1. ☎617-773-1290.* This granite Greek Revival structure, known as the "Church of the Presidents," is the final resting place of both John Adams and John Quincy Adams and their wives.

# ★★ SALEM
Pop 38,091

Map of Principal Sights p 3　　　　　　　　　Tourist Office ☎508-921-4990

Salem, a town tormented in the 17C by its fear of witchcraft and a seaport that launched nearly 1,000 ships in the following centuries, is a bustling and pleasant city where historic districts adjoin industrial sites. Today the city makes its living from revenues generated by tourism, manufacturing, the North Shore Medical Center and Salem State College.

Renewal programs in the heart of the downtown area, around **Essex Street**, have created the look of the colonial era with brick walkways and a pedestrian mall. A number of shops devoted to the occult offer tarot and psychic readings and sell witchcraft and New Age items. Operated by the National Park Service, the **visitor center**, housed in the town's renovated, turn-of-the-century armory, just off Essex Street, features a film *(27min)* on the history of Essex County *(2 New Liberty St; open year-round daily 9am–5pm; closed Jan 1, Thanksgiving Day, Dec 25; ☎508-741-3648).*

## HISTORICAL NOTES

**A City of Peace** – Founded in 1626 by Roger Conant, Salem derives its name from the Hebrew word *Shalom,* meaning peace. Ironically, intolerance and violence dominated the early days of this Puritan city. Roger Williams, persecuted by the authorities, fled to Rhode Island in 1636 *(p 202),* and thereafter zealous Salemites devoted their energies to driving the "evil ones" from the colony. With the intention of ridding the colony once and for all of evildoers, the notorious witch hunts of Salem began in the early 1690s.

**The Witchcraft Hysteria** – In 1692 several young girls, whose imaginations had been stirred by tales of voodoo told to them by the West Indian slave Tituba, began to have visions and convulsive fits. After examining the girls, a doctor declared them to be victims of "the evil hand." Impressionable and frightened, the young-sters accused Tituba and two other women of having bewitched them, and the women were immediately arrested and put into prison. From that point on, fear and panic spread through Salem, leaving no one free of suspicion. More than 200 persons were accused of witchcraft, 150 imprisoned and 19 found guilty and hanged. The hysteria, credited in retrospect to rivalries between several prominent Salem families, came to an abrupt end about a year later when Gov William Phips' wife was accused of witchcraft.

**An Era of Maritime Glory** – Salem's sizable fleet of vessels, important to colo-nial trade in the 17C, won special recognition during the Revolution. When the ports of BOSTON and New York were occupied by the British, it was Salem's ships that carried arms and supplies to the colonial troops. Operating as privateers, the town's vessels also weakened the enemy by raiding and capturing about 400 British ships before the war ended.

After the Revolution Salem's merchant craft were prominent in worldwide trade. In 1786 the *Grand Turk,* sailing out of Salem to China, returned home to New England laden with a cargo of luxury goods. To the many ships that followed the *Grand Turk,* the route to the Far East *(p 26)* became a familiar one; "To the farthest port of the rich East!" became Salem's motto. The Chinese, who saw great num-bers of vessels arriving in their ports bearing Salem's name, imagined Salem was a vast and magnificent country.

Two years after the *Grand Turk* set sail for China, trade between Salem and India was opened by another Salem ship, the *Peggy,* owned by Elias Hasket Derby (be-low). The China Trade brought such enormous wealth to Salem, that taxes paid in the town on imported goods alone provided eight percent of the nation's rev-enues. Salem merchants, including the Derbys, Peabodys and Crowninshields, were among the richest men in America; their mansions were filled with treasures retrieved from the Orient aboard their ships.

The decline of the port of Salem, due in part to the embargo on foreign trade en-forced by President Jefferson in 1807, was hastened by the development of new, deep-draft clipper ships that could only be outfitted in deep-water ports such as those of Boston and New York.

**Two Famous Men of Salem** – **Samuel McIntire** (1757-1811), carpenter, wood carver, sculptor, builder and architect, influenced much of Salem's architecture. His solid, four-square wood and brick mansions, such as the Peirce-Nichols house (1782) on Federal Street *(not open to the public)*, ornamented with handsome porches and balustrades, are among the finest examples of American Federal architecture. The masterfully carved doorways, ceilings, cornices and fireplaces for which McIntire is known, are adorned with a variety of classical motifs (garlands, rosettes, fruit baskets) that reflect his refined taste and attention to detail.

**Nathaniel Hawthorne** (1804-1864), a leading 19C American literary figure, was born in Salem, where he wrote his earliest stories. Salem often provided the inspiration or setting for Hawthorne's works, such as *The House of the Seven Gables.* Much of the atmosphere in his novel *The Scarlet Letter,* especially the descriptions of the Custom House, was influenced by the years he spent as surveyor of the port.

## SIGHTS  *2 days. Map p 169.*

### Seaside Salem  *3hrs*
*The historic district may be visited on foot; begin at the visitor center (below) on Central Wharf.*

After more than a century, Salem is once again alive with a vitality reminiscent of its days of maritime supremacy. **Pickering Wharf** boasts a concentration of restau-rants and specialty shops; just beyond it, on Derby Street, is the Salem Maritime National Historic Site.

★ **Salem Maritime National Historic Site** – *Open year-round daily 9am–5pm. Closed Jan 1, Thanksgiving Day, Dec 25.* & ☎508-745-1470. The city's historic wa-terfront site is administered by the National Park Service. The **visitor center** features a film *(18min)* on the seafaring history of Salem. At one time, more than 40 wharves reached out into the harbor from the town's shoreline. **Derby Wharf**, the longest (2,100ft), and for many years a busy mercantile center, still remains.

★ **Custom House [A]** – This Federal-style building with its symbolic eagle was construct-ed in 1819 to house the customs offices of Salem. Inside, several of the offices, including the one used by Nathaniel Hawthorne when he was an officer of the port, have been restored.

At the rear of the Custom House, the **Bonded Warehouse [B]** contains samples of car-goes carried by Salem vessels, cargo handling equipment and weighing devices.

**Derby House [C]** – *Visit by guided tour only.* This brick mansion was built in 1761 for merchant Elias Hasket Derby, whose ships opened trade with India and the Orient, making him very rich. From the waterfront location of this house, Derby could see his ships as they docked at or near Derby Wharf. Inside, the wave motif ornament-ing the stairway and the staircase balusters, carved to resemble a twisted rope, is an appropriate feature for the home of a man who earned his living from the sea.

★ **House of the Seven Gables** – *54 Turner St. Visit by guided tour (40min) only, Jul–Oct daily 9am–6pm, rest of the year 10am–4:30pm. $6.50.* ✕ ☎*508-744-0991.* A rambling 3-story Colonial with steeply pitched roofs, this house was immortalized by Hawthorne's novel of the same name. Built in 1668, the house was completely restored in 1968. Inside, scenes from Hawthorne's novel come alive as visitors pass from Hepzibah's Cent Shop to the parlor where the judge was found, and into Clifford's room, under the eaves, at the top of a secret staircase.

Other buildings in this garden setting include Hawthorne's Birthplace (c.1750, moved from its original location on Union Street), the Retire Becket House (1655, which contains the museum shop), the Hooper-Hathaway House (1682) and a counting house (c.1820).

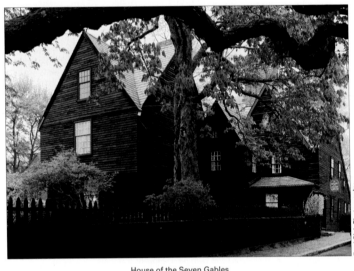

House of the Seven Gables

## ★★ Peabody Essex Museum   *1 1/2 days*

*East India Square. Open year-round Mon–Sat 10am–5pm (Thurs 8pm), Sun noon–5pm. Closed Jan 1, Thanksgiving Day, Dec 25. $7 (includes admission to on-site historic houses).* &. *Houses (p 169) can be visited by guided tour (45min) only; reservations suggested.* ☎*508-745-9500.*

The museum focuses on America's maritime history from the 17C to the present, and on the historical significance of the city of Salem and Essex County. It pays special tribute to Salem's great 18C and 19C maritime era, during which the town flourished as a major American port. The nearly 400,000 pieces in the museum's collection reflect the global range of Salem's ship captains, who returned from their travels with porcelains, carvings and other artifacts from the Far East, India, Africa and the Pacific Islands.

**A Museum for "Curiosities"** – In 1799, a group of local ship captains organized the **Salem East India Marine Society** and eventually the society built the East India Marine Hall. Still located on Essex Street, it originally housed a meeting hall, bank, insurance company and museum of "natural and artificial" curiosities from around the world. When the port declined, leaving Salem with serious economic problems, philanthropist George Peabody offered financial assistance. The society's museum was renamed for him in the early 20C, and in the latter half of the century, spacious modern galleries were added to the original hall. Two additions to the museum—a smooth-surfaced structure completed in 1976, and the Asian Export Wing dedicated in 1988—have greatly increased exhibition space.

In spring 1992, as part of the revitalization of historic Salem, the Peabody Museum was joined with the nearby Essex Institute, originally founded in 1821 to serve as the Essex County Historical Society. That society's holdings encompassed a museum of decorative arts, nine historic structures *(five currently open to the public)*, and a research library preserving rare manuscripts, log books, letters and diaries detailing life in early Salem. The combined museum displays art and artifacts from six curatorial departments.

**Maritime Art and History** – The collection of marine paintings includes works by major artists, such as Fitz Hugh Lane and Antoine Roux; port scenes illustrating commerce with the Orient; and ships' portraits commissioned by the vessels' owners. Portraiture and other paintings by such famed artists as John Singleton Copley and Gilbert Stuart are also featured, as are rare nautical instruments and charts and a dramatic collection of carved ships' figureheads.

**Asian Export Art** – Considered one of the most complete collections of its kind in the world, the collection features 19C and early 20C decorative and utilitarian porcelain, silver, furniture, textiles and precious objects. Created in China, Japan, India, the Phillipines and Ceylon (now Sri Lanka), the pieces were intended for export to England and America and therefore reflect a melding of Eastern artistry and Western tastes. The lacquer, ivory and mother-of-pearl work, as well as the items fashioned in gold and silver, are particularly impressive for their refined style and exquisite detail.

**Asian, Oceanic and African Art** – This section encompasses textiles, shields, ritual costumes, masks and pottery from the tropical Pacific Islands, Indonesia, Japan and Africa. The Edward S. Morse Collection of 19C Meiji costumes and crafts is reputedly the largest of its kind outside Japan.

**Native American Arts and Archaeology** – The collection includes artifacts from the Indian cultures of the Eastern seaboard, Great Lakes, Great Plains, Northwest Coast and South America.

**Natural History** – This section contains specimens of flora and fauna, predominantly from eastern America.

**American Decorative Arts** – The collection consists of furnishings, paintings, textiles, toys and costumes from the colonial period through the early 20C.

**Historic Houses** – *The following historic houses, located behind the museum in the former Essex Institute building, are open to the public (visit by 45min guided tour only; reservations suggested).*

★ **John Ward House [D]** – The Ward House (1684) is a good example of 17C American Colonial architecture, with its steep gables, clapboard exterior and small casement windows. The furnishings are of the same period.

**Crowninshield-Bentley House [E]** – The hipped roof, symmetrical windows, and pedimented doorway of this 1727 dwelling are typical of mid-18C New England architecture. The furnishings represent several different periods.

★★ **Gardner-Pingree House [F]** – The solid four-square silhouette of this handsome brick mansion (1804)—another of Samuel McIntire's designs—is lightened by its balustraded roof, numerous windows and curved entry porch supported by Corinthian columns.

Inside, the furnishings and decor create a mood of elegant refinement. In the front entrance hall, wave and rope motifs ornament the staircase. In the parlor, decorative motifs, including sheaves of wheat and baskets of fruit on the fireplaces and above the doorways reflect the work of master-carver McIntire. The bedchambers reveal the same refinement of taste. Most of the furniture was made in Salem.

The grounds also include the **Derby-Beebe Summer House [G]** (1799), designed by Samuel McIntire as a garden tea house, and the **Lyle-Tapley Shoe Shop [H]** (1830).

★ **Salem Common** – In the 19C a number of Federal mansions were built bordering the Common of colonial Salem, called Washington Square. A notable group of these residences stands on Washington Square North.

★★ **Chestnut Street** – This broad street lined with Federal-style mansions illustrates the wealth of 19C Salem. The majority of the dwellings on Chestnut Street were built between 1800 and 1820; their size and richly adorned facades are unrivaled. **Hamilton Hall** (no.9) was designed by Samuel McIntire *(p 167)*. The **Stephen Phillips Memorial Trust House** (no. 34), decorated with furnishings from around the world, is open to the public *(visit by 45min guided tour only, late May–mid-Oct Mon–Sat 10am–4:30pm; $2; ☎508-744-0440).*

**Goult-Pickman House** [J] – *Charter St. Not open to the public.* This Colonial dwelling (c.1680) is adjacent to Salem's old cemetery, the **Burying Point**, which contains interesting examples of early tombstones.

**Pioneer Village** – *Forest River Park, east of Salem State College, at the junction of Rtes 1A & 129. Visit by guided tour (1hr) only, May–Oct Mon–Sat 10am–5pm, Sun noon–5pm. $4.50. ☎508-745-0525.* This site features replicas of the diverse kinds of dwellings built by Salem's early settlers: thatched cottages, dugouts of mud and straw, and a wigwam that highlights the influence of the Indians on the first settlers. Costumed interpreters demonstrate the activities of 17C domestic life.

### Salem Bewitched  *2hrs*

In recent years Salem has become a center for adherents of the ancient religion of Wicca, a goddess and nature-based belief system. Several thousand witches, as followers of Wicca call themselves, currently live in the area, quietly practicing their religion and attempting to disspell long-held public opinions concerning witchcraft. To that end a Witches' League for Public Awareness was founded in 1986 by Laurie Cabot, who was named by former Gov Michael Dukakis as the "official Witch of Salem."

Several points of interest in or near Salem individually re-create the tale of the witch hunts and the story of their unfortunate victims. In 1992, the city celebrated the tercentenary of the witch trials. Each year at Halloween, Salem hosts Haunted Happenings, a ten-day festival that recalls the city's past.

**Salem Witch Museum** [M[1]] – *19 1/2 Washington Square North. Visit by guided tour (30min) only, year-round daily 10am–5pm (Jul–Aug 7pm). Closed Jan 1, Thanksgiving Day, Dec 25. $4. ⚐ 508-744-1692.* The museum presents a multimedia program *(30min)* of 13 life-size scenes that sensationalize the major events of the witchcraft hysteria from 1692 to its final days in 1693. Across from the museum stands Henry H. Kitson's statue of Salem's founder, **Roger Conant**.

**Witch House** – *310 1/2 Essex St. Visit by guided tour (30min) only, Mar–Dec 1 daily 10am–4:30pm (Jul–Aug 6pm). Closed Easter Sunday & Thanksgiving Day. $4. ☎508-744-0180.* This large dwelling (1642) was the home of Judge Corwin, one of the men who presided over the witch trials. The interior appears much as it did in the late 17C, when more than 200 persons accused of witchcraft were brought to the judge's chamber for preliminary hearings.

**Witch Dungeon Museum** [M[2]] – *16 Lynde St. Visit by guided tour (25min) only, Apr–Dec 1 daily 10am–5pm. $4. ☎508-741-3570.* A live stage presentation *(25min)*, based on historic transcripts of a 1692 witch trial, captures the hysteria that swept Salem in the late 17C. Following the presentation, visitors tour a re-creation of the dank dungeon where local "witches" were jailed in tiny, unlit cells.

**Rebecca Nurse Homestead** – *149 Pine St, in Danvers, 4mi north of Salem. Visit by guided tour (1hr) only, mid-Jun–Labor Day Tue–Sun 1–4:30pm. Mid-Sept–Oct weekends only 1–4:30pm. $3.50. ☎508-774-8799.* Rebecca Nurse, a victim of the Salem witch hunts, lived in this saltbox (c.1678). Accused of being a witch, Rebecca was tried, convicted and hanged, despite a petition in her favor that had been signed by many of the townspeople. A short walk from the house leads to the Nurse Burial Ground, where a monument marks Rebecca's presumed grave.

---

★ **SANDWICH**                                                    Pop 15,489

Map p 140                                             Tourist Office ☎508-362-3225

On the shores of Shawme Pond, tranquil and shaded by willow trees, are the Dexter Mill and the Hoxie House. Built in the 17C the house and the mill, which is still in use, evoke the colonial charm of Sandwich—the first settlement on Cape Cod, founded in 1637. Across from the village green stands the Sandwich Glass Museum.

**Boston and Sandwich Glass Company** – In 1825 Deming Jarves chose Sandwich as the site of his Boston and Sandwich Glass Co because of the region's vast forests, which provided the wood needed to fuel the furnaces in which he fired glass. An efficient administrator, Jarves brought skilled craftsmen from Europe to work in the factory, and built homes and company stores for them. He reintroduced the use of the three-part mold that had been used centuries before by the Romans, and developed a process to mass-produce clear, cut glass in a variety of shapes, forms and patterns. The delicate lacy pattern of the glass Jarves made became known as Sandwich glass *(p 35)* and brought fame to the factory and the town. By 1850, 500 workers were employed at the factory; but labor disputes in 1888 eventually forced the company to shut its doors permanently.

★ **Sandwich Glass Museum** – *129 Main St. Open Apr–Oct daily 9:30am–4:30pm. Nov–Mar Wed–Sun 9:30am–4pm. Closed Jan. $3.50.* & ☎508-888-0251. Founded in 1907, the museum owns an extensive collection of the glass made in Sandwich between 1825 and 1888. Moderately priced when it was produced in the 19C, Sandwich glass is today highly valued by collectors.

Before visiting the general exhibit rooms, pause at the diorama that illustrates the Sandwich factory and its craftsmen at work. Various stages of glassmaking are portrayed: sand is mixed with potash, carbonate of soda, or lime, heated in the furnace (at 2,500° F) and then blown, molded or pressed.

Exhibits display a variety of patterns in a wide range of Sandwich glass items, such as candlesticks, tableware, vases, furniture knobs and tiebacks. Examples of early pressed lacy glass, the colorful (canary, blue, green, opalescent) mid-period pattern glass, and the lesser-recognized blown, cut and engraved glassware are included. Note in particular the collections of decorative Sandwich paperweights and the one-of-a-kind presentation pieces made to commemorate special occasions or events.

★★ **Heritage Plantation of Sandwich** – *From the Sandwich green take Rte 130 to Pine St then turn left. Open mid-May–late Oct daily 10am–5pm. $7.* & ✗ ☎508-888-3300. The museum's collections of early American historical artifacts and folk art are arranged in several buildings designed to harmonize with the impeccably maintained 76-acre park setting. The plantation, formerly the estate of horticulturist Charles Dexter, who performed extensive research on rhododendrons in the 1920s and 1930s, is especially lovely during mid-May through mid-June when the plants are in bloom.

★★ **Automobile Museum** – This replica of the Round Stone Barn, constructed by the Shakers at Hancock *(p 149)*, contains antique automobiles in mint condition dating from 1899 to the 1930s, and includes the 1931 Duesenberg owned by Gary Cooper. Silent movies *(10min)* of the early days of the automobile are shown. The **Old East Mill** was built in Orleans c.1800.

★ **Military Museum** – This reproduction of the Publick House, a recreation hall built by the Continental Army (1783) in New Windsor, New York, contains antique firearms (including a rifle owned by Buffalo Bill Cody), flags and 2,000 hand-painted miniatures representing American military units from 1621 to 1900.

★ **Art Museum** – The superb collection of folk art comprises primitive portraits, wood carvings, metal work, glass, scrimshaw, birds carved by A. Elmer Crowell *(p 35)* and some 150 Currier and Ives prints. Children will enjoy riding on the carousel (1912).

# SPRINGFIELD
Pop 156,983

Map of Principal Sights p 2

Tourist Office ☎413-787-1548

Established on the banks of the Connecticut River in 1636 as a trading post, Springfield grew into an industrial center by the 19C. For more than 200 years, the city was known for the **Springfield Armory**, the government arsenal that turned out the first American musket (1795) and weapons used by the Union troops in the Civil War. A rich industrial past has contributed to making Springfield the hub of business, finance and industry in the Pioneer Valley *(p 160)* and the third largest city in Massachusetts, with tools and plastics among its leading products.

Each September the Springfield area hosts the **Eastern States Exposition**, the largest fair in the Northeast. Located on the 175-acre fairgrounds in West Springfield *(2mi west of the center of Springfield on Rte 147)*, the "Big E," as the annual fair is called, features exhibits, entertainment, the Eastern States Horse Show and an opportunity to tour **Old Storrowtown Village**, a restored colonial village on the fairgrounds.

Each June, the West Springfield fairground is also the site of the annual **American CraftFair**, formerly held in New York.

## SIGHTS  *4hrs*

★ **Basketball Hall of Fame** – *1150 W. Columbus Ave. Open Jul–Labor Day daily 9am–6pm, rest of the year daily 9am–5pm. Closed Jan 1, Thanksgiving Day, Dec 25. $7.* ☎413-781-6500. Basketball was originated by Dr James Naismith whose Springfield College team played the first game of basketball in 1891. Dr Naismith developed the game to provide students with an alternative to the monotonous exercise program practiced in physical education classes during the winter months. Equipment consisted of a ball and a peach basket; each time a team scored, someone had to climb a ladder to remove the ball from the basket. The game was adopted by the YMCA three years later, and by 1936 had gained international recognition and acceptance as an Olympic sport.

Exhibits trace the development of the sport from amateur to professional and international status. Life-size action photos of such basketball greats as Wilt Chamberlain and Bob Cousy, video tapes of unforgettable coaches in action on the sidelines, film clips of the celebrated Harlem Globetrotters, and a selection of uniforms, equipment and memorabilia constitute the displays. The Honors Court commemorates outstanding players, coaches, and contributors to the sport in a series of portrait medallions. Visitors may test their skill at the Shoot Out on the ground floor or play one-on-one against former stars in the virtual reality exhibit.

**Court Square** – This pleasant park in the heart of downtown Springfield is bordered by buildings representing a variety of styles. Diagonally opposite the square rises the **Municipal Group★** (1913), a complex consisting of a pair of classically inspired structures: City Hall and Symphony Hall, with identical columned porticoes, and an Italian Renaissance bell tower. The **First Church of Christ** (1819), at the west end of the square, is a 2-story wood frame meetinghouse surmounted by a gilded cock brought to America about 1750. Just beyond stands the **Hampden County Courthouse** (1871), a granite structure that has been substantially altered, yet retains the late Gothic character of its original H.H. Richardson design.

**The Quadrangle** – *Open year-round Thu–Sun noon–4pm. Closed major holidays. $4.* ☎413-739-3871. The Museum of Fine Arts, the George Walter Vincent Smith Art Museum, Connecticut Valley Historical Museum, Springfield Science Museum and the city library are grouped together on the Quadrangle bounded by Chestnut and State Streets.

**Museum of Fine Arts** – Holdings include European paintings of the 17C Dutch, 18C Italian, and 18C and 19C French schools. The American section contains canvases by eminent 19C painters, such as Winslow Homer and Frederick Edwin Church, and the finely detailed *Historical Monument of the American Republic,* painted by Erastus Salisbury Field to commemorate the nation's centennial.

**George Walter Vincent Smith Art Museum** – This building, designed to suggest an Italian Renaissance villa, contains a collection of Oriental and American art and furnishings, and Classical casts.
The collection includes American paintings, interesting examples of Japanese armor, screens, lacquers and ceramics and Chinese *cloisonné* (enamel poured into raised compartments).

**Connecticut Valley Historical Museum** – This building boasts a doorway similar to the type found throughout the Connecticut Valley. Inside, changing exhibits of the museum's collection of furniture, pewter, silver and portraits depict the social and cultural development of the Connecticut Valley from the 17C. The museum also contains a genealogy and local history library.

**Springfield Science Museum** – The museum contains a planetarium and a hands-on exploration center, as well as displays devoted to plant and animal life, geology and dinosaurs.

**Springfield Armory National Historic Site** – *1 Armory Sq. Open late May– Labor Day daily 10am–5pm, rest of the year Tue–Sun 10am–5pm. Closed Jan 1, Thanksgiving Day, Dec 25.* ☎413-734-8551. The main arsenal building of the defunct Springfield Armory—home of the Springfield rifle—contains a collection of small arms, edged weapons and related military items, dating from the 15C to the present, including examples some of the guns manufactured here.

## EXCURSION

**Stanley Park** – *400 Western Ave in Westfield. 15mi from Springfield by Rte 20, then turn left onto Elm St, left onto Court St, and bear left onto Granville Rd. Open mid-May–mid-Oct daily 8am–dusk. Summer concerts.* ☎413-568-9312. A 61-bell Flemish carillon, an English herb garden and a rose garden are among the many attractions in this 275-acre park. A covered bridge, old mill and blacksmith's shop are located in the pond area.

## ★★ STOCKBRIDGE

Pop 2,408

Map of Principal Sights p 2

Tourist Office ☎413-443-9186

Founded in the early 18C as an Indian mission, this quintessential New England town nestled in the heart of the Berkshires exudes a grace and charm that has traditionally endeared it to well-heeled Bostonians and New Yorkers as well as to artists and writers. The town's **Main Street★** is lined with a picturesque row of pedimented buildings bounded to the west by the sprawling white facade of the **Red Lion Inn**, a cozy country hostelry dating from colonial times. Beyond the inn, Main Street gives way to large clapboard dwellings rimmed by broad landscaped lawns. Owing to its prime location equidistant from BOSTON and New York *(both are accessible by car in 2hr30min)*, Stockbridge welcomes a steady stream of visitors throughout the year. In the summer performances of classic American drama are presented at the Berkshire Theater Festival housed in the Berkshire Playhouse, a 19C casino on Main Street designed by McKim, Mead and White.

**SIGHTS** *1 day. Map p 94.*

**Mission House** – *Rte 102 (Main St). Visit by guided tour (45min) only, late May–mid–Oct Tue–Sun 11am–4pm. Closed Tue after Mon holidays. $4.* ☎*413-298-3239.* John Sergeant, the first missionary sent to educate and convert the local Indians to Christianity, arrived in Stockbridge in 1734. This house, which Sergeant built five years later (1739) as a wedding present for his wealthy wife, Abigail, was extremely luxurious for its day. The elaborate front door made in the Connecticut Valley was hauled across the high mountains in an oxcart to adorn the entranceway of the Mission House. A tour of the interior, semi-dark from lack of electricity, suggests the conditions under which the pastor and his young bride lived in the early 18C. Most of the furnishings date from this period.

★★ **Norman Rockwell Museum** – *2.5mi from Stockbridge center. Take Rte 102 west (Main St, then Church St). After 2mi turn left onto Rte 183 and continue .6mi to museum entrance on left. Open May–Oct daily 10am–5pm; rest of the year Mon–Fri 11am–4pm, weekends 10am–5pm. Closed Jan 1, Thanksgiving Day, Dec 25. $8.* ☎*413-298-4100.* Occupying a 36-acre estate overlooking the Housatonic River Valley, this immensely popular museum is the repository of the largest collection of original works by America's premier 20C illustrator.

**An Illustrator of American Life** – Trained at the Art Student's League and the National Academy of Design in New York, **Norman Rockwell** (1894-1978) began his long and prolific career in his teens. At age 22, the artist drew his first cover for the *Saturday Evening Post*, thereby beginning a collaboration that would result in a total of 321 covers for the prestigious magazine over the next 47 years.

Rockwell's realistic paintings chronicle the changing times in America. His homespun scenes, often depicting the routines of day-to-day living, are seasoned with a sense of humor and wonder. A hallmark of Rockwell's works is the attention to detail: every wink of the eye, gesture and accessory reveals a meticulously conceived scheme. Rockwell often represented children, and in many cases his subjects were modeled on family, friends or neighbors. When Rockwell embarked upon a 10-year association with *Look* magazine in the 1960s, he focused on contemporary political figures and American social issues, such as the civil rights movement and poverty. In 1978 Rockwell died in Stockbridge, his home since 1953.

**Visit** – The core collection comprises Rockwell's personal holdings along with his studio and personal library and archives. In addition, the museum has acquired works through gifts or purchases, bringing the total holdings to over 500 paintings and drawings including 172 large-scale works. From 1969 until 1993, highlights from the collection were displayed in the small rooms of the Old Corner House on Stockbridge's Main Street.

The present facility was designed by the eminent post-Modern architect **Robert Stern** to provide a more spacious setting for the collection. The main building— a low-lying clapboard and fieldstone structure fronted by a pedimented entrance facade surmounted by a miniature "temple"—is clearly inspired by local Neoclas-

© 1958 Curtis Publishing Company

*The Runaway* by Norman Rockwell

173

sical architecture, and in particular the New England town hall. Its nine galleries display a selection of Rockwell's works including *Stockbridge Main Street at Christmas, Triple Self-Portrait* and *The Problem We All Live With*. The central octagonal gallery was specially designed as a sanctuary for the celebrated **Four Freedoms Series** (1943) inspired by President Franklin Delano Roosevelt's 1941 landmark speech rallying the nation to defend the rights of all people menaced by the Axis powers: feedom of speech, freedom of worship, freedom from want and freedom from fear. During World War II, these poignant images toured the nation on posters that formed the centerpiece of a fund-raising drive that yielded over $130 million in government bonds to support the war.

The museum also features temporary exhibits focusing on the work and life of Rockwell and, more largely, on the art of illustration.

Just a short stroll from the museum, on a rise overlooking the valley, stands **Rockwell's studio** *(open May–Oct)*, a simple red wooden building relocated from its original site in downtown Stockbridge.

**Chesterwood** – *3mi from Stockbridge center. Take Rte 102 west and turn left onto Rte 183. Continue .8mi and turn right onto Mohawk Lake Rd, then left on Willow St and continue .5mi to Chesterwood. Open May–Oct daily 10am–5pm. $6.* ☏413-298-3579. This large estate, formerly a farm, was acquired in the late 19C by the American sculptor Daniel Chester French (1850-1931). Although French achieved his first major success at the age of 25 with his statue of the *Minute Man* at Concord *(p 143)*, he is probably best remembered for the impressive seated *Abraham Lincoln* he sculpted for the Lincoln Memorial in the nation's capital. French executed more than 100 public monuments during his lifetime.

Models and casts of French's works, including the *Dupont Circle Fountain* he sculpted for Washington DC, occupy the **Barn Gallery**. The large Colonial Revival **house** (designed by Henry Bacon) replaced the farmhouse originally on the property. The house is furnished as it was when the artist lived here. Also on the grounds is Fench's spacious, well-lit **studio** (another Henry Bacon design), with its tall double doors and railroad tracks that allowed French to move large works outdoors, where he could work in the natural light.

A woodland walk *(20 min)* affords views of the hilly countryside.

**Naumkeag** – *2mi from Stockbridge center. From Main St turn right onto Pine St, then bear left at Shamrock St and continue on Prospect St. Visit of house by guided tour (45min) only, late May–mid-Oct Tue–Sun 10am–5pm. $6 (for house & garden).* ☏413-98-3239. This Norman-style mansion (1886, Stanford White) and its terraced hillside gardens were built for Joseph Choate (1832-1917), US ambassador to England. The unusual design of the entrance to the Chinese garden was intended to keep the devil out.

## ★★★ STURBRIDGE                                        Pop 7,775

Map of Principal Sights p 2                    Tourist Office ☏508-347-7594

Situated at the intersection of the Massachusetts Turnpike and I-84, Sturbridge has been a stopping place for travelers since colonial days. The town provides an ideal site for Old Sturbridge Village, one of New England's best-known attractions.

### ★★★ OLD STURBRIDGE VILLAGE   1 day. Map p 175.

*Open Apr–Oct daily 9am–5pm, rest of the year Tue–Sun 10am–4pm; closed Jan 1, Dec 25. $15 (2nd consecutive day free).* ☏508-347-3362.

Old Sturbridge Village is a living history museum that re-creates life between 1790 and 1840 in a rural New England community. Remarkable for the beauty of its woodsy site and the authenticity of its buildings and atmosphere, the village is the result of extensive research. Interpreters wearing 19C dress farm the land, cook and make tools and implements according to traditional methods.

The village was initiated by Albert and Joel Cheney Wells and their families to exhibit their collections of American antiques. When the museum was opened to the public in 1946, historic houses, farm buildings, and shops had been moved to and reconstructed on the Sturbridge site.

**Visitor Center** – *Map guide/schedule of events available.* Exhibits and a slide presentation *(15min)* introduce the visitor to farm and community life in 19C New England. Following the path to the Common, you will pass the small clapboard **Friends Meetinghouse** (1796), which typifies the simplicity that reflects the austere piety associated with the Quakers.

**The Common** – At the west end of the Common is a white Greek Revival **Center Meetinghouse**, its spire rising gracefully above the other village structures. Daylight, streaming in through large windows, illuminates the building's simple interior. Houses on the Common reflect a diversity of architectural styles. The **Fenno House** (1704), covered with wide rustic clapboards, is the oldest. Inside, the rooms are appointed with New England furnishings and the walls are covered with sheathing typical of the 18C. The more refined **Fitch House** (1737), furnished as the home of a

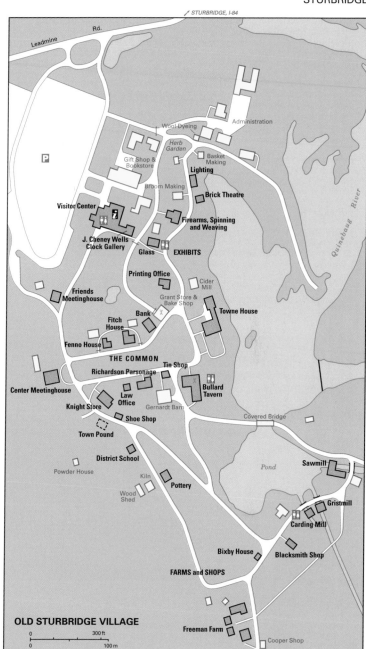

**OLD STURBRIDGE VILLAGE**

0    300 ft
0    100 m

prospering printer, contains double-hung sash windows. The **Richardson Parsonage** (1748), a white saltbox *(p 28)*, is the home of the village minister. In the **Tin Shop** next to the parsonage, a smith turns out utilitarian wares like those used in early 19C households. On the other side of the parsonage sits a tiny **law office** originally used by Connecticut lawyer John McClellan. Nearby is the well-stocked **Knight Store**, typical of the country store that was often the sole supplier of the farmer's needs and was indispensable in selling his surplus produce to urban consumers.

**Towne House** – Opposite the Center Meetinghouse and facing the Common, this attractively proportioned Federal-style house (1796) is similar to those dwellings built by the most prosperous rural families. Unusually comfortable and luxurious for residences in this community, the house contains period furnishings, delicately carved woodwork, English porcelains, a hand-painted floor cloth and woven carpets. The large meeting room/ballroom on the second floor is embellished with scenes painted directly on the plaster.

175

**Thompson Bank** – This modest Greek Revival building exemplifies the architectural style commonly used by financial institutions established throughout the region in the 19C to meet the needs of the rapidly expanding economy. In the 1830s commercial banks loaned money to emerging businesses and industries in New England.

**Printing Office** – The yellow wooden building beyond the bank is an early 19C printing office. Such offices usually printed books for urban publishers, as well as pamphlets and broadsides.

Cross the Common and follow the road that leads to the Pliny Freeman farm. You will pass the **Town Pound**, where stray animals were kept, the **Shoe Shop**, **the District School** and **Pottery Shop**.

**Freeman Farm** – This farm, with its livestock fields and farmhouse, is one of the liveliest areas in the village. Men and women in period dress cook, work in the fields and care for the animals as they did more than 150 years ago. Depending upon the season, the activities performed include plowing, cultivating and harvesting field crops, maple-sugaring, shearing sheep, preserving food, building fences and making butter and cheese.

**Bixby House** – Old Sturbridge Village's newest addition is the former home of a 19C blacksmith, moved from its original site in Barre, Massachusetts in 1986. Archaeological discoveries made during recovery and restoration provide an accurate picture of a craftsman's family in 1830's rural America.

Across the road, in a stone building, is the **Blacksmith Shop**; farther on are the **Carding Mill**, **Gristmill** and **Sawmill** located beside streams fed from the Mill Pond. Meals are served in the **Bullard Tavern** beyond the covered bridge.

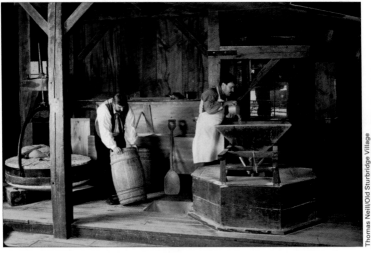

Thomas Neill/Old Sturbridge Village

The Gristmill

To reach the J. Cheney Wells Clock Gallery *(adjacent to the visitor center)* and the Formal Exhibits Area with its changing exhibits, cross the Common and continue past the Printing Office.

**Exhibits** – In one area of the village, small museums contain formal displays of traditional crafts and artifacts.

**Glass Exhibit** – Glassmaking was an important industry in New England in the 19C *(p 35)*. The collection at Sturbridge includes a wide variety of forms ranging from window glass to decorative paperweights. An interesting assortment of flasks features political, social and patriotic subjects as decorative motifs.

**Firearms, Spinning and Weaving Exhibit** – Exhibits and demonstrations illustrate 19C spinning and weaving techniques. A fine collection of guns and military equipment is accompanied by informative panels that present the detailed history of the New England militia.

Nearby, the **Brick Theatre** hosts storytelling, music performances and other forms of early 19C entertainment. *Check the map guide for the day's schedule.*

**Lighting Exhibit** – The exhibit presents lighting devices from prehistoric times to the 19C. Roman and Greek oil lamps, Betty Lamps (popular in early New England), whale oil lamps and kerosene lamps are among the interesting devices displayed.

Across the path, in the shop adjoining the herb garden, seasonal exhibits, such as brooms made from broom corn, are featured. Basketry and wool-dyeing exhibits complete the return walk to the visitor center.

**J. Cheney Wells Clock Gallery** – The collection contains more than 100 New England clocks, many in working order, produced between 1725 and 1850 by regional clockmakers. Thomas Claggett, Caleb Wheaton, Simon and Aaron Willard, Seth Thomas and Eli Terry are among the craftsmen represented.

## ★★ WILLIAMSTOWN                                                        Pop 8,220

Map of Principal Sights p 2                                    Tourist Office ☎ 413-664-6256

This beautiful colonial village nestles snugly in the northwest corner of Massachusetts, at the place where the MOHAWK TRAIL enters the BERKSHIRES. In 1753 the early settlement of West Hoosuck was established here by soldiers from Fort Massachusetts. Later, one of the soldiers, Col Ephraim Williams Jr, bequeathed part of his estate for the founding of a free school in West Hoosuck—provided the town be renamed in his honor. Soon after the Colonel's death, West Hoosuck was renamed Williamstown.

The Berkshires' verdant rolling hills provide a lovely setting for Williams College, as well as for the Sterling and Francine Clark Art Institute and the Williamstown Theater Festival, which is held each summer.

### SIGHTS   3hrs

★★★ **Sterling and Francine Clark Art Institute** – *225 South St. Open year-round Tue–Sun 10am–5pm. Closed Jan 1, Thanksgiving Day, Dec 25.* ♿ ☎*413-458-2303.* The institute's paintings, sculpture and decorative arts were gathered by Robert Sterling Clark and his wife, Francine, during the years between World War I and 1956. The collection, worthy of being compared with those of some of the world's finest museums, reflects the Clarks' early taste for classical art, which later turned to 19C paintings. The couple chose Williamstown as the site of their institute for its idyllic natural setting and its location far from urban centers (most likely to be threatened during wartime). The white marble building, designed to house the collection, suggests a private residence and provides a splendid setting for the collection. The red granite annex (1973, Pietro Belluschi) houses additional gallery space as well as the museum's auditorium.

**The Collections** – The earliest works are from the Renaissance period. Highlighting this section are the Italian paintings, including a seven-part panel altarpiece by Ugolino da Siena, a *Virgin and Child Enthroned with Four Angels* by **Piero della Francesca**, and Flemish portraits (*Portrait of a Man* by Jan Gossaert). The 17C and 18C are represented by masters of the European schools: the Spanish school by **Murillo** and **Goya**; the English school by **Gainsborough**, **Turner** and **Lawrence**; the Dutch and Flemish schools by **Ruisdael** and **Pynacker**; the French school by **Lorrain** and **Fragonard**; and the Italian school by **Tiepolo**.

However, it is in the realm of 19C French and American art that the collection excels. In the section devoted to the French school, the group of paintings by **Corot** shows the artist's skill in executing landscapes as well as figures. *The Trumpeter of the Hussars* by **Gericault**, the romantic, typifies his masterful style and contrasts with the muted tones used by **Millet**. Among the Impressionist canvases are more than 30 works by **Renoir**, including *Sleeping Girl with a Cat, The Blonde Bather, The Onions* and others painted between 1870 and 1890. **Degas'** treatment of his favorite subjects, dancers and horses, shows his extraordinary sense of movement. Shimmering with color, the paintings by **Monet** include one from his *Rouen Cathedral* series, and *The Cliffs at Etretat*. The post-Impressionist **Toulouse-Lautrec** is represented by several works, including his *Dr Péan Operating.*

In a room dedicated to works of Remington, Homer and Sargent, it is interesting to note the different personalities of these three American artists who lived in the late 19C. **Frederic Remington** was the painter of the American West. During his lifetime he created several thousand paintings and pieces of sculpture that portrayed his favorite subjects: cowboys, Indians and the cavalry, and their heroic way of life. **Winslow Homer**, also a student of the American scene, chose to depict the rugged New England landscape—the White Mountains of New Hampshire and the rocky Maine coast—in his paintings. In contrast to Remington and Homer, **John Singer Sargent** was a modern portraitist whose subjects, generally members of high society, were rendered with the artist's flair for sophistication. Sargent painted his famous *Fumé ed'Ambre Gris* while on a voyage to Tangiers.

Displays of porcelain, furniture and silver accompany the paintings and sculpture. The Clark collection of American and European silver, one of the finest in the world, includes pieces made by the 18C English silversmith **Paul de Lamerie**.

**Williams College** – Chartered in 1793 and named for Ephraim Williams, the college has more than 50 buildings from different periods, beginning in the late 18C. Set on the wide luxuriant campus lawns on Main and nearby streets are good examples of the Georgian, Federal, Gothic Revival (Thompson Memorial Chapel) and Greek Revival (Chapin Hall and Williams College Museum of Art) styles. On Main Street, note the president's house (Sloane House, 1801), an attractive well-proportioned Federal-style dwelling. Opposite is West College (1790), the free school that became Williams College.

**Williams College Museum of Art** – *On Main St between Spring & Water Sts. Open year-round Tue–Sun 10am–5pm. Closed Mon (except Memorial, Labor & Columbus Days), Jan 1, Thanksgiving Day, Dec 25.* & ☎413-597-2429. This building, one of the finest on campus, has evolved over the years from a brick Greek Revival octagon (1846) to its present size, which includes additions in 1983 and 1986 by renowned architect Charles Moore. The building's unassuming exterior belies the dramatic atrium and neatly sculpted, well-lit gallery spaces within.

The collection includes examples of European, non-Western and Ancient art, but its strength lies in American art: Copley, Homer, Eakins, Hopper, Inness, O'Keeffe and Wood are all represented. Changing exhibits of modern and contemporary art are also presented.

# WORCESTER
Pop 169,759

Map of Principal Sights p 2     Tourist Office ☎ 508-753-2920

Worcester, the second largest city in New England, is a modern industrial center with more than 350 manufacturing plants. Playing an important role in the rejuvenation of the downtown area are the Centrum, the city's civic center offering facilities for trade shows and concerts, and preservation projects such as the renovation of **Mechanics Hall** (1857), a 19C architectural gem now used as a concert hall. Between 1770 and 1776 the fiery anti-British newspaper, the *Massachusetts Spy,* was printed in Worcester by the patriot editor Isaiah Thomas. Following the Revolution Thomas helped establish the **American Antiquarian Society** (1812), which today owns an important collection of early American source material.

Educational institutions in the Worcester area include **Holy Cross College** and **Clark University.** The modernistic library on the Clark campus is named for physicist **Dr Robert Goddard** (1882-1945), a native of Worcester and former professor at Clark, who built and successfully fired the world's first liquid fuel rocket.

## SIGHTS *3hrs*

★★ **Worcester Art Museum** – *55 Salisbury St. Open year-round Tue–Fri 11am–4pm, Sat 10am–5pm, Sun 1–5pm. Closed major holidays. $5.* ✗ & ☎508-799-4406. The museum owns collections of paintings, sculpture and the decorative arts spanning 50 centuries from antiquity to the present. Displayed in a building inspired by Italian Renaissance architecture, the collections are arranged in galleries that surround a central court decorated with mosaics from Antioch (2-6C AD). The museum also provides gallery space for prints and drawings, 20C and contemporary art, changing exhibits, and an outdoor sculpture garden.

The **first floor** is devoted to ancient art, the art of the Middle Ages, and Asian art, including extensive holdings of Japanese prints from the Edo period. Note the 12C **Chapter House**, formerly part of a Benedictine priory in France, and *The Last Supper,* one of a group of 13C frescoes from Spoleto, Italy. In the central court is the large floor mosaic, *Hunting Scenes,* (6C) from Antioch.

On the second floor, the European schools of painting from the Middle Ages through the 20C are represented. Highlights include El Greco's intense *Repentant Magdalen, Rest on the Flight into Egypt* by the 16C Flemish painter Quentin Massys, a portrait by Gainsborough of his daughters, Gauguin's *Brooding Woman,* and in the Italian section, the dramatic *Calling of St Matthew* by Strozzi.

The **American wing** features the American school of painting with works by John Copley, Worcester native Ralph Earl, James McNeill Whistler, Winslow Homer, John Singer Sargent, Mary Cassatt, Childe Hassam and the landscapists George Inness, Albert Ryder and Samuel Morse. The portrait of **Mrs. Elizabeth Freake and Baby Mary** *(illustration p 33)* by an anonymous 17C artist, is considered one of the finest portraits of the colonial period. An unusual feature of the self-portrait by Thomas Smith (c.1680) is the naval battle scene that replaces the traditional landscape in the background. Another early work, *The Peaceable Kingdom* by Quaker Edward Hicks, is noteworthy for its simple, unsophisticated theme and treatment. A more contemporary work, *The Wave,* was painted by Marsden Hartley (1877-1943), an organizer of the 1913 New York Armory Show, which introduced the American public to trends in modern European painting, particularly cubism.

Worcester's sculpture collection includes an Egyptian female torso dating from the Fourth Dynasty and an 11-headed Japanese Kannon (9-10C AD).

The museum's distinguished **pre-Columbian collection** on the fourth floor is also worth viewing. Works in gold, jade, clay, stone, and ceramics represent various pre-Columbian cultures, such as Zapotec and Chimu.

★ **Higgins Armory Museum** – *100 Barber Ave. Open year-round Tue–Sat 10am–4pm, Sun noon–4pm. Closed major holidays. $4.75.* & ☎508-853-6015. This multi-storied steel and glass building constructed (1931) by John W. Higgins, former president of Worcester Pressed Steel Co, houses a prize collection of armor as well as early tools and weapons that Higgins gathered during his travels abroad and across the US. Presented in multimedia shows, live demonstrations and historical exhibits, these objects provide a unique perspective on knightly culture.

Principal displays are arranged in an enormous exhibition gallery, modeled after the Great Hall of an 11C Austrian castle. Paintings, furnishings, tapestries, banners and stained glass in the gallery add to the illusion of being in a medieval castle.

Along the walls stand more than 60 suits of parade, combat and jousting armor dating from the 14C to the 16C. Produced by highly skilled craftsmen, some of these suits are truly works of art, such as the suit of Maximilian armor named for **Emperor Maximilian**, who prefered fluted armor, and the **Franz von Teuffenbach** armor, with its elaborate decorative etching. Tools and weapons of the Stone and Bronze Ages and a rare gladiator's helmet (3C BC) are included in the other exhibits.

## EXCURSION

**Willard House and Clock Museum** – *11 Willard St in Grafton, 11mi southeast of Worcester. Take Rte 122, then Rte 140 to the center of Grafton. From there follow the signs 1.5mi. Visit by guided tour (1hr 30min) only, year-round Tue–Sat 10am–4pm, Sun 1–5pm. Closed major holidays. $3.* ☍ ☏*508-839-3500.* A collection of over 70 clocks made by the **Willard brothers** (Simon, Benjamin, Aaron and Ephraim) fills this house and clockshop (now a museum) where the Willards lived and worked in the 18C. Today these valuable clocks are sought by collectors and antique dealers.

Willard clocks were produced in a variety of styles (wall, shelf and tall case clocks). Simon became famous for his improved timepiece, the **banjo clock**, which resembles the musical instrument in shape.

# New Hampshire

Near New London / Fred Sieb Photography

# New Hampshire

**Area:** 9,304sq mi
**Population:** 1,109,252
**Capital:** Concord
**Nickname:** The Granite State
**State Flower:** Purple Lilac

Forests cover 80 percent of the land in this triangle, 168 miles long and 90 miles at its widest point. The mountainous relief of the Appalachian ridges to the west and north contrasts with the hilly coastal region that slopes gently down to the Atlantic Ocean. The southern section of the state, benefiting in recent decades from the overflow of businesses from the Boston area, is heavily industrialized and more densely populated than the rest of the state. Located here are New Hampshire's largest cities **Concord, Manchester, Nashua, Keene**, as well as its only seaport, **Portsmouth**.

**History** – "Here no landlords rack us with high rents. Here every man may be master of his land in a short time," wrote Capt John Smith about New Hampshire in 1614. Despite Smith's tribute, the colonization of New Hampshire proceeded slowly. The first settlement, established in 1623 on the coast, was followed by several other small settlements. New Hampshire was administered as a part of Massachusetts until 1679, when the region became a royal colony.

Its people, self-reliant, taciturn, industrious and independent, were staunch supporters of the Revolution. The New Hampshire colony declared its independence from Great Britain and set up its own government seven months before the Declaration of Independence was signed. The heroic words of Revolutionary War colonel John Stark, "Live free or die," are immortalized in the state motto.

The character of New Hampshire's early population, primarily of Anglo-Saxon stock, was altered in the 19C and 20C by an influx of French Canadians and Europeans to the region.

**Economy** – In the 19C factory complexes such as the **Amoskeag Mills** *(p 185)*, once the world's largest textile manufacturer, were built on the banks of the Merrimack River. Textiles are still produced, but have been replaced by leather goods, machinery, electronic equipment, plastics and paper as principal sources of income. Since the 1960s, more than 250 Massachusetts firms have established branches in New Hampshire, attracted to the state's favorable tax structure and proximity to Boston. Today tourism and industrial development share equal importance in New Hampshire's economy.

New Hampshire possesses an unusual tax structure. Lacking a state income tax or sales tax, New Hampshire obtains revenues from alternate sources, notably the state-operated liquor monopoly, pari-mutuel betting, and taxes on business profits, meals and rooms.

Farming is oriented chiefly toward dairy products, Christmas trees, specialty products such as apples and maple sugar, and vegetables, livestock

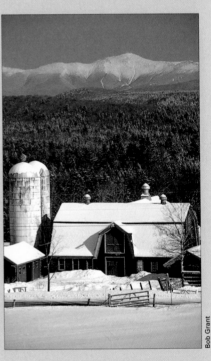

Bob Grant

and poultry. Sand, gravel and feldspar are among New Hampshire's most important minerals, and building granite is quarried on a limited scale. The introduction of concrete and steel construction has resulted in a decline of the granite industry that gave the state its nickname.

# ★ CANTERBURY CENTER

Pop 1,687

Map of Principal Sights p 2

Attracted by the serene countryside and the gift of a large tract of land in Canterbury, the Shakers *(p 148)* established a community in the 18C near the small village of Canterbury Center. The 24 original buildings still stand on 694 acres.

**★ Canterbury Shaker Village** – *15mi north of Concord. From I-93 take Exit 18, follow signs (7mi) to Shaker Village. Open May–Oct daily 10am–5pm; Nov, Dec & Apr Fri–Sun 10am–5pm. $8. ✗ & ☎603-783-9511.* The **Canterbury Shakers** farmed and made their own clothing, tools, furniture and machinery as did other Shaker communities. To obtain goods they were not able to produce, they specialized in the preparation of medicines and herbs that they sold throughout the US and abroad.

The **Meeting House** (1792), where the Shakers gathered for religious services, contains exhibits of their products: furniture, tools, wooden boxes and such Shaker inventions as the flat broom and the threshing machine. The simplicity of the Meeting House contrasts with the subtle ornamentation of the **Dwelling House**, with its pedimented porch and cupola. The well-equipped **Schoolhouse** reflects the commitment of the Shakers to educating the young people in their community.

# CONCORD

Pop 36,006

Map of Principal Sights p 2          Tourist Office ☎603-224-2508

The capital of New Hampshire since 1808, Concord boasts the largest state legislature in the nation, with 424 representatives. Originally called Rumford, this town was claimed by both the colonies of New Hampshire and Massachusetts. Following a royal declaration that settled the dispute by granting Rumford to New Hampshire in 1741, the town was appropriately renamed Concord. In the 19C Concord became known for its granite and for the **Concord coaches** that were built here from 1813 to 1900 by the Abbot-Downing Co. Offering increased riding comfort, the Concord coach encouraged passenger travel, and was later credited with having helped settle the West.

A modern center of government and commerce, the city is also a hub of railway and road systems linking all corners of the state. The gilded dome of the State House dominates the cluster of buildings that rise alongside the Merrimack River.

**State House** – *107 N. Main St. Open Sept–Oct Mon–Fri 8am–4:30pm, weekends 11am–4pm; Jul–Aug Mon–Fri 8am–4:30pm, Sat 11am–4pm; rest of the year Mon–Fri 8am–4:30pm. Closed major holidays. ✗ & ☎603-271-2154.* Completed in 1819, the New Hampshire State House is the oldest state capitol where the legislature still meets in its original chambers. Regimental colors hang in the Hall of Flags *(ground floor)*, while Barry Faulkner murals in the Senate Chamber *(second floor)* depict scenes from the state's history. Statues of New Hampshire sons John Stark, Daniel Webster and Franklin Pierce stand on the grounds.

**Museum of New Hampshire History** – *Eagle Sq. Open year-round Tue–Sat 9:30am–5pm (Thu 8:30pm), Sun noon–5pm. Closed major holidays $3.50. & ☎603-225-3381.* More than five centuries of New Hampshire history are depicted by the museum's exhibits, which include a 19C Concord coach made in the 19C by the Abbot-Downing Co.

**League of New Hampshire Craftsmen** – *205 N. Main St. Open year-round daily 9am–5pm. Closed major holidays. The retail shop is located at 36 N. Main St. & ☎603-224-3375.* The League of New Hampshire Craftsmen maintains its headquarters in Concord. Handcrafted textiles, glass and silver number among the items sold. The League Gallery features changing exhibits of handicrafts.

## EXCURSIONS

**Hopkinton** – *Pop 4,806. 8mi west of Concord by Rte 9.* Antique hunters haunt this appealing Concord suburb. The town's wide main street is lined with attractive dwellings and shops, the town hall and St Andrew's Church.

**Henniker** – *Pop 4,151. 15mi west of Concord by Rte 9.* This lively college town is home to New England College. From Route 114 between the college and the village center, the Henniker covered bridge can be seen.

**Hillsborough** – *Pop 4,498. 22mi west of Concord by Rte 9.* A small commercial center, Hillsborough has structures dating from the last century. From Route 9, a back road leads through **Hillsborough Center★** *(turn west onto School St)* a country hamlet with white buildings and rambling stone walls tucked among the trees.

*The ✗ symbol indicates that eating facilities can be found on the premises of the sight.*

# CONNECTICUT LAKES REGION

Map of Principal Sights p 2          Tourist Office ☎603-538-7405

The narrow section of New Hampshire near the Canadian border is a densely wooded lake region, a haven for hunters and fishermen because of its wide variety of animal life. South of the Canadian border, the **Third, Second** and **First Connecticut lakes** give rise to the Connecticut River, which continues southwest forming the Vermont-New Hampshire border. From Route 3, between Pittsburg and the Canadian border, there are glimpses of the lakes through the trees.

**Lake Francis State Park** – *7mi northeast of Pittsburg by Rte 3. Turn right onto River Rd. Park entrance is 2mi after passing the covered bridge. Open May–Oct daily 8:30am–8pm $2.50.* ⚠ ё ☎*603-538-6965. Facility information p 251.* The scenic shores of Lake Francis in New Hampshire's northern wilderness provide an ideal spot to camp or picnic.

# DIXVILLE NOTCH

Map of Principal Sights p 2          Tourist Office ☎603-237-8939

In northern New Hampshire, Route 26, between Colebrook and Errol, passes through an area of rugged cliffs and thick stands of evergreens called Dixville Notch. Here on the shores of Lake Gloriette, near the highest point (1,871ft) in the notch, stands the grand and luxurious **Balsams Hotel**, built in the 19C.
East of the hotel, there are two easy walks leading to waterfalls.The first walk begins at **Flume Brook Parking Area** on Route 26. The second, the **Cascades-Waterfalls Trail** to **Huntingdon Falls**, begins 1mi east of Flume Brook Parking at the Dixville Notch State Park wayside.

# GRAFTON CENTER                                        Pop 923

Map of Principal Sights p 2

South of the White Mountains, several areas have been exploited for their mineral resources. Among the mines no longer worked is the Ruggles Mine.

★ **Ruggles Mine** – *2mi from the village green at Grafton Center; follow signs. Open mid-Jun–mid-Oct daily 9am–5pm, mid-May–mid-Jun weekends only. $10. Insect repellent advised especially after periods of rain.* ☓ . The abandoned pegmatite mine on Isinglass Mountain is a curious and interesting place to explore, with its arched stone tunnels, winding passageways, large open pits and mine dumps. Sam Ruggles, a 19C Yankee farmer who discovered mica deposits on his property, worked the mine only at night and sold the mica outside the US to prevent other local landowners from learning his secret. The Ruggles Mine remained New Hampshire's first and only commercial mine until 1868.
Amateur rock hounds may wish to rent equipment and dig for mica, feldspar or one of the other 150 minerals that have been found here.

# ★ HANOVER                                            Pop 9,212

Map of Principal Sights p 2          Tourist Office ☎603-643-3115

Dartmouth College, one of the nation's prominent Ivy League schools, occupies this pretty colonial town on the banks of the Connecticut River. Since Hanover is a college community, it is often difficult to separate its buildings and activities from those of Dartmouth. Despite the town's growth into a regional center, Hanover's colonial charm and pleasant tree-lined streets remain essentially unspoiled.

## ★ DARTMOUTH COLLEGE

Established in 1769 by the Reverend Eleazar Wheelock "for the education of Youth of the Indian Tribes" and "English Youth and any others," Dartmouth today offers its 4,500 students undergraduate programs in the liberal arts and sciences, as well as graduate studies in medicine, engineering, sciences and business administration. Dartmouth's list of illustrious alumni includes the lawyer and orator Daniel Webster (1782-1852) and Nelson A. Rockefeller (1908-1979), the former governor of New York and US vice-president. The popular Dartmouth **Winter Carnival**, held each February, features skiing, skating, art shows and other special events.

★ **The Green** – The spacious green is bordered by the **Hanover Inn** and a number of college buildings. The corner of Main and Wheelock Streets commands a good view of Dartmouth Row, which is flanked by Hopkins Center *(right)* and Webster Hall *(left)*, originally built as an auditorium. Beyond Webster Hall is Baker Library.

**Hopkins Center** – The performing arts center (1962), recognizable by its multi-storied windows, houses theaters and two concert halls. The center provides the college and the entire Hanover region with a year-round program of cultural events.

**Hood Art Museum** – *Open year-round Tue–Sat 10am–5pm, Sun noon–5pm. Closed Jan 1, Thanksgiving Day, Dec 24 & 25.* ☓ ё ☎*603-646-2808.* Dartmouth's art museum connects the Romanesque Wilson Hall (1885) and the modern Hopkins Center. Opened in 1985, the Hood galleries contain works from the permanent collection, which features Native American, American, European, African and Ancient art. On the lower level, a special area displays a group of 9C BC Assyrian reliefs; on the upper level, contemporary art occupies a spacious loft gallery.

**Dartmouth Row** – This group of four Colonial buildings includes **Dartmouth Hall** *(center)*, a replica of the original building (1784) that was destroyed by fire in 1904.

**Baker Memorial Library** – *North end of the Green. Open year-round daily, hours vary. Closed major holidays.* ☎603-646-2560.

Dartmouth Hall, Dartmouth College

Fred Sieb Photography

The building houses **Epic of American Civilization★**, a series of murals painted by the Mexican artist José Clemente Orozco (1883-1949) between 1932 and 1934. Powerful and often brutal in their expression of the forces of good and evil, the murals are Orozco's interpretation of the 5,000-year history of the Americas.

# KEENE
Pop 22,430

Map of Principal Sights p 2      Tourist Office ☎603-352-1303

This commercial and manufacturing center has grown rapidly during the past several decades, largely because of its location near the industrialized areas of Massachusetts that have spilled over the border into New Hampshire. Keene's pottery and glassworks, which were major New Hampshire industries in the 19C and early 20C, have been replaced by the city's more than 50 manufacturing facilities that produce tools, machine parts, textiles and medical products.

**Historical Society of Cheshire County Museum** – *246 Main St. Open year-round Mon–Fri 9am–4pm. Contribution requested.* ☎603-352-1895. Glass and pottery made in Keene and the nearby village of Stoddard are on exhibit in this Italianate mansion (1872). Among the many pieces of locally made glass on display are the pictorial flasks embossed with patriotic themes, and one-of-a-kind pieces including walking sticks and miniatures. Light green or aqua color distinguishes the glass inks, bottles and flasks produced in Keene. Stoddard glass characteristically exhibits a deep shade of amber.

## EXCURSION

**Covered Bridges on the Ashuelot River** – Covered bridge enthusiasts will enjoy a side trip on Route 10 south to covered bridges **Nos. 2, 4** and **5.** *Roadside markers indicate directions to the bridges.*

# MANCHESTER
Pop 99, 567

Map of Principal Sights p 2      Tourist Office ☎603-666-6600

In the 19C the largest textile factory in the world, the **Amoskeag Mills**, was built here beside the Merrimack River. The 5mi-long stretch of brick buildings still standing along the river proves an awesome sight. The factory was the major employer in Manchester, and when the mills closed down permanently in 1935, the city was left financially destitute. The future appeared bleak until a group of investors, determined to revive the city, bought the mills with the idea of selling or leasing space to various businesses. Within ten years, dozens of industries relocated in the mill complex, starting Manchester on its way to economic recovery. Today financial services have replaced manufacturing as Manchester's main industry. The city's clothing and shoe outlets are attractions in themselves.

★ **Currier Gallery of Art** – *192 Orange St. Open year-round Tue–Sat 10am–4pm (Thu 9pm), Sun 1–5pm. Closed major holidays. $4.* & ☎603-669-6144. *Closed for renovation Jun 1995–Mar 1996.* A south entrance flanked by tall mosaic panels, and a north entry fronting a granite-paved courtyard provide access to this museum, known for its fine collection of paintings, sculpture and decorative arts.

The first floor west gallery contains the **European collection**: early Italian paintings; drawings by **Tiepolo**; Jan Gossaert's superb self-portrait, *Portrait of a Man;* and canvases from the French, Spanish, English and Dutch schools. In the west wing, 20C American paintings and sculpture are represented by **Andrew Wyeth, Edward Hopper,** O'Keeffe, Nevelson, Calder and others. Temporary exhibits are displayed in the east gallery and in the Henry Melville Fuller Gallery.

The second floor is devoted to **American decorative art** from the 17-19C, with emphasis on New Hampshire pieces. Among the paintings are portraits by Copley and Trumbull, and landscapes by Cole, Bierstadt and Church. Early portraits such as *Abraham Sleight and Ruth Rose Sleight* (1820-1825) by Ammi Phillips and Samuel Miller's *Emily Mouton* (1852) charm the viewer with their simplicity. An extensive collection of American silver and pewter is housed on this floor.

★ **Zimmerman House** – *Visit by guided tour (1hr) only, year-round Thu & Fri 2pm, Sat 11:30am, 1 & 3:30pm, Sun 11:30am, 12:45, 2:15 & 3:30pm. $5. 2-3-week advance reservations required.* ☎603-626-4158. Designed by Frank Lloyd Wright in 1950 and bequeathed to the Currier Gallery in 1988, this low-roofed, single story house made of brick, concrete and cypress typifies the famed architect's "Usonian" style, Wright's own term for the small, utilitarian, yet elegant houses he created late in his career to counter the housing shortage of the Depression. The interior contains Wright-designed textiles, and his built-in and freestanding furniture.

## EXCURSION

**"America's Stonehenge"** – *19mi from Manchester by I-93 south to Exit 3 then follow Rte 111 east 5mi; turn right onto Island Pond Rd to Haverhill Rd. Open mid-Jun–Aug daily 9am–6pm. Apr, May & Nov daily 10am–5pm. Mar & Dec weekends only. $6.50.* ✗ ⬥ ☎603-893-8300. The large standing granite slabs of this stone complex give this site its name. Many theories exist concerning the site's origin and function; the aligned slabs led scientists to speculate that this may be the remnant of a calendar laid out 4,000 years ago by an advanced civilization with a knowledge of the movement of the stars, moon and sun. Carbon datings were first conducted here in 1967 and, most recently, in 1989.

Names of the stone structures, such as the Oracle Chamber and the Sacrificial Table, suggest their possible use. It is especially interesting to follow the astronomical alignment trail on June 21 and September 22 to see the slabs that accurately indicate the summer solstice and the fall equinox.

# ★ MOUNT MONADNOCK REGION

Map of Principal Sights p 2                    Tourist Office ☎603-352-1308

Mt Monadnock (3,165ft), the isolated remnant of a range formed eons ago, looms above the tiny colonial villages with their white steepled churches and the farmland of southwestern New Hampshire. The word **monadnock**, derived from an Algonquian word meaning "a mountain that stands alone," has entered into the vocabulary of geographers to describe the residual relief of a landscape that has passed through various stages of evolution. Hiking to the top of Mt Monadnock for its spectacular view became popular in the 19C, and today it is one of the most frequently climbed peaks in the world. Each year some 125,000 persons scale its summit to enjoy the exhilarating view.

## FROM FITZWILLIAM TO HANCOCK  47mi. 1 day. Map p 187.

**Fitzwilliam** – Pop 2,011. Large clapboard structures, the old meetinghouse, the inn and a Congregational church, which is crowned by a wedding cake steeple, face the green. To the west *(1.5mi off Rte 119)*, **Rhododendron State Park** encompasses 16 acres of wild rhododendrons that provide a colorful spectacle when they burst into bloom during June and July.

*Take Rte 119 east; after the intersection with Rte 202, turn left onto an unmarked road, which leads to the cathedral.*

★ **Cathedral of the Pines** – *Open May–Oct daily 9am–5pm, grounds open rest of the year dawn–dusk. Contribution requested.* ⬥ ☎603-899-3300. Situated on the crest of a pine-carpeted hill, this outdoor cathedral, the work of a couple who lost their son in World War II, commemorates all Americans who were killed in battle. This place of worship welcomes persons of all faiths. Services are held at the **Altar of the Nation**, which faces Mt Monadnock; stones set into the altar were tributes from US presidents, military leaders and the 50 states and four territories. The **Memorial Bell Tower**, rising in a clearing, is dedicated to American women who served their country in wartime; Norman Rockwell *(p 173)* designed the plaques above the tower arches. The **museum** contains artifacts from around the world, including medals from World War I *(open May–Oct daily 9am–5pm, Nov–Dec Mon–Fri 9am–5pm)*.

*Turn left when leaving the Cathedral of the Pines; 1.5mi farther, at the fork, bear right onto Rte 124.*

**New Ipswich** – Pop 4,014. The **Barrett House**, a handsome Federal mansion on Main Street, and its sedate rustic surroundings have changed little over the years. Built in 1800 by wealthy mill owner Charles Barrett as a wedding gift for his son, the house is furnished with family pieces and features two turn-of-the-century bathrooms *(visit by 45min guided tour only Jun–mid-Oct Thu–Sun noon–5pm; $4;* ☎603-878-2517).

*Follow Rte 124 west to Jaffrey. Located at the foot of Mt Monadnock, Jaffrey provides easy access to Monadnock State Park. Continue on Rte 124.*

**Jaffrey Center** – Pop 2,558. A series of lectures held each year *(Jul–Aug Fri 7:30pm)* at the old meetinghouse (Rte 124) honors **Amos Fortune**, a former slave who bequeathed a sum of money to the Jaffrey School when he died. The tombstones of Fortune and his wife stand in the cemetery behind the meetinghouse. The inscription on Amos' tombstone reads: "to the memory of Amos Fortune who was born free in Africa, a slave in America, he purchased liberty, professed Christianity, lived reputably, and died hopefully."

*Take Rte 124 west and .5mi after the meetinghouse turn right.*

★ **Monadnock State Park** – *Open year-round daily 8am–dusk. $2.50.* ⛺ ♿ ☎603-532-8862. *Facility information p 251.* Trails to the summit of Mt Monadnock begin at the end of the tar road beyond the toll booth.

★★ **Mt Monadnock** – Of the 40 trails leading to this peak, the trail most frequently taken is the **White Dot Trail** *(several steep sections, round-trip 3-4hrs)*. A similar route, the **White Cross Trail**, is somewhat more difficult. **Pumpelly Trail** is the longest, but easiest path to the top. Longer and less popular connecting trails include **Cascade Link**, **Red Spot** and **Spellman** *(steepest trail)*. The far-reaching **view**★★ from the summit on a clear day includes Mt Washington *(north)* and the Boston skyline *(southeast)*. The summit is the only place in New England from which parts of all six of the region's states can be seen.

*As you leave the park, turn left onto Upper Jaffrey Rd.*

**Dublin** – Pop 1,474. Mark Twain summered in this hillside hamlet, today the home of *Yankee Magazine* and *The Old Farmers Almanac*.

*Continue north on Upper Jaffrey Rd, turn right on 101, then left onto New Harrisonville Rd.*

★ **Harrisville** – Pop 981. The handsome ensemble of modest brick buildings, dwellings, mills and Congregational church reflected in the village pond creates a pleasing tableau of an early rural mill town. To preserve the character of the village, residents of Harrisville restored these structures themselves. In 1970, when the textile industry that operated here for two centuries closed down, the town's residents succeeded in attracting several small companies to relocate in Harrisville.

*Follow the unmarked road east along the lakes, then turn left onto Rte 137.*

★ **Hancock** – Pop 1,604. The tranquility of this colonial village is disturbed only once a year on July 4th, when the bells of the meetinghouse peal from midnight to one o'clock in the morning to celebrate the anniversary of America's independence. The **John Hancock Inn** sits in the center of the village, opposite the general store. Headstones in the old **cemetery** at the end of the street provide good examples of the skill of early stonecutters.

# NASHUA

Pop 79,662

Map of Principal Sights p 2     Tourist Office ☎603-881-8333

Located 39mi northwest of BOSTON, Nashua has experienced a surge of industrial growth since the 1960s, making it the second largest city in New Hampshire.

## EXCURSION

**Anheuser-Busch Hamlet** – *221 Daniel Webster Hwy. 7mi from Nashua in Merrimack. Take Rte 3 to Exit 10, bear right, then turn left and continue to Hamlet (on the grounds of the Anheuser-Busch brewery). Visit by guided tour (45min) only, May–Oct daily 9:30am–5pm; rest of the year Wed–Sun 10am–4pm.* ಈ ☎603-595-1202. Budweiser Clydesdales clip-clop through the picturesque hamlet where they are raised and trained. The "white-stockinged" horses have been the symbol of Anheuser-Busch since 1933 when the company acquired its first team to celebrate the repeal of prohibition. Teams of Clydesdales tour the country, appearing in parades and at fairs and other events.

# The NEW HAMPSHIRE COAST

Map of Principal Sights p 3     Tourist Office ☎603-436-7678

Sandy beaches, rocky ledges and state parks alternate along New Hampshire's 18mi coastline. Coastal Route 1A from Seabrook to PORTSMOUTH winds past resort areas and elegant estates, affording views of the ocean.

**Hampton Beach** – *On Rte 1A, 1mi north of Seabrook.* This lively resort center claims a casino, large clusters of oceanfront hotels, motels and eating places, as well as a 3.5mi sandy beach. The **New Hampshire Marine War Memorial**, a granite statue of a seated maiden looking out to sea, borders Route 1A in the center of Hampton Beach. North of Hampton Beach the road skirts the waterfront estates of **Little Boars Head.**

**Fuller Gardens** – *On Rte 1A, just north of Rte 111 junction at Little Boars Head. Open May–Oct daily 10am–6pm. $4.* ಈ ☎603-964-5414. Redesigned by Olmsted Assocs in the 1930s, this formal garden occupies the summer estate of Alvan T. Fuller, a former governor of Massachusetts. A stroll through the formal rose beds, Japanese gardens, greenhouses, and beds of annuals and perennials is punctuated with glimpses of the sea beyond.

**Rye Harbor State Park** – *On Rte 1A in Rye. Open year-round daily 8am–6pm. $2.50 (May–Oct). ☎603-436-1552. Facilty information p 251.* This rocky headland overlooking the Atlantic Ocean provides good picnic and fishing grounds.

**Wallis Sands State Park** – *On Rte 1A in Rye. Open year-round daily 8am–6pm $5/car (weekends & holidays $8/car).* ಈ ☎603-436-1552. *Facility information p 251.* A gentle surf breaks onto the park's 1/4mi-long beach.

**Odiorne Point** – *On Rte 1A in Rye.* This location was the site of Pannaway Plantation, the first settlement in New Hampshire, established in 1623.

# ★ NEW LONDON

Pop 3,180

Map of Principal Sights p 2     Tourist Office ☎603-526-6575

New London's hilltop setting overlooks neighboring and far-reaching ridges and woodlands that flame with color during Indian summer. On the main street, Route 114, there is a comfortable old inn, the campus of **Colby Sawyer College** (1837) and a Baptist meetinghouse. Travelers are easily tempted to stop and spend a few days in this small, unspoiled New England village.

## EXCURSION

**Mt Sunapee State Park** – *13mi from New London by Rte 11 south. After crossing I-89, turn left onto Rte 103A south, then turn onto Rte 103 west.* Lake Sunapee and the mountain of the same name form the center of a year-round vacation resort. Opposite the entrance to the park is the entrance to the mile-long **State Beach** on the shores of Lake Sunapee *(open Jun–Aug daily 9:30am–8pm; $2.50;* ✕ ಈ ☎603-763-2356). The League of New Hampshire Craftsmen holds its annual Craftsmen's Fair at the park in early August.
The **chair lift** to the summit of Mt Sunapee (2,700ft) operates from North Peak Lodge during the summer and early fall, offering good **views★** of the region *(Jun–Labor Day Wed–Sun noon–7pm; late Sept–mid-Oct weekends only 9am–5pm; $4.50; ಈ).*

---

*Consult the **Practical Information** section (pp 242-257) for the Calendar of Events, travel tips and useful addresses and telephone numbers.*

# PLYMOUTH

Map of Principal Sights p 2                    Tourist Office ☎603-536-1001

Lying just outside the White Mountain National Forest is Plymouth, a small resort town that is home to Plymouth State College.

**Polar Caves Park** – *On Rte 25, 5mi west of Plymouth. Open mid-May–mid-Oct daily 9am–5pm. $8.50.* ✗ ☎*603-536-1888.* The Polar Caves consist of a series of caves and stone passageways that were formed during the last Ice Age, as freezing temperatures and ice caused gigantic boulders to break loose from the mountain. Five conveniently placed stations with taped commentaries allow visitors to tour the caves at their own pace.
Wooden walkways lead to the first cave, the Ice Cave, named for the cool air that rises from within to fill it. The walkways continue over, around and through four more caves to the last, Smugglers Cave, which is entered by the narrow Lemon Squeezer passage or the more comfortable corridor called Orange Crush. The Cave of Total Darkness contains an exhibit of fluorescent minerals.

## EXCURSION

★ **Hebron** – *Pop 386. 14mi from Plymouth by Rte 25 west, then Rte 3A.* Hebron possesses all the elements of a New England village: an emerald green, a church with its pointed steeple, a general store, post office, and nearby, a handful of attractive dwellings. Together, they form a harmonious and charming ensemble.

**Newfound Lake** – The tranquil setting of this spring-fed lake, nestled between two mountains, is best viewed from its western shore, site of **Wellington State Beach**, south of Hebron.

## ★★ PORTSMOUTH

Map of Principal Sights p 3                    Tourist Office ☎603-436-7678

New Hampshire's only seaport and the colonial capital until 1808, when the seat of government was moved to Concord, Portsmouth is a small, quiet city on the banks of the Piscataqua River. Vintage Georgian mansions, reminiscent of Portsmouth's past as a lumber and seafaring center, line the streets leading to the waterfront.
Since the 1950s, renewal projects aimed at preserving Portsmouth's colonial structures and character have been implemented in the older sections of the city. The most interesting of these projects is the transformation of **Strawbery Banke**, the city's early waterfront community, into a museum. In the **Old Harbor District—Bow, Market and Ceres Streets**—restored and freshly painted restaurants, craft studios and antique shops, as well as the tug boats tied up at the Ceres Street cove, remind visitors of a time when commerce was the mainstay of Portsmouth's economy. Although commerce still reigns as one of the city's most important industries, the **Portsmouth Naval Shipyard** (located in KITTERY, Maine) is the area's largest employer.

**Historical Notes** – In 1623 a group of English settlers arrived on the banks of the Piscataqua River. Noting that the riverbanks were covered with wild strawberries, they named their community "Strawbery Banke." Not until several decades later was the "port at the mouth of the river" renamed Portsmouth.

Portsmouth Harbor

Fred Sieb Photography

Fishing, shipbuilding and the region's many sawmills, which transformed New Hampshire's largest trees into timber for the British Navy, provided settlers with their livelihood. After the Revolution, maritime commerce brought increased prosperity to the city. Beginning in the 18C and continuing into the 19C, merchants and ship captains built dwellings that reflected their wealth. These residences were among the finest Georgian and Federal houses in the country.

In 1800 Portsmouth lent its name to the new naval base constructed in Kittery, Maine. The Treaty of Portsmouth, which ended the Russo-Japanese War, was signed at this base in 1905.

## ★★ STRAWBERY BANKE   *2hrs. Map below.*

This 10-acre restoration project involving **Puddle Dock**, the site of Portsmouth's Strawbery Banke settlement (1630), remains a living model of the techniques used to rehabilitate an entire district. Advised in the 1950s that renewal plans for the city included demolition of the Puddle Dock neighborhood, citizens urged that funds be made available to restore the district's old shops and dwellings. Their strong support never waned, and in 1957 they began the overhaul of the dock.

Eighteen of the 42 structures at Strawbery Banke have been restored and are open to the public; others can be viewed in varying stages of restoration.

**Visit** – *Open May–Oct daily 10am–5pm. $10. Map available at entrance (Marcy St). Guided tours offered on a variety of topics (included in museum admission); consult daily schedule distributed to ticket holders.* ✕ & ☏*603-433-1100.*

**Sherburne House [1]** – This medieval-looking timber structure with twin gables and small casement windows is the only remaining 17C building in Strawbery Banke.

**Lowd House [2]** – A plain Federal house (1810) featuring a fine exhibit on craftsmen's tools of the 18-19C.

**Joshua Jackson House [3]** – This unrestored house (c.1750) reveals the structural changes undertaken by its occupants over the last two centuries.

**Wheelwright House [4]** – A middle-class 18C dwelling with noteworthy paneling.

**William Pitt Tavern [5]** – This 3-story structure (1766) functioned as the center of the community's social life providing food, lodging and a gathering place for groups such as the Masons.

**Aldrich House [6]** – Fronted by a lovely flower garden, this house (late 18C) preserves the domestic atmosphere captured in the autobiography of Thomas Bailey Aldrich, who dwelled here in the mid-19C.

**Chase House [7]** – This handsome Georgian residence (c.1762), owned by a prosperous merchant family, is appointed with fine period furniture and elaborately carved woodwork.

**Walsh House [8]** – A late 18C house graced with a handsome curved staircase, period furniture and several examples of faux grain and marble.

**Goodwin Mansion [9]** – Behind a lovely garden rises the elegant 3-story residence (1811) of a former state governor. Victorian furnishings grace the interior.

**Jones House [10]** – The interior of this modest late 18C house features artifacts excavated on site and a small archeological lab.

Between Strawbery Banke and the river lies **Prescott Park**, which is planted with lush flower gardens during the summer. Opposite the entrance to Strawbery Banke is a **liberty pole [A]**, similar to those raised by the patriots during Revolutionary days to signify their opposition to the Crown. The old **Sheafe Warehouse**, located at the water's edge, contains temporary exhibits.

## HISTORIC HOUSES   *Map p 190*

★★ **Warner House** – *150 Daniel St. Open mid-Jun–Oct Tue–Sat 10am–4:30pm, Sun 1–4pm. Closed major holidays. $4. ☎603-436-5909.* This brick Georgian mansion was built in 1716 for the Scottish sea captain Archibald MacPheadris. Decorated with European- and New England-made furnishings, the house contains a group of Warner family portraits by Joseph Blackburn. The series of 18C murals adorning the walls of the stairwell includes life-size portraits of two Mohawk sachems who journeyed to London with Peter Schuyler in 1710.
Behind the house stands **St John's Church**.

★ **Moffatt-Ladd House** – *154 Market St. Visit by guided tour (45min) only, mid-Jun–mid-Oct Mon–Sat 10am–4pm, Sun 2–5pm. $4. ☎603-436-8221.* This elegant 3-story Georgian mansion, built in 1763 for local shipbuilder Samuel Moffatt, remained in the same family until 1913, when it was opened to the public as a house museum. Portsmouth furniture and family portraits grace the interiors. Highlights include the grand entrance hall with its period wallpaper and elaborate wood paneling. A pleasant terraced garden (mid-19C) adjoins the house.

**Wentworth-Gardner House** – *Mechanic & Gardner Sts. Visit by guided tour (1hr) only, mid-Jun–mid-Oct Tue–Sun 1–4pm. Closed major holidays. $4. ☎603-436-4406.* The facade of this lovely Georgian mansion, built in 1760, casts its reflection on the surface of the Piscataqua River. The pineapple carved above the doorway was the symbol of hospitality in colonial times *(illustration p 212)*. Inside, the paneling, balusters and cornices are flawlessly carved.

**Governor John Langdon Memorial** – *143 Pleasant St. Visit by guided tour (45min) only, Jun–mid-Oct Wed–Sun noon–5pm. $4. ☎603-436-3205.* This handsome Georgian mansion (1784) is known primarily for its original owner John Langdon, the first president of the US Senate and a former governor of New Hampshire. The interior features wood-carved embellishments, as well as 18C and 19C furniture that was made in Portsmouth.

**John Paul Jones House** – *43 Middle St. Visit by guided tour (45min) only, Jun–mid-Oct Mon–Sat 10am–4pm, Sun noon–4pm. $4. ☎603-436-8420.* The American naval hero John Paul Jones stayed in this Colonial-style home on two occasions during the Revolution. Early furnishings, china, clothing and historical memorabilia owned by the Portsmouth Historical Society are on display.

**Rundlet-May House** – *364 Middle St. Visit by guided tour (45min) only, Jun–mid-Oct Wed–Sun noon–5pm. $4. ☎603-436-3205.* This elegant 3-story Federal residence, perched on an artificial rise, reflects the taste and life-style of the merchant family who owned the property from its construction in 1807 until the 1970s. The interior is appointed with many of the original embellishments and amenities, such as fine pieces of Portsmouth furniture, English wallpaper and innovative early-19C kitchen conveniences. The attached outbuildings and garden further enhance the house's charm.

## EXCURSIONS

★ **Cruise to Isles of Shoals** – *Departs from Market St dock mid-Jun–Labor Day daily 7:30 & 11am. Limited schedule spring & fall. Round-trip 2hr 30min–5hr 45min (3hr stopover). Commentary. Reservations suggested. $8.50–16.50. ⚓ ⚙ Isles of Shoals Steamship Co. ☎603-431-5500.* The 10mi boat trip to this group of nine islands follows the banks of the Piscataqua for 5mi before heading out to sea. There are good views of sights along the river: the dry docks of the Portsmouth Naval Shipyard, the castle-like former maximum security prison that once held 3,500 inmates, **Fort McClary** (Kittery), **Fort Constitution**, and the lovely homes in the island town of New Castle.

Discovered by Capt John Smith in 1614, the Isles of Shoals were known briefly as Smith's Isles until they were renamed by fishermen for the vast shoals, or schools, of fish found in the offshore waters. When the boundary line was established in 1635 between Maine and New Hampshire, the islands were divided between the two states. In the 19C their stark beauty was popularized by author Celia Thaxter and other writers who gathered at her home on Appledore Island each summer. The most important islands are: **Appledore**, site of the marine labs of New Hampshire and Cornell Universities; **Smuttynose**, a private island linked by a breakwater to **Cedar Island**, and **Star Island**, dominated by a rambling old hotel operated by the Unitarian and Congregational churches as a summer religious conference center; and **White Island**, with its solitary setting and lighthouse, which delight photographers.

**New Castle** – Pop 815. *Take Pleasant St south to New Castle Ave (Rte 1B).* Built on an island linked to the mainland by a bridge and causeway, New Castle is a residential town known for its large number of colonial dwellings. Along the waterfront rises the sprawling white clapboard **Wentworth-by-the-Sea**, a 19C hotel complex that continued to draw visitors for almost a century until it closed its doors in the 1970s.

The walls of **Fort Constitution**, one of the oldest forts on the coast, overlook the point where the Piscataqua River enters the Atlantic Ocean.

**Wentworth-Coolidge Mansion** – *On Little Harbor Rd off Rte 1A, 2mi south from downtown Portsmouth. After crossing the Portsmouth city line (1/4mi, sign says "Welcome to Portsmouth") turn right just before the cemetery onto Little Harbor Rd. After 1mi, look for sign to mansion. Visit by guided tour (45min) only, mid-Jun–mid-Oct 10am–5pm. $2.50.* ☏603-436-6607. This 18C mansion on the banks of the Piscataqua River was the home of Benning Wentworth, the son of John Wentworth, New Hampshire's first colonial governor. Although only partially furnished today, the house remains an elegant example of the sophisticated early American architecture of the Portsmouth region.

**Exeter** – Pop 12,481. *13mi southwest of Portsmouth by Rtes 101 and 108.* The townspeople of Exeter were regarded as rebels against the Crown as early as 1734, when they stood their ground and prevented the king's agents from appropriating the tallest trees in the region for the British Navy. Exeter remained a patriot stronghold throughout the Revolution and served as the wartime capital of provincial New Hampshire in the 1770s. Tranquil and reserved today, the town is graced with wide, shaded streets and colonial dwellings, which identify Exeter as one of New Hampshire's earliest settlements.

The community is the home of **Phillips Exeter Academy**, a renowned preparatory school founded in 1781. The school's more than 100 buildings, many in the Georgian style, stand on the academy's broad, emerald-green campus. The Academy Building, a large Georgian structure set back on the lawn facing Front Street, is the main classroom building for the school's 990 students. The nine-level **library** was designed by Louis Kahn in 1965.

## SAINT-GAUDENS NATIONAL HISTORIC SITE

Map of Principal Sights p 2

Augustus Saint-Gaudens (1848-1907) was America's foremost sculptor in the 19C *(p 31).* Apprenticed to a cameo cutter as a boy, he later worked in Rome and studied at the Ecole des Beaux-Arts in Paris before establishing himself in New York, where he quickly became famous. He is remembered for the monumental Civil War memorials he created, such as the Shaw Memorial in Boston *(p 105),* and for his portrait reliefs, which brought him membership in the French Legion of Honor and the Royal Academy.

During the two decades he lived in Cornish, Saint-Gaudens produced about 150 sculptures. His home, studios and extensive gardens are maintained as a museum by the National Park Service.

**VISIT** *1hr 30min*
*In Cornish, 20mi south of Hanover. From Hanover, take Rte 10 south to Rte 12A. Travel approximately 15mi on Rte 12A and follow signs to site. Open May–Oct daily 8:30am–4:30pm. $2.* ☏603-675-2175. *Visit of the house by guided tour (25min) only.*

**The House** – Formerly a tavern before Saint-Gaudens bought and renovated it, the house (c.1800) was named "Aspet" after his father's birthplace in France.

**Studios and Galleries** – The Little Studio was Saint-Gaudens' workshop. A selection of his bas-relief portrait plaques, and the *Diana* he sculpted for the tower of the former Madison Square Garden are here. A cast of his statue *The Puritan* (Springfield, MA) stands among the other works in the gallery.

A cast of the enigmatic **Adams Memorial** (commissioned by Henry Adams for the grave of his wife, Marian, in 1885), regarded as an expression of the artist's interpretation of death, grief and divine peace, graces the grounds.

*Before planning your trip to New England be sure to consult:*
 •*the Map of Principal Sights pp 2-4*
 •*the regional driving tours presented on pp 5-6*

# ★★★ The WHITE MOUNTAINS

Map of Principal Sights p 2                    Tourist Office ☎603-745-8720

The most mountainous region in New England, the White Mountains spread across northern New Hampshire and into Maine. Named for the snow that blankets the area during most of the year, these mountains, dominated by Mt Washington (6,288ft), are characterized by their rounded summits, and deep broad U-shaped valleys known as **notches**.

Renowned for its spectacular natural attractions, picnic areas, campgrounds and more than 1,200mi of foot trails, the federally managed White Mountain National Forest encompasses 772,000 acres. The region's long winter offers numerous opportunities for skiing in the National Forest and in the valleys close by. Throughout the summer hikers and motorists enjoy the cool woods and waterfalls and the views from the mountain summits; in the fall, nature transforms the White Mountains into a leaf-looker's paradise.

## PRACTICAL INFORMATION ............................... Area Code: 603

**Getting There** – Access from the: south (**Boston** to **Lincoln** 295mi) I-93 north; west (**New York City** to **Warren/western White Mountains** 309mi) I-91 north to Rte 25A or (**New York City** to **Bretton Woods/Crawford Notch** 331mi) I-91 north to Rte-302 east; north (**Montreal** to **Franconia Notch** 233mi) Rte 10 west to Rte 55/I-91 south to I-93 south. International and domestic flights to **Portland International Airport** (Portland, ME) ☎207-774-7301. Major rental car agencies (p 248). Closest Amtrak **train** station: South Station, Boston MA ☎800-872-7245. Greyhound **bus** station: Stores St, Concord (transport to Franconia available) ☎800-231-2222.

**Getting Around** – Many scenic routes through National Forest including: I-93 from **Plymouth** to Exit 35 (30mi); Rte 112 from **Lincoln** to **Conway** (37mi); Rte 15 from **Milton Mills** (south of National Forest) to **Gorham** (86mi). Off-road vehicles prohibited, some sights accessible only on foot.

**Visitor Information** – **White Mountain National Forest** visitor centers: **headquarters** 719 Main St, Laconia ☎528-8721; **Saco Ranger Station** Kancamagus Hwy near Rte 16 ☎447-5448; **Androscoggin Ranger Station** 80 Glen Rd (Rte 16), Gorham ☎466-2713; **Ammonoosuc Ranger Station** Rtes 3 & 302 on Trudeau Rd, Bethelem ☎869-2626; **Evans Notch Ranger Station** Bridge St, Bethel ☎207-824-2134. Mailing address: PO Box 638, Laconia NH 03247. **Appalachian Mountain Club (AMC)** visitor center: Pinkham Notch Camp, Gorham ☎466-2725; *Appalachian Mountain Club White Mountain Guide*, available from AMC Books, PO Box 298, Gorham NH 03581 ☎800-262-4455. **Mt Washington Valley Chamber of Commerce** visitor center Main St, North Conway (open year-round Mon-Fri 9am-5pm). Mailing address: PO Box 2300, North Conway NH 03860 ☎356-3171.

**Accommodations** – Reservation service: **Country Inns in the White Mountains** PO Box 2025, North Conway NH ☎800-562-1300. **Mt Washington Valley Chamber of Commerce** (above) offers reservation assistance for towns located near the southeastern edge of the National Forest. **Appalachian Mountain Club** administers a system of huts and shelters, a lodge at the base of Mount Washington, and the **Crawford Notch Hostel** ☎466-2727. Year-round **camping** (advance reservations available for many campsites through MISTIX ☎800-283-2267). Permits not required for **backcountry camping**; information at ranger stations.

**Recreation** – Over 1,100mi of **hiking** trails: trail maps available at ranger stations and AMC visitor center. **Hunting** and **fishing** permitted; licenses and rental equipment available in neighboring towns. **Swimming, canoeing** and **kayaking** allowed on many lakes and rivers; contact ranger stations for more information. **Cross-country skiing** (p 255) trails throughout the area; **downhill skiing** (p 255) primarily in Mt Washington Valley, Waterville Valley and Franconia Notch. **Horse-drawn carriage** trips depart from North Conway area. Specialty **shopping** and supplies in North Conway. Outlet stores in Mt Washington Valley. *Contact organizations above for more information regarding recreation in the area.*

*Sudden and extreme changes in weather are not uncommon throughout the year; it is advisable to obtain current local weather forecast before departing. Hikers should heed warning signs and exercise extreme caution when hiking on Mt Washington.*

**Relief and Climate** – These mountains are remnants of ancient, primarily granite, mountain ranges. During the last Ice Age, they were covered by an immense icesheet grinding and carving the summits until they were rounded. As the ice sheet retreated, glaciers created steep-walled valleys, polishing them to smooth U-shaped notches, while the swirling action of melting glacial water sculpted giant potholes, such as the Basin found in Franconia Notch (p 198).

The climatic regime that dominates the upper slopes of Mt Washington is severe for mountains of this relatively low altitude. The harsh, sub-Arctic climate is responsible for the 4,000-5,000ft timberline of the White Mountains, which is low

# The WHITE MOUNTAINS

compared to the 8,000-9,000ft timberline of the Colorado Rockies. At the summit, the alpine vegetation resembles the flora of the Arctic tundra, and includes species found nowhere else in the Northeast.

**Historical Notes** – Giovanni da Verrazano sighted the White Mountains from the coast in 1524, and as early as 1642, a settler scaled the peak we now call Mt Washington. The artists and writers who visited the region in the early 19C depicted the rugged beauty of the White Mountains in their paintings, novels, short stories and poetry. During the same period, New Hampshire residents named Mt Washington and the other peaks in the Presidential Range after former US presidents. Shortly thereafter, tourists began to arrive. By the end of the century, with the construction of the railroad and the abundance of Victorian hotels that sprung up in the valley, tourism was established on a grand scale in the White Mountains. Many of the fine old hotels have since been destroyed by fire, and replaced by clusters of motels and cottages.

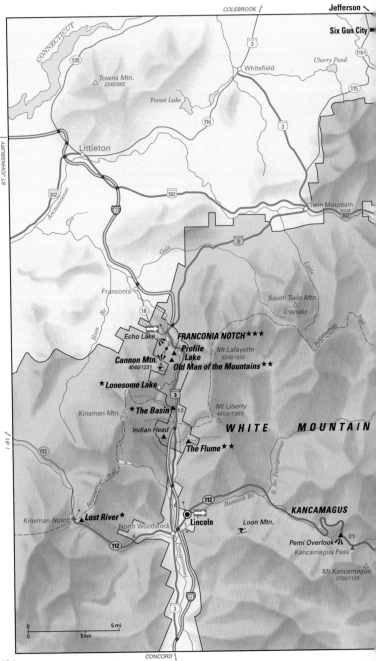

### ★★★ MOUNT WASHINGTON   *Map below*

Mt Washington is the highest point in New England (6,288ft) and the principal peak in the Presidential Range, which includes Mts Adams, Clay, Jefferson, Madison, Monroe and most recently, Mt Eisenhower. A sub-Arctic climate, similar to that of northern Labrador—characterized by bitter cold, wind and ice—predominates in the higher altitudes of this peak, influencing the plant and animal life capable of surviving near the summit. Tiny plants and dwarfed fir and spruce trees have adapted to this harsh environment and thrive in mountain crevices and amid the chaotic jumble of boulders that lie in the region above the timberline. The strongest winds ever recorded (231mph) swept across Mt Washington's summit on April 12, 1934.

Snow has fallen on this peak during every month of the year. Fogbound at least 300 days each year, the summit of Mt Washington, with its group of mountaintop buildings, has been dubbed the "City Among the Clouds."

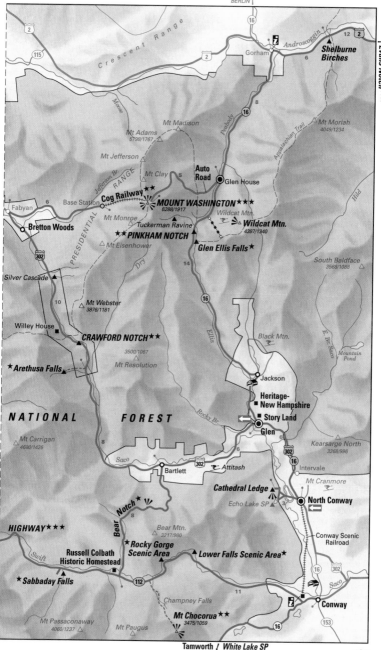

**The Summit** – *The Mt Washington Cog Railway (p 197) and the Auto Road (below) (closed during severe weather) are the quickest means of reaching the summit. Hikers in good condition with the proper equipment will want to try taking one of the four strenuous trails to the top.* Among the half dozen structures that cap Mt Washington are the stone-walled Tip Top House (1853), radio and TV broadcasting facilities, and the Summit Building. The summit and its facilities have served as testing grounds for items ranging from cold weather clothing to equipment used to control icing on aircraft engines.

The **Sherman Adams Summit Building**, a modern structure set into the mountain, is the home of the Mt Washington Weather Observatory, which operates a small museum with exhibits related to the weather, geology and history of the mountain *(open May–Oct daily 8am–8pm;* ✗ ⛄ ☎603-466-3347).

On a clear day, the rooftop deck of the building offers an impressive **panorama★★★** from the summit of Mt Washington. This 240mi vista, which encompasses the entire region, stretches north to Montreal.

**★★ Mt Washington Cog Railway** – *6mi east of Fabyan. Description p 197.*

**★★ PINKHAM NOTCH** – **North Conway to Glen House**
*26mi via Rtes 302 and 16. 1/2 day. Map p 195.*

**North Conway** – Pop 2,032. Situated on the edge of the White Mountain National Forest, North Conway is a gateway to the White Mountains. The town, located near Attitash, Mt Cranmore, Black Mountain and Wildcat Mountain ski areas *(ski information p 256)*, offers many facilities for tourists.

The Roman-style railroad station (1874) has been transformed into a museum and ticket office *(Rte 16)* for the **Conway Scenic Railroad**, which operates an 11mi ride on an antique train through the Saco Valley *(departs from North Conway depot early Jun–late Oct daily 10 & 11am, noon, 1, 2 & 4pm; spring & Nov–Dec hours vary; round-trip 1–2hrs; $7.50–12.50;* ✗ ⛄ *Conway Scenic Railroad;* ☎603-356-5251).

**Cathedral Ledge** – *From the Scenic Railroad turn left opposite the White Mountain Bank and continue 1.5mi to the sign for Cathedral Ledge, then turn left.* Towering 1,000 ft above the valley, this ledge commands a good **view★** of Echo Lake and the ruggedly beautiful Mt Washington Valley that surrounds it.

*Return to Rte 302/16 north. Mt Washington is visible from the road.*

**Glen** – Located at the intersection of Routes 16 and 302 (Crawford Notch), Glen has two popular attractions: Story Land and Heritage-New Hampshire.

**Story Land** – *Open mid-Jun–Labor Day daily 9am–6pm, after Labor Day–mid-Oct weekends only 10am–5pm. $15.* ✗ ⛄ ☎603-383-4293. This theme park features life-size characters and settings from children's stories and nursery rhymes, along with rides, a picnic grove and snack bars.

**Heritage-New Hampshire** – *Open mid-Jun–Labor Day daily 9am–6pm, after Labor Day–late Oct 9am–5pm. $7.50.* ⛄ ☎603-383-4293. Life-like scenes enhanced by special techniques allow visitors to experience significant events in New Hampshire's past. Beyond the building's classic white exterior, you will discover the state's mountainous landscape, walk through the grim interior of the Amoskeag Mills in 19C Manchester, and see Daniel Webster age as he tells the story of his life. The visit concludes with a simulated train ride through Crawford Notch.

*Continue north on Route 16 through the village of Jackson. Cross over the Jackson covered bridge to glimpse the village's old resort hotels.*

**★★ Pinkham Notch** – (2,032ft) In this gap between Mt Washington and Wildcat Mountain the valley narrows.

**★ Glen Ellis Falls**– *Parking lot on left side of the road.* The falls and its pools, located on the east side of the road *(take the underpass)*, are formed by the Ellis River.

**Wildcat Mountain** – *Parking area off Rte 16.* Ski trails that look across Pinkham Notch to Mt Washington have been cut on the slopes of Wildcat Mountain (4,397ft). A gondola lift provides access to the summit, which offers **views★★** of Mt Washington and the northern peaks of the Presidential Range *(gondola operates Jul–early Oct daily 9am–5pm; late May–Jun & early Oct–late Oct weekends only 9am–5pm; mid-Nov–Apr weekends only 9am–4pm; $8;* ✗ ☎603-466-3326).

**Auto Road** – The 8mi trek to the summit of Mt Washington begins at **Glen House**. You can drive your car or take a guided tour *(below)*. From the summit and scenic outlooks there are spectacular views of the Great Gulf Wilderness Area and the Presidential Range. *Open to private vehicles daily mid-May–mid-Oct (weather permitting). $12/car & driver; $5 each additional adult. Motorists planning to drive to the summit should be sure their car is in good condition before starting (check gas, brakes, water). The road, partially unpaved, can be narrow and steep in places. For safety reasons, mobile campers and overloaded vehicles not allowed. Guided tours (1hr 30min) depart from Glen House. $18.* ☎603-466-3988.

**Shelburne Birches** – *14mi from Glen House. Take Rte 16, then Rte 2 through Gorham.* This is a picturesque roadside stand of tall, slender white birch trees.

**★★ Evans Notch** – *12mi by Rte 2 from Shelburne Birches. Description p 68.*

## ★★ CRAWFORD NOTCH – Glen to Fabyan
*24mi via Rte 302. 3hrs. Map p 195.*

Route 302 follows the Saco River through Crawford Notch, a broad valley in the heart of the White Mountains. The road passes the **Attitash Ski Area**, a popular resort, and continues to **Bartlett**. In Bartlett a road located just past the library leads south through Bear Notch.

★ **Bear Notch** – *An additional 8mi between Bartlett and the Kancamagus Hwy.* This drive is especially scenic during the foliage season. At the point where the road leaves Crawford Notch *(3.5mi after Bartlett),* there is a beautiful **view** of the valley.

★★ **Crawford Notch** – (1,773ft) This pass was named for the Crawford family, White Mountain pioneers who cut the first trail to the summit of Mt Washington in the 19C, and whose home in the notch served as a shelter for hikers.

★ **Arethusa Falls** – *Parking lot on the left side of the road. Cross the railroad tracks, then follow the path (right) into the woods.* The trail *(round-trip 2hrs)* follows a brook, then crosses the brook just before reaching the falls, a refreshing forest setting.

Route 302 passes in front of the rustic **Willey House** and **Mt Webster**, its slopes covered in places with the rocky debris of recent landslides. Farther on you will pass the **Silver Cascade**, a roadside waterfall tumbling from a high ledge.

**Bretton Woods** – The slopes of the Presidential Range form the backdrop for the **Mount Washington Resort**, a sprawling complex that is one of the few 19C hosteleries still in existence. In 1944 the hotel was the site of the United Nations Monetary and Financial Conference (Bretton Woods Conference), which established the American dollar as the medium of international exchange and developed plans to establish the World Bank.

*Continue north on Rte 302. At Fabyan, turn right onto the road leading to the Cog Railway.*

Dusty Perin/Dembinsky Photo Assoc.

Mount Washington Cog Railway

★★ **Mt Washington Cog Railway** – *Departs from Marshfield Base Station 6mi east of Rte 302 Jul–Labor Day daily 8am–4pm. After Labor Day–Oct daily 9am–2pm (weather permitting); May weekends only 9am–2pm. Round-trip 3hrs. $35.* ✗ ₺ *Mt Washington Cog Railway ☎603-846-5404.* This small steam train is almost as famous as the mountain itself. Built in 1869, the 3.5mi railway represents an outstanding technological achievement for its day, and still offers passengers a thrilling ride to the summit of the mountain, especially as the train ascends **Jacob's Ladder**, the steepest grade (37 percent) on the trestle.
During the leisurely ride *(1hr 30min)* to the top, note how the vegetation and landscape change with increasing altitude.

## ★★ FRANCONIA NOTCH   *13mi via Rte 3. 1/2 day. Map p 194.*

Running along the floor of this scenic notch cradled between the Franconia and Kinsman Ranges, Route 3 offers easy access to **Echo Lake** *(Rte 18)* and to many of the area's natural attractions.

**Cannon Mountain** – Cannon Mountain is one of New Hampshire's finest ski areas. An **aerial tramway** travels to the summit (4,040ft), which overlooks Echo Lake and affords a **view★★** of the notch *(tramway operates mid-May–Oct daily 9am–4:30pm, rest of the year weekends only 9am–3:45pm; $9;* ✗ ₺ *☎603-823-5563).*

Located next to the tramway station, the **New England Ski Museum** illustrates skiing history with audio-visual presentations, photographs, equipment and memorabilia *(open late Dec–Mar & May–mid-Oct Thu–Tue noon–5pm; closed Jan 1; ☎603-823-7177).*

★★ **Old Man of the Mountains and Profile Lake** – A rocky formation that resembles a man's profile (40ft from chin to forehead) juts out from a mountainside above Profile Lake. The profile was discovered in 1805 by two men who compared it to a likeness of President Jefferson. Hawthorne described the profile in his short story *The Great Stone Face*, and when P.T. Barnum *(p 41)* toured the notch almost 20 years later, he was so impressed that he wanted to purchase the attraction for his circus. The Old Man of the Mountains is best viewed from a vantage point on the lakeshore.

★ **Lonesome Lake** – *Trail (3hrs) leaves from the parking lot at Lafayette Campground. Follow the yellow markers.* This lake occupies a clearing 1,000ft above Franconia Notch. A trail around the lake leads to the Appalachian Mountain Club Hut, which accommodates hikers in the summer.

★ **The Basin** – The action of churning waters rushing down from the falls above has formed this 30ft granite pothole.

★★ **The Flume** – *Open mid-May–late Oct daily 9am–5pm. $6. Bus transportation to Boulder Cabin (.5mi walk to Flume) is available from the visitor center. ☎603-745-8391.* A series of connecting paths forms a 2mi loop trail beginning at the visitor center. **Flume Path,** a system of boardwalks and stairways, guides visitors through the Flume, a deep, narrow granite chasm through which Flume Brook flows. **Ridge Path** leads to Liberty Cascade and then passes the **Sentinal Pine-Covered Bridge** that overlooks a clear natural pool. **Wildwood Path** completes the circuit, winding past mammoth boulders that were deposited here by glaciers thousands of years ago.

The Flume

Upon leaving the Flume, look across Route 3 for a rocky formation that resembles the profile of a human head. This rock is called **Indian Head**. Route 3 continues south toward the village of Lincoln.

**Lincoln** – Pop 1,229. Located at the southern entrance to Franconia Notch, Lincoln is a center for neighboring resorts, boasting a plentiful assortment of motels, restaurants, shops and commercial attractions.

★ **Lost River** – *7mi from Lincoln by Rte 112 west. Open May–Oct daily 9am–4pm (Jul–Aug 6pm). $7. ☎603-745-8031.* Located in Kinsman Notch, between the Connecticut and Pemigewasset Valleys, the Lost River Gorge is a steep-walled glacial ravine filled with enormous boulders that have been sculpted into potholes by the river. A system of boardwalks and staircases allows visitors to tour the caves, potholes and waterfalls in the gorge.

★★★ **THE KANCAMAGUS HIGHWAY** – Lincoln to Conway
*32mi. 3hrs. Map pp 194–195.*

This road through the White Mountain National Forest follows the **Hancock Branch** of the Pemigewasset River and the **Swift River**. It is one of the most spectacular drives in New England during the foliage season, when the maples and birch trees take on their fall colors. Picnic areas and campgrounds along the highways invite visitors to relax by the clear mountain streams interrupted by scenic rapids. The mountains south of the highway are named for some of New Hampshire's famous

Indians: the Passaconaway, Kancamagus ("a friend of the settlers") and Chocorua. The road passes in front of **Loon Mountain Recreation Area**, a year-round resort, then begins to climb to Kancamagus Pass. During the ascent, there is an exceptionally scenic **view★** from the **Pemi Overlook**. The road then dips into the Saco Valley.

★ **Sabbaday Falls** – *Parking area on south side of the road. Take the Sabbaday Brook Trail (round-trip 30min), an easy trail to follow.* The falls tumble over a series of ledges into two giant potholes, then through a flume.

**Russell Colbath Historic Homestead** – *House is open late May–mid-Oct daily 8:30–4:30pm. Craft demonstrations.* ♿ ☎603-447-5448. This is an information and nature center for the White Mountain National Forest. The short, self-guided **Rail 'N River Trail** begins here. Nicknamed for the former railroad bed it follows, the trail provides an introduction to the trees and shrubs in this part of the forest.

*The highway passes the road (on the left) to Bear Notch (p 197).*

★★ **Mt Chocorua** – *Round-trip 5hr hike to the summit from Champney Falls Trail parking area.* Follow the **Champney Falls Trail–Piper Trail**, which ascends gently the first 1.5mi and leads to a bypass *(on the left)* to Champney Falls. Return to the main trail, which becomes moderately difficult as it climbs rapidly through various stages of forest vegetation to the rocky summit of Mt Chocorua. From the summit, there are **views★★★** of the White Mountains on one side and of Chocorua Lake on the other.
Both the lake and the mountain are named in honor of the Indian chief, who according to legend, avenged the death of his son by killing the family of the man suspected of accidentally poisoning the boy. A group of angry settlers pursued the chief to the upper ledge of the mountain that today bears his name. Cornered, Chocorua uttered a curse on all white men then jumped to his death. Settlers recalled the Indian's curse when an epidemic killed many of their cattle; the cause was eventually traced to polluted drinking water.

*To return to the parking lot, follow the signs for Champney Falls Trail; there are many paths on Mt Chocorua, so it is easy to stray from the main trail.*

★ **Rocky Gorge Scenic Area** – The Swift River forms rapids at this point, where the valley narrows.

★ **Lower Falls Scenic Area** – The eastern end of the site affords the best view of the falls formed by the Swift River.

**Conway** – Pop 7,490. Conway is a resort for all seasons. Ski shops, motels and restaurants border Route 16, outside the town. The covered bridge spanning the Saco River can be seen from Route 16, about .5mi north of Conway.

**Tamworth** – Pop 2,165. *13mi from Conway. Take Rte 16 south.* After 10mi, there's a picture-postcard **view★★** of Mt Chocorua, reflected in the lake of the same name. A little farther south, pass through the tiny village of Chocorua. Route 113 west leads to the tranquil village of Tamworth, with its white houses and cozy inn. The **Barnstormers**, a local theater group, performs here during the summer.

## ADDITIONAL SIGHTS

**White Lake State Park** – *14mi south of Conway, .5mi north of West Ossipee on Rte 16. Open daily mid-May–Labor Day 8am–dusk, after Labor Day–mid-Oct weekends only. $2.50.* ⛺ ♿ ☎603-323-7350. *Facility information p 251.* Located south of the White Mountains, this park attracts swimmers and fishermen to its sandy beach.

**Mt Whittier** – *Rte 25 from West Ossipee.* From the summit (2,205ft) of this mountain, named for the poet John Greenleaf Whittier *(p 160)* who summered nearby, there is a view that includes the White Mountains and Mt Chocorua.

**Santa's Village** – *Rte 2 in Jefferson. Open Jun–Labor Day daily 9:30am–6:30pm, after Labor Day–Oct weekends only 9:30am–5pm. $13.* ✗ ♿ ☎603-586-4445. The village claims to be the summer home of Santa Claus, his reindeer and helpers. Its 40 gaily painted and decorated buildings are set in a grove of tall evergreens.

**Six Gun City** – *South of junction Rtes 2 and 115A, near Jefferson. Open Jun–Labor Day daily 9am–6pm, after Labor Day–Oct daily 9:30am–5pm. $9.25.* ✗ ♿ ☎603-586-4592. This replica of a small western town includes a blockhouse, jail, saloon and 35 other buildings. Visitors can enjoy the waterslide and ride logs through a mill.

*The* ⛺ *symbol indicates that campgrounds can be found on the premises of the sight described.*

# ★ Lake WINNIPESAUKEE REGION

Map of Principal Sights p 2                    Tourist Office ☎603-253-8555

New Hampshire's largest lake covers an area of 72sq mi, has a shore-line of 300mi, and is dotted with more than 200 tiny islands. The best way to view it is by taking a cruise*(below)*. On a clear day, the lake, set against the backdrop of the White Mountains, is a magnificent sight. The lake's name originated with an Indian legend about a brave who was canoeing on the lake one night. The sky suddenly darkened. Without warning, a brilliant ray of light shone on the water, guiding his boat safely to shore. He interpreted this light as a divine miracle, and named the lake Winnipesaukee, meaning "the smile of the Great Spirit."

**Lakeside Villages** – Each of the villages on the lake possesses its own character. **Laconia** is the industrial and commercial center of the region. The small charming village of **Wolfeboro★**, with its large homes overlooking the lake, has attracted summer vacationers for centuries. Unspoiled by industry, it is one of the prettiest communities on the shores of Lake Winnipesaukee. **Weirs Beach**, with its amusement arcade, souvenir shops and lakefront Victorian dwellings, is a lively resort; attractive **Center Harbor**, as well as Meredith, on bays at the northern end of the lake, serve as shopping centers for the resort cottages and campgrounds nearby.

Every summer thousands of vacationers enjoy boating on Winnipesaukee's waters. Public docks, marinas and launching ramps abound. Popular beaches include Weirs Beach and **Ellacoya State Beach**. For hikers, walking trails in the hills encircle the area. During the winter, **Gunstock Ski Area** *(ski information p 256)* and **Ragged Mountain Ski Area** teem with activity. Ice fishing, snowmobiling and the dogsled championships held each February in Laconia provide additional winter attractions.

**★★ Sightseeing Cruises** – *The following excursion boats are operated on the lake by Winnipesaukee Flagship Corp. ☎ 603-366-2628 (dinner cruises also available):*

**★★ M/S Mount Washington** – *Departs late May–mid-Oct from: Weirs Beach daily 9am & 12:15pm (Jul–late Aug additional 2hr 15min cruise 3:30pm; $10.50); Center Harbor Mon, Wed & Fri 9:45am; Alton Bay Tue, Thu, Sat & Sun 10:15am; Wolfeboro daily at 11am (Jul–late Aug additional 2hr 15min cruise 2:15pm; $10.50). Round-trip 3hr 15min. Commentary. $12.50.* ☒ ও.

**M/V Doris E.** – *Departs Jul–Labor Day daily from: Meredith 10am, noon, 2 & 6:30pm & Weirs Beach 10:30 & 11:30am, 12:30, 1:30, 2:30 & 7pm. Round-trip 2 hrs. Commentary. $9.* ☒.

**M/V Sophie C.** – *The Sophie C. is a mailboat that travels to the lake's upper islands. Departs from Weirs Beach early Jul–early Sept Mon–Sat 11am & 1:30pm, mid-Jun–early Jul 1:30pm only. Limited service spring & fall. Round-trip 2hrs. Commentary. $9.* ☒.

**★ Castle in the Clouds** – *In Moultonborough, 18mi north of Wolfeboro by Rte 109 then Rte 171. Open late May–Labor Day daily 10am–5pm, after Labor Day–late Oct daily 10am–4pm. $10.* ও ☎603-476-2352. This 6,000-acre estate was acquired in 1910 by the millionaire Thomas Plant, who made his fortune by developing machinery for use in the shoe industry. The residence Plant commissioned high on the slopes of the Ossipee Mountains overlooks the forests and lakes below. From the terrace, there is a **view★★** of Lake Winnipesaukee with its myriad tree-clad islands. Miles of foot and horse trails thread through the property *(horse rental $25/hr)*. A path *(.25mi)* beginning about 1mi from the entrance gate leads to two waterfalls, the **Fall of Song** and **Bridal Veil Falls**.

**★ Center Sandwich** – *5mi north of Moultonborough by Rte 109.* Situated at the foot of the White Mountains, Center Sandwich is one of New England's prettiest villages. In the fall a tapestry of brilliant autumn color frames its simple white clapboard structures. On the green sits the sales shop of the **Sandwich Home Industries**, the founding member of the state-wide guild of the League of New Hampshire Craftsmen.

# Rhode Island

Newport Harbor - O. Van der Wal/Stock Newport

# Rhode Island

**Area:** 1,214sq mi
**Population:** 1,003,464
**Capital:** Providence
**Nickname:** Ocean State
**State Flower:** Violet

The smallest state in the nation, Rhode Island measures only 48 miles long and 37 miles wide. In 1524 Italian navigator Giovanni da Verrazano sailed into Narragansett Bay and along the coast of the island known to the Indians as Aquidneck. Impressed by the brilliance of the natural light here, Verrazano noted the similarity in appearance between Aquidneck and the Greek isle of Rhodes. Over a century later, Aquidneck was renamed Rhode Island. Its official name, the State of Rhode Island and Providence Plantations, reflects the state's origin as a series of independent settlements. The Royal Charter of 1644 united "Providence Plantations" at the head of the Narragansett Bay with settlements at Newport and Portsmouth on Aquidneck Island. Today the state ranks as the third most densely populated state in the US.

Narragansett Bay, Rhode Island's dominant natural feature, extends 28 miles inland, nearly bisecting the state. The bay fostered the early commercial trade that contributed to the wealth of Newport, Providence and Bristol. Sprawling inland from the bay, the Providence metropolitan area remains the only large urban center in the state.

**A Land of Tolerance** – The earliest colonists came to Rhode Island in search of the religious freedom they could not find in Massachusetts. The first to arrive, in 1630, was the **Reverend Blackstone** *(p 96)*, fleeing the Puritans' invasion of his privacy on the Shawmut Peninsula. He was followed by the minister **Roger Williams**, who founded Providence in 1636. Exiled from Massachusetts for his "new and dangerous opinions," Williams established Providence Plantations, a farming community, on lands that he purchased from the Narragansett Indians. Two years later a group of disgruntled Bostonians bought the island of Aquidneck and started the colony of Portsmouth (north of present-day Newport). The religious leader **Anne Hutchinson** soon joined them, with her own adherents in tow. Newport was founded in 1639 by 11 former Portsmouth colonists who left after a factional dispute.

Relations between the colonists and the Indians remained friendly until 1675 when Philip, chief of the Wampanoags, led his tribe, along with the Narragansetts and Nipmucks, in raids against the settlers in **King Philip's War** (1675-1676). During the Great Swamp Fight (in Mt Hope, RI) on December 19, 1675, colonists launched a surprise attack on the Narragansetts, Rhode Island's most powerful tribe. The war dissipated the tribe's strength and greatly reduced the local Indian population.

**Economy** – Rhode Island's economy was at first based on the sea, with Newport and Providence vying for positions as the nation's leading seaports. By the 1650s Rhode Island had gained a portion of the trade between New England and the West Indies. The great fortunes resulting therefrom provided capital for the textile industry, which had its beginnings at Pawtucket *(p 214)* in 1793. One of the country's leading textile producers throughout the 19C, Rhode Island soon became the most heavily industrialized state in the US. The exodus of the textile factories to the South after World War II led to an emphasis on diversified manufacturing, which today ranks as the state's leading source of income and its largest employer. Rhode Island's early manufacture of machine tools gave rise in 1796 to the production of jewelry and silverware, now a major industry. Tourism generates over a billion dollars a year in revenues for the state. Health care, agriculture and the fishing industry provide additional sources of income.

# ★ BLOCK ISLAND

Map of Principal Sights p 2    Tourist Office ☎ 401-466-5200

This unspoiled island, 10mi south of the mainland, is covered with cliffs, sand dunes and grassy moors. Probably discovered in the 16C by Verrazano, Block Island was named for **Adrian Block**, the Dutch navigator who explored the region in 1614. The first permanent colonists to settle here arrived at the end of the 17C. They were followed by smugglers, pirates, and most likely those shipwrecked off the frequently

Jonathan Wallen

fogbound coast of Block Island. In the late 19C, the island developed into a summer resort with large, prim Victorian hotels, such as those that front **Old Harbor**. Tourists were attracted by the mild sea breezes and the refreshing climate. Visitors now enjoy the quiet island for its good beaches, deep-sea fishing and boating. **New Harbor** provides a superb haven for boats and a playground for water sports.

## PRACTICAL INFORMATION ............................... Area Code: 401

**Getting There** – From **Providence** to **Point Judith** (33 mi): I-95 south to Hwy 4 west to Hwy 1 south to Hwy 108; from **Newport** to **Point Judith** (20 mi): Hwy 138 west to Hwy 1 south to Hwy 108. International and domestic flights to **T. F. Green State Airport**, Providence ☎737-4000; bus service to Point Judith available ☎781-9400. Major rental car agencies p 248. Amtrak **train** station: New London CT ☎800-872-7245. Greyhound **bus** station: Newport ☎800-231-2222.

**Ferry Schedule** *advance reservations for vehicles strongly suggested*

| Departs From | Schedule | Duration (one-way) | Adult Fare | Company |
|---|---|---|---|---|
| Point Judith | year-round, daily | 1hr | $6.60 | Interstate Navigation ☎783-4613 |
| Newport | mid-Jun–Labor day, daily | | $9.25 | |
| Providence | mid-Jun–Labor day, daily | 4hrs | $10.65 | |
| New London, CT | mid-Jun–Labor day, daily | 2hrs | $13.50 | |
| Montauk, NY | early May–Sept, daily; weekends until mid-Oct | 1hr 30min | $15.00 | Viking Ferry ☎516-668-5709 |
| | early Jun–late Sept, daily | 1hr 45min | $15.00 | Jigger III ☎516-668-2214 |

**Getting Around** – Block Island is best visited by bicycle, as streets are often congested and parking may be difficult (especially in July and August). Bicycle and car rentals in Old and New Harbor areas.

**Visitor Information** – **Block Island Chamber of Commerce** visitor center: Old Harbor. Mailing address: Drawer D, Dodge St, Block Island RI 02807 ☎800-383-2474.

**Accommodations** – Information available from **chamber of commerce** *(above)*. Accommodations include historic hotels and bed & breakfasts ($85-$125/day). Camping is prohibited. *Average prices for a double room.*

**Recreation** – Swimming **beaches** stretch from Old Harbor to the north end of the island. **Hiking** trails throughout the island, including The Maze, a 128-acre preserve. **Fishing** licenses and rental equipment available in New Harbor. Most specialty **shopping** and supplies in Old Harbor. *Contact Chamber of Commerce for more information regarding shopping and recreation on Block Island.*

## SIGHTS 4hrs

★★ **Mohegan Bluffs** – The island's south shore is formed by a series of spectacular multicolored cliffs. Steep paths descend to the beach at the base of the cliffs.

★ **Sandy Point** – The northern end of the island has been set aside as a bird and wildlife preserve. A sandy path leads to the stone lighthouse. No longer in use, the old light with its 18in-thick walls, has managed to withstand the force of shifting sands and powerful gales over the years.

**Crescent Beach** – *Entrance off Corn Neck Rd. From Water St, turn left on Dodge St, and right on Corn Neck Rd at four-way stop.* Dressing rooms, showers and eating facilities are available at the locally owned, guarded section of Crescent Beach. *Swimming is advised at guarded beaches only because of the strong undertow and rough surf at some of the beaches.*

# BRISTOL                                                   Pop 21,625

Map of Principal Sights p 2                    Tourist Office ☎401-245-0750

Bristol survived the Revolution to become a leading seaport and shipbuilding center. Some of its wealthy citizens, who prospered from trade with Africa, the West Indies and the Orient, built mansions throughout the waterfront district.
For over 80 years the **Herreshoff** boatyards turned out steam and sailing yachts, among which were several successful America's Cup *(p 206)* defenders. A drive through **Colt State Park** *(off Rte 114)* affords views of Narragansett Bay.
Today Bristol is known for its Fourth of July parade, first held in 1785 and said to be the oldest in the country.

★ **Linden Place** – *500 Hope St. Visit by guided tour (45min) only, late May–mid-Oct Thu–Sun 10am–2pm. $4. ☎401-253-0390.* Notorious Rhode Island slave trader George DeWolf spent $60,000 to build this splendid 3-story clapboard mansion. Designed by Russell Warren, the Federal-style house, with its Corinthian columns and leaded fanlights, was completed in 1810. It contains DeWolf family furnishings.

**Blithewold Mansion & Gardens** – *101 Ferry Rd (Rte 114). Grounds open year-round daily 10am–5pm. $4. Mansion open Apr–Oct Tue–Sun 10am–4pm, Dec noon–8pm. Mansion closed major holidays. $7.50. ☎401-253-2707.* Flower gardens *(in season)*, and trees and shrubs from Europe and the Orient adorn the grounds of this former estate, built in 1907 for Augustus Van Wickle, a coal magnate. Even during the off-season, this is a delightful place for a stroll, with its spacious surroundings, harborside setting and expansive views of Narragansett Bay. A rock garden and water garden occupy clearings a short distance from the water's edge; near the mansion stands an 90ft-tall giant sequoia.
The mansion, a stone and stucco residence designed as an English manor house, is furnished with objects and artifacts acquired by the Van Wickles on their trips abroad. Twelve of the rooms in the house are open to the public.

**Haffenreffer Museum of Anthropology** – *Tower St. From Rte 136 take Tower Rd east and follow the signs. Open Jun–Aug Tue–Sat 10am–5pm, rest of the year weekends only. Closed major holidays. $2. ☎401-253-8388.* This small museum is part of Brown University's *(p 217)* Department of Anthropology. Exhibits are from Brown's rich collection of artifacts related to the cultures of aboriginal peoples of Africa, the Pacific and the Americas. The museum owns a selection of Arctic items gathered by a university-sponsored expedition to Alaska.

**Herreshoff Marine Museum** – *7 Burnside St, .5mi south of downtown. Open May–Oct Mon–Fri 1–4pm, weekends 11am–4pm. $3. �& ☎401-253-5000.* From 1863 to 1946 the waterside boatyards along Route 114 here were the site of the Herreshoff Manufacturing Co, designer of Naval torpedo boats, acclaimed wooden sailing and motor yachts, and seven America's Cup defenders (1893-1934).
Located in a 1-story warehouse, the museum offers an in-depth tribute to the company's glory days through photos, film, models and some 40 craft in various stages of restoration. The **America's Cup Hall of Fame** is also housed in the museum.

# LITTLE COMPTON                                            Pop 3,339

Map of Principal Sights p 3                    Tourist Office ☎401-849-8048

Located in the southeastern portion of the state known for its production of "Rhode Island Red" chickens, Little Compton is one of Rhode Island's prettiest villages, with its village green, white Congregational church and old cemetery. In the burial ground stands a monument honoring Benjamin Church, the Indian fighter who took part in the Great Swamp Fight and the capture and execution of King Philip *(p 202)*.
Marshes fringe the narrow roads (such as Route 77) that wind through the rural countryside and down to the coast.

# NARRAGANSETT PIER

Narragansett Pier and the coastal region extending south to Point Judith and Jerusalem possess some of the finest beaches in New England. **Scarborough's** lively atmosphere draws a young crowd, while surfers prefer **East Matunuck State Beach**. Families with young children are drawn to the calm waters at **Galilee Beach**.
Narragansett Pier began to develop into a fashionable seaside resort in the 19C, after Rhode Island governor William Sprague and his wife built their summer mansion in the area. All activity centered upon the pier (only the name survives), which extended from the southern end of Town Beach into the ocean. Beyond the beachfront Victorian hotels stood the vacation homes of American businessmen and political figures. The **Towers**, two stone structures joined by an arch extending across Ocean Road, are all that remain of the lavish Narragansett Casino, designed by McKim, Mead and White in 1884. The main section of the casino and many of Narragansett's grand hotels were destroyed by fire in 1900.

### The Coast from Narragansett Pier to Point Judith *6mi. 30min.*
*Drive south on Ocean Rd (Rte 1A), which passes under the Towers and skirts shorefront mansions that overlook the pounding surf. About 2mi after Scarborough Beach, you will enter Galilee.*

**Galilee** – In September this fishing village hosts the annual **Rhode Island Tuna Tournament**, a major sporting event. The Point Judith ferry to BLOCK ISLAND leaves from the State Pier at Galilee year-round *(p 203)*. On the opposite shore of Point Judith Pond is **Jerusalem**, another tiny fishing village.

**Point Judith** – The rocky headland with its octagonal-shaped lighthouse is a familiar landmark to mariners who sail these waters.

---

# ★★★ NEWPORT

An all-encompassing view of the city's beautiful setting in the midst of Narragansett Bay greets motorists arriving from the west by Newport Bridge *(passenger vehicles $2 one-way)*. A resort once devoted exclusively to the wealthy, Newport, today a major sailing center and home of the **Newport Music Festival**, is fascinating for its history and architecture.

**A Harbor of Refuge** – In the wake of a political dispute with Anne Hutchinson *(p 202)* in Portsmouth, **William Coddington**, another Boston exile, led a group of settlers to the southern part of Aquidneck Island in 1639. There, on the shore of a large harbor, they founded Newport. Other religious minorities—Quakers, Baptists and Jews—soon followed, seeking the religious tolerance for which the Rhode Island settlements were known. These settlers were talented entrepreneurs, and with their help, the colony rapidly developed .

**Newport's Golden Age** – By 1761 Newport had grown into a bustling port center second only to BOSTON. The colony's prosperity was due largely to the **triangular trade**. Vessels bearing cargoes of rum sailed to Africa, where the rum was exchanged for slaves. Merchants then transported the slaves to the West Indies and traded them for molasses used to produce rum. The slave market represented an important source of income to Newport. An import tax levied on each slave brought into the colony yielded sufficient revenue to build the roads and bridges needed to link the growing settlements. Rum was also exported to Europe, where it was exchanged for goods not available in the colonies.

The Breakers

Preservation Society of Newport County

**The Revolution** – Newport's fortunes were abruptly reversed with the outbreak of the American Revolution. Marked by the British for destruction, Newport was occupied from 1776 to 1779. Inhabitants were forced to quarter English soldiers, and looting and burning were widespread. Following the British defeat, French troops, allies of the Americans, occupied Newport. It was here that meetings between General Washington and Count Rochambeau took place (p 62).

By the end of the war, Newport lay in ruins. Most of its merchants had fled to Providence (p 215), and the colony would never again regain its commercial splendor.

**Summer Resort of the Wealthy** – During the years before the Revolution, planters from Georgia and the Carolinas escaped the heat of the southern summer by vacationing in Newport. In the mid-19C, with the introduction of steamboat travel between New York and Newport, an increasing number of visitors arrived each year. Following the Civil War, America's wealthiest families, the Astors, Belmonts and Vanderbilts, began to summer here. Impressed by the magnificence of the palaces and châteaux they had seen while touring Europe, they commissioned America's finest architects to design the mansion "cottages" that grace Ocean Drive and Bellevue Avenue.

In summer Newport's rich, part-time residents held fabulous picnics, dinner parties and balls, famed for their extravagance. Presiding over these events were Mrs William Astor, Mrs O.H. Belmont, Mrs Hermann Oelrichs and other high-society matriarchs. The search for unusual diversions led to such eccentricities as the champagne and caviar dinner given by Harry Lehr for his friends and their pets, during which masters and pets ate and drank at the same table; and the fleet of full-size model ships made for Mrs Oelrichs and placed on the ocean to convey the impression of a harbor.

Attracted by the latest fads and inventions, the affluent of Newport drove the first motor cars, built the first roads, filled the harbor with princely mahogany and brass-trimmed yachts, and introduced boat racing to the town.

**Newport and Sports** – Several sports owe their development and popularity to Newport society, whose favorite pastimes included tennis, golf and boating. In 1881 the first US tennis championships were held on the courts of the Newport Casino; annual tennis tournaments, including the **International Tennis Hall of Fame Grass Court Championships** (held in early July), are still played here. The first US amateur and open golf championships took place on a 9-hole course laid out on Brenton Point in 1894 by the 400 elite members of New York and Newport society (p 210).

It was, however, in the realm of sailing—especially yachting—that Newport became internationally famous. By the late 19C several yachting clubs had been established in Newport, and from 1930 to 1983 the city hosted the celebrated **America's Cup** races. These races, an international competition among the most sophisticated sailing yachts in the world, date from 1851, when the New York Yacht Club sent the schooner America across the Atlantic to compete against the British for the prestigious Hundred Guinea Cup. The America won the race and returned home with the Cup—actually an ornate silver pitcher thereafter known as the America's Cup.

Held only 26 times since 1851 because of the tremendous expense involved, the race was won consistently by the US until 1983 when the trophy passed into the hands of Australia. An American victory in 1987 by the challenger Stars and Stripes once again brought the cup home to the US, where it has remained. Newport is the point-of-origin of the biennial 685mi **Newport-Bermuda Race** and the destination of the **Single-Handed Transatlantic Race** that begins at Plymouth, England.

**Newport Music Festival** – The Newport Music Festival consists of a ten-day series of musical programs presented in the mansions (Rosecliff, Beechwood, The Elms and The Breakers) during the month of July. The **Newport Jazz Festival**, a celebrated annual event in the music world, first took place in Newport in 1954. Moved to New York during the 1970s, the festival has since returned to Newport and is currently known as the JVC Jazz Festival. Performances are held at Fort Adams State Park.

**Newport Architecture** – Newport provides an architectural sampler of the nation's most aesthetically pleasing building styles from the 17C to the 19C. The city's large group of colonial structures range from the simple and austere Quaker meetinghouse (p 210) to Trinity Church, inspired by the work of Christopher Wren. They also include Georgian structures designed by **Peter Harrison** (p 29): the Redwood Library, the Touro Synagogue and the Brick Market. Approximately 60 restored dwellings stand in the Easton's Point (p 212) and Historic Hill (in the vicinity of Trinity Church p 211) sections of town.

The sumptuous mansions on Bellevue Avenue and Ocean Drive are among the most impressive private residences in the US. The evolution in the style of these mansions begins with the eclecticism of the mid-19C Victorian period, as illustrated by Kingscote (1839) and Château-sur-Mer (1852). Displaying a splendor and magnificence never before expressed in American architecture, Marble House (1892), The Breakers (1895), The Elms (1901) and Rosecliff (1902) represent elaborate imitations of the châteaux of France and the palaces of Italy.

### ★★★ THE MANSIONS  *Map below*

*The mansions can be visited by guided tour (1hr each) only. Combination tickets are available for two to eight houses.* ☎401-847-1000. A number of the mansions can be seen by driving along **Bellevue Avenue★★★** and **Ocean Drive★★** *(10mi).* Ocean Drive follows the coast to the southern end of the island, and at sunset offers beautiful **views**, especially from **Brenton Point State Park**.

The **Cliff Walk★★** is a 3mi coastal path straddling the rocky shoreline that separates The Breakers, Rosecliff, Marble House and Salve Regina College from the sea. In the 19C, when fishermen protested against estate owners who attempted to close off the path, the state ruled in favor of the "toilers of the sea," and the walk has remained a public way ever since. Cliff Walk extends from Memorial Boulevard *(near Easton's Beach)* to Bailey's Beach *(private)* with an alternate access at the Forty Steps. *It is advisable to wear sturdy rubber-soled shoes on this path, especially after a rainstorm.*

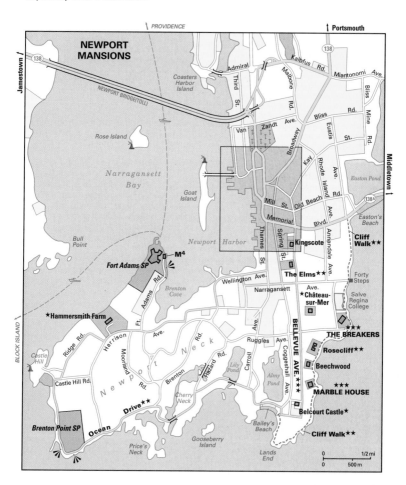

### ★★★ The Breakers – *Illustration p 205. Open Apr–Oct daily 10am–5pm. $8.* 🅿. In 1885 **Cornelius Vanderbilt II**, the grandson of the "Commodore," who had made his fortune in steamships and railroads, purchased the Ochre Point property and hired **Richard Morris Hunt** to design a summer residence on the site. Selecting a High Renaissance Italian palace as his model, Hunt created this opulent 70-room mansion. The palatial design with its elaborate use of French and Italian stone, marble and alabaster, reflected the Vanderbilts' great wealth. The exterior, heavily ornamented with arcades, columns and cornices, reveals the Italian influence. Within, The Breakers blends rich marbles and wooden trim with gilded plaster, mosaics and ceiling painting.

**Interior** – The **Great Hall**, more than two stories high, is a spectacular array of columns and pilasters, marble plaques and ornate cornices. In the **Grand Salon** (Music Room) the coffered ceiling bears a painting with figures representing Music, Harmony, Song and Melody. The **Morning Room** contains four corner panels painted in oil on silver leaf representing the Muses; the room looks out onto the loggia where there is a beautiful Italian mosaic. Most impressive of all the rooms is the **Dining Room** where the Vanderbilts entertained their guests amidst a setting of warm red alabaster, bronze and gilt. On the floor above lies Mrs Vanderbilt's spacious oval bedroom, one of a series of rooms on this floor decorated by Ogden Codman.

★★★**Marble House** – *Open Apr–Oct daily 10am–5pm. Nov–Mar weekends 10am–4pm. $6.50.* ▣ . A gracefully curved, balustraded drive leads to the columned façade of Marble House, one of several Newport mansions designed by **Richard Morris Hunt**. Built for millionaire yachtsman **William K. Vanderbilt**, Marble House is thought to have been inspired by the White House in Washington DC, or by the Petit Trianon at Versailles. Among the most lavish dinner parties and balls held at Marble House was the debut of Consuelo Vanderbilt, who, after the celebration, locked herself in her room to protest her upcoming marriage to the ninth Duke of Marlborough. The marriage nevertheless took place a short time later, in 1895.

**Interior** – The interior is as elegant as the exterior suggests. Gobelin's tapestries decorate the huge entrance hall, which is faced with yellow Siena marble. In the **Gold Ballroom**, the most ornate ballroom in Newport, gold gilt panels, pilasters, arches and doorways are reflected in the glittering crystal chandeliers and mirrors that capture every ray of light. In striking contrast to the Ballroom is the subdued mood of the **Gothic Room**, where the Vanderbilt collection of medieval art objects was displayed. The elaborate use of pink Numidian marble creates the luxuriant atmosphere of the **Dining Room**. The bronze Louis XIV chairs, weighing about 70lbs each, made it necessary for the host to provide each guest with a footman, who would move the chair when the guest wished to sit or leave the table. The tour includes a visit to the spacious basement **kitchen**, boasting an elegance all its own with its 25ft-long stove, built-in iceboxes, and shiny monogrammed cookware. The **Chinese Teahouse** *(open May–Oct),* designed by Hunt's sons, contains ten 8ft wooden panels decorated with scenes inspired by a 15C Chinese court painter.

★★ **The Elms** – *Open May–Oct daily 10am–5pm. Nov–Apr weekends 10am–4pm. $7.50.* ▣ . **Edward Julius Berwind**, the son of German immigrants, rose to prominence in the second half of the 19C as the "king" of America's coal industry. His coal fields in Pennsylvania, West Virginia and Kentucky supplied most of the coal for the US and other nations. In 1899, wealthy and powerful, he commissioned **Horace Trumbauer** to build a residence to rival the cottages of Newport's established millionaires, who regarded him as a *nouveau riche* outsider.

Inspired by the 18C Château d'Asnieres near Paris, Trumbauer created The Elms, a reserved and dignified country-style residence on the outside, a grandiose mansion within. The housewarming given by the Berwinds in August 1901 was the social highlight of the season; countless varieties of exotic plants were used to adorn the house, and monkeys scampered about the grounds.

**Interior** – The large-scale proportions of the rooms, especially of the entrance hall and **Ballroom**, are awesome. In the Ballroom, smoothly curved corners, restrained decoration, and an abundance of natural light create an inviting and pleasant atmosphere, despite the size of the room. The French classical style predominates: the **Conservatory** was intended to house tropical flora, the **Drawing Room** reflects the

Rosecliff Ballroom

Louis XVI style, the stucco reliefs and fine woodwork of the Ballroom suggest the earlier style of Louis XV. The four black and gold lacquer panels ornamenting the **Breakfast Room** date from the K'ang Hsi period (17C).

** **Rosecliff** – *Open Apr–Oct daily 10am–5pm. $6.50.* ▣. In 1891 **Mrs Hermann Oelrichs**, the daughter of a wealthy Irish immigrant who had discovered the Comstock Lode in Nevada, and her husband moved to Newport. They purchased the Rosecliff estate, named for its many rosebeds, and finding the house on the property too modest for their taste, engaged **Stanford White** to design a more elaborate residence. The result was a graceful imitation of the Grand Trianon at Versailles.

Outside, the off-white, glazed terra-cotta walls are finished to imitate stone.

Designed primarily for entertaining, Rosecliff has the largest **ballroom** (80ft x 40ft) in Newport. Windows open onto the terraces, allowing the outdoors to become an extension of the ballroom. Scenes from *The Great Gatsby* (1974) were filmed here. Mrs Oelrichs was one of society's most celebrated hostesses. The magnificent receptions she held at Rosecliff, including the official opening of the mansion in 1902, her famous Bal Blanc where everyone was required to wear white, and the "Mother Goose" Ball where guests dressed as fairy tale characters, were among the most spectacular events ever held in Newport.

A heart-shaped staircase leads upstairs to the sleeping quarters.

* **Château-sur-Mer** – *Open May–Sept daily 10am–5pm, Oct–Apr weekends only 10am–4pm. $6.50.* ▣. In 1877 Château-sur-Mer was considered the most "substantial and expensive residence in Newport." Constructed in the Second Empire style, this "Castle by the Sea," with its massive asymmetrical silhouette, was built in 1852 for **William S. Wetmore**, who earned his wealth in the China Trade. Extremely spacious and luxurious for its day, Château-sur-Mer was later enlarged in 1872 by **Richard Morris Hunt**.

Inside, several interesting decorative effects have been created. Light streams into the elaborately carved entrance hall through a colored-glass ceiling panel 45ft above its floor; the ballroom is embellished with decorative stucco moldings and trim fashioned to resemble wood. Illuminated by stained-glass windows, the stairwell is lined with canvas painted in the style of tapestry. In the Turkish sitting room, the blend of Oriental, European and American design elements and furnishings creates a style that is distinctly Victorian in character. The library and dining room were decorated in the Renaissance style by the Florentine Luigi Frullini.

* **Belcourt Castle** – *Open May–Sept daily 9am–5pm, rest of the year 10am–4pm. Closed Jan 1, Thanksgiving Day, Dec 25. $6.50.* ▣ ☏401-846-0669. Richard Morris Hunt chose one of Louis XIII's hunting lodges as the model for this castle (1896) designed for the 35-year-old bachelor **Oliver Hazard Perry Belmont** who, in 1898, married Alva Smith Vanderbilt, formerly the wife of William K. Vanderbilt *(p 208)*. The castle, owned since 1959 by the Tinney family, contains an outstanding collection of European furnishings.

The interior is inspired by different periods of French, Italian and English design. Decorated with plush red upholsteries and stained-glass windows, the huge **Banquet Hall** can comfortably accommodate 250 dinner guests. A huge crystal chandelier, which formerly graced a Russian palace, dominates the room.

From the oval Family Dining Room on the second floor there is a view out to the ocean. The spacious **French Gothic Ballroom**, also on this floor, contains stained-glass windows (13C), Oriental carpets, tapestries, distended vaults and the enormous castle-shaped fireplace.

* **Hammersmith Farm** – *Visit by guided tour (35min) only, late May–Labor Day daily 10am–7pm (Apr–late May 5pm; mid-Sept–mid-Nov 4pm). $7.50.* ▣ ☏401-846-7346. This estate was formerly owned by **Mrs Hugh Auchincloss**, whose daughter Jacqueline married John F. Kennedy here in 1953. The Kennedys returned to Hammersmith on numerous occasions after their wedding; following John Kennedy's election as President of the US, the farm served on occasion as the summer White House.

The mansion (1887) takes its name from the farm that has operated on the property since 1640. The modest exterior, covered uniformly with wooden shingles, exemplifies the Shingle style that was popular during the last several decades of the 19C. The bayside setting, enhanced with gardens designed by **Frederick Law Olmsted**, is especially scenic.

The interior is simple, yet comfortably furnished. Highlights of the tour include Hammersmith's many mementos relating to the years Jacqueline spent here, first as a young girl, then with her husband and children.

**Kingscote** – *Open May–Sept daily 10am–5pm, Apr & Oct weekends only. $6.50.* ▣. Designed in 1839 by **Richard Upjohn**, Kingscote was one of the earliest examples of a new trend in American architecture: the adaptation of Gothic Revival motifs and effects to private residences. Kingscote's irregular shape, expressed in wood rather than stone, and emphasized by gables, arches, eaves and varied roof lines, formed a striking contrast to the symmetrical, solid shape of earlier dwellings. This mansion was built for the southern planter **George Noble Jones**, then sold in the 1860s to **William H. King** after whom it (King's Cottage) was named.

The Victorian interior contains Tiffany windows, heavy furniture and somber rooms. Among the furnishings is a prized collection of Oriental paintings, rugs, porcelain and furniture attributed to Newport cabinetmakers Goddard and Townsend.

**Beechwood** – *580 Bellevue Ave. Open mid-May–Dec daily 10am–5pm; Feb–mid-May 10am–4pm. $7.75.* ▯ ☏*401-846-3772.* A tour of this Mediterranean-style villa, acquired in 1880 by **William** and **Caroline Astor**, is unlike that offered by its palatial neighbors. From the moment visitors are greeted at the door by the "butler," they are transported back to the 1890s by "servants" and "house guests" (portrayed by members of a theater group) who accompany callers throughout the house.

Named for the beech trees on the grounds, Beechwood was originally built by Calvert Vaux for the merchant Daniel Parish. Destroyed by fire in 1855, the mansion was rebuilt by Andrew Jackson Downing for Parish, and was later redecorated and refurnished by the Astors. The ballroom added at that time by Richard Morris Hunt was the largest in Newport when it was completed. Beechwood is famous as the home of Caroline Astor—*The* Mrs Astor as she insisted upon being called—whose husband was the grandson of John Jacob Astor. Mrs Astor, the grande dame of New York as well as Newport society, compiled the list of society's elite "400," the number of persons her ballroom could accommodate. A copy of Duran's portrait of Mrs Astor hangs in the entrance hall. Among the public rooms on the main floor is the light-filled **Ballroom**, ornamented with gilt and gesso relief, and containing more than 450 mirrors.

On the floor above, Mrs Astor's Victorian bedroom overlooks the ocean. She is reputed to have ordered the window that formerly looked out on Rosecliff sealed off, after she learned that Rosecliff's ballroom was larger than Beechwood's.

## ★★ COLONIAL NEWPORT  *4hrs. Map p 211.*

Newport's extraordinarily large group of colonial structures constitutes one of the nation's great architectural treasures. The itinerary below represents a selection of these dwellings and public buildings.

*From the Gateway Visitors Center, head south on America's Cup Ave and turn left on Marlborough St. Turn right on Thames St and walk one block south to the Brick Market.*

**★ Brick Market** – *Thames St.* Designed in 1762 by **Peter Harrison**, this handsome 3-story building with its arcaded base and massive pilasters above provides a fine example of the influence of the formality of the Palladian style on Georgian architecture. The market was the commercial center of Newport; open market stalls were located on the ground floor, while the upper floors were reserved for offices and storage.

Today two floors are occupied by the **Museum of Newport History [M¹]**, which includes displays on Newport's early colonial life, maritime commerce and naval history *(open year-round Mon, Wed–Sat 10am–5pm, Sun 1-5pm; $5; ☏401-841- 8770).*

**Washington Square** – Adjoining Brick Market Place, Washington Square was the crossroads of colonial Newport. At one end of the square stood the Old Colony House, at the other end was the marketplace. The homes, shops and warehouses of Newport's merchants clustered nearby.

**★ Old Colony House** – *Washington Square. Open by appointment only, 2-week advance reservation suggested.* ♿ ☏*401-277-6200.* This building designed by **Richard Munday** was the seat of Rhode Island's government from the colonial period through the early 19C. In 1781 General Washington and Count Rochambeau, the leader of the French troops, met here to discuss plans for the battle of Yorktown. Furniture made by Goddard and Townsend, and one of Gilbert Stuart's full-length portraits of George Washington decorate the interior.

*Turn left on Farewell St and continue to Marlborough St.*

**Friends Meeting House** – *Marlborough St. Open by appointment only, 2-week advance reservation suggested.* ☏*401-846-0813.* By the end of the 17C, Newport supported a large population of Quakers. This meetinghouse, constructed by the Society of Friends in 1699 and enlarged as the society grew, was the regional center for New England's Quakers. The building is architecturally interesting for its pulley-operated walls, large stone supports, which prevent the lower floor from resting directly on the ground, and the structure's remarkable vault.

*Walk back to Broadway and turn left.*

**Wanton-Lyman-Hazard House** – *17 Broadway. Visit by guided tour (30min) only, Jul–Aug Wed–Sun 10am–4pm. $3.* ☏*401-846-0813.* Prior to the Revolution, this house was the residence of Martin Howard, a tax collector whose official duties made him an unpopular person in town. During the Stamp Act riots, while the patriots ransacked his house, Howard fled Newport. Considering himself fortunate to have escaped, he eventually settled in England, never to see Newport again.

*Walk around the house to Spring St. Turn right and follow Spring St to Truro St. Turn left onto Touro St.*

★★ **Touro Synagogue** – *82 Touro St. Visit by guided tour (30min) only, mid-Jun–Labor Day Mon–Thu & Sun 10am–4:30pm, Fri 10am–3pm; rest of the year, hours vary, call before visiting.* ☐ ☎401-847-4794. The earliest members of Newport's Jewish community arrived from Lisbon and Amsterdam in 1650. However, it was not until a century later (1759), under the guidance of their leader, Isaac de Touro, that a synagogue—one of the earliest constructed in the US—was built.

The building, designed by architect **Peter Harrison**, successfully adapts the Georgian style to Sephardic Jewish tradition. Situated on a quiet street and set on a diagonal with the east wall facing the direction of Jerusalem, the exterior of the synagogue is almost stark in appearance. The interior is richly adorned with hand-carved paneling, balustrades and columns. Twelve columns support the galleries, and twelve columns support the ceiling, symbolizing the twelve tribes of Israel. The Scrolls of the Law, the Torah, are preciously guarded in the Holy Ark.

*Cross Spring St to Clarke St and turn left.*

**Armory of the Artillery Company of Newport** [M²] – *23 Clarke St. Open Jun–Sept Fri–Sun 9am–4pm, rest of the year by appointment only. $3.* �& 401-846-8488. The Newport Artillery Co participated in every principal American military campaign from the colonial period through World War I. This granite-walled Greek Revival building, constructed in 1836 as the company's armory, now houses American and foreign military weapons, uniforms and flags, as well as personal mementos of well-known military figures.

*At the end of Clarke St, turn left on Mary St and right onto Spring St.*

★ **Trinity Church** – *Queen Anne Sq. Open May–Oct daily 10am–4pm, Nov–Apr Mon–Fri 10am–1pm. Closed major holidays.* �& 401-846-0660. This white clapboard church (1725-1726) rising above **Queen Anne Square** was designed by Richard Munday and is contemporary with Boston's Old North Church *(p 112)*. Both were influenced by the designs of Christopher Wren. Trinity's arcaded belfry, surmounted by a tall colonial spire, is a distinct landmark. Inside, the original three-tiered pulpit remains the only one of its kind in the country. The left wall of the nave features two stained-glass windows by Tiffany, one of which commemorates Cornelius Vanderbilt; the face is said to be that of Vanderbilt himself.

The colonial dwellings bordering the square were moved to this location by the **Newport Restoration Foundation**, an organization established in 1968 to preserve Newport's early architecture.

*Continue south on Spring St and turn left on Mill St.*

**Old Stone Tower** – Nicknamed the Mystery Tower because of the various legends surrounding its origin, this stone structure has been attributed to the Vikings, the Portuguese, the Indians and the Irish. Less romantic, but perhaps a bit more realistic, is the theory that the tower is the remnant of a 17C mill.

*Continue east on Mill St and turn left on Bellevue Ave.*

**Redwood Library** – *50 Bellevue Ave.* Architect **Peter Harrison** selected a Roman temple as his inspiration for the library, his first important architectural achievement. The building's classical design, which includes a columned entranceway, seems out of proportion to its modest size, and the wooden exterior, painted and sanded to imitate stone, appears artificial. Yet in its day, the library—the first structure in the US to employ a freestanding portico—illustrated an impressive innovation in American architecture.

**Newport Art Museum** – *76 Bellevue Ave. Open late May–Labor Day daily 10am–5pm, rest of the year Tue–Sat 10am–4pm, Sun noon–4pm. Closed Thanksgiving Day, Dec 25. $4.* & 🖪 ☎*401-848-8200.* Designed by **Richard Morris Hunt**, the Griswold House provides an example of Stick-style architecture: sticks expressing the framing elements are used as exterior decoration. The house is reserved for changing exhibits. The adjacent building, Cushing Memorial Gallery, houses the museum's collection of American art, mainly 19C oil paintings, including works by Winslow Homer, George Inness, Fitz Hugh Lane and William Trost Richards.

*Continue on Bellevue Ave. Turn right on Pelham St, which is lined with colonial dwellings. Turn right on Thames St, then left on Mill St to the waterfront.*

★ **Bowen's Wharf** – Salty old dockside structures have been transformed into indoor and outdoor eating places. Along with neighboring craft shops and boutiques, they form the heart of this waterfront square.

## ADDITIONAL SIGHTS  *Map p 211*

★★ **Hunter House** – *54 Washington St. Visit by guided tour (1hr) only, May–Sept daily 10am–5pm. Apr & Oct weekends only. $6.50. Combination tickets available for other historic homes (p 177).* 🖪 ☎*401-847-1000.* This elegant dwelling, built in 1748 by a prosperous merchant, was purchased by ambassador William Hunter and subsequently served as the home of two governors and as the headquarters of Adm Charles de Ternay, commander of the French fleet during the Revolution. The house is a beautiful example of the 18C Colonial style. The carved pineapple ornamenting the doorway is a symbol of hospitality that originated during the colonial period when a sea captain, returning home from a voyage, placed a pineapple outside his home to announce his safe arrival and to invite everyone to share the refreshments that were waiting inside. The interior contains an exceptional collection of **Goddard** and **Townsend** furniture and skillfully carved woodwork.

**Easton's Point** – Most of the restored homes in this quiet residential neighborhood date from the 18C, when the point prospered as a mercantile community. Quakers, who lived in the area, named the streets for trees and numbers to avoid "man-worship." Washington Street was later renamed for George Washington.

**Old Colony and Newport Railway** – *America's Cup Ave. Departures late Jun–mid-Sept weekends & major holidays. May–mid-Jun Sun & major holidays. Late Sept–Nov Sun only. $5–$6. Old Colony Railway* ☎*401-624-6951.* Chartered in the 19C, the railway experienced its busiest year in 1913, when 24 trains daily, including the Boston "Dandy Express," arrived and departed from Newport.

Preservation Society of Newport County

Hunter House

Today the railway operates along the eastern shore of Narragansett Bay between Newport and Portsmouth. Round-trip excursions from Newport *(3hrs)* stop at the Navy base, the Bend Boat Basin at Melville, and Portsmouth. At Portsmouth a stopover *(1hr)* allows passengers to visit the Green Animals *(p 214)*.

**Samuel Whitehorne House** – *416 Thames St. Visit by guided tour (1hr) only, May–Oct Mon, Sat, Sun 10am–4pm, Fri 1–4pm. $5.* ☎401-847-2448. The four-square brick Federal dwelling, topped by a square cupola, was built (1811) for Samuel Whitehorne Sr, a sea captain. Later subdivided into apartments, the build-ing eventually deteriorated until the Newport Restoration Foundation acquired and restored the house. The interior is refurbished with a **collection★** of 18C furni-ture, many pieces of which were crafted in the workshops of Goddard and Townsend.

**Newport Casino** – *194 Bellevue Ave.* Facing Bellevue Avenue, this complex with its ground-floor shops gives the impression of a commercial block. The casino was the most exclusive country club in the East when it was built in 1880, during the height of Newport's "gilded age." Pass through the deeply arched entranceway to discover the casino's tennis courts and the Shingle-style buildings designed by **McKim, Mead and White**. The casino's grass courts hosted the first Men's US Lawn Tennis Association tournament (now the US Open) in 1881, which later moved to Forest Hills, New York. Tournaments are still held here in July.

**International Tennis Hall of Fame [M³]** – *In the casino. Open year-round daily 10am–5pm. $6.* ✗ ☎401-849-3990. Exhibits of tennis memorabilia, one of the largest col-lections in the country, focus on the history of the sport. Among the artifacts on display is the sterling silver punch bowl awarded to Bostonian Richard Sears, the first US men's singles champion in lawn tennis.

**Fort Adams State Park** – *Map p 207. Fort Adams Rd, off Ocean Dr. Open year-round daily dawn–dusk. $4/car non-residents (May–Sept).* ♿ 🅿 ☎401-847-2400. Fort Adams, its walls constructed of granite hauled from Maine by schooner, was originally built to guard the entrance to Narragansett Bay. The fort ultimately devel-oped into the command post for the coastal batteries in the northeast; until 1945 it was the center of a system of defenses to protect the bay and Long Island Sound. Today the fort is a state park where the JVC Jazz Festival is held each summer. From the park's roadways there is a sweeping **view★★** of the harbor, Newport Bridge and Newport, including the downtown area. *Due to unsafe conditions, the ruins of the old fort are closed to the public.*

The small, 2-story **Museum of Yachting [M⁴]** *(to relocate to Thames St in 1996)* houses classic small craft and displays on Newport yachting history. Videos focusing on 12-meter yachts and the museum's 1930s America's Cup sloop *Shamrock V*, which is moored offshore *(no boarding permitted)*, are shown continuously *(open mid-May–Oct daily 10am–5pm; $3;* ☎401-847-1018*)*.

## EXCURSIONS

**Jamestown** – *Pop 4,999. 3mi west of Newport via Newport Bridge (toll). On Co-nanicut Island in Narragansett Bay.* At the island's center, on North Road, is the 1787 **Jamestown Windmill** *(open mid-Jun–mid-Sept weekends 1–4pm;* ☎401-423-1798). From **Beaver Tail Lighthouse** *(at the end of Beaver Tail Rd)* there is a view along the south shore. An expansive vista across the bay to Newport can be admired from **Fort Wetherill** *(off of Rte 138 and Walcott Ave).* The fort's ramparts are built on granite cliffs that rise up to 100ft. The shores of picturesque **Mackerel Cove** are flecked with summer homes.

★ **Watson Farm** – *455 North Rd. Open Jun–mid-Oct Tue, Thu, Sun 1–5pm. $3.* ♿ ☎401-423-0005. Job Watson purchased this farm in 1789; it was operated by five successive generations of his family until 1979. Still a working farm, devoted to sheep and beef cattle, the property comprises some 230 acres of barnyard, hay fields, orchards and meadows. The site affords sublime **views★** of Narragansett Bay.

**Middletown** – *Pop 19,460. North of Newport by Memorial Blvd.* This small com-munity is a blend of long sandy beaches and rural countryside.

**Whitehall Museum House** – *311 Berkeley Ave. From Memorial Blvd, take Aquidneck Ave to Green End Ave. Travel east to Berkeley Ave and follow signs to the house. Open Jul–Labor Day daily 10am–5pm. $3.* ☎401-846-3116. This red clapboard Georgian-period farmhouse was built in 1729 by Anglican bishop and philoso-pher George Berkeley, who hoped the farm would finance a school he planned to establish in Bermuda. When his plans failed, Berkeley returned to Ireland in 1731 and left the farm to Yale University; the Colonial Dames of America took it over in 1902. The interior features furnishings of the period.

**Prescott Farm** – *2009 W. Main Rd (Rte114). Open Apr–Nov daily 10am–4pm. $3.* ☎401-847-6230. This pastoral setting features an herb garden and an assemblage of historic buildings (some moved here from other locations), including British general Richard Prescott's guardhouse (c.1730), a 19C wood-shingled windmill still used to grind cornmeal, and a former ferry-master's dwelling (c.1715), which now houses a country store.

**Portsmouth** – Pop 16,857. *North of Newport by Rte 114.* Settlers from Portsmouth moved south and founded Newport in 1639 *(p 205)*. Today this hilly township is a popular summer resort.

**Green Animals Topiary Gardens** – *From Rte 114, turn left onto Cory's Lane. Open May–Oct daily 10am–5pm. $6.50. Combination tickets available for public historic homes (p 207).* ☎401-847-1000. Colorful flowerbeds punctuate this group of 80 tree and shrub sculptures, which include representations of a giraffe, a lion and an elephant. The country house features a toy museum, dolls and doll houses.

# PAWTUCKET

Pop 72,644

Map of Principal Sights p 2

Tourist Office ☎401-274-1636

This bustling city just north of Providence gave birth to the Industrial Revolution in America. It was here, at the falls of Blackstone River in 1793, that the **Slater Mill**, the first US water-powered textile mill to successfully produce cotton yarn, was built. Construction of the mill resulted from an association between **Samuel Slater**, who had been employed in a textile factory in England, and **Moses Brown** *(p 215)*, a wealthy Providence Quaker. Combining their resources—Slater's technical knowledge and the Brown family capital—the two men laid the groundwork for the transition from handcraft to machine production. The mill they built pioneered the way for this change, as well as for the diffusion of the textile industry throughout New England.

Several years later, in 1810, another factory, the Wilkinson Mill, specializing in the production of machine parts and tools, was built nearby. The two factories and a dwelling of the same period have been restored and form a part of the 5-acre Slater Mill Historic Site devoted to the origins of the industrial age in America.

Slater Mill

★ **Slater Mill Historic Site** – *From I-95 south take Exit 29 (downtown Pawtucket); proceed straight ahead onto Broadway, cross Main St Bridge, then turn right on Roosevelt Ave. Visit by guided tour (1hr 30min) only, Jun–Labor Day Tue–Sat 10am–5pm, Sun 1–5pm. Mar–May & early Sept–mid-Dec weekends only 1–5pm. Closed major holidays (except Columbus & Veterans Days). $5.* ☎401-725-8638.

**Slater Mill** – Here, operating textile equipment (including a carding device, spinning frame and mule, power looms, and knitting and braiding machines) demonstrates the processes involved in transforming cotton from raw fiber to finished goods.

**Wilkinson Mill** – This mill contains a 19C machine shop with belt-driven machine tools: a jigsaw, lathes, drill pressers, planers and shapers. An 8-ton breast wheel has been reconstructed in the basement. Water from the Blackstone River is admitted to the wheel through restored raceways; the wheel drives the machine tools on the floor above. The mill originally housed a machine shop where textile machinery was built and repaired. Cotton and woolen thread were produced on the floor above.

**Sylvanus Brown House** – Furnished as it was in the early 1800s, this dwelling (1758) was the home of a millwright and pattern-maker. Demonstrations of hand spinning and weaving illustrate the tasks performed by household members.

The capital of Rhode Island, a center of business and industry, and the third largest city in New England, Providence occupies the hub of a metropolitan region that has more than 900,000 inhabitants.

The city's location on a natural harbor at the head of Narragansett Bay offered special advantages for the shipping and commercial activity that allowed Providence to prosper and expand. A result of this expansion was the development of the College Hill district with its lovely 18C and 19C structures. Today this tree-shaded residential neighborhood is the home of Brown University and the Rhode Island School of Design. On the hill across from College Hill, the majestic capitol building rises above the growing business area below. The famed **Trinity Repertory Company** stages performances from September through June (*Lederer Theater, 201 Washington St, ☎401-351-4242*).

## HISTORICAL NOTES

**Providence Plantations** – After **Roger Williams** was banished from his pastorate in Salem, Massachusetts, he traveled south with a group of his followers until they arrived on the banks of the Moshassuck (later the Providence) River in June 1636. Having decided to settle here, they bought the land from the Narragansett Indians and named it Providence, in honor of the divine providence that they believed had led them to this place. Williams declared that the new colony would be a safe and sure refuge for all persons seeking freedom of worship.

In 1644 he journeyed to England to obtain a charter for Providence and the Rhode Island (Newport) colony. The charter united the two colonies, but was declared void in 1660 following the restoration of the monarchy to the throne. Three years later, Charles II issued a royal charter granting "full liberty in religious concernments" to all Rhode Island inhabitants.

**The Development of Providence** – Originally a farming settlement, Providence rapidly developed into a commercial center, as its inhabitants turned to shipping and trade. By the mid-18C Providence vessels were engaged in the triangular trade (*p 205*), and in 1772, when Parliament passed legislation that threatened to limit American shipping, citizens were quick to react. One evening in June, they forced the British revenue schooner *Gaspee* aground at Warwick, burned the vessel and captured its crew. Despite a generous reward offered by the Crown, the culprits were never captured.

Strongly defended as the "backdoor to Boston" during the Revolution, Providence prospered as a privateering and supply depot. Following the war the city emerged as Rhode Island's leading port. In 1787 Providence resident **John Brown** (*below*) sent his first ship to China. Other merchants followed his lead and amassed great fortunes in the China Trade.

As maritime trade declined, capital investment shifted toward industry. Providence developed into a center for the manufacture of textiles, tools, files and steam engines, attracting thousands of immigrants to work at its many factories. The city underwent an economic crisis after World War II, when a number of factories moved to the South. Today Providence again enjoys an active business life as a manufacturer of a variety of products, including jewelry and silverware.

**The Brown Brothers** – The Brown name, closely associated with the industrial, cultural, political and commercial growth of Providence, identifies one of the city's oldest and most illustrious families. At the end of the 18C, the four Brown brothers were prominent among the leaders of Providence. **John**, bold and adventurous, a leader of the attack on the *Gaspee,* was a prosperous merchant. His was the first ship from Providence to reach China. **Joseph**, an architect, designed the Market House, the First Baptist Church and the John Brown House, among other buildings. **Moses**, a prosperous Quaker who established the Providence Bank, was the first to finance the development of the textile industry in the US (*p 214*). Finally, there was **Nicholas**, a successful businessman whose mercantile enterprise was internationally known.

## ** COLLEGE HILL    *1/2 day. Map p 216.*

In the early 18C the city's main thoroughfare—present-day **North** and **South Main Street**—bordered the waterfront and was crowded with warehouses, wharves and shops. To relieve the congestion, a dirt path running along the crest of the hill that rose behind the main street was widened for the "common benefit of all," thus creating Benefit Street. Wealthy merchants built their homes on Benefit Street, high above the waterfront, and by the beginning of the 19C, the hill had developed into a fashionable residential enclave. Chosen as the site of Rhode Island College (now Brown University) in 1770, the district came to be known as College Hill.

This area's charming, tree-shaded streets, lined with architecture ranging from Colonial to Italianate, represents one of the most beautifully preserved historic districts in the nation. High on the hill sits **Thayer Street**, the shopping center of the university community, with its bookstores, coffee shops, restaurants and many stores. Former warehouses and shops below the hill on South Main Street have been converted into boutiques and restaurants, adding to the aura of the past that pervades this section of the city.

## Walking Tour

*From the intersection of College and Main St, continue north on Main St.*

**Market House** – *4 S. Main St.* This was the commercial center of early Providence. Because of the building's location beside the river, boats could easily load and unload their cargoes here. Market House now belongs to the Rhode Island School of Design *(below)*.

*Continue on Main St past Waterman St.*

★ **First Baptist Church in America** – *75 N. Main St. Open year-round Mon–Fri 9am–4pm.* & ☎*401-454-3418.* The Baptist Church, founded by Roger Williams, dates back to 1638. The first house of worship built by the Baptists in America stood on North Main Street, a short distance from the present site of the wooden clapboard church (1775) designed by Joseph Brown. The handsome steeple rises 185ft. Inside, the paneling, scrolled pediments, lighted urns and arches are painted in soft tones of green and white. Enormous columns support the galleries and roof, leading the eye upward to the carved ceiling.

*Return to Waterman St and turn left. After one block, turn right on Benefit St.*

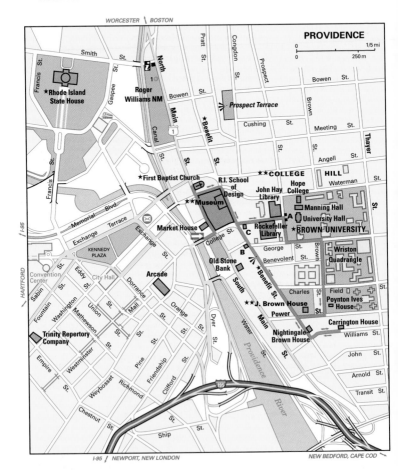

★ **Benefit Street** – At Benefit Street, pause to admire the graceful profile of the restored dwellings to the right and to the left. More than 100 homes, ranging from Colonial to Victorian in style, line the narrow streets and brick walks leading to the Rhode Island School of Design and to Brown University.

**Rhode Island School of Design** – Established in the 19C to train artisans for industry, RISD (RIZ-dee) is renowned as a teaching institution for design, architecture and the visual arts. Facilities available to the school's 1,990 students include sculpture, wood and metal labs, apparel design and textile workshops.

★★ **Museum of Art** – *224 Benefit St. Open early Sept–mid-Jun Tue, Wed, Fri, Sat 10:30am–5pm, Thu noon–8pm, Sun 2–5pm; rest of the year Wed–Sat noon–5pm. Closed Jan 1, Jul 4, Thanksgiving Day, Dec 25. $2.* & ☎*401-454-6500.* The museum presents, in an engaging manner, collections of art from various periods and civilizations: Egyptian, Greek, Roman, Asian, European, African and American. Many exhibits are arranged in chronological order, but often cross period boundaries to illustrate common trends in contemporary sculpture, painting and textiles. The fourth level *(entrance)* is devoted to medieval carvings, 19C American and French paintings, and Greek bronzes. On the fifth level is Oriental, Eastern, aboriginal and Egyptian art. The **Dainichi Buddha** (10C Japan), a wooden temple figure discovered in 1933 in the attic of a farmhouse, dominates one of the galleries. Adjoining the museum is **Pendleton House★**, built in 1904 to display the **Charles Pendleton Collection★★** of 18C American furnishings and decorative arts. The elegant interior with its rich mahogany woodwork features a large central hall and several luxurious rooms.

Constructed in 1993, the three-level Daphne Farago Wing features changing exhibits of contemporary art in all media.

In the museum courtyard there are several contemporary sculptures, including works by George Rickey and Clement Meadmore.

*Turn left on College St.*

**★ Brown University** – The seventh college established in the US (1764), this Ivy League school was founded at Warren as Rhode Island College, and renamed in 1804 for its principal benefactor, Nicholas Brown II.

Approximately 5,600 undergraduate and 1,700 graduate students are enrolled at Brown's 142-acre College Hill campus, which consists of some 245 buildings: large halls housing classrooms and administrative offices, student and faculty residences, libraries, and a sports complex that includes a 20,400-seat football stadium. The five university libraries contain more than 4.7 million volumes and related items, including distinguished collections of material printed prior to 1500 and sources related to colonial America. Pembroke College (1891), founded by the university as a separate school for women, merged with Brown in 1971.

At the main entrance to the university, on Prospect Street, are the **Van Wickle Gates [A]**, which are opened twice a year: inward on the first day of classes for freshmen, and outward on commencement day. From within the gates *(note campus map table to the left)*, Brown's oldest buildings are visible: **University Hall** (1770), a stately brick building known as the College Edifice, was the sole university structure until 1822; the building with the four granite columns is **Manning Hall** (1835), a Greek Revival structure that houses the University Chapel; **Hope College** (1822) serves as a dormitory.

On the west side of Prospect Street, opposite the gates, are the **John Hay Library** (1910) and the **Rockefeller Library** (1964). The "Rock" houses the university's general collection in the humanities and social sciences.

*Continue south one block on Prospect St and turn left on George St. After one block, turn right on Brown St.*

On Brown Street you will pass **Wriston Quadrangle** (1952), the campus residence of approximately 1,000 students.

*Continue south on Brown St to Power St.*

**Power Street** – At the corner of Brown and Power Streets stands **Poynton Ives House** (no. 66), a classic example of Federal architecture.

**★★ John Brown House** – *52 Power St. Visit by guided tour (1hr) only, Mar–Dec Tue–Sat 11am–4pm, Sun 1–4pm. Jan–Feb Sat 11am–4pm, Sun 1–4pm. Closed Jan 1, Easter Sunday, Dec 25. $5. ☎401-331-8575.* The 3-story brick mansion (1788), designed for John Brown by his brother Joseph, impressed many who came to see it. John Quincy Adams, who visited the house, proclaimed it to be: "the most magnificent mansion I have ever seen on this continent."

Inside, the carved doorways, columns, fireplaces, cornices, highly polished natural wood trim, and lavish plaster ornamented ceilings provide an appropriate setting for the treasured collection of Rhode Island furnishings, most of which are Brown family pieces. The unique **blockfront secretary** boasts nine shells carved into its front (shell secretaries normally have only six carved shells). Attributed to Rhode Island cabinetmaker John Goddard, this piece is one of the finest existing examples of American Colonial furniture.

*Continue west on Power St and turn left on Benefit St.*

Rhode Island Historical Society

Blockfront secretary (c.1760)

Note at no. 357 Benefit Street an attractive Federal dwelling, the **Nightingale-Brown House** set in pleasants grounds *(visit by 30min guided tour only, year-round Fri 1–4pm; closed major holidays; $3; ☎401-272-0357)*.

> *Continue south on Benefit St and then turn left on Williams St. At no. 66 stands another Federal-style mansion, the Carrington House. Return to Benefit St and continue north.*

Just beyond Benevolent Street, there is a good **view** of the gilded ribbed dome of the **Old Stone Bank**. A little farther, on the left, is the 18C red clapboard dwelling, the **Stephen Hopkins House** (no. 43) **[B]**, formerly the home of Quaker governor Stephen Hopkins, signer of the Declaration of Independence and ten-time governor of Rhode Island. Greek Revival style is represented by the **Providence Athenaeum [C]** (1838, William Strickland) where, after the death of his wife in 1847, Edgar Allen Poe courted poet Sarah Whitman, a resident of Benefit Street.

## ADDITIONAL SIGHTS  *Map p 216*

★ **Rhode Island State House** – *Smith St. Open year-round Mon–Fri 8:30am–4:30pm. Closed major holidays.* ✗ ⅋ *☎401-277-2357.* From its position on Smith Hill, the capitol building (1901), by McKim, Mead and White, commands a good view of downtown Providence. On a clear day the white marble exterior is especially impressive, set against the deep blue sky.

**The Dome** – The central section of the building is topped with the second largest freestanding dome in the world (the dome of St Peter's in Rome is the largest) and surmounted by a statue of the **Independent Man**, a symbol of Rhode Island's long-standing spirit of liberty and tolerance.

From the first floor, there is a good view of the dome mural portraying the history of Rhode Island and of the Latin inscription inside the dome: "Rare felicity of times when it is possible to think as you like and to say what you think."

**Legislative Chambers and Governor's Office** – *Second floor.* A full-length portrait of George Washington, painted by Gilbert Stuart, hangs in the Governor's Reception Room. The royal Charter of 1663 is among the historical documents on display.

**Roger Williams National Memorial** – *Between Smith St and Park Row. Visitor center (282 N. Main St) open year-round daily 8am–4:30pm. Closed Jan 1, Thanksgiving Day, Dec 25.* ⅋ *☎401-521-7266.* A 4.5-acre landscaped memorial park surrounds the site of the **spring [1]** around which, according to tradition, Roger Williams founded the Providence colony. The place where the spring once flowed to the surface is marked by a stone well curb.

**Prospect Terrace** – From this small park on Congdon Street, high on the slopes of College Hill, there is a **view**★ across the city to the State House.

**Providence Arcade** – Extending from Weybosset Street through to Westminster Street, this Greek Revival "temple of trade," designed by Russell Warren and James Bucklin in 1828, is one of the few surviving 19C shopping malls in the US.

## SAUNDERSTOWN

Map of Principal Sights p 2                    Tourist Office ☎401-789-4422

Gilbert Stuart, the celebrated early American portrait artist, was born in this rural corner of North Kingstown.

**Gilbert Stuart Birthplace** – *From Rte 1A, exit onto Gilbert Stuart Rd and continue 1.5mi. Open Apr–Oct Mon–Thu & weekends 11am–4:30pm. $3.* ☎401-294-3001. Born in the American colonies in 1755, Gilbert Stuart later studied in London and Dublin before he returned to the US, where he painted his most famous works *(p 33)*. Stuart is best known for his portraits of George Washington: two full-length portraits now hanging in the Rhode Island State House and the Old Colony House (Newport), and the Athenaeum Portrait, a likeness of which appears on the one-dollar bill.

Gilbert Stuart lived in this small frame dwelling until he was six years old. Located in a wooded setting, the house contains period furnishings and an old snuff mill formerly worked by the artist's father.

**Casey Farm** – *Rte 1A, 2mi south of Jamestown Bridge. Open Jun–mid-Oct Tue, Thu, Sat 1–5pm. $3.* ☎401-295-1030. A spartan but elegant mid-18C farmhouse *(visit by 30min guided tour only)* dominates this 300-acre farm, established in 1702, on the Narragansett Bay shore. The former dairy enterprise is now a community-supported farm where some 100 subscribing households raise organically grown produce and eggs. A stone-walled garden, the family cemetery and wooded trails enrich the visit.

*Admission prices and hours quoted in this guide were accurate at the time of publication.*

## WATCH HILL

Map of Principal Sights p 2                    Tourist Office ☎ 401-789-4422

Located at the southwesternmost point on the mainland of Rhode Island, Watch Hill is a fashionable seaside community with elegant summer houses, including several in late 19C Shingle style. Swimming, boating, golf and browsing in the fine shops are popular pastimes. From the **Watch Hill Lighthouse** *(south on Watch Hill Rd)*, you can see **Fishers Island**, a private island off the coast of Connecticut. A short distance from Watch Hill is **Misquamicut State Beach**.

## WICKFORD

Map of Principal Sights p 2                    Tourist Office ☎ 401-789-4422

This colonial village on the shores of Narragansett Bay developed in the 18C as a center for goods shipped to Newport from plantations on the mainland. Fishing and shipbuilding became principal activities after the Revolution, as Wickford grew into a bustling, prosperous shipping port. The large concentration of 18C and 19C white clapboard dwellings that distinguish Wickford date from this period.

**Smith's Castle** – *1.5mi north of Wickford by Rte 1. Visit by guided tour (30min) only, Jun–Aug Thu–Mon noon–4pm. May & Sept Fri–Sun noon–4pm; rest of the year by appointment only. $3 (No admission charge during current restoration of the house).* ♿ ☎ *401-294-3521.* In 1640 a garrison stood on this site, a short distance from the trading post established by Roger Williams. The Indians destroyed the garrison during King Philip's War, and two years later, in 1678, a small dwelling, later enlarged to its present 2.5-story size, was constructed here. The house contains 18C and 19C furnishings.

# Vermont

**Area:** 9,609sq mi
**Population:** 562,758
**Capital:** Montpelier
**Nickname:** Green Mountain State
**State Flower:** Red Clover

I n 1609 when the French explorer Samuel de Champlain first set eyes on the forested mountains extending southward from the lake that now bears his name, he reportedly exclaimed, *"Les verts monts!"* ("The green mountains!"). More than a century later, Champlain's description of these peaks was adopted as the official name of the state.

Pastoral and uncluttered, Vermont has no large cities or industrial centers (the largest city is Burlington with 39,127 inhabitants). Miles of back roads skirt rocky streams and cross the wooden covered bridges scattered throughout the open countryside. Dormant under a heavy cover of glistening white snow in winter, the region becomes a palette of rich greens in the spring and summer when the mountain streams run fastest, and blazes with color in autumn.

**An Independent State** – After many other parts of New England had been settled, Vermont remained virtually uninhabited and served as a battle-ground among the English, the French and the Indians. Not until the British defeated the French at Quebec in 1759 did colonists begin to arrive in large numbers. Prior to the outbreak of the Revolution, **Ethan Allen** and the Green Mountain Boys *(p 223)* (also known as the Bennington Mob), together with Benedict Arnold and his men, captured Fort Ticonderoga from the British. The artillery and supplies they seized at the fort were used by the Continental Army the following spring in the siege of Boston *(p 97)*. In 1777 Vermont declared itself independent, and a constitution was drawn up outlawing slavery and eliminating property ownership and personal wealth as voting requirements. Denied admission to the Union because of land claims by New York, Vermont remained independent for 14 years, coining its own money, operating its own post office and negotiating with foreign powers. In 1791, the dispute with New York settled, Vermont joined the Union as the 14th state. For generations since, Vermonters have guarded their spirit of independence and the principle of strong local government.

**Economy** – Although forests cover some 80 percent of the land, agriculture, primarily dairy farming, dominates the economy. Vermont's farms supply milk and dairy products, including the famous Vermont **cheddar cheese**, to the Boston region and to southern New England. **Maple syrup** is the state's other important product. In early spring, steam rises from small wooden sugarhouses, where farmers use evaporators to boil down the maple tree sap into rich, amber syrup.

**Granite** quarried near Barre and **marble** quarried in the Green Mountains near Danby are major state exports. Industrially Vermont is a producer of tools, computer components, furniture and paper. Year-round tourism is an important source of income (skiing alone generates some $290 million annually). Outdoor advertising is prohibited by law; a uniform statewide sign system indicates lodging and services.

C. Cochrane/State of New Hampshire Tourism

# BARRE

Map of Principal Sights p 2          Tourist Office ☎802-229-5711

Situated on the hilly, eastern flank of the Green Mountains, Barre (BER-rie) is the center of the largest granite industry in the nation. For over 150 years, this city's superior quality granite has been shipped to states across America, formerly to be used in the construction of public buildings, and today in the production of memorials, tombstones and industrial equipment. Dozens of quarries have been worked here since 1812, and in 1833 the capitol in Montpelier *(p 232)* was the first public building in the US to be constructed of Barre granite.

Two quarries on Millstone Hill are still active. These quarries and the manufacturing plant nearby are operated by the Rock of Ages Co.

★ **Rock of Ages Quarry** – *4mi from the Barre Information Center (Main St) by Rte 14 south. Turn left after 2mi onto Middle Rd and follow the signs for the Rock of Ages Visitor Center and Quarries (located in Graniteville). Open May–Oct daily 8am–5pm (rest of the year Sun noon–5pm). Closed major holidays.* ✗ ♿ *Bus tours (30min) of the quarry available Jun–mid-Oct Mon–Fri 9:30am–3pm. $2.50.* ☎802-476-3119.

**The Quarries** – From the edge of the quarry, the view 475ft down to the bottom of the quarry is awesome. Enormous derricks, capable of hauling stone blocks weighing up to 100 tons, are used to lift massive granite slabs out of the quarry. Use of modern machinery, such as jet-channeling flame machines and pneumatic drills, has increased efficiency; yet quarrying remains a formidable task.

**Craftsmen Center** – *Open year-round Mon–Fri 8am–3:30pm. Closed Jul & major holidays.* Visitors may observe the workers at this manufacturing plant as they skillfully cut, polish and carve the granite, transforming it from rough stone into finished monuments and sculptures.

★ **Hope Cemetery** – *On Rte 14 north of Barre center. Open year-round daily 7am–dusk.* ☎802-476-6245. The cemetery has come to be regarded as an outdoor museum of granite memorial sculpture. Gravestones carved by craftsmen for departed members of their families reflect their sculptors' artistry and originality. Note in particular the memorials adorned with scenes depicting rural landscapes.

## EXCURSION

**Brookfield** – Pop 1,089. *15mi south of Barre by Rte 14, then Rte 65 west.* Lying off the beaten path, this tiny picturesque community on the shores of Sunset Lake is sought out primarily for its inn, lakeside restaurant (formerly a pitchfork factory) and **floating bridge**, which carries traffic across the lake. The bridge is buoyed by a network of 380 barrels that rise and fall with the water level. The present bridge, completed in 1973, is the latest replacement for the original floating structure constructed in 1832.

*To enjoy New England's glorious fall colors, consult the driving itineraries on pp 10-13 for selected foliage tours.*

# ★ BENNINGTON

Map of Principal Sights p 2          Tourist Office ☎802-447-3311

This southern Vermont community, surrounded by the Taconic Range and the Green Mountains, includes commercial North Bennington; Old Bennington, an historic district with a rich ensemble of early American architecture; and **Bennington College**, a liberal arts school distinguished for its progressive ideas and programs. During the early days of the nation, Bennington was the home of Revolutionary War hero Ethan Allen and his Green Mountain Boys.

**The Battle of Bennington** – Bennington was an important rallying point and supply depot for colonial troops even before the outbreak of the Revolution. In May 1775 Ethan Allen and the Green Mountain Boys gathered here before they marched north to attack Fort Ticonderoga *(p 225)*.

Two years later, in August 1777, Bennington was once again associated with an important military victory for the patriots: the Battle of Bennington. On August 11, desperately in need of supplies for his army, British Gen John Burgoyne dispatched Lt Col Friederich Baum and his troops to Bennington to seize the arms and munitions stored there. Forewarned of the British plan, New Hampshire's **Gen John Stark** led the colonial militia from Vermont into New York to head off the enemy. There they encountered Baum and his men at the present-day site of Wallomsac Heights, New York. General Stark led his men into battle with the shout: "There are the Red Coats and they are ours, or Molly Stark sleeps a widow tonight!"

The fight was a disaster for the British. For the Americans, the battle served as a prelude to the defeat of General Burgoyne's army at the Battle of Saratoga (October 17) that same year.

## ★★ OLD BENNINGTON *3hrs*

*A walking tour brochure is available from the Chamber of Commerce, Veterans Memorial Dr ☎802-447-3311.*

★ **Old First Church** – *Monument Ave. From the junction of Rtes 9 and 7, take Rte 9 west and turn left onto Monument Ave. Open Jul–mid-Oct Mon–Sat 10am–noon & 1–4pm, Sun 1–4pm. Late May–Jun weekends only. ☎802-447-1223.* This white clapboard church (1805), with its graceful lines and three-tiered steeple, has been the subject of numerous paintings and photographs. The interior, including box pews and six tall columns, each fashioned from a single pine tree, has been restored to its 19C appearance.

Old First Church

*Vermont Dept. of Travel & Tourism*

The old cemetery in the rear is the resting place of Revolutionary War soldiers and early founders of Vermont. One white marble tombstone marks the grave of poet **Robert Frost** (1874-1963) *(p 36)*, who penned his own epitaph: "I had a lover's quarrel with the world."

**Bennington Battle Monument** – *From Rte 9 west turn right onto Monument Ave. Open mid-Apr–Oct daily 9am–5pm. $1. ☎802-447-0550.* This 306ft obelisk was erected in 1891 to commemorate the Battle of Bennington *(p 223)*. The **view**★★ from the observation deck *(accessible by elevator)* includes the Berkshires, the Green Mountains and New York state.

★ **Bennington Museum** – *1mi west of Bennington center on Main St (Rte 9). Open year-round daily 9am–5pm. Closed Jan 1, Thanksgiving Day, Dec 23-31. $5. ☎802-447-1571.* The museum's diverse collections are related to Vermont and New England history and life. Highlights include choice examples of fine American glassware, furniture, 19C Bennington pottery and the Bennington Flag, one of the oldest Stars and Stripes in existence. A large group of paintings by **Grandma Moses** hangs in a ground-floor gallery.

**Grandma Moses Schoolhouse** – *Adjacent to and part of the Bennington Museum.* The story of Anna Mary Robertson Moses' *(p 34)* career as a painter is as memorable as her paintings. Grandma Moses, as she became known, lacked formal training; she did not begin to paint until the age of 70. Her simple scenes of the countryside and farm life appealed to the public, and her first show, in 1940, won her immediate fame. Grandma Moses was received by President Truman when she was 90, and she continued to paint until her death at 101. Her works have been shown throughout the US and Europe and are familiar subjects of prints and greeting cards. Several paintings by Grandma Moses and memorabilia of her life are exhibited in this schoolhouse, where she attended classes as a young girl.

## EXCURSIONS

★ **Park-McCullough House** – *North Bennington. From Bennington center, take Rte 7 north to Rte 7A. Continue on Rte 67A 3mi. Turn left on West St. Visit by guided tour (1hr) only, mid-May–mid-Oct daily 10am–4pm. $5. ☎802-442-5441.* Situated on six pleasantly wooded acres, this 35-room Second Empire mansion was home to the respected Vermont families of Hall, Park and McCullough, whose members were governors, Bennington College founders and recognized corporate figures. Built by Trenor Park as a summer home in 1865, the richly panelled house contains art glass, European and American paintings, decorative arts and family heirlooms.

**Molly Stark Trail** – Route 9 between Bennington and BRATTLEBORO *(40mi)* is named for the wife of Gen John Stark *(p 223)*. From the turnout on Hogback Mountain (2,410ft), there are views east to Mt Monadnock (3,165ft) in New Hampshire and south to the Berkshire Hills and the Holyoke Range in Massachusetts.

**Woodford State Park** – *10mi east of Bennington on Rte 9. Open late-May–mid-Oct daily 10am–dusk. $1.50. △ �& ☎802-241-3655 (summer) 802-447-7169 (rest of the year). Facility information p 251.* The 400-acre park hugs the shores of Adams Reservoir, a peaceful site encircled by trees.

# ★ BRANDON and MIDDLEBURY GAPS

*81mi. 1 day. Map below.*

Broad vistas unfold as you follow this itinerary through mountain gaps and past the open farmlands of the Lake Champlain Valley.

*From Rte 100 in Rochester take Rte 73 through Brandon Gap.*

Route 73 passes tidy houses and tranquil meadows along the White River Valley as it enters the Green Mountain National Forest and skirts the base of **Mt Horrid** (3,216ft), with its rocky face, before reaching **Brandon Gap★** (2,170ft). From this point there is a **view★** of the Lake Champlain Valley, with the Adirondacks as a backdrop. Descending west through the gap, the road continues to the village of **Brandon**, anchored by its historic inn. Begun as a one-room tavern in 1786, the current stone and wood hostelry features a late-19C Dutch Colonial interior. Behind the inn is the fledgling **Vermont Ski Museum**, displaying vintage skis and memorabilia from Vermont's Olympians *(open May–Oct Tues–Sun 9am–4pm; $2; ☎802-247-8080)*. After Brandon Route 73 continues west to LAKE CHAMPLAIN, yielding vistas of rock-studded pasturelands, dairy farms and the Adirondack Mountains to the west.
The ferry *(schedule p 227)* from **Larrabees Point** crosses Lake Champlain, which is very narrow at this point, and provides access to Fort Ticonderoga in New York.

★★ **Fort Ticonderoga** – *Rte 74 in Ticonderoga, New York. Open mid-May–mid-Oct daily 9am–5pm (Jul & Aug 6pm). $7. Fife & drum corps performances Jul & Aug daily.* ✗ ☎518-585-2821. Built in 1755 by the French, Fort Ticonderoga was captured by the British in 1759. The fort is famous for the surprise attack launched here against the British on May 10, 1775 by **Ethan Allen** and the Green Mountain Boys along with **Benedict Arnold** and his men. The supplies captured were used the following spring by General Washington to drive the British out of Boston.
At Fort Ticonderoga, guides outfitted in French Army uniforms perform artillery drills daily *(Jul & Aug)*. The **Military Museum** houses a fine collection of 18C firearms, polearms and artifacts from the French and Indian, and Revolutionary Wars.

*Take the ferry to Vermont, follow Rte 74 east through Shoreham and West Cornwall to Cornwall, and then take Rte 30 north.*

★ **Middlebury** – *Description p 231.*

*From Middlebury take Rte 125 east, named Robert Frost Memorial Dr for the well-known New England poet.*

On Route 125, 2mi beyond Ripton, the **Robert Frost Interpretive Trail** offers a 1mi loop through scenic marshland and forest, punctuated by markers containing poems by the renowned poet.

*Continue east on Rte 125 for about 1mi.*

The crisp buff and green clapboard cottages of Middlebury College's Bread Loaf mountain campus, formerly a 19C resort, serve as the setting for the respected Writers' Conference, whose instructors have included Robert Frost, Willa Cather, Sinclair Lewis and other 20C literary figures. The road then continues on through **Middlebury Gap★** (2,149ft).

**Texas Falls Recreation Area** – *Left from Rte 125.* A short trail leads to a series of falls that tumble over rocks and giant holes formed by glaciers.

The itinerary ends in the tiny crossroads community of Hancock.

# BRATTLEBORO
Pop 12,241

Map of Principal Sights p 2
Tourist Office ☎802-254-4565

Located at the southeastern tip of Vermont beside the Connecticut River, Brattleboro is a commercial and industrial center with a number of motels and restaurants. Brattleboro was the site of the first permanent settlement in Vermont (1724) and during the following century the town grew, largely because of industry and tourism. Handsome 19C brick structures form the nucleus of the town center and preserve the atmosphere of that period, when Brattleboro was evolving from a country village into an urban community. The sixth most heavily populated city in the state, Brattleboro is today home to wood and paper plants and produces furniture, leather goods and precision tools.

**Brattleboro Museum and Art Center** – *Main and Vernon Sts. Open mid-May–mid-Nov Tue–Sun noon–6pm. Closed major holidays. $2. ☎802-257-0124.* Changing displays of the work of Vermont artists, as well as permanent exhibits of Rudyard Kipling's years in the state (1892-1896) and of locally manufactured Estey organs are held in this former railroad station.

*When driving the back roads of Vermont, speeds in excess of 30mph are generally unsafe since many of these roads are unpaved and have sharp curves, steep grades and uneven surfaces. Take special care during the spring thaw or after a rainfall, as unpaved roads will be muddy. Distances may be long between gas stations; begin with a full tank of gas.*

# BURLINGTON
Pop 39,127

Map of Principal Sights p 2
Tourist Office ☎802-863-3489

Located on Lake Champlain, Burlington, the most populous city in the state, reigns as the urban and industrial heart of Vermont. Its successful past as an industrial center and commercial port in the 19C is evidenced in the lovely residences remaining from this period. With the establishment of facilities by IBM, Digital Equipment Corp and General Electric in the area, the city's industrial sector has been revived. The lively downtown is anchored on the east by the University of Vermont and on the west by the shoreline of Lake Champlain, with the Adirondack Mountains of New York rising in the distance. A four-block downtown pedestrian mall, **Church Street Marketplace**, bustles with cafes, boutiques and a marked student atmosphere. **Battery Park** and **Ethan Allen Park** *(North Ave to Ethan Allen Pkwy)*, and boat rides *(p 227)* offer opportunities for viewing the lake and its surroundings. Each year Burlington hosts the **Vermont Mozart Festival** *(p 245)*, and benefits from the programs of art, music and theater presented by the university.

**University of Vermont** – As old as the state itself, the university was chartered in 1791 as the fifth college in New England. Throughout its 200-year history, it has pursued a strong commitment to such social concerns as religious freedom and equality for women and minorities. From the campus green *(between S. Prospect St and University Pl)*, the grounds rise to a line of buildings that includes the landmark **Ira Allen Chapel** (1925), a neo-Georgian edifice designed by McKim, Mead and White. The adjacent **Billings Center** (1885) reflects the arched, ashlar Richardsonian Romanesque style of its designer Henry Hobson Richardson.

★ **Robert Hull Fleming Museum** – *Open May–Aug Mon noon–4pm, Tue–Fri 9am–4pm, weekends 1–5pm. Rest of the year weekends 1–5pm. $2. ☎802-656-2090.* Also designed by McKim, Mead and White, this Colonial Revival building was constructed in 1930 and renovated in 1984. Original funds for its construction were provided by the heir to the estate of Robert Hull Fleming, a Chicago businessman and graduate of the university. The museum's collection includes Egyptian, Asian and Native American artifacts, as well as an **American gallery** of 18C and 19C paintings and decorative arts, and a **European gallery** of 17C to 19C works. On the grounds, note the abstract, five-figure sculpture entitled *Lamentations Group, 1989* by Vermont resident Judith Brown (1931-1992).

## EXCURSIONS

★★★ **Shelburne** – *12mi south on Rte 7. Description p 236.*

**Ethan Allen Homestead** – *2mi north on Rte 127. From Burlington, take Rte 7 north, turn left on Pearl St, then right on N. Champlain St to road's end. Turn left, then immediate right onto Rte 127 north and exit at North Ave Beaches. Take the first right at the sign for the homestead. Open mid-May–Labor Day daily 10am–5pm, after Labor Day–mid-Oct daily 1–5pm. Mid-May–Jun 19 Tue–Sun 1–5pm. $3.50. ☎802-865-4556.* Dedicated to the legendary folk hero, this 5-acre site threaded by the Winooski River includes a reconstructed frame house (c.1785) believed to have been the final home of Ethan Allen *(p 222)*. The visitor center houses exhibits on regional history and the escapades of Allen and his Green

Mountain Boys. A re-created tavern in the center serves as the setting for a multi-media presentation *(15min)* in which Allen is remembered by friends and associates. Trails lead along the river.

## JAY PEAK

Map of Principal Sights p 2

Located only 8mi from the border crossing into southern Quebec at North Troy, Jay Peak (3,861ft) is an important ski area in northern Vermont and attracts both Americans and Canadians during the winter *(ski information p 257)*. An **aerial tram** lifts passengers to the peak's summit *(open late Jun–Labor Day daily 10am–5pm; $6;* ✗ & ☏ *800-451-4449)*. From the top, there are sweeping **views**★★ of Lake Champlain, the Adirondacks, the White Mountains and, to the north, Canada.
Several drives in the area are especially picturesque during Indian summer; in particular, **Route 242** from Montgomery Center to Route 101, and **Route 58** from Lowell to Irasburg, offer views of northern Vermont against the backdrop of the surrounding mountain ranges.

## LAKE CHAMPLAIN

Map of Principal Sights p 2                                Tourist Office ☏802-524-2444

This immense lake (125mi long) that straddles the Vermont/New York border was discovered by Samuel de Champlain in 1609. Following the last Ice Age, a vast salt-water sea (Champlain Sea) invaded the Champlain Lowlands, separating northern New England from the rest of the continent. As the land began to rise, free from the weight of the glaciers, the sea gradually receded, forming the largest lake in the US after the Great Lakes.
Cradled in a broad valley between the Adirondacks and the Green Mountains, this lake and its surroundings have become a popular recreation and vacation area. At the northern end of Lake Champlain, bridges provide access to the islands of Isle la Motte, North Hero and Grand Isle. In recent years North Hero has become the summer residence of the famed **Royal Lipizzan Stallions** *(p 244)*.

**Isle la Motte** – A **shrine** honoring Saint Anne marks the site of Fort Saint Anne (1666), built by the French as a defense against the Mohawk Indians. The 12ft **statue of Champlain** was sculpted by a Vermonter, Ferdinand Weber, for Expo '67 in Montreal *(open mid-May–mid-Oct daily dawn–dusk;* ☏*802-928-3362)*.

★ **Cruise** – The stern-wheeler *Spirit of Ethan Allen* offers narrated scenic cruises on Lake Champlain with views of the islands and the Adirondacks. *Departs from Burlington Boathouse, College St, Burlington late-May–mid-Oct daily 10am–4pm. Round-trip 1hr 30min. $7.75.* ✗ & *Green Mountain Boat Lines Ltd.* ☏*802-862-9685.*

**Ferries** – Ferry services operating on Lake Champlain afford lake crossings between Vermont and New York state. *Rates quoted below are for car and driver, except for Larrabees Point to Fort Ticonderoga Ferry (car and passengers included). Winter service, conditions permitting. Connecting points north to south are:*

**Grand Isle to Plattsburgh** – *Departs from Gordon Landing (Rte 314) year-round daily 5–1am (7:40am–11pm holidays). Round-trip 24min. $10.75.* ✗ & *Lake Champlain Transportation Co.* ☏*802-864-9804.*

**Burlington to Port Kent** – *Departs from King St dock late Jun–end-Aug daily 7:15am–7:45pm. Limited service spring & fall. Round-trip 2hrs. $21.* ✗ & *Lake Champlain Transportation Co.* ☏*802-864-9804.*

**Charlotte to Essex** – *Departs from Ferry Rd mid-May–mid-Oct daily 6:30am–10pm. Limited service spring & fall. Round-trip 40min. $10.75.* & *Lake Champlain Transportation Co.* ☏*802-864-9804.*

**Larrabees Point to Fort Ticonderoga** – *Departs from Shoreham (Rte 74) Jul–Aug daily 7am–8pm. May–Jun & Sept–Oct 8am–6pm. Round-trip 20min. $10. Shorewell Ferries, Inc.* ☏*802-897-7999.*

## ★ MAD RIVER VALLEY

Map of Principal Sights p 2

Remote, rural, and set in the midst of broad expanses of rolling, mountainous terrain, the Mad River Valley is a premier four-season resort famed for its ski areas, **Sugarbush** and **Mad River Glen** *(ski information p 257)*. The metamorphosis of this once quiet, secluded farm community into a sophisticated vacation getaway followed swiftly after the opening of Mad River Glen in 1947. Sugarbush began operating in the late 1950s, and in the mid-1960s became Sugarbush North. The lovely setting, abundant accommodations and superb downhill and cross-country skiing facilities have contributed to its great success.
Driving north on Route 100 from **Granville**, or along Route 17 through the **Appalachian Gap** (2,356ft), **views**★★ of the region's unspoiled beauty unfold. Especially scenic is the East Warren Road from Warren to Waitsfield.

## ★ FROM WARREN TO WAITSFIELD  *8mi. Allow 1hr.*

*From Rte 100 turn east onto the road to Warren.*

**Warren** – Pop 1,172. This small village contains crafts shops and a country store frequented for its fresh-baked goods and salads. The Warren covered bridge is reflected in the Mad River, which flows underneath it.

*Leave the village heading east and drive north on East Warren Rd.*

The drive along East Warren Road parallels the Mad River and the Green Mountains to the west. After 5mi, you will pass the **Round Barn** (1908-1909), one of several built in the valley, and now part of an inn.

*The road continues straight ahead over the Waitsfield covered bridge (1833) crossing the Mad River into Waitsfield.*

Round Barn near Waitsfield

Dennis Curran (f/STOP PICTURES)

**Waitsfield** – Pop 1,422. The town has been a commercial center since the 19C, when the daily stagecoach from Waitsfield linked the valley with the railroad in nearby Middlesex. Two shopping centers today provide the inhabitants and visitors in the area with a variety of stores and services. Farming continues to be a principal activity in Waitsfield, despite the influx of professionals and artists in recent years.

## ★ MANCHESTER                                                    Pop 3,622

Map of Principal Sights p 2                     Tourist Office ☎802-362-2100

Favored as a summer resort and cultural center for more than a century, Manchester has become popular during the winter as well, with the development of Bromley and Stratton ski areas *(ski information p 257)*.
**Manchester Center** is a busy place year-round, with its rows of restaurants and shops, while farther south off Route 7A, countrified estates nestle among the foothills of the Taconic Range. In **Manchester Village★** the **Equinox Hotel**, a stately 19C hostelry that catered to an elite clientele including Presidents Harrison, Grant, Theodore Roosevelt and Taft, has been renovated to combine modern comforts with the traditions and gracious service reminiscent of an earlier era.
Manchester is the home of the Orvis Co, one of the oldest surviving (1856) fishing tackle manufacturers in the US. In the past two decades, it has been joined by numerous clothing outlet stores along Routes 7A and 11.

### SIGHTS

★ **Hildene** – *Map p 230. On Rte 7A, 2mi south of the junction of Rtes 7 and 11/30. Visit by guided tour (1hr 30min) only, mid-May–late Oct daily 9:30am–5pm; Nov–mid-May 9am–4pm $6. ✗ & ☎802-362-1788.* This 412-acre "hill and valley" estate was the home of **Robert Todd Lincoln** (1843-1926), the eldest of four children of Abraham and Mary Lincoln. The Lincoln family vacationed in Manchester during Robert's college years. Robert, who eventually became chairman of the board of the Pullman Co, chose this place, tucked between the Taconic and Green Mountains, as the site of his new country home. Hildene was occupied by succeeding generations of Lincolns until the 1970s.

In the main house, a 24-room Georgian Revival mansion, an elegant staircase leads from the entrance hall to the floor above. To the left of the entrance, in the dining room, the unusual layered wall covering creates a collage effect; while in the library to the right, the dark, mahogany-stained paneling conveys a subdued atmosphere. The furnishings are family pieces.

From the gardens there are **panoramas** of the mountains and the valley below.

**American Museum of Fly Fishing** – *Seminary Ave. North of the Equinox Hotel at Rte 7A. Open May–Oct daily 10am–4pm, rest of year weekdays only. Closed major holidays. $2.* ☎802-362-3300. Novice and serious anglers alike will be interested in this museum devoted to the history and lore of fly fishing. Early books on the subject, an extensive array of multicolored artificial flies, and fly-fishing tackle belonging to Daniel Webster, Andrew Carnegie, Ernest Hemingway and other well-known Americans, are among the artifacts in the collection.

**Southern Vermont Art Center** – *West Rd. From the village green, take West Rd 1mi north. Open May–Oct Tue–Sat 10am–5pm, Sun noon–5pm. Dec–Mar Mon–Sat 10am–4pm. Closed major holidays. $3.* ⚔ & ☎802-362-1405. Changing exhibits of paintings, sculpture, prints and photography are held in the 2-story, Georgian-style mansion on this mountainside estate.

★ **Dorset** – *Pop 1,918. Map p 230. 6mi north of Manchester by Rte 30.* The abandoned **quarry** on the right, 4.5mi north of Manchester, was one of the first commercially exploited marble quarries in Vermont. It is now a popular swimming hole in the summer.

Dorset is an artists' colony of painters and writers attracted by the charm of the village's mountain setting. Summer theater is presented at the **Dorset Playhouse**.

**Equinox Skyline Drive** – *Map p 230. 5mi south of Manchester by Rte 7A. Open May–Oct daily 8am–10pm. $6/car.* ⚔ ☎802-362-1114. The 5.5-mile drive leads to the crest of Mt Equinox (3,816ft), the highest point in the Taconic Range. From the road, the Carthusian monastery *(not open to the public)*, completed in 1970, is visible in the distance. At the summit there is a communications center and an inn. The **view★** reaches from the Hudson River Valley deep into the Green Mountains.

**Arlington** – *Pop 2,299. Map p 230. 8mi south of Manchester by Rte 7A.* This tranquil village and its residents served as models for illustrator **Norman Rockwell** *(p 173)*, who lived here at one time.

The **Batten Kill River** provides Arlington with some of the best trout fishing grounds in New England. From Route 7A, you can admire the St James Episcopal Church and the gravestones and monuments in its old churchyard.

## ★★ THE VILLAGES OF SOUTHERN VERMONT
*97mi. 1 day. Map p 230.*

*Leave Manchester Village by Rte 7A. At Manchester Center take Rte 30 east and continue on Rte 11.*

**Bromley Mountain** – The Bromley ski area *(ski information p 257)* has become popular during the summer season because of its **Alpine Slide** *(open Jun–mid-Oct daily 9:30am–5pm; $4.50;* ⚔ & ☎802-824-5522). Bromley's summit (3,260ft) can be reached by hiking trails *(below)* and offers **views** of the Green Mountains. *A chair lift operates late May–mid-Oct daily 9:30am–5pm $4.50.* ⚔ & ☎802-824-5522.

**Long Trail to Bromley Summit** – *From the Bromley ski area, follow Rte 11 approximately 2mi east. A small sign indicates the Long Trail. Parking is on the right. Round-trip 5.6mi, 3hrs.* From the parking lot, a dirt road leads to the trail *(left)*, which is a segment of both the Long Trail *(p 252)* and the Appalachian Trail. After gently ascending through forest for 2mi, the trail climbs steeply, then crosses open meadowland. A **panorama★★** of Stratton Mountain (to the south) and the surrounding Green Mountains is afforded from an observation tower.

*Two miles after Bromley, take the road on the left through Peru. At the fork bear left and continue through North Landgrove, turning left in front of the town hall. After passing the Village Inn, bear right at the fork and continue to Weston.*

★ **Weston** – Pop 488. With its attractive village green, craft shops and general stores, Weston is a popular tourist stop on Route 100. Looking out on the green is the **Farrar-Mansur House**, a late 18C tavern that serves as the local history museum *(visit by 1hr guided tour only, late May–Labor Day daily 12:30–4pm; mid-Sept–mid-Oct weekends only; $2)*.

Behind the house, the **Weston Mill Museum** displays 19C cooperage, milling and tinsmithing tools, weaving and farm implements *(open late May–Labor Day daily 11am–4pm; mid-Sept–mid-Oct weekends only)*. Nearby is the **Weston Playhouse**, modeled after a church that burned in 1963. *Summer theater is presented at the playhouse.* The popular **Vermont Country Store** enjoys a statewide reputation for its varied merchandise, from local cheeses to long underwear *(open year-round Mon–Sat 9am–5pm* ☎802-824-3184).

*From Weston follow Rte 100 past the green, then bear right at the sign for Chester. Continue through Andover, then east on Rte 11.*

**Chester** – Pop 2,832. The wide main street of this community is lined with lodgings and shops, several of which are housed in historic buildings *(walking tour brochure available from information booth on the village green Jun–Oct)*. The National Survey, a New England cartographic institution, has made its home here since 1912.

*From Chester take Rte 35 to Grafton.*

★ **Grafton** – Pop 602. In the 19C this village on the old post road between Albany and BOSTON was a prosperous community with sheep farms, woolen, grist- and sawmills, tanneries and a soapstone quarry. By mid-century the town's economic prospects began to fade and continued to decline. In 1963 the Windham Foundation was established by a private benefactor "to restore...economic vitality in the village." Today more than half the 19C buildings have been renovated by the foundation, which also owns the **Grafton Village Cheese Co** *(tours on request ☎802-843-2221)*; the **Red Barns**, housing antique carriages and exhibits on the sheep farming and blacksmithing; and the **Old Tavern** (1801). Once frequented by such luminaries as Ulysses S. Grant, Oliver Wendell Holmes and Rudyard Kipling, this 3-story brick structure, fronted by a 2-story porch, has been restored to its innkeeping tradition. The interior is furnished with Federal and country-style antiques and 19C artwork. *Horse-drawn carriage tours of the town available year- round Fri–Mon. Wilbur's Horse Drawn Rides ☎802-875-3643.*

*In Grafton turn right, cross the bridge, turn left before the tavern. Follow this road to Rte 35, which leads to Townshend, then take Rte 30 south to Newfane.*

**Newfane** – Pop 1,555. Situated deep in the Green Mountains, this town has grown little since the 18C, when it was selected as the Windham county seat. Newfane's village green★, with its white Congregational Church, **Windham County Courthouse** and two old inns, is pretty at any time of year, but it becomes a spectacular sight in the fall, when the leaves on the surrounding trees take on hues of red, gold and rust.

*Take Rte 30 back through Townshend. Between Townshend and West Townshend you will pass a covered bridge on the left. Continue through Jamaica into Bondville, where a road to the left leads to the Stratton Mountain Ski Area.*

**Stratton Mountain** – (3,936ft). With 92 slopes and trails accessible by a gondola and 14 chair lifts, this is one of the major ski areas in Vermont *(ski information p 257)*. The annual Stratton Arts Festival featuring the work of Vermont artists and craftspeople is held at the base lodge in September and October.

*Return to Manchester by Rte 30.*

*Strict laws keep Vermont's roadways free of billboards. Only black and white roadside signs posted by the State mark local attractions and services.*

# ★ MIDDLEBURY — Pop 8,034

Map of Principal Sights p 2

Tourist Office ☎802-388-7951

Set amid gently sloping hills and rolling countryside, Middlebury is a pleasant town, with its pristine Congregational Church, and Victorian-style buildings converted into stores and restaurants. It is the site of stately Middlebury Inn (1827) and Middlebury College.

## SIGHTS

★ **Middlebury College** – Chartered in 1800 and considered a member of the "Little Ivy League," this respected college is well-known for its fine liberal arts curriculum, its foreign language summer schools and its Bread Loaf Writers' Conference *(p 225)*, which Robert Frost was instrumental in founding. *Summer visitors are asked to speak quietly if conversing in English; students are pledged to speak only foreign languages on campus.* The main campus covers some 500 acres and features impressive stone and marble buildings of eclectic architectural styles. Notable are **Painter Hall** (1815), the oldest surviving college building in the state, and **Le Château** (1925), modeled after a pavilion of the French Château de Fontainebleau. The Starr Library contains the **Frost Room**.

**Center for the Arts** – Incorporating elements of traditional Vermont barns and silos into a bold, modern building of granite and clapboard, this center (1992) houses a dance and studio theater, a concert hall and the college's **museum of art★**. The museum's permanent collection includes works by such notables as Vermont native Hiram Powers, Gilbert Stuart, Alexander Calder and John Frederick Kensett *(open year-round Tues–Fri 10am–5pm, weekends noon–5pm. & ☎802-388-3711).*

**Sheldon Museum** – *1 Park St. Open year-round Mon–Fri 10am–5pm, Sat 10–4pm. $3.50. & ☎802-388-2117.* In 1882 Henry Sheldon moved into this brick house with his pianos, old clocks and books and hung out a sign that read: "Sheldon Art Museum Archaeological and Historical Society." His museum, the first of many local museums and historical societies that have since sprung up throughout New England, today includes 19C furnishings, Victorian toys and personal records.

**Frog Hollow** – This attractive area *(Main & Mill Sts)* of small boutiques perched above the cascading waters of Otter Creek that tumble through the center of town, is an appropriate setting for the **Vermont State Craft Center**. Located in a renovated mill, the center displays and sells fine blown glass, metalwork, jewelry, wooden ware and handwoven fabrics made by leading Vermont craftspeople *(open year-round Mon–Sat 9:30am–5pm (Fri 7pm), Sun noon–5pm; & ☎802-388-3177).*

## EXCURSIONS  *Map p 225*

**Morgan Horse Farm** – *In Weybridge, 2.5mi northwest of Middlebury. From the center of Middlebury bear right onto College St (Rte 125), then turn right onto Rte 23 (Weybridge St). Follow the signs to the farm, bearing left at the fork with the covered bridge. Open May–Oct daily 9am–4pm. $3.50. & ☎802-388-2011.* When Vermont schoolmaster **Justin Morgan** obtained a colt in payment for a debt in the 1780s, little did he suspect that the colt would sire the first American breed of horse: the Morgan horse. Strong, thick-muscled and fast, the stallion was capable of out-pulling draft horses in clearing logs and could outrun some of the best thoroughbreds. His descendants have been bred, raised and trained in Vermont ever since the 1790s. An important US export in the 19C, the Morgan was named Vermont's official state animal in 1961.

Owned by the University of Vermont *(p 226)*, the farm operates as a breeding, training and instructional facility. Visitors may tour the 19C barn where descendants of the original Morgan are housed *(20min slide presentation shown hourly).*

★ **Branbury State Park** – *Near Brandon, 10mi southeast of Middlebury by Rte 7 south, then Rte 53. Open late May–mid-Oct daily 10am–dusk. $1.50. △ ⚔ & ☎802-247-5925 (summer), 802-483-2314 (rest of the year). Facility information p 251.* This popular warm-weather destination has a large sandy beach on Lake Dunmore *(boat rentals available)*, and hiking trails to the **Falls of Llana** *(round-trip 1.1mi, 45min, some difficult sections)* and to **Silver Lake** *(round-trip 3mi, 1hr 30min).*

**Vergennes** – *Pop 2,578. 13mi northwest of Middlebury by Rte 7 north.* Vergennes, covering 1.8sq mi, is hailed as the smallest incorporated city in the US.

**Button Bay State Park** – *6mi west of Vergennes by West Main St to Panton Rd, turn right onto Basin Harbor Rd, then left on unmarked road. Open late May–mid-Oct daily 10am–dusk. $1.50. △ $12 ⚔ ☎802-475-2377. Facility information p 251.* Named for the unusual geological formations, resembling buttons, found in the clay banks, the park offers views of LAKE CHAMPLAIN and the Adirondacks. The nature center displays "buttons" of different sizes, and has exhibits on local geology.

★ **Lake Champlain Maritime Museum** – *In Basin Harbor, 21mi northwest of Middlebury by Rte 7 to Vergennes, then West Main St to Panton Rd. Turn right onto Basin Harbor Rd. Open early May–mid-Oct daily 10am–5pm. $3. ☎802-475-2022.* Five exhibit buildings, including a stone schoolhouse (c.1818), trace the history of the lake and its maritime traditions. A variety of boats are displayed, and a replica of the *Philadelphia*, a 54ft Revolutionary gunboat, is anchored along the museum's lake shoreline.

# MONTPELIER                                      Pop 8,247

Map of Principal Sights p 2   Tourist Office ☎802-229-5711

This small city, the capital of Vermont since 1805, sits among the wooded hill-sides that rise above the Winooski River. The golden dome of the State House, ablaze in the afternoon sun, dominates the city and is a magnificent sight when the trees change color in autumn. The granite industry, which enabled the city to develop and prosper, has been supplanted in importance by state government and the insurance industry.

## SIGHTS   1hr

**State House** – *State St. Open Jul–mid-Oct Mon–Fri 8am–4:15pm, Sat 11am–3pm. Rest of the year weekdays only. Closed major holidays.* ✗ ᪿ ☎802-828-2228. This elegant Neoclassical edifice, built in 1857, is the third state house erected on this site; the first (1808) and second (1836) were destroyed by fire. The present structure incorporates the Doric columns and portico of the second state house, which was modeled after the Temple of Theseus in Greece. A 14ft statue of Ceres, the Roman goddess of agriculture, rises from the pinnacle of the golden dome.

★ **Vermont Museum** – *109 State St, in the Pavilion Office Building. Open year-round Tue–Fri 9am–4:30pm, Sat 9am–4pm, Sun noon–4pm. $3.* ᪿ ☎802-828-2291. The Victorian facade of this building was modeled after the Pavilion Hotel, which stood on the site between 1876 and 1965. Inside, the 19C lobby has been recon-structed. Beyond it are the rooms occupied by the Vermont Historical Society. Displays relate to the history, economy and traditions of Vermont.

# ★★ NORTHEAST KINGDOM

Map of Principal Sights p 2

This region of forests, lakes, wide-open valleys and back roads that girdle tiny vil-lages includes the three northeastern counties (Caledonia, Essex and Orleans) that surround St Johnsbury *(p 235)* and extend to the Canadian and New Hampshire borders. The region is busiest in the fall, when the countryside is a symphony of color: shades of copper, gold, and everywhere the vibrant reds of the maple trees. During this period, harvest suppers, bazaars, flea markets and auctions are held in many villages.
Seven villages in the region, Barnet, Cabot, Groton, Marshfield, Peacham, Plain-field and Walden, participate in the week-long **Northeast Kingdom Foliage Festival** during which a different village, each day, hosts activities ranging from church breakfasts to house tours and craft shows *(late Sept–early Oct; reservations rec-ommended).*
Two other interesting villages are **Craftsbury Common**, with its immense hilltop vil-lage green that appears to meet the sky at the horizon, and Danville *(p 233)*, home of the American Society of Dowsers.

## ★ LAKE WILLOUGHBY AND BROWNINGTON
*Circle tour north of St Johnsbury – 87mi. Allow 1 day, if including hike.*

*From St Johnsbury, take Rte 5 north through Lyndonville to Rte 114, and con-tinue north on Rte 114 to East Burke. There, follow an unmarked road to Burke Hollow and West Burke.*

**The Burkes** – East Burke, Burke Hollow and West Burke are tiny communities at the base of Burke Mountain, a ski area *(ski information p 257)*. The gentle moun-tain landscape is especially scenic when viewed from the road that leads to the summit of Burke Mountain (3,262ft). In the distance, note Lake Willoughby to the northwest through the gap. *Access to the Burke Mountain Auto Road (toll) is from Rte 114 in East Burke.*

*From West Burke take Rte 5A to Lake Willoughby.*

★ **Lake Willoughby** – Two mountains rising abruptly opposite each other in a for-mation resembling the entrance to a mountain pass, signal the location of Lake Willoughby *(swimming in season)*. The taller mountain, towering above the south-eastern end of the lake, is **Mt Pisgah** (2,751ft).

**South Trail to Mt Pisgah** – *Trailhead parking off Rte 5A at south end of lake, 5.6mi north of West Burke. Trail begins across the road from the parking area. Round-trip 4mi, 2hrs 30min.* Crossing a picturesque wetland, the trail climbs through a mixed northern forest, with views of Lake Willoughby on the way. Leaving the lake, it as-cends more steeply through a birch and evergreen forest to the summit, with **views★★** of the surrounding mountains and New Hampshire's Mt Washington in the distance. A 2mi spur trail leads to a fine overlook of the lake.

*Follow Rte 5A north along the lake shoreline to Rte 58 west. Continue approx-imately 4mi on Rte 58 to the village of Evansville.Turn right on the road marked Brownington Center, which becomes a dirt road. Take the second left and continue to Brownington Center. There, bear right up the hill 1.5mi to Brownington Village Historic District.*

★ **Brownington Village Historic District** – A once thriving community, this charming hamlet has changed little since the early 19C, when it was home to the Brownington Academy. The private institution was founded by The Reverend Alexander Twilight (1795-1857), an alumnus of Middlebury College, and believed to be the country's first black college graduate. The academy served as the main school for neighboring communities for 25 years. The dormitory building, the **Old Stone House** (1836), a 4-story granite edifice, now functions as a museum, with period rooms and exhibits on the school *(open Jul–Aug daily 11am–5pm; mid-May–Jun & Sept–mid-Oct Fri–Tue 11am–5pm; $3; ☎802-754-2022).* At the north edge of the village, an observatory platform on Prospect Hill affords a **panorama★★** of Willoughby Gap (southeast), Mt Mansfield (southwest), Jay Peak (west) and Lake Memphremagog (north).

> *From Prospect Hill, turn right, continue past the Congregational Church and follow the unmarked road 2mi west to the junction with Rte 58. Turn right and continue through the town of Orleans (1mi). Take Rte 5 south for 5mi to Rte 16 south. Take Rte 16 through the town of Glover, and then turn left on Rte 122 south for about 1mi to the Bread and Puppet Museum.*

**Bread and Puppet Museum** – *Rte 122. Open mid-May–mid-Oct daily 10am–5pm. ☎802-525-6972.* In a cavernous barn built in 1863, the socially committed Bread and Puppet Theater Company dramatically displays its larger-than-life puppets. These head masks and mannequin-like creations are the result of almost 30 years of work by founder Peter Schumann, a Silesian-born sculptor and choreographer.

> *Return to St Johnsbury via Rte 5 south.*

★ **PEACHAM AND BARNET CENTER**
*Tour south of St Johnsbury – 65mi. Allow 3hrs 30min.*

> *From St Johnsbury take Rte 2 west to Danville.*

**Danville** – Pop 1,917. Because of its high elevation, this rural agricultural community enjoys refreshing breezes and clear air even on hot summer days. The village is the home of the **American Society of Dowsers**. The society's annual 4-day convention, held in Lyndonville in August, attracts dowsers (dowsers use a forked twig, or divining rod, to search for underground water and minerals) from across the nation.

> *Continue south on Rte 2 to Marshfield. Turn right onto Rte 215 to Cabot.*

**Cabot** – Pop 1,043. This small community is associated with the production of cheese. The **Cabot Creamery**, in business since 1919, is perhaps the best known purveyor of Vermont daily products, particularly its variety of cheeses *(free samples available)*. A tour *(30min, $1)* of the plant operations, opening with a video presentation *(15min)* explains in detail how cheese, yogurt and butter are made *(open mid-Jun–mid-Oct Mon–Sat 9am–5pm; rest of the year 9am–4pm ☎802-563-2231).*

> *Return to Danville via Rtes 215 and 2. Take the unmarked road south through Harvey and Ewell Mills to Peacham.*

Doug Locke/Dembinsky Photo Assoc.

Peacham

★ **Peacham** – Pop 627. Surrounded by a breathtaking hill-and-dale setting, Peacham may be the most photographed of all Vermont's villages during the fall. Lovely white dwellings stand near the church, the general store and Peacham Academy.

*Continue to Barnet Center through South Peacham, turning left to West Barnet. At Barnet Center, turn left before the church and continue up the hill.*

**Barnet Center** – Pop 1,415. From a vantage point past the church near the top of the hill, you can look down on a beautiful pastoral scene of a large barn with its silo. Beyond the barn, there is a **view★★** of the countryside stretching into the distance.

*Return to the foot of the hill and turn left in the direction of Barnet. There, take Rte 5 to St Johnsbury.*

## ★ PLYMOUTH                                                   Pop 440

Map of Principal Sights p 2

This tiny hamlet abutting the hills of the Green Mountains was the birthplace of **Calvin Coolidge** (1872-1933), the 30th President of the US. It was here, on August 3, 1923 that Vice President Coolidge, upon receiving the news of the death of President Warren Harding, was sworn into office by his father John Coolidge, a notary public. This was the first and only occasion in the history of the nation on which a President was administered the oath of office by his father.
*Several buildings in the Plymouth Notch Historic District on Rte 100A (in the village of Plymouth Notch) relate to the life of Calvin Coolidge, and may be visited mid-May–mid-Oct daily 9:30am–5:30pm. $4. ✗ & ☎802-672-3773.*

**Coolidge Birthplace** – Calvin Coolidge was born in this small, modest dwelling. The house is attached to the country store once owned by his parents.

**Coolidge Homestead** – Vice President Coolidge was sworn into the presidency in 1923 in this house, where the family lived from the time Calvin was a youngster.

Also in the historic district are a barn that has been transformed into a museum of early American tools and the Coolidge family's **Plymouth Cheese Corp**, a small operation where visitors can observe the making of traditional granular curd cheese. Coolidge's **grave** lies in the village cemetery, across Route 100A.

## ★ PROCTOR                                                  Pop 1,979

Map of Principal Sights p 2

With its string of quarries from Dorset to LAKE CHAMPLAIN, Vermont was once the nation's leading producer of marble. The Vermont Marble Co, formerly based in Proctor, operated most of the state's quarries.

★ **Marble Exhibit** – *62 Main St. Open mid-May–Oct daily 9am–5:30pm, rest of the year Mon–Sat 9am–4pm. $3.50. & ☎802-459-2300.* The exhibit presents the origin, quarrying and finishing of marble. Polished marble slabs from Vermont and around the world are used to illustrate the rich diversity of colors and graining characteristic of this stone. Visitors may view a video about marble *(13min)*, observe a sculptor at work and see marble sculptures. Marble bas-relief portraits of the US Presidents occupy a special gallery.

**Wilson Castle** – *West Proctor Rd, 4mi south of Proctor. Visit by guided tour (45min) only, late May–mid-Oct daily 9am–6pm. $6. ☎802-773-3284.* This massive brick mansion (1867), built by a Vermont doctor, offers a glimpse of the opulence that characterized the private homes of 19C America's upper classes. Luxurious furnishing and art pieces are enhanced by the surrounding heavily carved woodwork, stained-glass windows and hand-painted and polychromed ceilings. Note the Louis XVI Crown Jewel case.

## RUTLAND                                                   Pop 18,230

Map of Principal Sights p 2                        Tourist Office ☎802-773-2747

Situated at the junction of Otter and East Creeks, Rutland, settled in the 1770s, is Vermont's second-largest city. The town developed into a railroad center in the 19C and marble quarrying flourished, giving Rutland the nickname "the marble city." Many small industries now thrive, producing a variety of goods.
Rutland's mountains and lakes make the region a year-round playground for those who love the outdoors. Killington, one of the largest ski resorts in the East, and Pico are among the nearby recreation areas *(ski information p 257)*.

**Norman Rockwell Museum** – *2mi east of Rutland on Rte 4. Open year-round daily 9am–6pm. Closed Jan 1, Easter Sunday, Thanksgiving Day, Dec 25. $2.50. &. ☎802-773-6095.* The museum contains hundreds of examples of the work of

Norman Rockwell *(p 34)*, illustrator, humorist and chronicler of more than half a century of American life. The series of over 300 magazine covers that Rockwell created for the *Saturday Evening Post* and for which he is best remembered, is displayed together with other magazine covers, movie and war posters, advertising work, calendars and greeting cards, which also brought him fame.

## EXCURSIONS

★ **Proctor** – *6mi from Rutland by West St, then Rte 3 north. Description p 234.*

**Hubbardton Battle Site** – *18mi northwest of Rutland in East Hubbardton. Take Rte 4 west to Exit 5. Follow the signs north.* A monument and visitor center commemorate the Revolutionary War battle that occurred at Hubbardton in 1777. Early in July 1777 American troops, which had held Fort Ticonderoga for two years, were forced by the British to surrender control of the fort. Pursued by the British, the Americans retreated into Vermont, where a small colonial force had been stationed to form a rear guard. When the two armies clashed on July 7 on a hillside in East Hubbardton, the battle left both sides with hundreds of casualties. After the fight, the British decided to halt their pursuit of the colonists and return to the fort. For the Americans, tired and reduced in number, this was victory enough as they withdrew deeper into Vermont.

Visitor Center – *Open mid-May–mid-Oct daily 11am–5pm. $1.* & ☎*802-759-2412.* This building contains a small museum and a diorama of the battle.

**Killington** – *10mi east of Rutland on Rte 4; gondola station 15mi east of Rutland on Rte 4.* Killington, with 155 trails cut on six interconnecting mountains, is one of New England's most popular ski resorts *(ski information p 257).* The Killington gondola is the longest *(2.5mi)* ski lift of its kind in the US *(reduced rates for fall foliage viewing mid-Sept–mid-Oct;* ✗ ☎*802-422-3333).* A ride on the gondola affords views★★ of the Green Mountains.

**Lake St Catherine State Park** – *20mi southwest of Rutland. On Rte 30 south of Poultney. Take Rte 4 to Exit 4, then Rte 30 south. Open Jun–Oct daily 10am–9pm. $1.50.* △ & ☎*802-287-9158. Facility information p 251.* Cool breezes sweep the calm surface of Lake St Catherine, making this a popular spot for windsurfing, sailing and fishing for trout and northern pike.

# ST JOHNSBURY                                   Pop 7,608

Map of Principal Sights p 2                    Tourist Office ☎802-748-3678

This small city began to prosper in the 1830s when a grocer named Thaddeus Fairbanks invented and began to manufacture the platform scale here; Fairbanks scales have been produced and shipped around the world ever since. The St Johnsbury Athenaeum and the Fairbanks Museum and Planetarium, both in the downtown area, were established by the Fairbanks family, devoted patrons of their hometown. Manufacturing and maple syrup production are major occupations in St Johnsbury.

★ **Athenaeum** – *30 Main St. Open year-round Mon–Fri 10am–5:30pm (Mon, Wed 8pm), Sat 9:30am–4pm. Closed major holidays.* & ☎*802-748-8291.* Horace Fairbanks built this brick Second Empire building as a public library in 1871, adding an art gallery to the rear in 1873. Still hung in the style of a Victorian salon, the gallery is dominated by Albert Bierstadt's monumental *Domes of Yosemite.* Also represented are Asher B. Durand and other painters of the Hudson River school as well as Vermont natives Hiram Powers and Thomas Waterman Wood. The library features ornate woodwork and reading mezzanines.

**Fairbanks Museum and Planetarium** – *Main and Prospect Sts. Open year-round Mon–Sat 10am–4pm (Jul & Aug 6pm), Sun 1–5pm. Closed Jan 1, Easter Sunday, Thanksgiving Day & Dec 25. $4.* & ☎*802-748-2372.* This institution was founded in 1891 by Franklin Fairbanks, who donated his collection of taxidermy wildlife to the museum. Today the museum houses 4,500 mounted birds and mammals, a large collection of antique dolls, and artifacts from many lands. The ornate Romanesque Revival building, designed by Vermont architect Lambert Packard, is carved of red sandstone, and the interior features a magnificent barrel-vaulted ceiling. A wainscoted circular staircase leads to cultural history exhibits in the second-floor gallery.

**Maple Grove Farms** – *On Rte 2 east of the city center. Open year-round Mon–Fri 8am–5pm. Sugarhouse open May–Oct daily 8am–5pm. Closed major holidays.* ☎*802-748-5141.* Exhibits and brief films illustrate how maple syrup is harvested and produced. The factory tour *(15min, $.75)* introduces visitors to the step-by-step procedures involved in transforming maple syrup into Maple Grove candies; the sugarhouse contains a continuously operating sap boiler.

## EXCURSION

★★ **Northeast Kingdom** – *Description p 232.*

# ★★★ SHELBURNE

Pop 5,871

Map of Principal Sights p 2

Shelburne town comprises Shelburne Village, Shelburne Falls and Shelburne Harbor, sedate pastoral communities on LAKE CHAMPLAIN with sweeping vistas of the Adirondacks and the Green Mountains. During the glory days of steamboat travel, a shipyard on Shelburne Bay turned out vessels that carried passengers and freight on the lake. The *SS Ticonderoga (p 237)*, the last of these steamers, was launched from a local pier in 1906. A lakeshore resort for many years, Shelburne today is known primarily for the Shelburne Museum, whose fine collection of American folk art preserves the early spirit of the nation.

## ★★★ SHELBURNE MUSEUM   *1 day. Map below.*

The Shelburne Museum possesses a preeminent collection of home crafts, folk arts, trade tools, transportation, fine arts, furnishings and architecture representing three centuries of American life, history and art. These varied collections are well-presented in the 37 buildings spread across 45 acres near Lake Champlain.

The museum was established in 1947 by **Electra Havemeyer Webb** and her husband **J. Watson Webb**. An avid collector of American crafts and folk art, Mrs Webb assembled varied collections of Americana over the years, then purchased a number of historic structures and had them moved to Shelburne to house the collections. Within ten years, Shelburne had its own church, school, jail, barns, houses, a general store, and even a lighthouse, railway depot and steamboat.

### VISIT

On Rte 7. Open  late May–late Oct daily 10am–5pm. $15. Rest of the year by guided tour (2hrs) only, daily 1pm. $6. Hands-on tours Sat 11am (reservations required). $6. Closed major holidays. ✗ & ☎802-985-3346.

★★ **Round Barn** – Built in 1901, this is one of the few remaining round wooden barns in Vermont. The labor-saving design of the 3-story barn became popular around the turn of the century, prior to the developments of modern technology. Hay was

SHELBURNE MUSEUM

0      300 ft
0    100 m

BURLINGTON

Printing and Weaving Shops
Shaker Shed
★★Hat and Fragrance Textile Gallery
Jail
Variety Unit★★
★★★HORSESHOE BARN
Smokehouse
Stone Cottage
★Vergennes Schoolhouse
Vermont House
Charlotte Meeting House
★★Stagecoach Inn
Meeting House Shed
Administrative Offices
Blacksmith Shop
Dutton House
Covered Bridge
★★General Store
Family Center
★Dorset House
★Stencil House
Sawyer's Cabin
Prentis House
Sawmill
Pleissner Gallery and Garden
★Webb Gallery
Diamond Barn Store
Bostwick Garden
★★Colchester Reef Lighthouse
★★Ticonderoga
★★Electra Havemeyer Webb Memorial Building
★★Shelburne Station
Shelburne Road
Beach Lodge
Beach Gallery
★★Round Barn
Museum Store
Carousel
★Circus Building
P

MIDDLEBURY

loaded into the huge central silo from the upper level, and the animals, held in stalls surrounding the silo on the middle level, could be easily fed by one person. The barn, which houses the visitor center, contains agricultural exhibits, equipment and an orientation slide show *(14min, lower level)*.

**★ Circus Parade Building** – The semicircular building houses carousel horses, circus posters, and the hand-carved Kirk Bros. 5,000-piece miniature circus.

**Beach Gallery and Beach Hunting Lodge** – Nature and hunting are the themes of these collections. Western landscape and wildlife paintings, trophies and Plains and Northwest Coast Indian artifacts are shown.

**★★ Shelburne Railroad Station** – This structure exemplifies the Victorian-style railroad stations that were built across America in the 19C. The private car, *Grand Isle* (outside the station), was owned by former Vermont governor William C. Smith.

**★★ The Ticonderoga** – After steaming along on Lake Champlain for almost 50 years hauling passengers, freight and other tourist traffic, this side-wheeler, known as the *"Ti,"*—the last vertical-beam, side-wheel steamship left intact in the US—was saved from the scrap heap in the 1950s by Electra Havemeyer Webb.
A specially constructed dike allowed workers to transfer the *Ti* out of the water to a series of tracks that extended several miles overland to Shelburne; a film *(10min)* shown continuously on board illustrates this feat. Inside, the exhibits and plush decor recall the *Ti's* past as a luxurious steamship.

**★★ Colchester Reef Lighthouse** – Located at one time off Colchester Point in Lake Champlain, the lighthouse (1871) was moved to Shelburne, where it now serves as a gallery of marine art. Paintings, photos, figureheads, scrimshaw and lithographs depict whaling and the great days of sail.

**Prentis House** – This 18C house (1733) is impeccably furnished with antiques.

**★ Stencil House** – The interior of this dwelling (1790) contains splendid examples of decorative wall stenciling.

Tuckaway General Store

Ken Burris/Shelburne Museum

**★★ Tuckaway General Store** – This brick building (1840), which originally stood in Shelburne, houses a general store, post office, barbershop, dentist's and doctor's offices, a tap room and an apothecary shop. On the first floor, every imaginable item necessary for daily farm living will be found on the shelves, hanging from the ceiling, or tacked onto the timbered posts of the store.
Upstairs in the doctor's and dentist's offices are displays of their instruments. The apothecary shop contains all types of remedies and a sizeable collection of razors.

**Charlotte Meeting House** – The simple brick meetinghouse (1840) has been refurbished with new wooden pews and trompe l'œil wall panels.

**Vermont House** – Furnished like the home of a New England sea captain, this dwelling (1790) contains colorful hand-painted wallpapers illustrating port scenes.

VERMONT

★★★**Horseshoe Barn** – This barn (1949), in the shape of an enormous horseshoe, contains more than 140 horse-drawn carriages and sleighs. Among the phaetons and coaches on the second floor is a calèche and a luxurious **Berlin** with an exquisite satin interior. Concord coaches, buggies, a Conestoga wagon, and brightly painted peddlers' wagons fill the Annex.

★★ **Hat and Fragrance Textile Gallery** – This early 19C building contains a superb group of American quilts: appliqué, pieced work, and reverse appliqué, dating from the 17C through the present. With their intricate patterns and needlework, these quilts are admired as works of art.
Victorian dollhouses, Parisian gowns designed in the 19C for America's richest women, hooked rugs, lace samplers and an assortment of needlecraft are also displayed.

★★ **Variety Unit** – This building (c.1835), the only original structure on the museum grounds, houses numerous examples of pewter, porcelain, clocks and amusing figure jugs known as Toby mugs. On the second floor there is a multitude of dolls: porcelain, bisque, wax, dried-apple, wood and papier-mâché.

★ **Vergennes Schoolhouse** – The books, charts, maps and chalkboard are arranged in this one-room brick schoolhouse (1830) as though students were expected to arrive at any moment.

★★ **Stagecoach Inn** – Formerly an inn on the stage route linking southern New England with Canada, the building (1783) contains an outstanding collection of American folk sculpture. An enormous wooden eagle carved for the Marine Base at PORTSMOUTH, New Hampshire numbers among the many other eagles, weather vanes, ships' figureheads, sternboards, trade signs, cigar store Indians and carousel figures found throughout the inn.

★ **Dorset House** – The house (c.1840) contains Shelburne's collection of more than 1,000 decoys, including ducks, geese, swans and shorebirds. The realism and artistry attained by the carvers of some decoys benefited the hunter; other decoys, such as those executed by A. Elmer Crowell, were intended for decorative purposes only.

★ **Webb Gallery** – Three hundred years of American painting are represented in the gallery. Works range from the simple, anonymous, primitive portraits of the colonial period through the classic seascapes (Fitz Hugh Lane) and landscapes (Hudson River school) of the 19C. Canvases by 20C artists, such as Andrew Wyeth and Grandma Moses, are also included.

★★ **Electra Havemeyer Webb Memorial Building** – This imposing Greek Revival mansion dedicated to Mrs Webb contains works of art acquired by her parents, and six complete rooms from the Webbs' Park Avenue apartment.
Inside, the warm understated elegance is enhanced by the English paneling, European furnishings and the paintings by Rembrandt, Corot, Manet, Degas and Monet that hang in the rooms and hallways.

## ADDITIONAL SIGHT

**Shelburne Farms** – *Follow Harbor Rd 1.5mi east from traffic light at Shelburne Village. Visit by guided tour (1hr 30min) only, late May–mid-Oct daily 9am–5pm. ☎802-985-8442. $6.50. Visitor center open year-round daily 9am–5pm.* This agricultural estate exemplifying the grand style of the 19C was the country home of railroad tycoon **William Seward Webb** and his wife **Lila Vanderbilt Webb**, granddaughter of Cornelius Vanderbilt (known as the "Commodore"), who founded the Vanderbilt dynasty. The Webbs were attracted to this beautiful setting on the shore of Lake Champlain.
After acquiring the 30-odd farms that originally stood on the property, they turned to the architect Robert Robertson, the landscape designer Frederick Law Olmsted, and Gifford Pinchot, one of the nation's first conservationists, to plan and build Shelburne Farms. The terrain was leveled, buildings razed, and in their place appeared a new park-like landscape of undulating knolls and forest studded with Queen Anne structures.
At its peak the Webb estate, which encompassed some 3,800 acres of fields, pastures and woodlands, was the family residence and a working "model" farm, known for its advanced methods and experimentation in such fields as animal husbandry and crop-raising.
Reduced in size over the years to about 1,000 acres, the farm operates as a nonprofit environmental education center, with a working dairy on the premises. The **Farm Barn** (1888), an enormous turreted structure enclosing a 2-acre courtyard, and the **Coach Barn** (1901) serve as centers for conservation programs.
**Shelburne House** (1899), a 110-room country manor house with **views**★★ of Lake Champlain and the Adirondacks, is completely restored and now operates as an inn. The house also serves as a gracious setting for educational and cultural events and summer lawn concerts.

## EXCURSION

**Vermont Wildflower Farm** –
*On Rte 7 in Charlotte, 5mi south
of Shelburne. Open May–Oct
daily 10am–5pm. $3.* &. ☎*802-
425-3500. An audio-visual presentation (15min) on New
England wildflowers is included
in the admission fee.* The many
species of wildflowers growing
in the farm's field and woodland habitats transform the
landscape into a wonderful display of changing color spring
through fall. The familiar Jack-
in-the-pulpit, black-eyed Susan,
aster and Devil's paintbrush
grow here in abundance, together with dozens of lesser-
known varieties. Descriptive
panels accompany the plants,

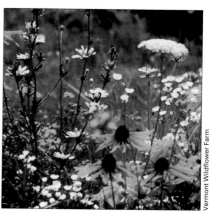

Vermont Wildflower Farm

providing facts and anecdotes (the name *daisy* derives from "day's eye," a reference to the flower's golden center believed by the ancients to represent the sun)
regarding the history, legends and uses of the flowers.

★ # STOWE                                          Pop 3,433

Map of Principal Sights p 2                    Tourist Office ☎802-253-7321

As Route 108 winds through this small village, situated at the foot of Stowe's distinctive landmark, Mt Mansfield, the slender white spire of Christ Community
Church comes into view. The valley's exceptionally long snow season, and abundance of Swiss-style chalets, lodgings and restaurants account for Stowe's
sobriquet, "the ski capital of the east." During the winter up to 8,000 skiers use the
trail systems on the slopes of Stowe's two interconnected mountains, **Mt Mansfield**
(4,393ft), Vermont's highest peak, and **Spruce Peak** (3,320ft) *(Stowe ski information
p 257).* In the summer, Stowe features horseback riding, hiking, swimming, mountain climbing, summer theater and concerts. *Maps & information on area recreation available at The Green Mountain Club, Rte 100 in Waterbury Center, south of
Stowe* ☎*802-244-7037.*

## SIGHTS  *3hrs*

**Trapp Family Lodge** – *Take Rte 108 north 2mi, then turn left at the Trapp Family
sign in front of the white church.* The Trapp family of *Sound of Music* fame chose
this setting for their home because it reminded them of their native Austria. The
mountain resort comprises a Tyrolean chalet-style lodge, guest houses and condominiums. It offers 60 miles of cross-country skiing trails *(ski information p 257).*

★★ **Mt Mansfield** – From the summit there is a sweeping **view**★★ of the entire region,
including JAY PEAK to the northeast, LAKE CHAMPLAIN and the Adirondacks of New
York to the west and the WHITE MOUNTAINS of New Hampshire to the east. On a clear
day, Montreal can be seen to the north.
During the 1930s when a skier had to climb the mountain before skiing down,
Stowe's unplowed toll road was the only ski trail on Mt Mansfield. Today a network of well-groomed ski and hiking trails lace the mountain's slopes.

**Mt Mansfield Auto Road** – *Rte 108, 7mi north of Stowe. Open mid-May–mid-Oct daily
10am–5pm (weather permitting). $12.* ⋇&. ☎*802-253-3000.* The Auto Road *(toll)* is
a 4.5mi gravel road that leads to the summit.

**Mt Mansfield Gondola** – *Rte 108, 8mi north of Stowe. Operates mid-Jun–mid-Oct
daily 10am–5pm. Late May–mid-Jun & mid-Oct–late Oct weekends only. $9.*
☎*802-253-3000.* The 8-passenger gondola lift provides access to the Cliff House
near the summit.

**Bingham Falls** – *.5mi north of the Auto Rd there is a path (difficult to find) to the
right that leads through the woods to the falls.* The West Branch forms a series of
waterfalls here as it spills through a ravine.

★★ **Smugglers Notch** – *Rte 108, 7mi north of Stowe; closed in winter.* The road linking Stowe and Jeffersonville is extremely narrow and climbs rapidly as it twists
through the rugged scenic notch (2,162ft) between Mt Mansfield and Spruce Peak.
The forest admits little light, even on a bright day. *Exercise caution when proceed-
ing between the large roadside boulders that have split from the walls of the
notch.* Smugglers Notch earned its name because of the slaves and contraband
items that were smuggled from the US into Canada through this pass during the
War of 1812.

★ **Ben & Jerry's Ice Cream Factory** – *Rte 100, 9mi south of Stowe. Open year-round daily 9am–5pm (Jul–Aug 8pm).* ✗ ☎*802-244-6957.* Now a Vermont land-mark and headquarters for the nationally recognized gourmet ice cream, this play-ful building, with its Holstein polka dots, reflects the fun-loving, "caring capitalism" approach of its founders Ben Cohen and Jerry Greenfield. The two men began their business in 1977 with a $5 correspondence course on ice-cream making. In 1978 they opened their first scoop shop in a renovated Burlington gas station. Their products are now sold worldwide, with 1993 sales totaling $140 million. Tours *(30min, $1)* include a slide presentation *(10min)* on the history and social ac-tivism of the company and a look at the ice-cream making and packaging plant.

**Moss Glen Falls** – *Rte 100, 3mi north of Stowe. From Rte 100, take Randolph Rd, then the first right to the small parking area.* A short trail leads to the falls and con-tinues somewhat steeply *(not well marked)* upstream to a brook where it is possible to take a dip in the cool water.

**Alpine Slide** – *Spruce Peak. Rte 108, 8.5mi north of Stowe. Open mid-Jun– Labor Day daily 10am–5pm. Mid-May–mid-Jun & mid-Sept–mid-Oct weekends only. $6.* ☎*802-253-3000.* Stowe is one of the ski areas in New England where an alpine slide operates on the mountain slopes during the mild seasons.

## WINDSOR                                                                Pop 3,714

Map of Principal Sights p 2                               Tourist Office ☎802-674-5910

This historic town on the banks of the Connecticut River was the birthplace of Ver-mont in 1777. Representatives meeting here that year agreed upon the state's official name *(p 222)*, declared Vermont an independent republic, and drew up its first constitution—the first constitution in the nation to prohibit slavery and grant the right to vote without regard to property ownership or individual wealth.
In the 19C, the hydraulic pump, the coffee percolator and other inventions were de-veloped in Windsor, which today is a center for the machine tool industry.

**Constitution House** – *16 N. Main St. Open mid-May–mid-Oct daily 11am–5pm. $1.* ☎*802-672-3773.* Delegates, meeting in this old tavern in July 1777, drew up Vermont's first constitution. Exhibits arranged in the tavern rooms include the development of the state's constitution and examples of early Vermont crafts.

**Vermont State Craft Center in Windsor** – *Main St. Open Jun–Dec Mon–Fri 10am–6pm (Fri 8pm), Sun 11am–4pm. Jan–May Mon–Fri 11am–4pm, Sat 10am–5pm.* ☎*802-674-6729.* Located in Windsor House, a restored 19C Greek Revival hotel, the center features the work of Vermont's finest craftspeople. Pottery, weav-ings, jewelry, leather goods, glassware and food products are among the hundreds of original items displayed in the retail galleries on the first and second floors.

**American Precision Museum** – *196 Main St. Open mid-May–Nov Mon–Fri 9am–5pm, weekends and holidays 10am–4pm. $3.50.* ☎*802-674-5781.* This cav-ernous brick building was constructed as the Robbins and Lawrence Armory (1846), an innovative machine mill where interchangeable-parts manufacturing was first widely used. The museum displays a large collection of precision machines tools and firearms that trace the history of American industrialization techniques from the mid-19C through the mid-20C.

**Windsor-Cornish Covered Bridge** – *South of the Constitution House; after two sets of lights, turn left.* Spanning the Connecticut River between New Hampshire and Vermont, this is the longest covered bridge (460ft) in New England.

## ★★ WOODSTOCK                                                         Pop 3,212

Map of Principal Sights p 2                               Tourist Office ☎802-457-3555

A touch of urban elegance has characterized this pretty village since the 18C, when it was selected as the Windsor County seat. Businessmen, lawyers, doctors and teachers settled here during the next 200 years, building frame, brick, and stone dwellings and shops that reflected the wealth of the community. A lack of indus-trial development in the 19C and the devotion of the town's residents to Woodstock's architectural heritage have ensured the preservation of the gracious 18C and 19C structures bordering the village green, and lining Elm, Pleasant and Central Streets.

### HISTORICAL NOTES

Established in 1761 by settlers from Massachusetts, Woodstock developed quickly after it was selected as the county seat. Mills were built on the outskirts of town, and tradesmen, working in shops surrounding the village green, provided most of the goods needed for daily living. Woodstock was self-sufficient and prosperous. During the heyday of the 19C water cures, the village became a fashionable vaca-tion spot.

In 1934 skiers experimenting with a Model T motor and a piece of cable on a hill near Mt Tom *(outside Woodstock)* developed the nation's first ski tow. Twenty years later, a poma lift, then more modern lifts such as chairs and aerial trams, were adopted by Vermont's burgeoning ski industry. While the ski tow devised 50 years ago near Mt Tom is still remembered for the role it played in the history of skiing in the US, today the most modern equipment is used at **Suicide Six**, a ski area nearby *(ski information p 257)*.

The **Woodstock Inn**, facing the village green, was opened in 1969. The hotel's lodging and conference facilities attract business travelers as well as tourists. F.H. Gillingham & Sons has been the town's general store since 1886 and stocks handmade Vermont products as well as hardware, housewares and specialty foods.

## SIGHTS *2hrs*

To enjoy Woodstock, stroll along **Elm** and **Pleasant Streets**, browse in the emporia and galleries on **Central Street**, and walk across the covered bridge *(in the middle of town)* that spans the Ottauquechee River. The Town Crier bulletin board, located near the corner of Elm and Central Streets, posts notices of auctions, flea markets and other community events.

★ **The Green** – The oval village green is fringed with buildings of different styles: Federal mansions, the Greek Revival **Windsor County Courthouse** and the Romanesque-style **Norman Williams Library**.

★ **Dana House Museum** – *26 Elm St. Visit by guided tour (1hr) only, Jun–Oct Mon–Sat 10am–5pm, Sun 2pm–5pm. $3.50. ☎802-457-1822.* Constructed in 1807 by the merchant Charles Dana, this house is the headquarters of the Woodstock Historical Society. Exhibits include furnishings, clocks, dolls and clothing formerly owned by Woodstock families.

★★ **Billings Farm & Museum** – *River Rd. Follow Elm St, cross the bridge, turn right, then .2mi on River St. Open May–Oct daily 10am–5pm. Nov–Dec weekends only 10am–4pm. $7. ✕ & ☎802-457-2355.* A slide show *(8min)* provides a good introduction to life in rural Vermont in the late 19C. The complex is both an operating modern-day dairy farm and a museum depicting life on a Vermont farm in 1890. The farm was established in 1871 by lawyer/businessman **Frederick Billings**, whose interest in animal husbandry and conservation led him to stock the farm with purebred Jersey cattle. The Billings' herd, a prize-winner over the years, continues to earn blue ribbons to this day.

The 1890 **farmhouse**, restored and appointed with period furniture, features tile-decorated fireplaces and a basement creamery.

Life-size displays in several restored barns illustrate the daily and seasonal activities performed by a 19C Vermont family.

Located in the fields just below the farmhouse, a 19C garden features a variety of vegetables and flowers.

## EXCURSIONS

★ **Plymouth** – *14mi southwest of Woodstock by Rtes 4 & 100A. Description p 234.*

**Quechee Gorge** – *6mi east of Woodstock on Rte 4.* Quechee Gorge, formed over thousands of years by the erosive action of the Ottauquechee River, is spanned by the Route 4 highway bridge. The sheer walls of the gorge rise approximately 165ft from the river below. The gorge is best seen from the bridge on Route 4.

A trail, steep in sections *(round-trip 1.5mi, 45min)*, leads to the bottom of the gorge, a popular swimming area *(in season)*. Hikers can park at the gift shop on the east side of the bridge.

Two miles beyond the gorge, in the appealing village of Quechee, is the popular **glass shop** of designer Simon Pearce. Housed in the town's historic woolen mill on the edge of the river, the retail store allows visitors to watch glassblowers and potters at work *(open year-round daily 10am–5pm. ✕ ☎802-295-2711)*.

**Silver Lake State Park** – *In Barnard, 10mi north of Woodstock by Rte 12. Open mid-May–Labor Day daily 10am–dusk. $1.50. △ ☎802-234-9451. Facility information p 251.* The park, within walking distance of Barnard village, contains a small lakefront beach, picnic area, country store and campsites set in a pine grove.

# Practical Information

# CALENDAR OF EVENTS

Listed below is a selection of New England's most popular annual events; some dates may vary from year to year. For detailed information contact local tourism (☎ numbers listed under the blue-banded entry headings) or state tourism (p 246) offices.

| Date | Event | Location |
|------|-------|----------|

## Spring

| Date | Event | Location |
|------|-------|----------|
| early Apr | **Legends of Freestyle Tournament** | *Newry (ME)* |
| 3rd Mon in Apr | **Boston Marathon** (p 103) | *Boston (MA)* |
| | **Patriots' Day Celebrations** | *Lexington & Concord (MA)* |
| early May | **Dogwood Festival** | *Fairfield (CT)* |
| May–Jun | **Art of the Northeast** (p 60) | *New Canaan (CT)* |
| mid-May | **Dogwood Festival** | *Fairfield (CT)* |
| | **Sheep & Wool Festival** | *New Boston (NH)* |
| mid-May, Jul & Sept | **Brimfield Outdoor Antiques Show** | *Brimfield (MA)* |
| late May | **Lilac Sunday** | *Shelburne (VT)* |
| late May–mid-Jun | **Gaspee Days Festival** | *Cranston & Warwick (RI)* |
| Memorial Day weekend | **Lobsterfest** | *Mystic (CT)* |

## Summer

| Date | Event | Location |
|------|-------|----------|
| 1st Sat in Jun | **Yale-Harvard Regatta** | *New London (CT)* |
| early Jun | **Festival of Historic Houses** | *Providence (RI)* |
| | **Market Square Days Celebration** | *Portsmouth (NH)* |
| mid-Jun–Aug | **Williamstown Theater Festival** (p 177) | *Williamstown (MA)* |
| mid–late Jun | **American CraftFair** (p 171) | *West Springfield (MA)* |
| late Jun | **St Peter's Fiesta** (p 135) | *Gloucester (MA)* |
| | **Block Island Race Week** | *Block Island (RI)* |
| | **Rose Arts Festival** (p 60) | *Norwich (CT)* |
| | **Portsmouth Jazz Festival** | *Portsmouth (NH)* |
| late Jun–late Aug | **Berkshire Theater Festival** | *Stockbridge (MA)* |
| last weekend in Jun | **Windjammer Days** (p 69) | *Boothbay Harbor (ME)* |
| Jul–late Aug | **Tanglewood Music Festival** (p 93) | *Lenox (MA)* |
| Jul–Sept | **Royal Lipizzan Stallions** (p 227) | *North Hero (VT)* |
| early Jul | **Riverfest** | *Hartford (CT)* |
| | **Harborfest** | *Boston (MA)* |
| | **Oyster Festival** | *Damariscotta (ME)* |
| early to mid-Jul | **International Tennis Hall of Fame** (p 213) | *Newport (RI)* |
| | **Grass Court Championships** | |
| early Jul–late Aug | **Jacob's Pillow Dance Festival** (p 93) | *Becket (MA)* |
| Jul 4 | **Bristol Civic, Military & Fireman's Parade** | *Bristol (RI)* |
| 1st weekend after Jul 4th | **Great Schooner Days** | *Rockland (ME)* |
| 2nd weekend in Jul | **Vermont Quilt Festival** | *Northfield (VT)* |
| mid-Jul | **Open House Tour** | *Litchfield (CT)* |
| | **Newport Music Festival** (p 206) | *Newport (RI)* |
| late Jul | **Friendship Sloop Days** | *Boothbay Harbor (ME)* |
| | **Blessing of the Fleet** | *Galilee (RI)* |
| | **Black Ships Festival** | *Newport (RI)* |
| each Fri in Aug | **Pilgrim Progress Procession** (p 162) | *Plymouth (MA)* |
| early Aug | **Lobster Festival** (p 87) | *Rockland (ME)* |
| | **Craftsmen's Fair** (p 188) | *Newbury (NH)* |
| | **Southern Vermont Craft Fair** | *Manchester (VT)* |
| 2nd weekend in Aug | **JVC Jazz Festival** (p 206) | *Newport (RI)* |
| mid-Aug | **Mystic Outdoor Art Festival** | *Mystic (CT)* |
| | **Retired Skippers' Race** (p 72) | *Castine (ME)* |

244

| Date | Event | Location |
|------|-------|----------|

## Fall

| Date | Event | Location |
|------|-------|----------|
| Sept–early Oct | **South Mountain Concert Festival** *(p 93)* | *Pittsfield (MA)* |
| early Sept | **Tuna Tournament** *(p 205)* | *Galilee & Narragansett (RI)* |
| | **Vermont State Fair** | *Rutland (VT)* |
| | **Woodstock Fair** | *South Woodstock (CT)* |
| mid-Sept | **Eastern States Exposition** *(p 171)* | *West Springfield (MA)* |
| mid-Sept–mid-Oct | **Stratton Arts Festival** *(p 230)* | *Stratton (VT)* |
| late Sept | **Banjo Contest** | *Craftsbury Common (VT)* |
| | **Old Time Fiddlers Contest** | *Barre (VT)* |
| late Sept–early Oct | **Northeast Kingdom Fall Foliage Festival** *(p 232)* | *Northeast Kingdom (VT)* |
| last weekend in Sept | **Old Fashioned Harvest Market** | *Underhill (VT)* |
| Halloween week | **Haunted Happenings** *(p 170)* | *Salem (MA)* |
| Thanksgiving Day | **Pilgrim Progress Procession** *(p 162)* | *Plymouth (MA)* |

## Winter

| Date | Event | Location |
|------|-------|----------|
| Dec 24 | **Torchlight Parade** | *Old Saybrook (CT)* |
| mid-Jan | **Annual Winter Carnival** | *Stowe (VT)* |
| late Jan–Feb | **Chinese New Year Parade** *(p 125)* | *Boston (MA)* |
| Feb | **Dartmouth Winter Carnival** *(p 184)* | *Hanover (NH)* |
| early–mid-Feb | **World Championship Sled Dog Derby** | *Laconia (NH)* |
| mid-Feb–mid-Mar | **Vermont Mozart Festival** *(p 226)* | *Burlington (VT)* |
| early Mar | **New England Spring Flower Show** | *Boston (MA)* |

Vermont State Fair, Rutland

Alan L. Graham (f/STOP PICTURES)

The following symbols are used throughout this section:

🆕 New England  ⓒ Connecticut  ⓜ Maine  ⓜ Massachusetts
ⓡ Rhode Island  ⓝ New Hampshire  ⓥ Vermont.

Consult the pages shown for detailed practical information about:

**Block Island** *(p 203)*, **Boston** *(pp 102-103)*, **Cape Cod** *(p 138)*, **Martha's Vineyard** *(p 153)*, **Monhegan Island** *(p 77)*, **Mount Desert Island** *(p 80)*, **Nantucket Island** *(p 157)*, **Northern Maine** *(p 78)*, **Portland** *(p 84)*, **White Mountains** *(p 193)*.

# PLANNING YOUR TRIP

State tourism offices provide information and brochures on points of interest, seasonal events and accommodations, as well as road and city maps. In this guide local tourism office telephone numbers are listed (if available) under the blue-banded entry headings. Information centers are indicated on maps by the symbol 🖸.

| State | Tourism Offices | ☎ |
|---|---|---|
| ⓒ | **Department of Economic Development**<br>865 Brook St<br>Rocky Hill CT 06067 | (worldwide) 800-282-6863 |
| ⓒ | **Maine Publicity Bureau**<br>PO Box 2300<br>Hallowell ME 04347 | 207-623-0363<br>800-533-9595 |
| ⓜ | **Office of Travel & Tourism**<br>100 Cambridge St<br>Boston MA 02202 | 617-727-3201<br>(North America only) 800-447-6277 |
| ⓝ | **Office of Travel & Tourism Development**<br>PO Box 1856<br>Concord NH 03302-1856 | 603-271-2666<br>800-386-4664 |
| ⓡ | **State Tourism Division**<br>7 Jackson Walkway<br>Providence RI 02903 | 401-277-2601<br>(North America only) 800-556-2484 |
| ⓥ | **Department of Travel & Tourism**<br>134 State St<br>Montpelier VT 05602 | 802-828-3236 |

**Outside the US** – Foreign visitors can request additional tourist information from the nearest US embassy or consulate in their country of residence.

| US Embassies (selected) | | ☎ |
|---|---|---|
| **Australia** | Moonah Place, Canberra ACT 2600 | 6-270-5000 |
| **Canada** | 100 Wellington St, Ottawa ON K1P ST1 | 613-238-4470 |
| **Germany** | 5300 Bonn 2, Deichmanns Aue | 228-3391 |
| **United Kingdom** | 24/31 Grosvenor Square, London,<br>W. 1A 1AE; PSC 801 Box 40,<br>FPO AE 09498-4040 | 499-9000 |

**Foreign Visitors** – Canadian citizens are not required to present a passport or visa to enter the US, although identification and proof of citizenship may be requested at any time (the best proof of citizenship is a passport, but a Canadian birth certificate and photo ID are usually acceptable). Naturalized Canadian citizens should carry their citizenship papers. Citizens of countries participating in the Visa Waiver Pilot Program (VWPP) are not required to obtain a visa to enter the US for visits of less than 90 days. For a list of countries participating in the VWPP, contact the US consulate in your country of residence. Citizens of non-participating countries must have a visitor's visa. Upon entry, non-resident foreign visitors must present a valid passport and round-trip transportation ticket. Inoculations are generally not required (contingent upon country of residence and countries recently visited). Check with the US embassy or consulate before departing. Many countries have consular offices in Boston.

**Health Insurance** – Before departing, visitors from abroad should check with their insurance company to determine if their medical insurance covers doctor's visits, medication and hospitalization in the US. Prescription drugs should be properly identified, and accompanied by a copy of the prescription.

**US Customs** – All articles brought into the US must be declared at the time of entry. For information about US Customs, contact the US embassy or consulate before departing. It is also recommended that visitors contact the customs service in their country of residence before departing to determine re-entry regulations.

**Currency Exchange** – Most main offices of national banks offer currency exchange and charge a small fee for this service; contact main or branch offices for exchange information and locations. Private exchange companies generally charge higher fees. Exchange facilities tend to be limited in rural areas; carrying US currency or traveler's checks is recommended.

**Disabled Travelers** – Recent Federal law requires that existing businesses (including hotels and restaurants) increase accessibility and provide specially designed accommodations for the disabled. It also requires that wheelchair access, devices for the hearing impaired, and designated parking spaces be available at newly constructed hotels and restaurants.

## WHEN TO GO

A resort area for more than a century, New England continues to attract vacationers to its mountains and shores in every season. **Summer** months are generally mild. Daytime temperatures along the coast and in the north average 70-80°F/21-27°C; in the central area they rarely climb above 90°F/32°C, July being the warmest month. Summer nights tend to be cool and comfortable.

| Average Daily Temperatures | | |
|---|---|---|
| | January | July |
| Connecticut | 27°F (-2.5°C) | 73°F (23°C) |
| Maine | 16°F (-9°C) | 67°F (19°C) |
| Massachusetts | 26°F (-3°C) | 70°F (21°C) |
| New Hampshire | 13°F (-10°C) | 60°F (15°C) |
| Rhode Island | 30°F (-1°C) | 71°F (21.5°C) |
| Vermont | 16°F (-9°C) | 70°F (21°C) |

In the north, the long summer days begin to fade into the clear, crisp days of autumn by late August. **Indian summer** (a period of warm, mild weather in late autumn or early winter) is considered the glory of New England and often accompanies the spectacle of blazing **autumn** color. Foliage reports (p 253) track the procession of color as it advances from the northern regions southward. In autumn the countryside teems with activity: country fairs (p 253), auctions (p 253) and flea markets.

Skiers and other snow enthusiasts await the long New England **winter**, typically lasting from late November through April. Daytime temperatures in the south and along the coast average 20°-30°F (-7° to -1°C). In the north and at higher elevations, temperatures may stay below 0°F/-18° for 60 days annually. Snowfall is heavier in the higher elevations, with an annual average of 60in/154cm, the greatest snowfall occurring in January. There are more than 100 ski areas (pp 256-257) in the region, and opportunities abound for ice-skating and snowmobiling (p 255) as well. New England's infamous **"Northeaster"** storms, typically lasting two to three days, can dump 10 or more inches (25cm) of snow in a single day.

The **spring** thaw, a mixture of warm days and cold nights, brings forth budding flowers, often peeking through an unexpected layer of snow, and is the perfect weather for the cultivation of maple syrup (p 253).

Most attractions are open from Memorial Day to mid-October only (except in large cities), although many sights extend their season from mid-April through late October.

Sharon Cummings/Dembinsky Photo Assoc.

Metcalf Pond, Vermont

# GETTING THERE & GETTING AROUND

**By Air** – Most flights to New England stop at La Guardia or JFK International Airports in New York, or Logan International Airport in Boston before making connecting flights to the principal New England airports: Bradley International (**Hartford** CT), Bangor International (**Bangor** ME), Portland International (**Portland** ME), Manchester Airport (**Manchester** NH) and T. F. Green State Airport (**Providence** RI).

The **Travelers Aid Society**, located in Terminal E outside Customs at Logan Airport, provides assistance to travelers in crisis situations. They also offer language/translation services (minimum one week notice requested) ☎617-542-7286.

**By Train** – With access to over 44 communities in New England, the Amtrak rail network offers a relaxing alternative for the traveler with time to spare. Advance reservations are recommended to ensure reduced fares and availability of desired accommodations. First class, coach and sleeping accommodations are available; fares are competitive with the airlines. The *New England Express* travels from New York City to Boston in just over five hours. Travelers from Canada should ask their local travel agents about Amtrak/Via Rail connections. **All-Aboard Pass** allows travel over any distance within 45 days (limited to three stops). **USARailPass** (not available to US or Canadian citizens or legal residents) offers unlimited travel within Amtrak-designated regions at discounted rates; 15- and 30-day passes available. Schedule and route information: ☎ 800-872-7245 (North America only; other travelers should contact their local travel agent).

**By Bus** – Greyhound, the largest bus company in the US, offers access to most communities in New England at a leisurely pace. Overall, fares are lower than other forms of public transportation. **Ameripass** allows unlimited travel for 7, 14 or 21 days. Some travelers may find long-distance bus travel uncomfortable due to the lack of sleeping accommodations. Advance reservations suggested. Schedule and route information: ☎ 800-231-2222 (worldwide).

**By Car** – New England has an extensive system of well-maintained major roads. In remote areas, minor roads tend to be unmarked and may be confusing. It is advisable to plan itineraries along numbered state routes and interstates. Exercise caution when driving in mountainous areas or on back roads. Roads tend to be narrow, steep and twisting; many are unpaved. Observe cautionary road signs and posted speed limits.

Foreign visitors are not required to obtain an International Driver's License; a valid license issued by the country of residence is sufficient. Drivers must carry vehicle registration and/or rental contract; proof of automobile insurance may also be required by law.

**Gasoline** is sold by the gallon (1 US gal = 3.8l). Gas stations are usually found in clusters on the edge of a city, where two or more highways intersect. Self-service gas stations do not offer car repair, although many sell standard maintenance items.

**Rental Cars** – Most major rental car agencies have offices at airports and in major cities in New England. Rental agencies offering worldwide reservation services for New England include:

| | | | |
|---|---|---|---|
| Avis | 800-331-1212 | Budget | 800-527-0700 |
| Dollar | 800-421-6868 | Hertz | 800-654-3131 |
| National | 800-227-7368 | | |

**Road Regulations** – The maximum speed limit on major freeways is 65mph (105km/h) in rural areas and 55mph (90km/h) in and around cities (in Connecticut and Rhode Island maximum speed limits are 55mph). Speed limits range from 30-40mph (45-65km/h) within cities, and average 20-30mph (30-45km/h) in residential areas. Use of seat belts is mandatory for all persons in the car (except New Hampshire, only for passengers under 12 and Maine, only for passengers under 19).

Child safety seats are required in Vermont for children under 6 years, Connecticut and Massachusetts for children under 5 years, Maine, Rhode Island and New Hampshire for children under 4 years (seats available from most rental car agencies). School bus law in effect for the six-state area requires motorists to bring vehicles to a full stop when warning signals on a school bus are activated. Unless otherwise posted, it is permissible to turn right at a red traffic light after coming to a complete stop. Parking spaces identified with ♿ are reserved only for handicapped persons. Anyone parking in these spaces without proper identification is subject to ticketing.

**Turnpikes** – Principal toll roads in New England are: I-95 connecting with I-495 from York to Augusta, Maine; I-95 from the Massachusetts border to Portsmouth, New Hampshire; I-90 (Massachusetts Turnpike) from the New York/Massachusetts state border to Boston; and I-93 from Nashua to Concord, New Hampshire.

**In Case of Accident** – If you are involved in an accident resulting in personal or property damage, you must notify the local police, and remain at the scene until dismissed. If blocking traffic, vehicles should be moved if possible.

*Unless otherwise indicated, telephone numbers listed in this guide that start with "800" are toll free and accessible only in the US.*

# ACCOMMODATIONS

Luxury **hotels** are generally found in major cities, **motels** in clusters on the edge of town, or where two or more highways intersect. In rural areas motels are found on roads frequently traveled by tourists. **Bed & breakfasts** (B&Bs) can be found in residential areas of cities and villages.

Local tourist offices provide detailed accommodation information *(telephone numbers listed under blue-banded titles in the main section of this guide)*. In season and during weekends, advance reservations are recommended. Always advise reservations clerk of late arrival; rooms, even though reserved, might not always be held after 6pm otherwise. Off-season and weekday rates are usually lower. Many New England facilities offer either: the American Plan, three meals included; or the Modified American Plan (MAP), breakfast and dinner included.

**Hotels/Motels** – Major hotel chains with locations throughout New England include (toll-free numbers valid worldwide):

| | | | |
|---|---|---|---|
| Best Western | 800-528-1234 | Howard Johnson | 800-446-4656 |
| Comfort Inn | 800-228-5150 | Marriott | 800-228-9290 |
| Days Inn | 800-325-2525 | Radisson | 800-333-3333 |
| Hampton Inn | 800-426-7866 | Ramada Inn | 800-272-6232 |
| Holiday Inn | 800-465-4329 | Westin Hotels | 800-228-3000 |

Accommodations range from luxury hotels to budget motels. Rates vary with season and location; rates tend to be higher in cities and in coastal and vacation areas. Many hotels and motels offer packages (including meals, passes to local sights and access to facility-sponsored events) and weekend specials. Amenities include television, restaurant, swimming pool, and smoking/non-smoking rooms. The more elegant hotels also offer in-room dining and valet service. **Reservations Service:** International Reservations Services Limited ☎800-365-6962 or 203-792-6772.

**Inns and Bed & Breakfasts** – Many B&Bs are privately owned and located in historic homes. Some inns have been in operation since colonial times. Breakfast is usually included; private baths are not always available. Smoking indoors may not be allowed. Some establishments may charge 10-15% gratuity (inquire when reserving). Inns often include a restaurant that serves three meals a day. The price of breakfast may not be included in the lodging fee, as it is with B&Bs. Many inns and B&Bs participate in one-day and weekend Inn-to-Inn tours for bikers, hikers and cross-country skiers.

**Referral services** – ⓘ: Bed & Breakfast Inns of New England Reservation Service, 329 Lake Dr, Guilford CT 06437 ☎800-582-0853, 203-457-0042. ⓘ Covered Bridge B&B Reservation Service, 69 Maple Ave, PO Box 447, Norfolk CT 06058 ☎203-542-5944. ⓘ Maine Innkeepers Association Lodging & Food Guide, 305 Commercial St, Portland ME 04101 ☎207-773-7670. ⓘ Bed & Breakfast Rhode Island, PO Box 3291, Newport RI 02840 ☎800-828-0000 or 401-849-1298. ⓘ Vermont Bed & Breakfast, Main St, East Fairfield VT 05048 ☎802-827-3827.

Longfellow's Wayside Inn, Sudbury, Massachusetts

Dianne Dietrich Leis

**Camping** – *State park list p 251.* Campsites are located in national and state parks, national forests, and in private campgrounds. Amenities range from full RV hookups to rustic backcountry sites. Most camping areas provide recreational and sporting amenities. Advance reservations are recommended from mid-May through mid-October. **Wilderness camping** is available on most public lands. Topographic maps of most wilderness areas are available. Contact desired location or state tourism offices *(p 246)* for further information.

**Hostels** – A simple, economical alternative, hostels average $12/night; amenities include community living room, showers, laundry facilities, full service kitchen and dining room, and dormitory-style rooms (blankets and pillows are provided, but guests are required to bring their own linens). Membership cards are recommended. **American Youth Hostels**, 733 15th St, NW, #840, Washington DC 20005 ☎202-783-6161.

**Farm Vacations** – Host farms allow paying visitors the opportunity to participate in the daily activities of a working farm. Rates vary from $28-$60/night. For more information contact: ⓘ Dept of Agriculture, 165 Capitol Ave, Rm 263, Hartford CT 06106 ☎203-566-4845, ⓘ Maine Farm Vacation B&B Association, RR1, Box 1145, Hallowell ME 04347 ☎207-622-2708 ⓘ *Vermont Farm Vacations*, from Dept of Agriculture, 116 State St, Montpelier VT 05620-2901 ☎802-828-2416.

# BASIC INFORMATION

**Business Hours** – Mon-Fri 9 or 10am–5pm; some retail shops may stay open unti 9pm on Thursday. Shopping centers: Mon–Sat 9:30am–8 or 9pm, Sun 11am–6pm. Banking hours: Mon–Thur 10am–3 or 4pm, Fri 10am–5pm; some close later on Friday. Banks in larger cities may open on Saturday morning.

**Electricity** – Voltage in the US is 120 volts AC, 60 HZ. Foreign-made appliances may need AC adapters and North American flat-blade plugs.

**Liquor Laws** – The legal age for purchase and consumption of alcoholic beverages is 21 throughout New England; proof of age may be required. Liquor stores and many grocery and drug stores sell liquor. Almost all grocery stores sell beer and wine. Alcoholic beverages may be sold during the following hours: ⬡ Mon–Sat 8am–8pm; ⬡ Mon–Sat 6–1am, Sun noon–1am; ⬡ locally regulated, times vary; ⬡ daily 6am–11:45pm; ⬡ Jun–Oct Mon–Sat 7am–11pm (rest of the year 10pm) ⬡ Mon–Sat 7am–7pm, Sun 10am–4pm (beer and wine may be sold any time).

**Mail** – First class rates within the US: letter $.32 (1oz), post card $.20. Overseas: letter $.50 (1/2oz), postcard $.40. Inquire at post offices for further information.

**Major Holidays** – Most banks and government offices in the New England states are closed on the following legal holidays *(many retail stores and restaurants remain open on days shown with \*)*:

| Holiday | States Observing | Date |
| --- | --- | --- |
| New Year's Day | ⬡ | January 1 |
| Martin Luther King's Birthday* | ⬡ ⬡ ⬡ ⬡ ⬡ | 3rd Monday in January |
| Lincoln's Birthday* | ⬡ ⬡ | 2nd Monday in February |
| George Washington's Birthday (Presidents' Day)* | ⬡ | 3rd Monday in February |
| Town Meeting Day | ⬡ | 1st Tuesday in March |
| Patriots' Day | ⬡ ⬡ | Monday nearest April 19 |
| Fast Day | ⬡ | Last Monday in April |
| Memorial Day | ⬡ | Last Monday in May or May 30 |
| Independence Day | ⬡ | July 4 |
| Victory Day | ⬡ | 2nd Monday in August |
| Bennington Battle Day | ⬡ | August 16 |
| Labor Day | ⬡ | 1st Monday in September |
| Columbus Day* | ⬡ | 2nd Monday in October |
| Election Day | ⬡ | 2nd Tuesday in November |
| Veterans Day* | ⬡ | November 10 or 11 |
| Thanksgiving Day | ⬡ | 4th Thursday in November |
| Christmas Day | ⬡ | December 25 |

**Measurement** – New England states follow the US Customary system of measurement. Weather temperatures are given in Fahrenheit (F°), liquids are sold by the pint, quart or gallon, and grocery items are measured in ounces or pounds. All distances and speed limits are posted in miles. Some useful examples of metric equivalents are:

| | | |
| --- | --- | --- |
| 1 mile (mi) = 1.6 kilometers | 1 foot (ft) = 30.5 centimeters | 1 pound (lb) =.4 kilograms |
| 1 inch (in) = 2.5 centimeters | 1 gallon (gal) = 3.8 liters | 1 ounce (oz) = 31.1 grams |

**Smoking Regulations** – Many New England cities have ordinances that prohibit smoking in public places or confine smoking to designated areas.

## State Sales Tax

| State | General Tax | Room Tax | Restaurant Tax | Exemptions |
| --- | --- | --- | --- | --- |
| ⬡ | 6% | 12% | 6% | Clothing purchases under $50, grocery items |
| ⬡ | 6% | 7% | 7% | Grocery items |
| ⬡ | 5% | 5.7-9.7% | 5% | Clothing purchases under $175, grocery items |
| ⬡ | none | 8% | 8% | None |
| ⬡ | 7% | 12% | 7% | Clothing & grocery items |
| ⬡ | 5% | 8% | 8% | Grocery items |

**Telephone** – **Emergencies** (police, fire, ambulance): dial 911. Instructions for using public telephones are listed on or near the phone. The cost of a local call is $.25 (Boston $.10). Coins should be inserted before dialing (any combination of nickels, dimes or quarters is accepted). Some public telephones accept credit cards. All public phones will accept long-distance calling cards. Most hotels add a surcharge for local and long-distance calls. For further information dial "0" for operator assistance.

**Time Zone** – New England is on Eastern Standard Time (EST). Daylight Savings Time (clocks advanced 1hr) is in effect for most of the US from the first Sunday in April until the last Sunday in October.

**Tipping** – It is customary in restaurants to tip the server 15% of the bill. At hotels, $1 per suitcase should be given to the porter. Taxi drivers are usually tipped 15% of the fare.

# SPORTS & RECREATION

| Selected State Parks | ☎ | △ | ⅄ | ! | 🏊 | 🎣 |
|---|---|---|---|---|---|---|
| **Connecticut** | area code: 203 | | | | | |
| Office of State Parks & Recreation, 165 Capital Ave, Hartford CT 06106 | 566-2304 | | | | | |
| Fort Shantok SP (p 61) | 848-9876 | | • | • | | • |
| Gillette Castle SP (p 41) | 526-2336 | | • | • | | |
| Housatonic Meadows SP (p 50) | 927-3238 | • | • | • | | • |
| Kent Falls SP (p 50) | 927-3238 | | • | • | | |
| Macedonia Brook SP (p 49) | 927-3238 | • | • | • | | • |
| Sleeping Giant SP (p 57) | 566-2305 | • | • | • | | |
| Talcott Mountain SP (p 48) | 677-0662 | | • | • | | |
| **Maine** | area code: 207 | | | | | |
| Bureau of Parks & Recreation, Station 22, Augusta ME 04333 | 287-3821 | | | | | |
| Baxter SP (p 66) | 723-5140 | • | • | • | • | • |
| Camden Hills SP (p 71) | 236-3109 | • | • | • | | |
| Cobscook Bay SP (p 73) | 726-4412 | • | • | | | • |
| Crescent Beach SP (p 87) | 767-3625 | | • | | • | • |
| Grafton Notch SP (p 67) | 824-2912 | | • | • | | |
| Mt Blue SP (p 87) | 585-2347 | • | • | • | • | • |
| Popham Beach SP (p 66) | 389-1335 | | • | | • | • |
| Quoddy Head SP (p 73) | 773-0911 | | • | • | | |
| Rangeley Lake SP (p 87) | 864-3858 | • | • | • | • | • |
| Sebago Lake SP (p 87) | 693-6615 | • | • | • | • | • |
| Two Lights SP (p 87) | 799-5871 | | • | | | |
| Wolfe's Neck Woods SP (p 75) | 865-4465 | | • | • | | |
| **Massachusetts** | | | | | | |
| Division of Forests & Parks, 100 Cambridge St, 19th Floor, Boston MA 02202 | 617-727-318 | | | | | |
| Halibut Point SP (p 137) | 508-546-2997 | | • | • | | • |
| Natural Bridge SP (p 155) | 413-663-6312 | | • | • | | |
| Nickerson SP (p 139) | 508-896-3491 | • | • | • | • | • |
| Skinner SP (p 161) | 413-586-0350 | | • | • | | |
| Western Gateway Heritage SP (p 155) | 413-663-8059 | | • | | | |
| **New Hampshire** | area code: 603 | | | | | |
| Division of Parks & Recreation, PO Box 1856, Concord NH 03301 | 271-3556 | | | | | |
| Lake Francis SP (p 184) | 538-6965 | • | • | | | |
| Monadnock SP (p 187) | 532-8862 | • | • | • | | |
| Mt Sunapee SP (p 188) | 736-2356 | | • | • | • | |
| Rhododendron SP (p 186) | | | • | • | | |
| Rye Harbor SP (p 188) | 436-1552 | | • | | | • |
| Wallis Sands SP (p 188) | 436-1552 | | | | • | |
| Wellington SP (p 189) | | | • | | • | • |
| White Lake SP (p 199) | 323-7350 | • | • | • | • | • |
| **Rhode Island** | area code: 401 | | | | | |
| Department of Parks & Recreation, 2321 Hartford Ave, Johnston RI 02919 | 277-2632 | | | | | |
| Brenton Point SP (p 207) | 847-2400 | | • | | | • |
| Colt SP (p 204) | 253-7482 | | • | • | | • |
| Fort Adam's SP (p 213) | 847-2400 | | • | | | • |
| **Vermont** | area code: 802 | | | | | |
| Department of Parks & Recreation, 103 S. Main St, Waterbury VT 05671-0301 | 241-3660 | | | | | |
| Branbury SP (p 231) | 247-5925 | • | • | • | • | |
| Button Bay SP (p 231) | 475-2377 | • | • | • | • | |
| Lake St Catherine SP (p 235) | 287-9158 | • | • | • | • | |
| Silver Lake SP (p 241) | 234-9451 | • | • | • | • | |
| Woodford SP (p 224) | 241-3655 | • | • | • | • | |

△ camping; ⅄ picnic area; ! hiking; 🏊 swimming; 🎣 fishing.

# Sports

**Hiking/Biking** – Many trail systems lace the region. State and local parks provide opportunities for hiking and biking. The **Long Trail** (265mi/427km) in Vermont runs north to south along the Green Mountains from the Canadian to Massachusetts borders; the **Appalachian Trail** extends in New England from Mt Katahdin in Maine to the Connecticut/New York border. **Acadia National Park** *(p 80)* offers 35,000 acres/14,000ha of moderately easy hiking trails. The 202,000 acre/82,000ha wilderness trails of **Baxter State Park** *(p 66)* and 772,000 acre/313,000ha **White Mountain National Forest** *(p 193)* are more challenging. In addition, 455mi/734km of former railroad tracks throughout New England have been converted into paved and dirt paths for bikers and pedestrians (contact **Rails-to-Trails Conservancy**, 1400 16th St NW, Suite 300, Washington DC 20036 ☎ 202-797-5400 for maps and information). **Llama tours** provide a novel way to enjoy the terrain while allowing these gentle creatures to carry the meals and gear: Northeast Kingdom Llama Expeditions, RR 2 Box 71-A, Groton VT 05046 ☎ 802-584-3198; Northern Vermont Llama Co, Rd 1, Box 544, Waterville VT 05492; Telemark Inn's Llama Treks, RFD 2, Box 800, Bethel ME 04217 ☎ 207-836-2703.

When hiking in the backcountry stay on marked trails. Taking shortcuts is dangerous and causes erosion. If hiking alone, notify someone of your destination and proposed return time.

Bicycles are prohibited on most unpaved trails. Riders should stay on paved paths and roads (on public roads, stay to the right and ride in single file). Bicyclists are encouraged to wear helmets and other protective gear.

Both hikers and bicyclists are cautioned to be well equipped (including detailed maps of the areas to be explored), and alert to weather conditions, particularly in higher elevations. For more information on trails, and on local mountain biking regulations contact local tourism offices.

**Tours & Trail Information** – ⊕ New England Hiking Holidays, PO Box 1648, North Conway NH 03860, ☎ 603-356-9696. Cycle America PO Box 485-O, Cannon Falls MN 55009 ☎ 800-245-3263 or 507-263-2665. Appalachian Mountain Club, Five Joy St, Boston MA 02108 ☎ 617-523-0636. Appalachian Trail Conference, PO Box 807, Harpers Ferry, WV 25425-0807 ☎ 304-535-6331. ⊕ Back Country Excursions, RFD 2, Box 365, Lemerick ME 04048 ☎ 207-625-8189. ⊕ Bike Vermont Inc, Box 207 TL, Woodstock VT 05091 ☎ 800-257-2226 or 802-457-3553. Vermont Bicycle Touring, PO Box 711, Bristol VT 05443 ☎ 802-453-4811. Vermont Department of Forests, Parks & Recreation, Waterbury VT 05671-0601 ☎ 802-241-3655. Green Mountain National Forest, Supervisor, PO Box 519, Rutland VT 05702 ☎ 802-747-6700. The Green Mountain Club, RR 1, Box 650, Waterbury Center VT 05677 ☎ 802-244-7037.

**Hunting & Fishing** – With an abundance of game and fish (including deer, moose, trout, and deep sea fishing), New England is a sportsmen's paradise. Licenses are required to hunt and fish in all six states. One-day non-resident fishing licenses are available in fishing supply stores (some offer rental equipment). Non-resident hunting licenses tend to be considerably more expensive than resident licenses. Many fish are in season year-round, whereas most game can only be hunted seasonally. When transporting a rifle or shotgun it must be unloaded and in a secure case (no permit required). Contact the following agencies for additional information (including regulations on transporting game out of the state(s)): ⊕ Dept of Environmental Protection, Wildlife Division, 79 Elm St, Hartford CT 06106 ☎ 203-566-4683. ⊕ Department of Inland Fisheries and Wildlife, 284 State St, August ME 04333 ☎ 207-287-2871. *Maine Guide to Hunting and Fishing*, published by the Maine Publicity Bureau *(p 75)*. ⊕ Division of Fisheries and Wildlife, Field Headquarters, Westboro MA 01581 ☎ 508-792-7270 ⊕ Fish & Game Dept, 2 Hazen Dr, Concord NH 03301 ☎ 603-271-3421. ⊕ Division of Fish & Wildlife, Government Center, Tower Hill Rd, Wakefield RI 02879 ☎ 401-789-3094. ⊕ Department of Fish and Wildlife, 103 South Main St, Waterbury VT 05671-0501 ☎ 802-241-3700.

**Ocean Swimming** – Beaches along the coast of New England are generally clean and sandy; several are rocky, the beaches a mixture of sand with pebbles (walking barefoot may be uncomfortable). Summer water temperatures vary: Connecticut and Rhode Island waters range from 65°-75°F/18°-24°C; southern Massachusetts (including Cape Cod) water temperatures average 65°-75°F/18°-24°C; northern Massachusetts, New Hampshire and Maine beaches average a brisk 50°-65°F/10°-18°C. Excellent surfing can be found along Rhode Island, Massachusetts and Maine coastlines. Swimmers should be aware of the occasional riptide or undertow (strong underlying currents that pull seaward away from shore). Many New England communities employ lifeguards seasonally. Care should be taken when swimming at an unguarded beach. Children should be supervised at all times.

*To enjoy New England's glorious fall colors, consult the driving itineraries on pp 10-13 for selected foliage tours.*

# Recreation

**Antiquing** – Displayed in elegant Boston shops or simple roadside stands along rural roadways, New England antiques will delight both the seasoned and novice collector in variety and quality. Auctions, typically listed in Thursday and weekend editions of local newspapers, are a bargain hunter's dream.

The following organizations provide dealer listings: ⓐ ⓑ ⓒ Vermont Antiques Dealers' Association Directory, c/o James Harley, Yellow House Antiques, RR1, Box 155, Reading VT 05062 (include self-addressed stamped envelope). ⓓ ⓔ *Antique Hunter's Guide to Route 7*, A&L Travel Guides, Box 6, Ripton VT 05766. ⓕ Maine Antique Dealers' Association, PO Box 253, Newcastle ME 04553. ⓖ New Hampshire Antiques Dealers Association RFD 1, Box 305 C, Tilton NH 03276 ☎ 603-286-7506.

**Fall Foliage Tours** – *Maps pp 10-13.* New England's grand foliage season traditionally begins in early September along the Canadian border and higher elevations, and moves progressively southward until the end of October. Advance reservations (2-3 months) are recommended for accommodations. Lovely views can be seen on most rural routes. Many tour companies offer weekend packages that include accommodations and guided tours.

**Foliage Hotlines** – Telephone the numbers below for up-to-date fall color information (Sept–Oct):

ⓐ 203-566-5348    ⓒ 800-533-9595    ⓔ 800-447-6277

ⓑ 800-556-2484    ⓓ 800-258-3608    ⓕ 802-828-3239

**Farmers Markets** – During the New England harvest (mid-to-late June through early October), many farmers sell fresh-grown produce at modest prices at roadside stands. Visitors can also pick their own fruits and vegetables (for a small fee) at farms open to the public. Contact the following agencies for a list of roadside stands and 'pick your own' farms: ⓐ Dept of Agricultural, Marketing Division, 165 Capital Ave, Hartford CT 06106 ☎ 203-566-4845. ⓑ Dept of Agricultural, PO Box 2042, Concord NH 03302-2042 ☎ 603-271-3788. ⓒ Dept of Agricultural, 116 State St, Drawer 20, Montpelier VT 05620-2901 ☎ 802-828-2416.

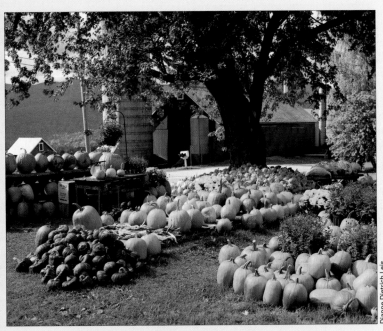

A Vermont farm

**Maple syrup** is harvested in the spring. Farmers collect sap from maple trees in groves commonly called 'sugar bushes' and boil down the watery substance into syrup. Visitors are welcome at a number of sugarhouses (to obtain list, contact the Vermont Dept of Agriculture, 116 State St, Montpelier VT 05620-2901 ☎ 802-828-2416, or the Greater Springfield Convention & Visitors Bureau, 34 Boland Way, Springfield MA 01103 ☎ 800-723-1548 or 413-787-1548). **Country Fairs** offer a lively opportunity to view (and purchase) prize livestock, produce and local crafts.

**Historic Tours** – The following organizations offer their members free admission to their historic properties in New England: ⊕ ⊕ ⊕ ⊕ ⊕ Society for the Preservation of New England Antiquities 141 Cambridge St, Boston MA 02114 ☎ 617-227-3956, yearly dues $25; ⊕ The Antiquarian and Landmarks Society 394 Main St, Hartford CT 06103-9857 ☎ 203-247-8996, yearly dues $25; National Trust for Historic Preservation (sights located nationwide) 1785 Massachusetts Ave, NW Washington DC 20036 ☎ 202-673-4166, yearly dues $20.

**Whale Watching** – Because of the abundance of plankton, whales can be seen in large numbers on their migration route from the Caribbean to Greenland and Newfoundland from early spring to mid-October, primarily along the Stelwegon Bank (27mi east of Boston) in the Gulf of Maine.

### Selected Cruise Companies

| Company | Location | ☎ | Season |
|---|---|---|---|
| ⊕ **Massachusetts** | | | |
| Boston Harbor Cruises | Boston | 617-227-4321 | May–mid-Oct |
| Boston Harbor Whale Watch | Boston | 617-345-9866 | mid-Jun–Labor Day |
| New England Aquarium | Boston | 617-973-5277 | Apr–mid-Oct |
| Cape Ann Whale Watch | Gloucester | 508-283-5110 | mid-Apr–mid-Oct |
| Captain Bill's Whale Watch | Gloucester | 508-283-6995 | May–Oct |
| Seven Seas Whale Watching | Gloucester | 508-283-1776 | May–mid-Oct |
| Yankee Whale Watch | Gloucester | 508-283-0313 | Apr–Oct |
| Hyannis Whale Watcher Cruises | Hyannis | 508-362-6088 | Apr–Oct |
| Captain John Boats | Plymouth | 508-746-2643 | Apr–Oct |
| Cape Cod Cruises | Provincetown | 508-747-2400 | Apr–Oct |
| Provincetown's Portuguese Princess Whale Watch | Provincetown | 508-487-2651 | Apr–Oct |
| East India Cruise Co | Salem | 508-741-0434 | May–Oct |
| ⊕ **Maine** | | | |
| Acadian Whale Watcher | Bar Harbor | 207-288-9794 | May–Oct |
| Frenchman Bay Co | Bar Harbor | 207-288-3322 | late May–late Oct |

**Puffins** – Puffins can be seen in their summer colonies in the Gulf of Maine on Eastern Egg Rock, Matinicus Rock and Machias Seal Island usually between June and early August (prime viewing time: July). On-land viewing is allowed only on Machias Seal Island by the following companies (binoculars recommended): Cap'n Fish Boat Cruises, Boothbay Harbor, ☎ 207-633-3244; Hardy Boat Cruises, New Harbor ☎ 207-677-2026.

Eric Le Bel/Parks Canada

Puffins

## Winter Activities

**Skiing** – The primary ski areas in New England are the Green Mountains of Vermont, and the White Mountains of New Hampshire; there are also excellent ski resorts in northwestern Maine, western Connecticut and the Berkshires of Massachusetts *(ski charts pp 256-257)*. Many ski area communities offer a variety of accommodations *(p 249)* including major hotel chains, B&Bs and alpine lodges. Discount packages for stays of 3 or more days, which can include lift tickets, equipment rental, meals and transportation to the slopes, are often available.

Radio stations throughout the northeast report local ski conditions. Most ski resorts have snow-making equipment.

Killington, Vermont

**Cross-Country Skiing** – Many local parks and recreation departments maintain trail systems through recreation areas and forests. Always ask permission before skiing on private land. Some of the trail systems have warming huts, while others offer cabins with sleeping accommodations. Most backcountry trails are ungroomed.

### Trail Conditions & Information

| State | Downhill | Cross-Country |
|-------|----------|---------------|
| Massachusetts | 800-632-8038 | |
| New Hampshire | 800-258-3608 | 800-262-6660 |
| Rhode Island | | 401-277-2632 |
| Vermont | 802-229-0531 | 802-828-3239 |

**Snowmobiling** – New England offers enthusiasts miles of maintained trails on both public and private lands. Many outfitters *(see below)* provide guided tours and rental equipment.

The Vermont Association of Snow Travelers (VAST) maintains a 3,500mi trail system for its members ($57/year) that extends from the northern to southern borders of the state. Contact: VAST, PO Box 839, Montpelier VT 05601 ☎ 802-229-0005. ⓖ Snowmobile Assocs., PO Box 77, Augusta ME 04330 ☎ 207-622-6983.

**Trail Information** – ⓖ Office of State Parks & Recreation *(p 251)* ⓖ Trails Bureau, Div of Parks & Recreation *(p 251)*. Snowmobile Association, PO Box 38, Concord NH 03301 ☎ 207-224-8906. ⓖ Dept of Parks & Recreation *(p 251)*.

**Dogsledding** – This ancient mode of transportation offers a unique way to view the winter beauty of Maine's wilderness. Trips vary from one-hour excursions to day and overnight trips. **Mahoosuc Mountain Adventures**, Bear River Rd, Newry ME 04261 day and overnight trips in the Rangley Lakes region ☎ 207-824-2073. **White Howling Express**, PO Box 147, Stratton ME 04982 hour-long rides at Sugarloaf Ski Center near Farmington ☎ 207-246-4461.

| Selected Ski Areas City | ☎ | Vertical Drop (ft) | Total Runs | Downhill Trails Beginner | Intermediate | Advanced | Cross Country Trails |
|---|---|---|---|---|---|---|---|
| **❄❄❄ Connecticut** / area code: 203 | | | | | | | |
| **Cedar Brook** West Suffield | 668-5026 | | | | | | 10km |
| **Mohawk Mountain** Cornwall | 672-6100 | 660 | 23 | 20% | 60% | 20% | 400 acres |
| **Mount Southington** Southington | 628-0954 | 425 | 14 | 33% | 33% | 33% | |
| **White Memorial Foundation** Litchfield | 567-0857 | | | | | | 56km |
| **Woodbury Ski & Racquet** Woodbury | 263-2203 | 300 | 12 | 33% | 33% | 33% | 32km |
| **❄ Maine** / area code: 207 | | | | | | | |
| **Sunday River Ski Resort** Newry | 824-3000 | 2,300 | 102 | 25% | 40% | 35% | |
| **Sugarloaf** *(p 74)* Farmington | 237-2000 | 2,820 | 101 | 33% | 33% | 33% | 90km |
| **Saddleback** *(p 74)* Rangley | 864-5671 | 1,826 | 41 | 33% | 33% | 33% | 40km |
| **Squaw Mountain** *(p 79)* Greenville | 695-2272 | 1,750 | 18 | 33% | 33% | 33% | Yes |
| **❄ Massachusetts** / area code: 413 | | | | | | | |
| **Mt Tom Ski Area** *(p 161)* Holyoke | 536-0416 | 680 | 15 | 33% | 47% | 20% | |
| **Butternut Basin** Great Barrington | 528-2000 | 1,000 | 22 | 20% | 60% | 20% | 7km |
| **Brodie Mountain** New Ashford | 443-4752 | 1,250 | 28 | 33% | 33% | 33% | 25km |
| **❄ New Hampshire** / area code: 603 | | | | | | | |
| **Attitash** *(p 197)* Bartlett | 374-2368 | 1,750 | 40 | 13% | 57% | 30% | |
| **Balsams/Wilderness** Dixville Notch | 255-3951 | 1,000 | 15 | 25% | 50% | 25% | 90km |
| **Black Mountain** *(p 196)* Jackson | 383-4490 | 1,150 | 26 | 30% | 40% | 30% | |
| **Bretton Woods** Bretton Woods | 278-5000 | 1,500 | 30 | 30% | 43% | 27% | 90km |
| **Cannon Mountain** *(p 197)* Franconia | 823-7771 | 2,146 | 38 | 21% | 53% | 26% | |
| **Mt Cranmore** N. Conway | 356-5543 | 1,200 | 32 | 22% | 53% | 25% | Yes |
| **Franconia Inn** Franconia | 823-5542 | | | | | | 65km |
| **Gunstock** *(p 200)* Gilford | 293-4345 | 1,400 | 40 | 25% | 50% | 25% | 50km |
| **Highland Mtn Ski Area** Tilton | 286-2414 | 800 | 21 | 40% | 30% | 30% | Yes |
| **Jackson Ski Touring Foundations** Jackson | 383-9355 | | | | | | 154km |
| **King Ridge** New London | 526-6966 | 850 | 23 | 57% | 22% | 22% | |
| **Loon Mountain** Lincoln | 745-8111 | 2,100 | 41 | 27% | 49% | 24% | 35km |
| **McIntyre** Manchester | 624-6571 | 169 | 3 | 50% | 50% | | Yes |
| **Mt Sunapee** Sunapee | 763-2356 | 1,510 | 36 | 24% | 60% | 16% | |
| **Mt Washington Valley Ski Touring** Intervale | 356-9920 | | | | | | 20km |
| **Nordic Skier** Wolfeboro | 569-3151 | | | | | | 20km |
| **Norsk Cross-Country Center** New London | 526-4685 | | | | | | 90km |
| **Pat's Peak** Henniker | 428-3245 | 710 | 19 | 58% | 16% | 26% | |
| **Ragged Mountain** Danbury | 768-3475 | 1,250 | 23 | 30% | 40% | 30% | |
| **Sugar Shack Nordic Village** Thornton | 726-3867 | | | | | | 32km |
| **Sunset Hill Nordic Center** Sugar Hill | 823-5522 | | | | | | 30km |
| **Temple Mountian** Peterborough | 924-6949 | 600 | 15 | 40% | 40% | 20% | 40km |
| **Waterville Valley** Waterville Valley | 236-8311 | 2,020 | 53 | 20% | 60% | 20% | 105km |
| **Wildcat Mountain** *(p 196)* Jackson | 466-3326 | 2,100 | 31 | 20% | 45% | 35% | |
| **Windblown Cross-Country** New Ipswich | 878-2869 | | | | | | 40km |

| Selected Ski Areas City ☎ | Vertical Drop (ft) | Total Runs | Downhill Trails Beginner | Intermediate | Advanced | Cross Country Trails |
|---|---|---|---|---|---|---|

| **Selected Ski Areas** | | Vertical Drop (ft) | Total Runs | Beginner | Intermediate | Advanced | Cross Country Trails |
|---|---|---|---|---|---|---|---|
| **City** ☎ | | | | | | | |

## ❄ Rhode Island / area code: 401

| Name | City | Phone | Vertical Drop (ft) | Total Runs | Beginner | Intermediate | Advanced | Cross Country Trails |
|---|---|---|---|---|---|---|---|---|
| **Yawgoo Valley** | Exeter | 294-3802 | 240 | 12 | 60% | 20% | 20% | |

## ❄ Vermont / area code: 802

| Name | City | Phone | Vertical Drop (ft) | Total Runs | Beginner | Intermediate | Advanced | Cross Country Trails |
|---|---|---|---|---|---|---|---|---|
| **Ascutney Mountain Resort** | Brownsville | 484-7711 | 1,530 | 31 | 26% | 39% | 35% | 32km |
| **Blueberry Hill** | Goshen | 247-6735 | | | | | | 60km |
| **Blueberry Lake** | East Warren | 496-6687 | | | | | | 23km |
| **Bolton Valley** | Bolton | 434-2131 | 1,625 | 48 | 28% | 49% | 23% | 100km |
| **Brattleboro Outing Club** | Brattleboro | 254-4081 | | | | | | 20km |
| **Bromley** *(p 229)* | Manchester Ctr | 824-5522 | 1,334 | 36 | 35% | 34% | 31% | |
| **Burke Mountain** *(p 232)* | East Burke | 626-3305 | 2,000 | 30 | 30% | 40% | 30% | 65km |
| **Camel's Hump Nordic** | Huntington | 434-2704 | | | | | | 70km |
| **Catamount Family Ctr** | Williston | 879-6001 | | | | | | 40km |
| **Craftsbury Nordic** | Craftsbury Common | 586-7767 | | | | | | 120km |
| **Edson Hill Manor** | Stowe | 253-8954 | | | | | | 25km |
| **Green Mountain** | Randolph | 728-5575 | | | | | | 35km |
| **Green Trails** | Brookfield | 276-3412 | | | | | | 34km |
| **Hazen's Notch** | Montgomery Ctr | 326-4708 | | | | | | 45km |
| **Hermitage** | Wilmington | 464-3511 | | | | | | 50km |
| **Hildene** | Manchester | 362-1788 | | | | | | 18km |
| **Jay Peak** *(p 227)* | Jay | 988-2611 | 2,153 | 61 | 20% | 55% | 25% | 10km |
| **Killington** *(p 235)* | Killington | 422-3261 | 3,150 | 162 | 50% | 18% | 32% | |
| **Lake Morey Inn** | Fairlee | 333-4800 | | | | | | 65km |
| **Mad River Glen** *(p 227)* | Waitsfield | 496-3551 | 2,000 | 33 | 30% | 30% | 40% | |
| **Maple Valley Ski Area** | W. Dummerston | 254-6083 | 1,000 | 17 | 25% | 50% | 25% | |
| **Middlebury College Snow Bowl** | Middlebury | 388-4356 | 1,200 | 13 | 23% | 54% | 23% | |
| **Mount Snow/Haystack** | Wilmington | 464-3333 | 1,700 | 127 | 21% | 62% | 17% | |
| **Mountain Meadows** | Killington | 775-7077 | | | | | | 50km |
| **Mountain Top** | Chittenden | 483-6089 | | | | | | 110km |
| **Nordic Inn** | Landgrove | 824-6444 | | | | | | 26km |
| **Okemo** | Ludlow | 228-4041 | 2,150 | 83 | 30% | 50% | 20% | |
| **Pico** *(p 234)* | Rutland | 775-4345 | 1,967 | 42 | 20% | 60% | 20% | |
| **Prospect Ski Mountain** | Woodford | 442-2575 | | | | | | 40km |
| **Rikert's** | Ripton | 388-2759 | | | | | | 42km |
| **Round Barn Farm** | Waitsfield | 496-2276 | | | | | | 30km |
| **Sitzmark** | Wilmington | 464-3384 | | | | | | 24km |
| **Stowe Mountain Resort** | Stowe | 253-3000 | 2,360 | 45 | 16% | 59% | 25% | 70km |
| **Stratton** *(p 230)* | Stratton Mtn | 297-2200 | 2,003 | 92 | 23% | 27% | 50% | 70km |
| **Sugarbush** *(p 227)* | Warren | 583-2381 | 2,600 | 110 | 23% | 48% | 29% | 21km |
| **Suicide Six** *(p 241)* | Woodstock | 457-1666 | 650 | 19 | 33% | 33% | 33% | |
| **Tater Hill** | Chester | 875-2518 | | | | | | 25km |
| **Topnotch** | Stowe | 253-8585 | | | | | | Yes |
| **Trapp Family Lodge** *(p 239)* | Stowe | 253-8511 | | | | | | 60km |
| **Viking Ctr** | Londonderry | 824-3933 | | | | | | 40km |
| **White House** | Wilmington | 464-2135 | | | | | | 45km |
| **Wild Wings** | Peru | 824-6793 | | | | | | 25km |
| **Wilderness Trails** | Quechee | 295-7620 | | | | | | 18km |
| **Woodstock** | Woodstock | 457-2114 | | | | | | 60km |

# INDEX

**New Haven**      City, town, region or other point of interest
Paul Revere      Person, historic event or term
*Accommodations*      Practical information
74, **89**, *95*      Page reference, **principal reference**, *illustration*

Place and sight names are followed by state abbreviations: **CT** Connecticut, **ME** Maine, **MA** Massachusetts, **NH** New Hampshire, **RI** Rhode Island, **VT** Vermont. **Newport Mansions** RI and selected sights in **Boston** MA, **Hartford** CT and **Providence** RI are listed under those headings. **Beaches** and historic **Ships/Boats** are also grouped separately. **State parks** are listed on page 251. **Maps** are listed on page 9.

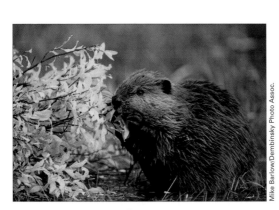

Beaver

Mike Barlow/Dembinsky Photo Assoc.

Baily Island, Maine

© Dick Dietrich

**MANUFACTURE FRANÇAISE DES PNEUMATIQUES MICHELIN**
Société en commandite par actions au capital de 2 000 000 000 de francs
Place des Carmes-Déchaux – 63 Clermont-Ferrand (France)

R. C. S. Clermont-Fd B 855 200 507
© Michelin et Cie, Propriétaires-Éditeurs 1995
Dépôt légal 9-1995 — ISBN 2-06-156907-2 — ISSN 0763-1383

Printed in the United States of America 09-95-40 by Motheral Printing Company, Fort Worth  TX